Guidelines
for Design and Construction
of Health Care Facilities

2006

Guidelines
for Design and Construction
of Health Care Facilities

The Facility
Guidelines Institute

The American
Institute of Architects
Academy of Architecture
for Health

With assistance from the
U.S. Department of Health
and Human Services

This publication supersedes the *Guidelines for Design and Construction of Hospital and Health Care Facilities*, 2001 edition.

To order copies of the Guidelines, call 202-626-7541 or 1-800-242-3837 (menu option 4) or visit the AIA Bookstore Web site at www.aia.org/books.

A CD of the content of this book is enclosed. Upon removing and using the CD, the user is bound by the license agreement that appears on the CD. For questions about appropriate use of the CD, contact the publisher.

Art Direction: Zamore Design
Design: Gretchen Maxwell, GLM Design

Facility Guidelines Institute
www.fgi-guidelines.org

Published by The American Institute of Architects
1735 New York Avenue, NW
Washington, DC 20006

ISBN: 1-57165-013-X

Printed in the United States of America on archival quality recycled paper.

On the occasion of his retirement from the Health Guidelines Revision Committee, the committee members dedicate this Guidelines edition to Chairman Emeritus J. Armand Burgun, FAIA, FACHA, in grateful acknowledgment of his 50 years of extraordinary leadership, dedication, and vision in the development and use of many generations of this document.

Contents

Tables

Preface

The 2006 edition is the latest in the 59-year history of this Guidelines document to aid in the design and construction of health care facilities.

The original *General Standards* appeared in the *Federal Register* on February 14, 1947, as part of the implementing regulations for the Hill-Burton program. The standards were revised from time to time as needed. In 1974 the document was retitled *Minimum Requirements of Construction and Equipment for Hospital and Medical Facilities* to emphasize that the requirements were generally minimum, rather than ideal standards. The 1974 edition was the first to request public input and comment. Requirements relating to the preparation of plans, specifications, and estimates or to site survey and soil investigation, which had been a part of all previous editions, were removed. These requirements were published in a document entitled *Technical Manual on Facility Design and Construction* published by the Department of Health, Education, and Welfare's (DHEW) Office of Facilities Engineering.

In 1984 the Department of Health and Human Services (DHHS) removed from regulation the requirements relating to minimum standards of construction, renovation, and equipment of hospitals and medical facilities, as cited in the *Minimum Requirements*, DHEW Publication No. (HRA) 81-14500. Since the federal grant and loan programs had expired, there was no need for the federal government to retain the guidelines in regulation format. To reflect its nonregulatory status, the title was changed to *Guidelines for Construction and Equipment of Hospital and Medical Facilities*. However, the document was, and still is, used by many state authorities having jurisdiction for licensure or registration. Further, the Guidelines are used by DHHS staff to assess Department of Housing and Urban Development applications for hospital mortgage insurance and for Indian Health Service construction projects. Therefore, regulatory language has been retained. The 1983–84 edition of the Guidelines was the last one revised and published by the federal government; at the same time, DHHS published and distributed an addendum to the Guidelines entitled *Energy Considerations for Hospital Construction and Equipment.*

At the conclusion of the revision cycle that resulted in the 1983–84 edition, DHHS asked the American Institute of Architects Committee on Architecture for Health (AIA/CAH) to form an advisory group to work with, and be funded by, the Public Health Service for the next revision. When the revisions to the document were complete, the federal government declined to publish it. The AIA/CAH asked several nonprofit agencies and professional associations to publish and distribute the Guidelines. An agreement was finally reached with the American Institute of Architects (AIA) to publish the 1987 edition. At this point, revision of the Guidelines would have ceased, or even its existence, if three people had not taken it upon themselves to approach the Public Health Service and the Health Care Financing Administration and request a federal grant to fund a revision cycle. These same three people, working with AIA/CAH, put together the first Steering Committee, which in turn set up the first Health Guidelines Revision Committee (HGRC) not under the aegis of the federal government.

The members of this multidisciplinary group came from the federal and state governments and the private sector and offered expertise in design, operation, and construction of health care facilities. The 1992–93 edition of the Guidelines was published and distributed by the AIA. The Steering Committee from the 1992–93 cycle requested and received federal funding from DHHS for another cycle. Substantial funding was also provided by the American Hospital Association and the AIA/CAH. The consensus process was enhanced and the input base broadened by asking the public to propose changes to the Guidelines and then to comment on the proposed changes. Approximately 2,000 proposals and comments were received and processed. Three HGRC meetings—one on the East Coast, one on the West Coast, and one in the middle of the country—were held to discuss the merits of all proposals and comments. More than 65 experts attended these sessions and reached a consensus on the content of the 1996–97 edition of the Guidelines. A letter ballot was sent to all eligible members of the HGRC and the document was approved by a unanimous vote. To better reflect its content, the title of the document was changed to *Guidelines for Design and Construction of Hospital and Health Care Facilities.*

It was during this revision cycle that the AIA Committee on Architecture for Health became the AIA Academy of Architecture for Health (AIA/AAH).

In an effort to create a more formal procedure and process and to keep the document current, the Facility Guidelines Institute (FGI) was founded as an independent, not-for-profit 501(c)(3) corporation in 1998. The main objectives of FGI are (1) to see that the Guidelines are reviewed and revised on a regular cycle with a consensus process carried out by a multidisciplinary group of experts from the federal, state, and private sectors, (2) to stimulate research in support of evidence-based guidelines, and (3) to reinvest all of the net revenue derived from FGI's share of the sale of Guidelines documents in research and development for improved future editions of the Guidelines. FGI, in its role as a promulgator of health care facility guidelines and standards, contracts with the American Institute of Architects for support of the consensus revision process and publication of the document.

FGI is primarily interested in consensus methodology and in overseeing the Guidelines revision process. Specifically, FGI wants to make sure the Health Guidelines Revision Committee

- is properly funded,

- has a balance of stakeholder representation from individuals with expertise or jurisdiction,

- uses the consensus process,

- requests public input in the form of proposals for change and comments on proposed changes,

- reviews and revises the Guidelines on a timely basis to maintain a balance between minimum standards and the state of the art in health care design and construction, and

- operates under a formal set of bylaws governing its purpose, scope, membership, and goals that includes standing rules governing voting procedures, recognized duties and responsibilities for committee members, and established rules regarding appointments, terms, and officers.

FGI monitors requests for interpretations from the public. Goals are to make sure that requests are answered in a timely manner, interpretations are rendered by the individuals best equipped to reflect the intent of the committee when the document was written, and interpretations are made available to the public.

The 2001 edition of the Guidelines resulted from the first revision cycle to be completed under the aegis and direction of FGI. It received major funding from DHHS/Health Care Financing Administration and the AIA/AAH. The American Society for Healthcare Engineering (ASHE), the National Institutes of Health (NIH), and the AIA provided staff and technical support. The HGRC met in Washington, D.C., and reviewed the 1996–97 edition of the Guidelines line by line to ascertain issues that needed to be addressed, including infection control, safety, and environment of care. The membership for this revision cycle included an increased number of state authorities having jurisdiction (AHJs), consistent with the increasing number of states utilizing all or portions of the Guidelines as state regulation by adoption. The work of the HGRC was greatly enhanced by the attendance and participation of these AHJs.

At the beginning of the 2001 revision cycle, an announcement requesting proposals for change to the document was made in health care industry publications. The HGRC received and gave serious consideration to 539 proposals to modify the document. After the HGRC meeting in Irvine, California, a document containing proposed changes was made available for public comment. The HGRC received and gave careful consideration to 1,030 comments on the proposed changes. For the first time, the Internet was used extensively to distribute the draft of the document and to receive proposals and comments.

The 2001 Guidelines were the result of many hours spent at three meetings, each attended by 82 to 86 members of the 97-member HGRC. Committee members spent countless hours in subcommittee and focused task groups reviewing the proposals for change and comments on them. Text for the 2001 edition of the Guidelines formally adopted at the final HGRC meeting in Denver was sent to the HGRC members for letter ballot. The result of the ballot process was an overwhelming endorsement of the document. The adopted Guidelines were approved by FGI and turned over to the AIA for publication and distribution. A major change in format was adopted for this edition, placing appendix material at the foot of the relevant pages in the main text. A glossary of terms and a form to request an interpretation were added to the book.

The 2006 edition of the Guidelines also received major funding from DHHS/Centers for Medicaid and Medicare Services, ASHE, and NIH, and the AIA again provided staff and technical support. This edition was also the result of many hours of formal and informal meetings on the part of more than 107 HGRC members. There were never fewer than 85 members present at the three "all-hands" meetings in Washington, D.C.; Austin, Texas; and Irvine, California; and 67 individuals faithfully attended every session. Committee members spent untold hours at "all-hands" meetings and subcommittee and focused task group meetings, as well as time outside the meetings, writing proposals and reviewing proposed changes and comments. They reviewed 797 proposals for change and 1,156 comments on proposed changes. The HGRC reached a consensus at its final meeting and unanimously endorsed the revised guidelines to be sent out for letter ballot. The result of the letter ballot was unanimous approval of the 2006 document. The HGRC also elected a new Steering Committee for the 2010 revision cycle.

The 2006 HGRC took on the challenge of two goals stated in the preface of the 2001 edition: to prepare more committee-generated changes to reflect the collective knowledge and experience of the members and to improve the format, readability, and indexing or searchability of the document to make it a more useful and user-friendly tool. The HGRC developed a number of work groups and added time to the revision cycle to draft proposals for new language. The committee also approved a complete reorganization to make the Guidelines more accessible to users. This time-intensive effort has resulted in a book presented in four parts: one with information applicable to all health care facility types, one on hospitals, one on ambulatory care facilities, and one for other health care facilities. (Details about the reorganization appear in the Major Additions and Revisions section that follows this preface.)

When possible, the Guidelines standards are performance oriented for desired results. Prescriptive measurements, when given, have been carefully considered relative to generally recognized standards. For example, experience has shown that it would be extremely difficult to design a patient bedroom smaller than the size suggested and still have space for the normally expected functions and procedures.

Authorities adopting the Guidelines should encourage design innovation and grant exceptions where the intent of the standard is met. These standards assume that appropriate architectural and engineering practice and compliance with applicable codes will be observed as part of normal professional service.

The Guidelines change to keep pace with evolving health care needs and in response to requests for up-to-date guidance from health care providers, designers, and regulators. It is recognized that many health care services may be provided in facilities not subject to licensure or regulation, and it is intended that these Guidelines be suitable for use by all health care providers. It is further intended that when used as regulation, some latitude be granted in complying with these Guidelines so long as the health and safety of the occupants of the facility are not compromised.

In some facilities, areas, or sections, it may be desirable to exceed the Guidelines standards for optimum function. For example, door widths for inpatient hospital rooms are noted as 3 feet 8 inches (1.11 meters), which satisfies applicable codes, to permit the passage of patient beds. However, widths of 3 feet 10 inches (1.22 meters) may be desirable to reduce damage to doors and frames when beds and large equipment are frequently moved. The decision to exceed the standards should be included in the functional program of the health care facility.

The Guidelines and the methodology for revising them have been, and still are, evolving. When first published, the document comprised a set of regulations developed by a single department of the federal government as a condition for receiving a federal hospital construction grant under the Hill-Burton Act. Even in those early days, the document was highly respected and influential throughout the world. From the time it was first issued and enforced, U.S. hospitals have become the ideal and the goal to be achieved by those building hospitals in all nations.

Gradually, state hospital authorities and other federal agencies were added to the HGRC, then private, nongovernmental health care professional societies, practitioners, and designers. Educational programs and seminars were introduced in the 1980s to inform the public about the subjects addressed in the Guidelines and the reasons for inclusion of certain requirements. Very slowly, public input was requested by the committee in the form of comment on proposed changes. This has now exploded into the current avalanche of proposals and comments. In each succeeding cycle, the committee has been enlarged to increase the base of expertise and to allow more public representation. Further, the consensus procedure was adopted for all decision-making.

As the process became more complex, as the committee grew larger, as more and more public proactive and reactive input was requested and received, as the practice of health care delivery and the buildings that house them began to change at an ever faster rate, a more formal and expeditious process became mandatory. Adding to the complexity of the process is the expansion in the scope of the document from covering only acute care general hospitals to including nursing homes, rehabilitation facilities, ambulatory care facilities, psychiatric hospitals, mobile health care units, hospice care, assisted living, and so on.

It is the desire of the Health Guidelines Revision Committee to continue working with the American Institute of Architects and the Facility Guidelines Institute to make certain the Guidelines and the revision process continue. The HGRC does, however, wish to maintain its independence as an objective, multidisciplinary committee, operating without pressure from any organization and arriving at conclusions candidly, fairly, and knowledgeably through an open consensus process.

It is also the desire of the HGRC to see that the process continues to improve with each passing cycle. Some goals for the future follow:

- Seek more public input from a wider base, not only from professionals but from patients and other consumers.

- Encourage and sponsor research projects to support the evidence-based decision-making process.

- Allow more time to study and evaluate proposals for changes and to comment on recommended changes.

- Improve the committee's ability to communicate and receive information electronically, making full use of the Internet and other formats and programs as they become available. This would include requests for interpretation, tentative interim amendments, etc.

- Work constantly to improve the process and the content of the Guidelines to keep it a dynamic document that truly reflects the state of the art.

- Continue to have the courage and wisdom to adopt requirements that are forward looking and address the needs of the future, looking backward only to discover what not to do.

- Continue to strive for a document that is credible, reasonable, and knowledge-based and that will maintain the tradition of the American hospital as the role model for the rest of the world.

This publication supersedes the *Guidelines for Design and Construction of Hospital and Health Care Facilities,* 2001 edition.

Inquiries or questions about interpretations of the Guidelines may be addressed to:
The Facility Guidelines Institute
1919 McKinney Avenue
Dallas, TX 75201
www.fgi-guidelines.org

Questions about the Guidelines revision process may be addressed to:
The American Institute of Architects
Knowledge Resources Department
1735 New York Avenue, N.W.
Washington, DC 20006
202-626-7367 or 800-242-3837
healthcareguidelines@aia.org

To order copies of the Guidelines, call 202-626-7541 or 1-800-AIA-3837 (menu option 4) or send an e-mail to bookstore@aia.org.

Major Additions and Revisions

On picking up the 2006 edition, users of previous editions of the Guidelines will notice a change in the cover design. The colorful new cover is a harbinger of much more that is new.

First, the book is three-hole punched so those who prefer to have a document that lies flat can have the glue binding cut off and place the pages in a binder. In addition, for the first time, a searchable electronic CD version of the book is included for use on laptops and other personal computers.

Inside the book, users will find the document has been completely reorganized to make it easier to access the information they need. Previously, the contents comprised a list of facility types in more or less the order the topics were added to the book. In this edition, the content has been arranged in four parts that group similar facilities together. Part 1 provides information applicable to all facility types. Part 2 contains all of the chapters on hospitals, and Part 3 the chapters on a variety of ambulatory care facility types. Part 4 comprises "other" health care facility types and in this edition includes nursing, hospice, assisted living, and adult day health care facilities. Within each chapter, the content is also presented differently than in the 2001 edition. The text has been broken into smaller paragraphs with more subheads and placed in basically the same order in every chapter. A second color has been introduced for headings to help users follow the text.

The reorganization of the Guidelines is accompanied by a new numbering system that reflects the division of the content into parts. The first part of each paragraph reference is the chapter number, which appears at the top of the page. This is followed by a hyphen and the paragraph number. For instance, the reference to typical patient rooms in a hospital medical/surgical unit is 2.1-3.1.1. For users who are accustomed to the previous numbering system, a matrix at the back of the book lists the paragraph numbers in the 2001 edition and their corresponding numbers in the 2006 edition. So the document will be easy to peruse, full-length references appear only in cross-references, the matrix, and the index. However, references to the content of the 2006 Guidelines in other documents must be complete, showing the chapter and the paragraph number.

This major reorganization effort was instigated by a study of the Guidelines document commissioned by the Facility Guidelines Institute (FGI) in 2003. The Clemson University School of Architecture was contracted to review the Guidelines thoroughly under the direction of David J. Allison, AIA, associate professor and coordinator of the Graduate Program in Architecture + Health, and Barbara Heifferon, associate professor of professional communication and rhetoric. After consulting with a task force of the Health Guidelines Revision Committee Subcommittee on Research and Development, led by J. Armand Burgun, FAIA, a group of graduate students made suggestions about ways to improve the usability, clarity, and consistency of the Guidelines document. The resulting report presented 13 general recommendations. The Steering Committee of the Health Guidelines Revision Committee (HGRC) chose to institute eight of these in the 2006 edition.

In addition to the reorganization and renumbering of the Guidelines text, which was a monumental editorial effort, the 2006 edition provides an updated version of the content, including both completely new material and revisions to the text of the 2001 edition. As explained in the preface, the HGRC is the body responsible for considering proposals to change the 2001 document presented by the public, as well as for generating proposals based on their multidisciplinary discussions. After the draft 2006 edition was posted for public comment, the HGRC reviewed the comments and finalized the text.

The major additions and revisions that resulted from the 2006 edition revision cycle are outlined below. As in past editions, significant changes are marked throughout the book with a vertical line beside the text.

Part 1: General
Chapter 1.1 provides a useful introduction and adds information about how to use the Guidelines and request interpretations of its requirements. Like the former Chapter 1, which it replaces, it explains how the Guidelines are applied to renovation projects and outlines provisions for disasters and federal requirements for protecting patient privacy.

The Environment of Care chapter (formerly Chapter 2, now Chapter 1.2) has been significantly expanded. The goal of the chapter is to identify the overall components and specific elements that directly affect the experience of participants in the health care delivery system. The functional program, as the key document used to identify a provider's goals and objectives for the environment of care and to describe specific strategies for achieving them during design and construction, receives expanded coverage in this chapter.

The contents of former Chapters 5 and 6 have been consolidated into the new Chapter 1.5, which covers planning, design, construction, and postconstruction considerations. Language relating to the infection control risk assessment (ICRA) has been reworked and expanded, and a revised section on infection control risk mitigation recommendations has been included. Information about the design process, finishes and surfaces, construction phasing, critical ventilation requirements during construction, commissioning, and record drawings and manuals have been introduced and combined to address the entire planning, design, and construction (PDC) process.

Chapter 1.6 is a new chapter intended to capture requirements that are common to all or nearly all health care facility types. Chapters on individual facility types will refer back to this chapter and identify any instances in which the common requirements do not apply to a particular facility type. Other chapters contain references to material in Chapter 1.6 that applies to them. This approach makes it easier to update technical information, which can be changed in only one location rather than in multiple chapters. This chapter will receive significant attention during the 2010 revision cycle, and the Steering Committee expects the public and the HGRC members to make substantial proposals to expand its content.

Part 2: Hospitals

Part 2 contains the chapters on general hospitals, psychiatric hospitals, and rehabilitation facilities from the 2001 edition of the Guidelines, along with a completely new chapter on small inpatient primary care hospitals. This new chapter was added to address smaller facilities that are more commonly constructed in rural areas or inner city communities to serve smaller populations.

Perhaps the most widely anticipated change in the text in the General Hospitals chapter (now Chapter 2.1) is the change in room capacity in medical/surgical (including postpartum) units. The 2006 edition specifies that the single-bed room is the minimum standard in new construction. Approval of a two-bed arrangement is still permitted if a facility's functional program demonstrates it is necessary. In addition, when an organization undertakes a major renovation, the patient room bed compliment is permitted to remain the same.

The text of the General Hospitals chapter includes the following completely new and significantly revised material:

- New section on intermediate care units

- Bed clearances in critical care units and neonatal intensive care units (NICUs)

- Bedside documentation areas in critical care units

- Expanded lighting requirements for NICUs

- Revised text for in-hospital psychiatric nursing units

- New section on in-hospital skilled nursing units

- Appendix language on surge capacity in emergency departments

- Revised language on decontamination areas in emergency departments

- New section on observation units in emergency departments

- New section on freestanding emergency facilities

- Addition of electrophysiology labs in cardiac catheterization labs

- Requirements for patient toilets in diagnostic x-ray facilities

- Appendix language regarding magnetic shielding for MRI facilities

- New language on waste management and processing

- New language specifying the use of ducted systems for all return ventilation in patient care areas

- New language on ventilation for airborne infection isolation rooms (AIIRs) and protective environment rooms

- New description of electronic surveillance systems

Part 3: Ambulatory Care Facilities

Chapter 9 of the 2001 edition, Outpatient Facilities, has been divided into 11 chapters for the 2006 edition. Chapter 3.1 offers guidelines for outpatient facilities in general, with some notations about facility types to which parts of the chapter do not apply. The sections on specific facility types that previously appeared in Chapter 9 have all been made into individual chapters. In addition, the former Chapter 12, Mobile, Transportable, and Relocatable Units, is located in Part 3.

Significant content changes to chapters in this part of the book are mentioned here. First, the section on "Freestanding Emergency Service" has been moved to the General Hospitals chapter, and a new classification, "Freestanding Urgent Care Facilities," appears in Part 3. This arrangement reserves the term "emergency department" for use in the chapter covering hospitals and makes the requirements for the two types of emergency departments similar. Urgent care facilities are distinguished as those facilities providing basic care for non-emergency conditions on a less-than-24-hour-per-day schedule.

The second major content change is in the chapter containing guidelines for outpatient surgical facilities. This chapter has been greatly expanded and improved to create guidelines that require outpatient surgery facilities to provide the same environmental design functions, controls, and finish materials as those found in the surgery departments of inpatient facilities. These changes will help mandate a similar standard of care for all perioperative patients, no matter where a procedure is performed.

A new chapter has been created for office surgical facilities. As more and more procedures are performed on an outpatient basis, concern about unregulated set-tings has increased. Minimum standards are set for this classification, recognizing that the patients served are ambulatory but that they often need a similar environment of care to ensure positive outcomes.

Minimum dimensions have been defined for clean and sterile supply rooms, operating rooms, post-anesthesia care areas, and storage rooms.

Other new chapters added in this part of the book cover these facility types:

- Gastrointestinal endoscopy facilities

- Renal dialysis centers

- Psychiatric outpatient centers

Part 4: Other Health Care Facilities

Part 4 includes chapters on nursing facilities, hospice facilities, assisted living facilities, and adult day health care facilities.

Chapter 4.1 (formerly Chapter 8), Nursing Facilities, was not extensively revised, but some significant changes were made:

- Clarification of maximum room occupancy in renovation projects as two (unless the room already accommodates up to four residents)

- A new requirement that rooms for ventilator-dependent residents provide for the administration of oxygen and suction

- Use of noncentral air-handling systems (e.g., through-the-wall fan coil units) for recirculation only

- Provision of a central ventilation system capable of providing the minimum outdoor air requirements for each individual space in all new facilities

- New minimum requirements for ambient and task lighting levels consistent with standards developed for senior living by the Illuminating Engineering Society of North America

Requirements for the remaining facility types in Part 4 were nonexistent in previous editions, with chapter placeholders consisting only of brief descriptions of the program and/or appendix language. However, because hospice, assisted living, and adult day health care facilities have become increasingly relevant in today's health care environment, the HGRC focused its efforts on developing reasonable minimum standards to assist in the design of these facilities.

The hospice facility requirements in Chapter 4.2 recognize a programmatic similarity between nursing and hospice facilities. Using the minimum nursing facility requirements as a basis, design requirements were developed to reflect a keen understanding of the unique nature of residential hospice programs and the need to accommodate special relationships between the hospice resident, family members, and caregivers. Although the text is based on nursing facility requirements, there is no expectation that residential hospice facilities will look like nursing homes; the performance focus of the new hospice requirements allows for a smaller, resident-focused environment that can accommodate numerous programmatic philosophies, with less emphasis on the institutional perspective assumed for most nursing facilities.

The assisted living facility requirements in Chapter 4.3 resulted from an intense collaborative effort between HGRC members, including several state authorities, and representatives from a number of national associations representing both the assisted living industry and consumers. The requirements represent a general consensus that recognizes the residential and consumer focus of assisted living, while setting basic standards for the functionality and safety of assisted living facilities.

The growing interest in adult day health care facilities reflects the increasing importance of this care modality as the continuum of care for the elderly expands to accommodate the movement toward increased alternatives to nursing home care. Although adult day health care programs can vary greatly in scope, the requirements in Chapter 4.4 are directed toward significant programs that are state licensed and must cater to an increasingly frail elderly population. The requirements are performance-based wherever possible and can appropriately accommodate programs of various size and scope of services.

Glossary

The glossary, which first appeared in the 2001 edition, has been expanded. Definitions of commonly used terms that appear throughout the Guidelines have been added to facilitate understanding, clarify issues; and help maintain consistency in the document.

Coming Up: More Research and White Papers

As a not-for-profit, 501(c)(3) corporation, the Facility Guidelines Institute is dedicated to, and reinvests its share of the net proceeds derived from sales of Guidelines documents in, research and development projects that inform and help produce improved editions of the Guidelines. Two such major research efforts instigated, organized, and funded by FGI informed significant changes in Guidelines 2006— (1) a study by the Clemson University School of Architecture that led to total reorganization and reformatting of the document, and (2) a study by Simon Frazer University that led to adoption of the single-bed room as the minimum standard for new medical/surgical and postpartum inpatient units. Additional research is already under way, and more studies are anticipated to inform the development of Guidelines 2010 about numerous subjects that play a vital role in health facility design and construction, including the following:

- Implementation of the remaining Clemson recommendations

- Outcome measures and life-cycle costs related to single-bed rooms

- Windows, daylighting, and views

- Space requirements for dining and recreation

- Impact of proper humidity control on residents of long-term care facilities

- Universal definition of new construction versus renovation

- Impact of therapeutic patient care environments

- Evidenced-based design criteria

- Surge capacity and disaster preparedness

In addition, during the public review and comment period for the first draft the 2006 edition, a number of new proposals were received on subjects of critical interest to many health facility providers, designers, and regulators that could not be processed so late in the revision cycle. Subjects of immediate concern that were introduced too late to develop draft consensus recommendations for public review and comment included these:

- Bariatric design

- Design for safe use of patient lifts and transport devices

- Acoustics and speech privacy

- Inpatient and outpatient oncology facilities

- Interventional radiology

Recognizing that both the public and the HGRC need a minimum of four years to use, digest, critique, and develop true consensus recommendations for modifications to each new edition of the Guidelines, and that the industry probably cannot afford to wait another four years to receive useful guidance on some of these emergent issues, FGI has organized task groups that are working on the development of draft white papers or monographs on several of them. The results of these efforts will be reviewed at the first full meeting of the HGRC for the 2010 revision cycle. After due consideration and modification at that meeting, FGI plans to issue draft documents for public consideration about as many of these subjects as possible.

Such research monographs and white papers will be published for information purposes only. However, individual state authorities having jurisdiction may adopt or refer to them before these draft recommendations have moved through the complete consensus development process (involving public review and comment, followed by committee review and modification). Since these papers may be published at least two years ahead of the next edition of the Guidelines, they may also serve other beneficial purposes, including the following:

- Stimulation of early action, research, development, and dissemination of information for consideration and discussion

- Provision of admittedly preliminary drafts on subjects about which very little else may then be available

- Receipt of feedback that can better inform the Guidelines to be developed and published for jurisdictional adoption and use in 2010

To prepare for the issuance of such research monographs and white papers, and to give purchasers of Guidelines 2006 a place to access them when they are published, FGI has developed a Guidelines Web site. It is the authors' and publisher's mutual intent to offer such papers free of charge to all users of Guidelines 2006 by making them available for download from the FGI and AIA Web sites, as well as the Web sites of other interested organizations, with a feedback mechanism to be developed and advertised when the papers become available.

Acknowledgments

The revision cycle that resulted in the 2006 edition of the *Guidelines for Design and Construction of Health Care Facilities* embodied much work on the part of many dedicated individuals committed to providing up-to-date information on health care facility design and construction. The Facility Guidelines Institute (FGI) and the American Institute of Architects (AIA) extend sincere thanks to all those who worked to produce this document.

FGI and the AIA express sincere gratitude to all those who took the time to submit proposals for change and comments on those proposals for consideration by the Health Guidelines Revision Committee (HGRC). Many thanks are due the members of the HGRC, a multidisciplinary group of individuals dedicated to improving the environment in which health care is delivered. The committee members—architects, engineers, doctors, nurses, and health facility managers and consultants from the private sector, state authorities having jurisdiction, and representatives of federal agencies—worked for many hours discussing, writing, and voting on proposals to change the 2001 edition of the Guidelines to better reflect the practice of health care in the 21st century.

Appreciation is also extended to the organizations that supported the travel and work of the HGRC members. Listed are the members of the HGRC who attended at least two meetings during the revision cycle and thus were eligible to vote on the final document. Some participants were physically able to attend only one meeting, but their speakerphone input at other sessions and contributions between meetings greatly benefited the document. In particular, Lorraine G. Hiatt, Ph.D., of Innovage Consultants, and Ellie Ward, RN, of Dare Home Health & Hospice, deserve recognition for their assistance on rewrites of the adult day health care and hospice facility chapters, respectively. In addition, representatives of the following organizations gathered with HGRC members and spent many hours determining the best way to address assisted living facilities in this document: the American Association of Homes and Services for the Aging, AARP, the Assisted Living Federation of America, the Alzheimer's Association, the National Center for Assisted Living (of the American Health Care Association), and the AIA Design for Aging Knowledge Community.

After the HGRC completed the work of updating the content of the Guidelines, a massive effort was undertaken to reorganize and renumber the document. Martin Cohen was retained to provide his expertise and work with AIA editor Pamela James Blumgart to think through the purpose of the reorganization, arrive at a new structure for the document, and ultimately reorganize and review the entire text to implement and refine the new structural concept. Together, they carefully reworked the final draft manuscript to incorporate many of the recommendations presented in the Clemson University research study on how to improve the document, without changing the intent of the draft as approved by the HGRC. Their work was aided by a continuous virtual dialogue with Steering Committee and other HGRC members, who reviewed particular sections and chapters via e-mail.

Of those HGRC members who reviewed the reorganization while it was in process, a particular debt is owed to Douglas Erickson, who reviewed the manuscript for all of Parts 1, 2, and 3. The following individuals reviewed portions of the document according to their expertise: Kurt Rockstroh, Judene Bartley, Albert S. Buck, Jon Cechvala, Ramona Conner, Roger Gehrke, Thomas Jung, William Lindeman, Robert Loranger, Margaret Montgomery, Chris Rousseau, Wade Rudolph, Arthur St. André, Alberto Salvatore, Judy Smith, David Uhaze, and Enrique Unanue. Lee Mickle of EEI Communications, Inc., prepared the final draft manuscript that resulted from the meetings of the full HGRC, constructed the relocation matrix, and reviewed the new numbering system, especially correcting the cross-references. Great thanks are extended to all!

At each of the three meetings of the full HGRC, local architecture firms kindly sent individuals supplied with computers and projectors to help record the decisions that resulted from committee members' discussions in subcommittees. The following individuals (followed by the firms that sent them) were much appreciated participants in the 2006 revision cycle: In Washington, D.C.—Kathy Dixon, AIA (McKissack & McKissack); Jennifer Jackson, AIA (SmithGroup); Alison Parks, Assoc. AIA (SmithGroup); and Michael Smyser, AIA, ACHA (HDR). In Austin, Texas: Richard

Burnight, AIA, ACHA (O'Connell Robertson & Associates); Sean H. Carlson, AIA (Graeber, Simmons & Cowan); Alan D. Felder, AIA (Felder Group Architects); and William P. Peeples, AIA (Bower Downing Partnership). In Irvine, California: Edward G. Avila, AIA (HMC); Bruce MacPherson, AIA, LEED AP (Puchlik Design Associates); Caroline Sheridan, LEED AP (Taylor); and Russell Triplett, AIA (Perkins + Will).

Special thanks are also extended to the Centers for Medicare and Medicaid Services of the U.S. Department of Health and Human Services for funding of the revision cycle and to the American Society for Healthcare Engineering, the National Institutes of Health, and the American Institute of Architects, which provided staffing and other support throughout the revision cycle and the reorganization effort.

Joseph G. Sprague, FAIA, FACHA, FHFI
Chairman
Health Guidelines Revision Committee

Executive Committee

Chairman
Joseph G. Sprague, FAIA, FACHA, FHFI
HKS Architects, Inc.

Vice Chairman
Douglas S. Erickson, FASHE
American Society for Healthcare Engineering (of the American Hospital Association)

Vice Chairman
Martin H. Cohen, FAIA, FACHA
Design for Aging and Health Care Architecture Consultant

Chairman Emeritus
J. Armand Burgun, FAIA, FACHA

Steering Committee

Judene Bartley, MS, MPH, CIC
Epidemiology Consulting Services, Inc.

Alfred S. Buck, MD, FACS
Martin, Blanck & Associates, Inc.
Joint Commission on Accreditation of Healthcare Organizations

Roger W. Gehrke
Idaho Department of Health & Welfare

Thomas M. Jung, RA
New York State Department of Health

Robert A. Loranger, PE, CHFM
New England Medical Center

James Merrill, PE
Centers for Medicare & Medicaid Services

Juanita M. Mildenberg, FAIA
National Institutes of Health

Emilio Pucillo, RA
Health Resources & Services Administration, DHHS

Kurt A. Rockstroh, AIA, ACHA
Steffian-Bradley Architects

Arthur St. André, MD, FCCM
Washington Hospital Center

Mayer D. Zimmerman
Centers for Medicare & Medicaid Services

Revision Committee

Paul Evans Acre, PE
Arkansas Department of Health & Human Services

Maria Allo, MD, FACS
Santa Clara Valley Medical Center
American College of Surgeons

Donald C. Axon, FAIA, FACHA
DCA/FAIA, Inc.
International Congress of Building Officials

Donald E. Baptiste
Sturdy Memorial Hospital, Inc.

Michael Bayley, RA
Texas Department of State Health Services

Chad E. Beebe, AIA
Washington State Department of Health

Chris Bettlach
Sisters of Mercy Health System–St. Louis

Elizabeth A. Bolyard, RN, MPH
Centers for Disease Control & Prevention

William J. Bonn III, AIA
Utah Department of Health

John A. Braeckel, MS
Indiana State Department of Health

Roger V. Brown, PE
United Health Services Hospitals

Christopher M. Burney, MS, CPE
Hartford Hospital

Dale B. Carr
Mississippi Department of Health

Kenneth N. Cates
Northstar Management Company

Jon F. Cechvala, RA
Wisconsin Department of Health & Family Services

Robert A. Cochran, AIA, ACHA
Weller Architects

Ramona Conner, RN, MSN, CNOR
Association of Perioperative Registered Nurses

ACKNOWLEDGMENTS

Michael D. Coppedge, AIA, ACHA
Weller Architects

Kenneth N. Dickerman, AIA,
ACHA, FHFI
Leo A Daly Company

John M. Dombrowski, PE
H. F. Lenz Company

Brian Madden Dubey, AIA, CSI
Maryland Department of Health
& Mental Hygiene

Jennifer M. Dunaway
Nevada Health Division

Glenn S. A. Gall, AIA
California Office of Statewide
Health Planning
& Development

David L. Ginsberg, FAIA
Larsen Shein Ginsberg Snyder,
Architects

Warren N. Goodwin, FAIA

Thomas C. Gormley
HCA

James R. (Skip) Gregory, RA
Florida Agency for Health Care
Administration

Robin Guenther, FAIA
Guenther 5 Architects

Jeffery M. Hardin, PE
U.S. Army Corps of Engineers

Maurene Harvey, RN
Consultants in Critical Care, Inc.

Daniel L. Hightower, AIA
BBH Design
(U.S. Public Health Service, ret.)

Andrea V. Hyde, ASID
Hyde Inc. Interior Design

Gerald R. Inglett, RA
Indian Health Service, DHHS

Thomas W. Jaeger, PE
Jaeger & Associates, LLC
American Health Care Association

Paul A. Jensen, PhD, PE, CIH
Centers for Disease Control &
Prevention

John P. Kouletsis, AIA
Kaiser Permanente

Robert G. Larsen, FAIA
Larsen Shein Ginsberg Snyder
Architects

John Larson, AIA
Larson & Associates, Inc.

Rod Laucomer, RA
Nebraska Health & Human
Services System

Rebecca J. Lewis, AIA, CID, ACHA
DSGW Architects

William E. Lindeman, AIA
WEL Designs PLC
Accreditation Association for
Ambulatory Health Care

James T. Lussier
St. Charles Medical
Center/Cascade Health Services

Linda Lybert
DuPont

Stephan G. Lynn, MD, FACEP
St. Luke's Roosevelt Hospital
Center
American College of Emergency
Physicians

Rita Rael Meek, RA
New Mexico Department
of Health

Farhad Memarzadeh, PhD, PE
National Institutes of Health

James F. Miller Jr., RA
Arkansas Children's Hospital

Richard D. Moeller, PE, SASHE
CDi Engineers

Margaret Montgomery, RN, MSN
American College of Emergency
Physicians

R. Gregg Moon, AIA, ACHA
M. D. Anderson Cancer Center

Hugh O. Nash Jr., PE, FIEEE
Nash Lipsey Burch

Gaius G. Nelson, AIA
Nelson-Tremain Partnership–
Architecture & Design for Aging
Society for the Advancement of
Gerontological Environments

Paul T. Ninomura, PE
Indian Health Service, DHHS

Richard K. Nolen, AIA
HCR ManorCare, Inc.
American Health Care Association

Pamela Ward O'Malley, RA
The Children's Hospital of
Philadelphia

Robin Orr, MPH
The Robin Orr Group

Eric T. Overton
Sparling

Peter P. Petresky
Pennsylvania Department of
Health

Michael P. Pietrzak, MD, FACEP
KMS/Project ER One

Donald Pyskacek, AIA
Universal Health Services, Inc.

Christopher P. Rousseau, PE
Newcomb & Boyd

Wade Rudolph, CBET
North Central Health Care
Wisconsin Healthcare Engineering
Association

Alberto Salvatore, AIA
Salvatore Associates

James D. Scott, PE
Michigan Department of
Community Health

William B. Selan, AIA
RBSD Architects

Lloyd H. Siegel, FAIA
U.S. Department of Veterans
Affairs

David M. Sine, CSP, ARM
National Association of Psychiatric
Health Systems

Judith Smith, MHA
Smith Hager Bajo, Inc.

Joseph J. Strauss, AIA, ACHA
Mitretek Systems

Andrew J. Streifel
University of Minnesota
Department of Environmental
Health & Safety

Dana E. Swenson, PE
UMass Memorial Health Care
System

Tom A. Thliveris, AIA
Arizona Department of Health
Services

Dan R. Thompson, MD, MA
Albany Medical College

George R. Tingwald, MD, AIA,
ACHA
Skidmore, Owings & Merrill

David B. Uhaze, RA
New Jersey Department of
Community Affairs

Enrique J. Unanue, AIA, ACHA
Illinois Department of Public
Health

Marjorie Underwood, RN, BSN,
CIC
Three Rivers Community Hospital
Association for Professionals in
Infection Control & Epidemiology

Christopher Upton, AIA, FAAMA,
CSI
Kirksey

Walter Vernon, PE
Mazzetti & Associates

Marjorie E. Vincent, RN, MBA,
CNOR, CASC
Woodrum/ASD

Ronald J. Vitori, MD
Axis Construction Corporation

Robert D. White, MD
Memorial Hospital
Consensus Committee to Establish
Recommended Standards for
NICU Design

Dale Woodin, CHFM, SASHE
American Society for Healthcare
Engineering (of the American
Hospital Association)

M. Judy Zumbo, RN, BSN, JD
Delaware Office of Health Facilities
Licensing & Certification

1

General

1.1 Introduction

Appendix material, which appears in shaded boxes at the bottom of the page, is advisory only.

1 General Considerations

1.1 Applicability

1.1.1 The provisions of this chapter shall apply to all health care facility projects.

1.1.2 This document covers health care facilities common to communities in the United States.

1.1.3 Facilities with unique services will require special consideration. However, sections herein may be applicable for parts of any facility and may be used where appropriate.

1.2 About This Document

These *Guidelines for Design and Construction of Health Care Facilities* (Guidelines) are developed through a consensus process similar to one approved by the American National Standards Institute. This process brings together the members of the Health Guidelines Revision Committee (HGRC) of the Facility Guidelines Institute Inc. (FGI). The HGRC is a balanced group of volunteers representing varied viewpoints and interests in health care facility planning, design, and construction. It considers proposals for change received from the public; achieves consensus on health care facility planning, design, and construction issues; and develops proposed revisions to the previous edition of these Guidelines. The proposed revisions are then published for public comment and revised by the HGRC, as needed, in response to those comments. The product of this revision process is then compiled and published as a new edition of the Guidelines by the American Institute of Architects (AIA).

1.2.1 Uses of This Document

These Guidelines are made available for a wide variety of public and private uses. These include reference in laws, codes, rules, and regulations, as well as use in private self-regulation and standardization of space and equipment requirements and the promotion of safe practices and methods in planning, design, and construction for various types of health care facilities.

1.2.1.1 Regulatory use. Use of these Guidelines or any portion thereof for regulatory purposes should be accomplished through adoption by reference. The term "adoption by reference" means the citing of title, edition, and publishing information only.

(1) Any deletions, additions, and changes desired by the adopting authority should be noted separately in the adopting instrument.

(2) In order to assist FGI in following the uses made of this document, adopting authorities are requested to notify FGI when they adopt these Guidelines or use them in any other regulatory fashion.

1.2.2 Disclaimers

1.2.2.1 While FGI administers the process and establishes rules to promote fairness in the development of consensus, it does not independently test, evaluate, or verify the accuracy of any information or the soundness of any judgments or advice contained in these Guidelines.

1.2.2.2 FGI endeavors to develop performance-oriented minimum requirements as suggested standards for American health care facility design, without prescribing design solutions. FGI disclaims liability for any personal injury or property or other damages of any nature whatsoever, whether special, indirect, consequential, or compensatory, directly or indirectly resulting from the publication, use of, or reliance on this document. FGI also makes no guaranty or warranty as to the accuracy or completeness of any information published herein.

1.2.2.3 In issuing and making this document available, FGI and the AIA are not undertaking to render professional or other services for or on behalf of any person or entity. Nor are FGI and the AIA undertaking to perform any duty owed by any person or entity to someone else.

1.2.2.4 Anyone using this document should rely on his or her own independent judgment or, as appropriate, seek the advice of a competent professional in determining the exercise of reasonable care in any given circumstance.

1.2.2.5 Neither FGI nor the AIA has any power, nor do they undertake, to police or enforce compliance with the contents of this document. Nor do FGI or the AIA list, certify, test, or inspect designs or construction for compliance with this document.

1.2.2.6 Any certification or other statement of compliance with the requirements of this document shall not be attributable to FGI or the AIA and is solely the responsibility of the certifier or maker of the statement.

1.2.3 Copyright

The content of this document, in both book and CD form, is copyrighted by the Facility Guidelines Institute, Inc. (FGI), and its compilation is copyrighted by the American Institute of Architects (AIA). By making this document available for use and adoption by public authorities and private users, FGI and the AIA do not waive any rights in copyright to this document.

1.3 How to Use These Guidelines

1.3.1 Basic Organization

1.3.1.1 Main body. The main body of this document comprises four parts:

(1) Part 1 contains chapters that address considerations applicable to all health care facilities, except as noted or modified in specific facility-type chapters in the remaining parts.

(2) Part 2 addresses inpatient care, with chapters devoted to general hospitals, small primary care hospitals, rehabilitation facilities, and psychiatric hospitals.

(3) Part 3 addresses ambulatory care, including chapters devoted to same day outpatient facilities and adult day care facilities.

(4) Part 4 addresses other health care venues, including long-term, residential, and other care settings. Chapters are devoted to nursing facilities; hospice care; assisted living; and mobile, transportable, and relocatable units.

1.3.1.2 Appendix. An appendix is associated with each chapter in the main body of the text.

(1) An asterisk (*) preceding a paragraph number indicates that explanatory or educational material can be found in an appendix item located at the bottom of the page.

(2) Appendix items are identified by the letter "A" preceding the paragraph number in the main text to which they relate.

1.3.1.3 Front and back matter

(1) Informative introductory sections, including a preface, a summary of major additions and revisions to the previous edition, acknowledgments, and the table of contents precede the main body of the document.

(2) A glossary of terms and a detailed index follow the main body of the text, together with forms for use in submitting requests for formal interpretations and proposals to change these Guidelines. For Guidelines 2006, a "where to find it" matrix of relocated information has been added to help readers familiar with previous editions of these Guidelines find information that has been moved to a different location in the reorganized document.

1.3.2 Minimum Standards for New Facilities

Each chapter in this document contains information intended as minimum standards for designing and constructing new health care facility projects.

1.3.2.1 Standards set forth in these Guidelines shall be considered as minimum.

1.3.2.2 Insofar as practical, these standards relate to desired performance or results or both.

1.3.3 Code Language

For brevity and convenience, these standards are presented in "code language." Use of words such as shall indicates mandatory language only where the text is applied by an adopting authority having jurisdiction (AHJ). However, when adopted by an AHJ, design and construction shall conform to the requirements of these Guidelines.

1.3.4 Other Codes

These Guidelines address certain details of construction and engineering that are important for health care facility design and construction, but they are not intended to be all-inclusive, nor shall they be used to the exclusion of other guidance. When applicable, other details of construction and engineering that are part of good design practice and building regulation shall be consulted in addition to these Guidelines.

1.3.4.1 Local codes. For aspects of design and construction not included in these Guidelines, local governing building codes shall apply.

1.3.4.2 Model codes. Where there is no local governing building code, the prevailing model code used within the relevant geographic area is hereby specified for all requirements not otherwise specified in these Guidelines.

1.3.4.3 Life Safety Code. The Centers for Medicare and Medicaid Services, which is responsible for Medicare and Medicaid reimbursement, has adopted the National Fire Protection Association Life Safety Code, NFPA 101. Facilities participating in Medicare and Medicaid programs shall comply with that code.

1.3.4.4 AHJ verification. Some projects may be subject to the regulations of several different jurisdictions, including local, state, and federal authorities. While coordination efforts have been made, these Guidelines may not always be consistent with all applicable codes, rules, and regulations. Therefore, it is essential that individual project requirements be verified as appropriate with all authorities having jurisdiction. Should requirements be conflicting or contradictory, the authority having primary responsibility for resolution should be consulted.

1.3.5 Deviations

These Guidelines are not intended to restrict innovations and improvements in design or construction techniques. Accordingly, authorities adopting these standards as codes may approve plans and specifications that contain deviations if it is determined the applicable intent or objective has been met. Final implementation of these Guidelines may be subject to requirements of the authority having jurisdiction.

2 Interpretations of Requirements

Although the ultimate interpretation of information contained in this document is the responsibility of the adopting authority having jurisdiction, where applicable, the value of advisory commentary has been recognized.

2.1 Purpose of Interpretation

2.1.1. Interpretations of the language in the document are intended to provide clarification; a summary of any background and previous discussion, if appropriate; and a rationale for the interpretation rendered.

2.1.2. It is understood that any such interpretation is advisory in nature, intended to assist the user and adopting authority having jurisdiction to maximize the value of these Guidelines.

2.2 Requesting an Interpretation

2.2.1. The interpretation of a specific standard contained in these Guidelines may be requested from the Facility Guidelines Institute (FGI) with a detailed request.

2.2.2. Requests for interpretation should be submitted to FGI following the directions at the back of the book or by including the information requested in the directions in an e-mail message to interpretations@fgi-guidelines.org.

3 Renovation

3.1 Compliance Requirements

Where renovation or replacement work is done within an existing facility, all new work or additions or both shall comply, insofar as practical, both with applicable sections of these Guidelines and with appropriate parts of NFPA 101, covering New Health Care Occupancies.

3.1.1 Exceptions

Where major structural elements make total compliance impractical or impossible, exceptions should be considered.

3.1.1.1 This recommendation does not guarantee that an exception will be granted, but does attempt to minimize restrictions on those improvements where total compliance would not substantially improve safety but would create an unreasonable hardship.

3.1.1.2 These standards should not be construed as prohibiting a single phase of improvement. (For example, a facility may plan to replace a flammable ceiling with noncombustible material but lack funds to do other corrective work.) However, they are not intended as encouragement to ignore deficiencies when resources are available to correct life-threatening problems. (See Section 1.1-7.3.)

3.1.2 Temporary Waivers

When parts of an existing facility essential to continued overall facility operation cannot comply with particular standards, those standards may be temporarily waived if patient care and safety are not jeopardized.

3.2 Affected Areas

In renovation projects and additions to existing facilities, only that portion of the total facility affected by the project shall comply with applicable sections of these Guidelines and with appropriate parts of NFPA 101 covering New Health Care Occupancies.

3.3 Unaffected Areas

Those existing portions of the facility that are not included in the renovation but that are essential to the functioning of the complete facility, as well as existing building areas that receive less than substantial amounts of new work, shall, at a minimum, comply with the relevant section of NFPA 101 for Existing Health Care Occupancies

3.4 Functional Requirements and Safety

When construction is complete, the facility shall satisfy functional requirements for the appropriate classification (general hospital, skilled nursing facility, etc.), in an environment that will provide acceptable care and safety to all occupants.

3.5 Conversion

When a building is converted from one occupancy to another, it shall comply with the new occupancy requirements.

3.5.1 For purposes of life safety, conversion from a hospital to a nursing facility or vice versa is not considered a change in occupancy.

3.5.2 Conversion to other appropriate use or replacement should be considered when cost prohibits compliance with acceptable standards.

3.6 Undiminished Safety

Renovations, including new additions, shall not diminish the safety level that existed prior to the start of the work; however, safety in excess of that required for new facilities is not required.

3.7 Long-Range Improvement

3.7.1 Nothing in these Guidelines shall be construed as restrictive to a facility that chooses to do work or alterations as part of a phased long-range safety improvement plan.

3.7.2 All hazards to life and safety and all areas of non-compliance with applicable codes and regulations shall be corrected as soon as possible in accordance with a plan of correction.

4 Design Standards for the Disabled

4.1 Federal Standards

4.1.1 Regulations

4.1.1.1 The Americans with Disabilities Act (ADA), which became law in 1990, extends comprehensive civil rights protection to individuals with disabilities. Under Titles II and III of the ADA, public, private, and public service hospitals and other health care facilities are required to comply with the Accessibility Guidelines for Buildings and Facilities (ADAAG) for alterations and new construction.

4.1.1.2 The Uniform Federal Accessibility Standards (UFAS) also provides criteria for the disabled.

4.1.2 Implementation

Implementation of UFAS and ADAAG for federal facilities is handled in the following ways:

4.1.2.1 Compliance with UFAS

4.1.2.2 Compliance with ADAAG

4.1.2.3 Compliance with a combination of UFAS and ADAAG using the most stringent criteria

4.1.3 Applicability
Individual federal agencies will provide direction on applicable criteria to be used for the design of federal facilities.

4.2 State and Local Standards

4.2.1 Many state and local jurisdictions have adopted American National Standards Institute (ANSI) A117.1, "American National Standard for Accessible and Usable Buildings and Facilities," which is also available for use in providing quality design for the disabled.

4.2.2 State and local standards for accessibility and usability may be more stringent than ADA, UFAS, or ANSI A117.1. Designers and owners, therefore, must assume responsibility for verification of all applicable requirements.

4.3 Special Needs in Health Care Facilities
The users health care facilities often have very different accessibility needs than the typical adult individual with disabilities addressed by the model standards and guidelines mentioned above. Hospital patients, and especially nursing facility residents, due to their stature, reach, and strength characteristics, typically require the assistance of caregivers during transfer maneuvers. Many prescriptive requirements of model accessibility standards place both older persons and caregivers at greater risk of injury than do facilities that would be considered noncompliant. Thus, flexibility may be permitted for the use of assistive configurations that provide considerations for transfer assistance.

5 Provisions for Disasters

5.1 Needs Assessment
In locations where there is recognized potential for hurricanes, tornadoes, flooding, earthquake, or other regional disasters, planning and design shall consider the need to protect the life safety of all health care facility occupants and the potential need for continuing services following such a disaster.

5.1.1 Facility Assessment
Owners of existing facilities should undertake an assessment of their facility with respect to its ability to withstand the effects of regional natural disasters. The assessment should consider performance of structural and critical nonstructural building systems and the likelihood of loss of externally supplied power, gas, water, and communications under such conditions.

5.1.2 Facility Planning
Facility master planning should consider mitigation measures required to address conditions that may be hazardous to patients and conditions that may compromise the ability of the facility to fulfill its planned post-emergency medical response.

5.1.3 Seismic Considerations
Particular attention should be paid to seismic considerations in areas where the seismic design classification of a building would fall into Seismic Design Categories C, D, E, or F as described in American Society of Civil Engineers/Structural Engineering Institute (ASCE/SEI) 7-05, "Minimum Design Loads for Buildings and Other Structures." (See Section 1.1-7.5.1.)

5.2 NBC Hazards Control
When consistent with their functional program and disaster planning, acute care facilities with emergency services can serve as receiving, triage, and initial treatment centers in the event of nuclear, biological, or chemical (NBC) exposure. These facilities shall designate specific area(s) for these functions.

5.2.1 Facilities may designate an outdoor parking lot adjacent to the emergency department to serve as a primary decontamination area, which should include appropriate plumbing fixtures (e.g., hot and cold water) and drainage.

5.2.2 Utilization of screens and tents may be needed.

5.2.3 Other contingencies may require airborne infection isolation, application and removal of therapeutic chemical substances, and temporary container storage of contaminated materials.

5.2.4 Hand-washing and shower capabilities will usually be of paramount importance in biohazard control efforts.

5.3 Wind- and Earthquake-Resistant Design for New Buildings

5.3.1 Regulations
5.3.1.1. ASCE/SEI 7. The seismic provisions in ASCE/SEI 7 are based on the National Earthquake Hazards

Reduction Program (NEHRP) provisions developed by the Building Seismic Safety Council (BSSC) for the Federal Emergency Management Agency (FEMA). Facilities shall be designed to meet the requirements of ASCE/SEI 7-05 or the building codes specified in Section 1.1-7.5.1, provided their requirements are substantially equivalent to ASCE/SEI 7.

5.3.1.2. Other seismic standards. The following seismic standards are essentially equivalent to the ASCE/SEI 7 provisions:

(1) NEHRP Recommended Provisions for Seismic Regulations for New Buildings

(2) International Building Code

5.3.1.3. Executive Order 12699, dated January 5, 1990, specified the use of the maps in the most recent edition of ANSI A58 for seismic safety of federal and federally assisted or regulated new building construction.

5.3.2 Design for Continued Operation
For those facilities that must remain operational in the aftermath of a disaster, special design is required to protect systems and essential building services such as power, water, medical gas systems, and, in certain areas, air conditioning. In addition, special consideration must be given to the likelihood of temporary loss of externally supplied power, gas, water, and communications

5.3.3 Seismic Construction Inspection
The owner shall provide special inspection during construction of seismic systems described in Section 11A.1.3 and testing described in Section 11A.2 of ASCE/SEI 7-05.

5.3.4 Roof Considerations
5.3.4.1 Roof coverings and mechanical equipment shall be securely fastened or ballasted to the supporting roof construction and shall provide weather protection for the building at the roof.

5.3.4.2 Roof covering shall be applied on clean and dry decks in accordance with the manufacturer's instructions, these Guidelines, and related references.

5.3.4.3 In addition to the wind force design and construction requirements specified, particular attention shall be given to roofing, entryways, glazing, and flashing design to minimize uplift, impact damage, and other damage that could seriously impair functioning of the building.

5.3.4.4 If ballast is used it shall be designed so as not to become a projectile.

5.4 Flood Protection
Flood Protection, Executive Order No. 11988, was issued to minimize financial loss from flood damage to facilities constructed with federal assistance. In accordance with that order:

5.4.1 Possible flood effects shall be considered when selecting and developing the site.

5.4.2 Insofar as possible, new facilities shall not be located on designated floodplains.

5.4.3 Where locating a facility on a floodplain is unavoidable, consult the Corps of Engineers regional office for the latest applicable regulations pertaining to flood insurance and protection measures that may be required.

5.5 Emergency Supply Storage

5.5.1 Required Supplies
Should normal operations be disrupted, the facility shall provide adequate storage capacity for, or a functional program contingency plan to obtain, the following supplies:

5.5.1.1 Food

5.5.1.2 Sterile supplies

5.5.1.3 Pharmacy supplies

5.5.1.4 Linen

5.5.1.5 Water for sanitation

5.5.2 Storage Capacity
Such storage capacity or plans shall be sufficient for at least four continuous days of operation.

6 National Standards for the Protection of Certain Health Information

6.1 HIPAA
The Health Insurance Portability and Accountability Act (HIPAA) became law in 1996. HIPAA consists of three major parts: the Privacy Rule, Transaction and Code Sets, and the Security Rule.

6.1.1 The U.S. Department of Health and Human Services (HHS) issued the Privacy Rule to implement the requirement of HIPAA. Within HHS, the Office of Civil Rights (OCR) has responsibility for enforcement of the HIPAA regulations. HHS may provide direction and clarification on the Privacy Rule and Security Rule.

6.1.2 HIPAA does not preempt or override laws that grant individuals even greater privacy protection. Additionally, covered entities are free to retain or adopt more protective policies or practices.

6.1.3 HIPAA provides for civil and even criminal penalties for violations.

6.1.4 Ultimately, designers and owners must assume responsibility in developing policies and procedures for verification of all applicable requirements that appropriately limit access to personal health information without sacrificing the quality of health care.

7 Codes and Standards

7.1 Safe Environment
Every health care facility shall provide and maintain a safe environment for patients, personnel, and the public.

7.2 Code Compliance
In the absence of state or local requirements, the project shall comply with approved nationally recognized building codes except as modified in the latest edition of NFPA 101 and/or herein.

7.2.1 References made in these Guidelines to appropriate model codes and standards do not, generally, duplicate wording of the referenced codes.

7.2.2 National Fire Protection Association (NFPA) standards, especially NFPA 101, are the basic codes of reference; but other codes and/or standards may be included as part of these Guidelines (see Section 1.1-7.5.1).

7.2.3 Referenced code material is contained in the issue current at the time of this publication.

7.2.4 The latest revision of code material is usually a clarification of intent and/or general improvement in safety concepts and may be used as an explanatory document for earlier code editions.

7.2.5 Questions of applicability should be addressed as the need occurs. The actual version of a code adopted by a jurisdiction may be different. Confirm the version adopted in a specific location with the authority having jurisdiction.

7.3 Equivalency

7.3.1 Performance Standards
Insofar as practical, the minimum standards in these Guidelines have been established to obtain a desired performance result.

7.3.2 Prescriptive Standards
Prescriptive limitations (such as exact minimum dimensions or quantities), when given, describe a condition that is commonly recognized as a practical standard for normal operation. For example, reference to a room or area by the patient, equipment, or staff activity that identifies its use avoids the need for complex descriptions of procedures for appropriate functional planning.

7.3.3 Technical Standards
7.3.3.1 NFPA document 101A is a technical standard for evaluating equivalency to certain requirements of NFPA 101, the Life Safety Code.

7.3.3.2 The Fire Safety Evaluation System (FSES) has become widely recognized as a method for establishing a safety level equivalent to that of the Life Safety Code. It may be useful for evaluating existing facilities that will be affected by renovation. For purposes of these Guidelines, the FSES is not intended to be used for new construction.

7.3.4 Equivalency
While these Guidelines are adopted as a regulatory standard by many jurisdictions, it is the intent of the document to permit and promote equivalency concepts.

7.3.4.1 When contemplating equivalency allowances, the authority having jurisdiction may use a variety of expert sources to make equivalency findings and may document the reasons for approval or denial of equivalency to the requester.

7.3.4.2 Alternate methods, procedures, design criteria, and functional variations from these Guidelines, because of extraordinary circumstances, new programs, or unusual conditions, may be approved by the authority having jurisdiction when the facility can effectively demonstrate that the intent of the Guidelines is met and that the variation does not reduce the safety or operational effectiveness of the facility below that required by the exact language of the Guidelines.

7.3.4.3 In all cases where specific limits are described, equivalent solutions will be acceptable if the authority having jurisdiction approves them as meeting the intent of these standards.

7.3.4.4 Nothing in this document shall be construed as restricting innovations that provide an equivalent level of performance with these standards in a manner other than that which is prescribed by this document, provided that no other safety element or system is compromised in order to establish equivalency.

7.4 English/Metric Measurements

7.4.1 Where measurements are a part of this document, English units are given as the basic standards, with equivalent metric units in parentheses.

7.4.2 Either method shall be consistently used throughout a given design.

7.5 Referenced Codes and Standards

Codes and standards that have been referenced in whole or in part in the various sections of this document are listed in Section 1.1-7.5.1. Names and addresses of the originators are included in Section 1.1-7.5.2 for information.

7.5.1 Publication References

Users of these Guidelines are encouraged to use these publications for further information as may be necessary to achieve the final product. The issues available at the time of publication are cited. Later issues will

normally be acceptable where requirements for function and safety are not reduced; however, editions of different dates may have portions renumbered or retitled. Care must be taken to ensure that appropriate sections are used.

Access Board (an independent federal agency) (http://www.access-board.gov/ufas/ufas-html/ufas.htm). *Uniform Federal Accessibility Standard* (UFAS).

American Conference of Governmental Industrial Hygienists (www.acgih.org).
   Industrial Ventilation: A Manual of Recommended Practice, 25th ed.

American Society of Civil Engineers (http://www.pubs.asce.org).
   ASCE/SEI 7-05 *Minimum Design Loads for Buildings and Other Structures.*

American Society of Heating, Refrigerating and Air-Conditioning Engineers (ASHRAE) (http://www.ashrae.org).
   ASHRAE *Handbook of Fundamentals.*
      2003 ASHRAE Handbook–HVAC Applications.
   Humidity Control Design Guide for Commercial and Institutional Buildings.
   Standard 52.1-1992, *Gravimetric and Dust-Spot Procedures for Testing Air-Cleaning Devices Used in General Ventilation for Removing Particulate Matter.*
   Standard 52.2, *Method of Testing General Ventilation Air-Cleaning Devices for Removal Efficiency by Particle Size.*
   Standard 55-2004, *Thermal Environmental Conditions for Human Occupancy.*
   Standard 62-1999, *Ventilation for Acceptable Indoor Air Quality.*
   Standard 90.1, *Energy Standard for Buildings Except Low-Rise Residential Buildings.*
      Standard 154-2003, *Ventilation for Commerical Cooking Operations.*

American Society of Mechanical Engineers (ASME) (http://www.asme.org/cns/departments/Safety/Public/A17/ or www.ansi.org).
   ANSI/ASME A17.1, *Safety Code for Elevators and Escalators*, 2000.

ANSI/ASME A17.3, *Safety Code for Existing Elevators and Escalators*, 2002.

American Society for Testing and Materials (ASTM) (www.astm.org)
C1071-05, *Standard Specification for Fibrous Glass Duct Lining Insulation (Thermal and Sound Absorbing Material)*, 2005

American Water Works Association (AWWA) (www.awwa.org).
Recommended Practice for Backflow Prevention and Cross-connection Control, 2004.

Americans with Disabilities Act. U.S. Department of Justice ADA Information Line, 1-800-514-0301 or 1-800-514-0383 (TDD). (http://www.usdoj.gov/disabilities.htm).

Association for the Advancement of Medical Instrumentation (www.aami.org).
ANSI/CDV-1 RD62, 2001, *Water Treatment Equipment for Hemodialysis Applications.*

Building Seismic Safety Council (National Institute of Building Sciences) (http://www.bssconline.org).
NEHRP (National Earthquake Hazards Reduction Program) Recommended Provisions for Seismic Regulations for New Buildings, 2000 ed.

Centers for Disease Control and Prevention (CDC) (www.cdc.gov).
"Guidelines for Preventing the Transmission of Mycobacterium tuberculosis in Health-Care Settings, 2005." *Morbidity and Mortality Weekly Report (MMWR)* 2005:54 (No. RR-17). (http://www.cdc.gov/mmwr/PDF/rr/rr5417.pdf)
"Guidelines for Preventing Health Care-Associated Pneumonia, 2003." *Morbidity and Mortality Weekly Report (MMWR)* 53 (RR03); 1-36. (http://www.cdc.gov/ncidod/dhqp/gl_hcpneumonia.html)

College of American Pathologists. 1-800-323-4040 (www.cap.org).
Medical Laboratory Planning and Design, 1985.

Compressed Gas Association (CGA). (http://www.cganet.com/Pubs/CGA_Publications).

Publication #E-10, *Maintenance of Medical Gas and Vacuum Systems in Health-Care Facilities*, 2001.

Defense Standardization Program, U.S. Department of Defense (http://www.dsp.dla.mil).
MIL STD 282, *Filter Units, Protective Clothing, Gas-Mask Components and Related Products: Performance-Test Methods.* (http://assist.daps.dla.mil —Click "Quick Search" and enter "MIL-STD-282" as the document ID.)

Food and Drug Administration (http://www.fda.gov).
FDA Food Code, 2001. (http://www.cfsan.fda.gov/~dms/fc05-toc.html).

Hydronics Institute Division of the Gas Appliance Manufacturers Association (http://www.gamanet.org/).
I-B-R Boiler Ratings Procedural Guide, 2002.
I-B-R Testing and Rating Standards for Baseboard Radiation, 1990.
I-B-R and Rating Standards for Finned Tube (Commercial) Radiation, 1990.

Illuminating Engineering Society of North America (IESNA) (http://www.iesna.org).
ANSI/IESNA RP-28-01, *Lighting and the Visual Environment for Senior Living.*
ANSI/IESNA Publication RP-29-06, *Lighting for Hospitals and Health Care Facilities.*

Industrial Safety Equipment Association (ISEA) (www.ansi.org).
ANSI-Z-358.1-2004, *American National Standard for Emergency Eyewash and Shower Equipment.*

National Association of Psychiatric Health Systems (www.NAPHS.org).
"Guidelines for the Built Environment of Behavioral Health Facilities" (http://www.naphs.org/Teleconference/safetystandards.html)

National Council on Radiation Protection and Measurements (NCRP). (http://www.ncrp.com/ncrprpts.html)
Report #102, *Medical X-Ray, Electron Beam and Gamma-Ray Protection for Energies Up to 50 MeV (Equipment Design, Performance and Use)*, 1989.

Report # 144, *Radiation Protection Design for Particle Accelerator Facilities*, 2003.

Report # 147, *Structural Shielding Design for Medical Use of X Ray Imaging Facilities*, 2004.

National Fire Protection Association
(http://www.nfpa.org/categoryList.asp).

NFPA 13, *Installation of Sprinkler Systems*, 2002.

NFPA 20, *Standard for the Installation of Stationary Fire Pumps for Fire Protection*, 2003.

NFPA 70, *National Electrical Code*, 2005.

NFPA 72, *National Fire Alarm Code*, 2002

NFPA 80, *Standard for Fire Doors, Fire Windows*, 1999.

NFPA 82, *Standard on Incinerators and Waste and Linen Handling Systems and Equipment*, 2004.

NFPA 90A, *Standard for the Installation of Air Conditioning and Ventilating Systems*, 2002.

NFPA 90B, *Standard for the Installation of War Air Heating and Air-Conditioning Systems*, 20002.

NFPA 96, *Standard for Ventilation Control and Fire Protection of Commercial Cooking Operations*, 2004.

NFPA 99, *Standard for Health Care Facilities*, 2005.

NFPA 101, *Life Safety Code*, 2003.

NFPA 110, *Standard for Emergency and Standby Power Systems*, 2005.

NFPA 253, *Standard Method of Test for Critical Radiant Flux of Floor Covering Systems Using a Radiant Heat Energy Source*, 2000.

NFPA 255, *Standard Method of Test of Surface Burning Characteristics of Building Materials*, 2000.

NFPA 258, *Standard Research Test Method of Determining Smoke Generation of Solid Materials*, 2001.

NFPA 418, *Standard for Heliports*, 2001.

NFPA 701, *Standard Methods of Fire Tests for Flame Propagation of Textiles and Films*, 2004.

NFPA 801, *Standard for Fire Protection for Facilities Handling Radioactive Materials*, 2003.

Nuclear Regulatory Commission (NRC)
(http://www.nrc.gov/reading-rm/doc-collections/cfr/).

Code of Federal Regulations (CFR) Title 10—Energy, Chapter 1—Nuclear Regulatory Commission Part 20 (10 CFR 20), Standards for Protection Against Radiation.

Part 35 (10 CFR 35), Medical Use of Byproduct Material.

Occupational Safety and Health Administration, U.S. Department of Labor (www.osha.org).

Code of Federal Regulations (CFR) Title 29—OSHA Regulations. Part 1910 (29 CFR 1910), Occupational Safety and Health Standards. (http://www.osha.gov/pls/oshaweb/owastand.display_standard_group?p_toc_level=1&p_part_number=1910)

Plumbing-Heating-Cooling Contractors—National Association (PHCC—National Association) (http://www.phccweb.org/).

National Standard Plumbing Code, 2000.

7.5.2 Resources for Codes and Standards

Providers of some of the codes and standards used in this publication are listed here. Unless otherwise noted in Section 1.1-7.5.1, federal publications may be obtained from the Government Printing Office in Washington, D.C.

Air Conditioning and Refrigeration Institute
4100 North Fairfax Drive, Suite 200
Arlington, VA 22203
Tel. 703-524-8800
Web: http://www.ari.org

Architectural and Transportation Barriers Compliance Board
Office of Technical and Information Services
1331 F St., N.W., Suite 1000
Washington, DC 20004-1111
Tel. 202-272-5434, 1-800-872-2253
Web: http://www.access-board.gov

Americans with Disabilities Act
U.S. Department of Justice
950 Pennsylvania Ave., N.W.
Washington, DC 20530-0001
Tel. 202-514-2000
Web: http://www.usdoj.gov/crt/ada/adahom1.htm

American National Standards Institute (ANSI)
1819 L Street, N.W., Sixth floor
Washington, DC 20036
Tel. 202-293-8020
Web: http://www.ansi.org

American Society of Civil Engineers
1801 Alexander Bell Drive
Reston, VA 20191-4400
Tel. 1-800-548-2723, 703-295-6300
Web: http://www.asce.org

American Society of Heating, Refrigerating and
Air-Conditioning Engineers
1791 Tullie Circle, N.E.
Atlanta, GA 30329
Tel. 1-800-527-4723, 404-636-8400
Web: http://www.ashrae.org

American Society of Mechanical Engineers (ASME)
Three Park Avenue
New York, NY 10016-5990
Tel. 1-800-843-2763
Web: http://www.asme.org

American Society for Testing and Materials
100 Barr Harbor Drive
West Conshocken, PA 19428-2959
Tel. 610-832-9585
Web: http://www.astm.org

Association for the Advancement of Medical
Instrumentation
1110 N. Glebe Road, Suite 220
Arlington, VA 22201-5762
Tel. 1-800-332-2264, 703-525-4890
Web: http://www.aami.org

Building Seismic Safety Council
National Institute of Building Sciences
1090 Vermont Avenue, N.W., Suite 700
Washington, DC 20005-4905
Tel. 202-289-7800
Web: http://www.bssconline.org

Centers for Disease Control and Prevention
Hospital Infection Control Practices (HICPAC)
Center for Infection Control
1600 Clifton Road
Atlanta, GA 30333
Tel. 404-639-3311, 1-800-311-3435
Web: http://www.cdc.gov

College of American Pathologists
325 Waukegan Road
Northfield, IL 60093-2750
Tel. 1-800-323-4040
Web: http://www.cap.org

Compressed Gas Association
4221 Walney Road, Fifth floor
Chantilly, VA 20151-2923
Tel. 703-788-2700
Web: http://www.cganet.com

Food and Drug Administration (FDA)
Center for Food Safety and Applied Nutrition
5100 Paint Branch Parkway
College Park, MD 20740-3835
Tel. 1-888-SAFEFOOD
Web: http://cfsan.fda.gov

General Services Administration
1800 F Street, N.W.
Washington, DC 20405
Web: http://www.gsa.gov

Hydronics Institute (Division of Gas Appliance
Manufacturer Association (GAMA))
35 Russo Place, P.O. Box 218
Berkeley Heights, NJ 07922
Tel. 908-464-8200
Web: http://www.gamanet.org

Illuminating Engineering Society of North America
(IESNA)
120 Wall Street, Floor 17
New York, NY 10005
Tel. 212-248-5000
Web: http://www.iesna.org

International Code Council
5203 Leesburg Pike, Suite 600
Falls Church, VA 22041-3401
Tel. 703-379-1546
Web: http://www.iccsafe.org

National Council on Radiation Protection and
Measurement
7910 Woodmont Avenue, Suite 400
Bethesda, MD 20814-3095
Tel. 301-657-2652
Web: http://www.ncrponline.com

National Fire Protection Association (NFPA)
1 Batterymarch Park
P.O. Box 9101
Quincy, MA 02169-7471
Tel. 617-770-3000
Web: http://www.nfpa.org

National Institute of Standards and Technology
(formerly National Bureau of Standards)
100 Bureau Dr., Stop 3460
Gaithersburg, MD 20899-3460
Tel. 301-975-6478
Web: http://www.nist.gov

National Technical Information Service (NTIS)
U.S. Department of Commerce Technology
Administration
5285 Port Royal Road
Springfield, VA 22161
Tel. 703-605-6858
Web: http://www.ntis.gov

Nuclear Regulatory Commission
One White Flint North
11555 Rockville Pike
Rockville, MD 20852-2738
Tel. 301-415-7000
Web: http://www.nrc.gov

Occupational Safety and Health Administration
U.S. Department of Labor
200 Constitution Avenue, N.W., Room N3647
Washington, DC 20210
Tel. 1-800-321-6742
Web: http://www.osha.gov

Plumbing-Heating-Cooling Contractors—
National Association
180 South Washington Street, P.O. Box 6808
Falls Church, VA 22040
Tel. 1-800-533-7694
Web: http://www.phccweb.org
Underwriters Laboratories, Inc.
333 Pfingsten Road
Northbrook, IL 60062-2096
Tel. 847-854-3577
Web: http://www.ul.com

1.2 Environment of Care

Appendix material, which appears in shaded boxes at the bottom of the page, is advisory only.

1 General Considerations

The goal of the Environment of Care chapter is to identify overall environment of care components (including key elements of the physical environment) and functional requirements that directly affect the experience of all people involved in the health care delivery system. These components and requirements influence patient outcomes and satisfaction, dignity, privacy, confidentiality, and safety, and the incidence of medical errors, patient and staff stress, and facility operations. (While the environment of care is the focus of this chapter, it is also an element in individual chapters where the demonstrated value and necessity of such features are unique to individual requirements.)

1.1 Applicability

The provisions of this chapter shall apply to all health facility projects.

*1.2 Framework for Health Facility Design

Because the built environment has a profound effect on health, productivity, and the natural environment, health care facilities shall be designed within a framework that recognizes the primary mission of health care (including "first, do no harm") and that considers the larger context of enhanced patient environment, employee effectiveness, and resource stewardship.

2 Functional Program

2.1 Requirements

The health care provider shall supply for each project a functional program for the facility that describes the purpose of the project, environment of care components (including key elements of the physical environment), functional requirements, and other basic information related to fulfillment of the institution's objectives, including but not limited to the projected demand or utilization, staffing patterns, departmental relationships, and space requirements. Projects that only involve equipment replacement, fire safety upgrades, or minor renovations do not require a functional program.

2.1.1 Required Services

A description of those services necessary for the complete operation of the facility shall be provided in the functional program.

2.1.2 Environment of Care Components

The relationships between the following environment of care components (including key elements of the physical environment) and the functional requirements shall be addressed in the functional program:

*2.1.2.1 Delivery of care model (concepts)

(1) The delivery of care model shall be defined in the functional program.

(2) The functional program shall support the delivery of care model to allow the design of the physical environment to respond appropriately.

2.1.2.2 Facility and service users (people). The physical environment shall support the facility and service users in their effort to administer the delivery of care model.

*2.1.2.3 Systems design. The physical environment shall support organizational, technological, and building systems designed for the intended delivery of care model.

*2.1.2.4 Layout/operational planning. The layout and design of the physical environment shall enhance operational efficiencies and the satisfaction of patients or residents, families, and staff.

2.1.2.5 Physical environment. The physical environment shall be designed to support the intended delivery of care model and address the key elements listed below:

*(1) **Light and views.** Use and availability of natural light, illumination, and views shall be considered in the design of the physical environment.

*(2) **Clarity of access (wayfinding).** Clarity of access shall be addressed in the overall planning of the facility, individual departments, and clinical areas.

APPENDIX

A2.1.2.3 Systems design
Physical relationships between services or new aggregations of services should be clearly defined and supported. Clustering of related services affects the criteria for design of the physical environment.

Information technology, medical technology, and/or staff utilization and cross training are issues that should be addressed.

A2.1.2.4 Layout/operational planning
Criteria for evaluation of the layouts should be consistent with the delivery of care model to allow each optional layout and operational plan to be reviewed appropriately.

A2.1.2.5 (1) Light and views
Natural light, views of nature, and access to the outdoors should be considered in the design of the physical environment wherever possible.

a. Siting and organization of the building should respond to and prioritize unique natural views and other natural site features.

b. Access to natural light should be achieved without going into private spaces (i.e., staff should not have to enter a patient/resident room to have access to natural light). Examples include windows at the ends of corridors, skylights into deep areas of the building in highly trafficked areas, transoms, and door sidelights.

c. In residential health care occupancies, dining areas, lounges, and activity areas should be designed to include natural light.

d. Hospitals and long-term care facilities should provide a garden or other controlled exterior space that is accessible to building occupants. Consider specifically designed therapeutic and restorative gardens for patients and/or caregivers as a component of the functional program, as appropriate.

e. Artificial lighting strategies. The Illuminating Engineering Society of North America (IESNA) has developed two publications that apply to health care facilities; both are American National Standards Institute (ANSI) standards. ANSI/IESNA RP-29, Lighting for Hospitals and Health Care Facilities addresses lighting for the general population and special lighting for medical procedures. ANSI/IESNA RP-28, Lighting and the Visual Environment for Senior Living addresses the special lighting needs of older adults.

f. Lamp selection should address color rendering properties.

A2.1.2.5 (2) Clarity of access (wayfinding)
a. Entry points to the medical facility should be clearly defined from all major exterior circulation modes (roadways, bus stops, vehicular parking).

b. Clearly visible and understandable signage and visual landmarks for orientation should be provided.

c. Boundaries between public and private areas should be well marked, and clearly distinguished.

d. A system of interior "landmarks" should be developed to aid occupants in cognitive understanding of destinations. These may include water features, major art, distinctive color, or decorative treatments at major decision points in the building. These features should attempt to involve tactile, auditory and language cues, as well as visual recognition.

e. Signage systems should be flexible, expandable, adaptable, and easy to maintain.

*(3) Control of environment. Patient/resident/staff ability to control their environment shall be addressed in the overall planning of the facility consistent with the functional program.

*(4) Privacy and confidentiality. The level of patient or resident privacy and confidentiality shall be addressed in the overall planning of the facility consistent with the functional program.

*(5) Safety and security. The safety and security of patients or residents, staff, and visitors shall be addressed in the overall planning of the facility consistent with the functional program.

*(6) Finishes. The effect of materials, colors, textures, and patterns on patients or residents, staff, and visitors shall be considered in the overall planning and design of the facility. Maintenance and performance shall be considered when selecting these items.

*(7) Cultural responsiveness. The culture of patients or residents, staff, and visitors shall be considered in the overall planning of the facility.

APPENDIX

A2.1.2.5 (3) Control of environment

a. Every effort should be made to allow individual control over as many elements of the environment as possible and reasonable, including but not limited to temperature, lighting, sound, and privacy.

b. Lighting in patient and staff areas should allow for individual control and provide variety in lighting types and levels.

c. Building design should address individual control over the thermal environment through carefully considered zoning of mechanical systems.

d. Noise has been proven to be a negative environmental stressor for patients, families, and staff. Noise should be minimized by the design of the physical environment and the selection of operational systems and equipment.

A2.1.2.5 (4) Privacy and confidentiality

a. Public circulation and staff/patient circulation should be separated wherever possible.

b. Waiting areas for patients on stretchers or in gowns should be located in a private zone within the plan, out of view of the public circulation system.

c. Private alcoves or rooms should be provided for all communication concerning personal information relative to patient illness, care plans, and insurance and financial matters.

d. In facilities with multi-bed rooms, family consultation rooms, grieving rooms, and/or private alcoves in addition to family lounges should be provided to permit patients and families to communicate privately.

A2.1.2.5 (5) Safety and security

a. Attention should be given to balancing readily accessible and visible external access points to the facility with the ability to control and secure all access points in the event of an emergency. Factors such as adequate exterior lighting in parking lots and entry points to the facility and appropriate reception/security services are essential to ensuring a safe environment.

b. Since the strict control of access to a medical facility is neither possible nor appropriate, safety within the facility should also be addressed through the design of circulation paths and functional relationships. Provisions for securing the personal belongings of staff, visitors, and patients or residents should be addressed.

c. The physical environment should be designed to support the overall safety and security policies and protocols of the institution. Safety and security monitoring, when provided, should respect patient privacy and dignity.

A2.1.2.5 (6) Finishes

a. In any design project, the selection of a color palette should be based upon many factors, including the building population, anticipated behavior in the space, time of encounter, and level of stress. The color palette selected should be suitable and appropriate for the specific environment, taking into account the specific activities conducted in that environment.

b. Finishes and color palettes should respond to the geographic location of the health care facility, taking into account climate and light, regional responses to color, and the cultural characteristics of the community served.

A2.1.2.5 (7) Cultural responsiveness

Organizational culture is defined by the history of the organization, leadership philosophy, management style, and caregivers' dispositions.

Regional culture is defined by the physical location and demographics (including age, nationality, religion, and economics) of the communities served.

*(8) Water features. Where provided, open water features shall be equipped to safely manage water quality to protect occupants from infectious or irritating aerosols.

*2.1.2.6 Design process and implementation. Groups (stakeholders) affected by and integral to the design shall be included in the planning and implementation process.

2.1.3 Functional Requirements

The facility shall incorporate the following information into the functional program commensurate with the scope and purpose of the project.

2.1.3.1 The size and function of each space and any other design feature

(1) Include the projected occupant load, numbers and types of staff, patients, residents, visitors, and vendors.

APPENDIX

A2.1.2.5 (8) Water features

Fountains and other open decorative water features may represent a reservoir for opportunistic human pathogens; thus, they are not recommended for installation within any enclosed spaces in health care environments.

a. If a water feature is provided, the design should limit human contact with the water and/or allow for the application of water disinfection systems. Materials used to fabricate the water feature should be resistant to chemical corrosion. Water features should be designed and constructed to minimize water droplet production. Exhaust ventilation should be provided directly above the water feature.

b. If aquariums are used, they should be enclosed to prevent patient or visitor contact with the water. Aquariums are not subject to exhaust ventilation recommendations.

A2.1.2.6 Design process and implementation

An interdisciplinary design team should be assembled as early as possible in the design process. The design team should include but not be limited to administrators, clinicians, infection control specialists, safety officers, support staff, patient advocates/consumers, A/E consultants, and construction specialists. (Also see Section 1.5-A1.3.)

---

(2) Describe the types and projected numbers of procedures for treatment areas.

2.1.3.2 Equipment requirements

(1) Describe building service equipment.

(2) Describe fixed and movable equipment.

2.1.3.3 Circulation patterns

(1) Describe the circulation patterns for staff, patients or residents, and the public.

(2) Describe the circulation patterns for equipment and clean and soiled materials.

(3) Where circulation patterns are a function of asepsis control requirements, note these features.

2.1.3.4 Consideration of potential future expansion that may be needed to accommodate increased demand

2.2 Nomenclature

2.2.1 Use the same names for spaces and departments as used in these Guidelines. If acronyms are used, they shall be clearly defined.

2.2.2 The names and spaces indicated in the functional program shall be consistent with the submitted floor plans.

2.3 Use

2.3.1 Following approval, the functional program shall be made available for use in the development of project design and construction documents.

2.3.2 The facility shall retain the approved functional program with other design data to facilitate future alterations, additions, and program changes.

*3 Sustainable Design

Sustainable design, construction, and maintenance practices to improve building performance shall be considered in the design and renovation of health care facilities.

3.1 Components
The basic components of sustainable design to be considered shall include:

*3.1.1 Site Selection and Development
Design to minimize negative environmental impacts associated with buildings and related site development.

*3.1.2 Waste Minimization
Design to support the minimization of waste in construction and operation.

*3.1.3 Water Quality and Conservation
3.1.3.1 Evaluate potable water quality and conservation in all phases of facility development or renovation.

3.1.3.2 Design for water conservation shall not adversely affect patient health, safety, or infection control.

*3.1.4. Energy Conservation
Proper planning and selection of mechanical and electrical systems, as well as efficient utilization of space and climatic characteristics, can significantly reduce overall energy demand and consumption.

APPENDIX

A3 Sustainable Design
A growing body of knowledge is available to assist design professionals and health care organizations in understanding how buildings affect human health and the environment and how these effects can be mitigated through a variety of strategies.

The U.S. Green Building Council's LEED® Green Building Rating System (www.usgbc.org) has established a third-party certification framework for the design of sustainable buildings; the Green Guide for Health Care™ (www.gghc.org) is a voluntary self-certification metric tool that specifically addresses the health care sector. An increasing number of states and municipalities have individual high performance guidelines or standards. These tools establish "best practice" criteria for site design, water and energy usage, materials, and indoor environmental quality.

To meet these objectives, health care organizations should develop an interdisciplinary design process to guide facility design. The intent of an interdisciplinary design process is to improve building performance by integrating design considerations from project inception.

A3.1.1 Site Selection and Development
Site development considerations include land use, storm water management, habitat preservation, landscape design and irrigation systems, and effects from heat islands.

A3.1.2 Waste Minimization
A 1998 memorandum of understanding between the Environmental Protection Agency (EPA) and the American Hospital Association (AHA) targeted a 33 percent reduction in solid waste by 2005, 50 percent by 2010. As hospitals develop environmentally preferable purchasing standards and implement significant recycling programs to achieve this goal, facilities should consider the space needs associated with these activities.

A3.1.3 Water Quality and Conservation
Potable water consumption reductions may be achieved through the use of low consumption fixtures and controls, landscape design (xeriscaping) and irrigation systems, and replacement of potable water sources for items such as water-cooled pumps and compressors, with non-potable sources or non-evaporative heat rejection equipment (air cooled or ground source).

A3.1.4 Energy Conservation
Health care facilities should consider energy conservation strategies that include but are not limited to the following examples:

1. On major new projects, consider the use of computer modeling to assist in developing and assessing energy conservation strategies and opportunities.

2. Reduce overall energy demand. Examples of strategies include high-efficiency building envelope; low-energy sources of lighting (including use of daylighting); advanced lighting controls; use of high-efficiency equipment, both as part of building mechanical/electrical systems (chillers, air handlers) and for plug loads (EnergyStar copiers, computers, medical equipment).

3. Optimize energy efficiency. Mechanical/electrical control systems should optimize consumption to the minimum actual needs of the building. Consider co-generation systems for converting natural gas to both heat (or cooling) and electricity. Select equipment with improved energy efficiency ratings.

4. Reduce environmental impacts associated with combustion of fossil fuels and refrigerant selection. Consider various renewable sources of energy generation, including purchase of green power, solar and wind energy, or geothermal/ground source heat pumps.

3.1.4.1 Energy conservation shall be considered in all phases of facility development or renovation. Architectural elements that reduce energy consumption shall be considered as part of facility design.

3.1.4.2 The quality of the health care facility environment must be supportive of the occupants and function served. Therefore, design for energy conservation shall not adversely affect patient health, safety, or accepted personal comfort levels.

*3.1.5. Indoor Air Quality
3.1.5.1 The impact of building design and construction on indoor air quality shall be addressed.

3.1.5.2 Impact from both exterior and interior air-contamination sources shall be minimized.

3.1.6. Environmental Impact of Selected Building Materials
The environmental impacts associated with the life cycle of building materials shall be addressed.

APPENDIX

A3.1.5 Indoor Air Quality
Carpeting, upholstery, paint, adhesives, and manufactured wood products may emit volatile organic compounds (VOCs), including formaldehyde and benzene. Substitute low or zero VOC paints, stains, adhesives, sealants, and other construction materials, where practical, for building products that emit formaldehyde and other known carcinogens and irritants.

Materials or construction systems that trap moisture may promote microbial growth. All permeable building materials should be protected from exposure to moisture prior to and during construction. Permeable materials exposed to moisture should be dried within 72 hours or removed.

High-volume photocopiers, portable sterilizing equipment, and aerosolized medications have been identified as important sources of indoor air pollution in health care settings. Dedicated exhaust ventilation may be necessary for specialty areas such as housekeeping, copying rooms, sterilization areas, etc., in which such chemical use occurs.

1.3 Site

Appendix material, which appears in shaded boxes at the bottom of the page, is advisory only.

1 General Considerations

1.1 Applicability
The provisions of this chapter shall apply to all health facility projects.

2 Location

2.1 Access
The site of any health care facility shall be convenient both to the community and to service vehicles, including fire protection apparatus, etc.

*2.2 Availability of Transportation
A transportation plan shall be established.

2.3 Security
Health facilities shall have security measures for patients, families, personnel, and the public consistent with the conditions and risks inherent in the location of the facility.

2.4 Availability of Utilities
Facilities shall be located to provide reliable utilities (water, gas, sewer, electricity).

APPENDIX

A2.2 Availability of Transportation
Facilities should be located so they are convenient to public transportation where available, unless acceptable alternate methods of transportation to public facilities and services are provided. The transportation plan should support alternatives to fossil-fueled single-occupancy vehicles, including preferred van/carpool parking, bike parking and changing facilities, alternative vehicle fueling stations, and nearby transit access.

A3.4 Other vehicular or pedestrian traffic shall not conflict with access to the emergency station.

A4 Release of Toxic Substances from Equipment
Equipment should minimize the release of chlorofluorocarbons (CFCs) and any potentially toxic substances that may be used in their place. For example, the design of air conditioning systems should specify CFC alternatives and recovery systems as may be practicable.

2.4.1 Water Supply
The water supply shall have the capacity to provide for normal usage and to meet fire-fighting requirements.

2.4.2 Electricity
The electricity shall be of stable voltage and frequency.

3 Facility Site Design

3.1 Roads
Paved roads shall be provided within the property for access to all entrances and to loading and unloading docks (for delivery trucks).

3.2 Pedestrian Walkways
Paved walkways shall be provided for pedestrian traffic.

3.3 Parking
Parking shall be made available for patients, families, personnel, and the public, as described in the individual sections for specific facility types. Signage shall be provided to direct people unfamiliar with the facility to appropriate parking areas.

*3.4 Emergency Access
3.4.1 Hospitals with an organized emergency service shall have the emergency access well marked to facilitate entry from the public roads or streets serving the site.

3.4.2 Access to emergency services shall be located to incur minimal damage from floods and other natural disasters.

*4 Environmental Pollution Control

4.1 Environmental Pollution
The design, construction, renovation, expansion, equipment, and operation of health care facilities are all subject to provisions of several federal environmental pollution control laws and associated agency regulations. Moreover, many states have enacted substantially equivalent or more stringent

statutes and regulations, thereby implementing national priorities under local jurisdiction as well as incorporating local priorities (e.g., air quality related to incinerators and gas sterilizers; underground storage tanks; hazardous materials and waste storage, handling, and disposal; storm water control; medical waste storage and disposal; and asbestos in building materials).

4.1.1 Federal Regulations

The principal federal environmental statutes under which health care facilities may be regulated include, most notably, the following:

4.1.1.1 National Environmental Policy Act (NEPA)

4.1.1.2 Resource Conservation and Recovery Act (RCRA)

4.1.1.3 Superfund Amendments and Reauthorization Act (SARA)

4.1.1.4 Clean Air Act (CAA)

4.1.1.5 Safe Drinking Water Act (SDWA)

4.1.1.6 Occupational Safety and Health Act (OSHA)

4.1.2 State and Local Regulations

Consult the appropriate U.S. Department of Health and Human Services (DHHS) and U.S. Environmental Protection Agency (EPA) regional offices and any other federal, state, or local authorities having jurisdiction for the latest applicable state and local regulations pertaining to environmental pollution that may affect the design, construction, or operation of the facility, including the management of industrial chemicals, pharmaceuticals, radionuclides, and wastes thereof, as well as trash, noise, and traffic (including air traffic).

APPENDIX

A4.2 Mercury Elimination

Health care facilities should collect and properly store, recycle, or dispose of mercury encountered during construction or demolition (such as mercury accumulated in P-traps, air-handling units, sumps, etc.).

4.1.3 Permits

Health care facilities regulated under federal, state, and local environmental pollution laws may be required to support permit applications with appropriate documentation of proposed impacts and mitigations.

4.1.3.1 Such documentation is typically reported in an Environmental Impact Statement (EIS) with respect to potential impacts on the environment and in a Health Risk Assessment (HRA) with respect to potential impacts on public health. The HRA may constitute a part or appendix of the EIS. The scope of the EIS and the HRA is typically determined by consultation with appropriate regulatory agency personnel and, if required, a "scoping" meeting at which members of the interested public are invited to express their particular concerns.

4.1.3.2 Once the EIS and/or HRA scope has been established, a Protocol document shall be prepared for agency approval.

(1) The Protocol shall describe the scope and procedures to be used to conduct the assessment(s).

(2) The EIS and/or HRA shall be prepared in accordance with a final Protocol approved by the appropriate agency or agencies. Approval is most likely to be obtained in a timely manner and with minimum revisions if standard methods are initially proposed for use in the EIS and/or HRA. Standard methods suitable for specific assessment tasks are set forth in particular EPA documents.

*4.2 Mercury Elimination

4.2.1 Applicability

4.2.1.1 New construction. In new construction, health care facilities shall not use mercury-containing equipment, including thermostats, switching devices, and other building system sources.

4.2.1.2 Renovation. For renovation, health care facilities shall develop a plan to phase out mercury-containing sources and upgrade current mercury-containing lamps to low or no mercury lamp technology.

4.2.2 Local Codes and Standards

Many states and municipalities have enacted bans on the sale of mercury-containing devices and equipment. Health care facility projects shall comply with local codes and standards.

1.4 Equipment

Appendix material, which appears in shaded boxes at the bottom of the page, is advisory only.

1 General Considerations

Equipment will vary to suit individual construction projects and therefore will require careful planning.

1.1 Applicability
The provisions of this chapter shall apply to all health facility projects.

1.2 Equipment List
An equipment list shall be included in the contract documents to assist in overall coordination of the acquisition, installation, and relocation of equipment.

1.2.1 The equipment list shall show all items of equipment necessary to operate the facility.

1.2.2 The equipment list shall include the classifications identified in Section 1.4-2 below.

1.2.3 The equipment list shall specify whether the items are new, existing to be relocated, owner provided, or not-in-contract.

1.3 Drawing Requirements

*1.3.1 Provisions for Equipment
1.3.1.1 The drawings shall indicate provisions for the installation of fixed or movable equipment that requires dedicated building services or special structures and illustrate how the major equipment will function in the space.

1.3.1.2 An equipment utility location drawing shall be produced to locate all services for equipment that requires floor space and mechanical connections.

1.3.2 Not-in-Contract (NIC) Equipment
Some equipment may not be included in the construction contract but may require coordination during construction.

1.3.2.1 Design development documents. Equipment that is not included in the construction contract but requires mechanical or electrical service connections or construction modifications shall, insofar as practical, be identified on the design development documents to provide coordination with the architectural, mechanical, and electrical phases of construction.

1.3.2.2 Construction documents. Such equipment shall be shown in the construction documents as owner-provided or not-in-contract for purposes of coordination.

1.3.3 Final Equipment Selections
Adjustments shall be made to the construction documents when final selections are made.

2 Equipment Classification

Equipment to be used in projects shall be classified as building service equipment, fixed equipment, or movable equipment.

2.1 Building Service Equipment
Building service equipment shall include items such as heating, ventilating, and air conditioning equipment; electrical power distribution equipment; emergency power generation equipment; energy/utility management systems; conveying systems; and other equipment with a primary function of building service (e.g., humidification equipment, filtration equipment, chillers, boilers, fire pumps, etc.).

2.2 Fixed Equipment
Fixed equipment includes items that are permanently affixed to the building or permanently connected to a service distribution system that is designed and installed for the specific use of the equipment. Fixed equipment may require special structural designs, electromechanical requirements, or other considerations.

2.2.1 Fixed Medical Equipment
This includes, but is not limited to, such items as fume hoods, sterilizers, communication systems, built-in casework, imaging equipment, radiotherapy equipment, lithotripters, hydrotherapy tanks, audiometry testing chambers, and surgical and special procedure lights.

2.2.2 Fixed Nonmedical Equipment
This includes, but is not limited to, items such as walk-in refrigerators, kitchen cooking equipment, serving lines, conveyors, mainframe computers, laundry, and similar equipment.

2.3 Movable Equipment
Movable equipment includes items that require floor space or electrical and/or mechanical connections but are portable, such as wheeled items, portable items, office-type furnishings, and diagnostic or monitoring equipment. Movable equipment may require special structural design or access, electromechanical connections, shielding, or other considerations.

2.3.1 Movable Medical Equipment
This includes, but is not limited to, portable X-ray, electroencephalogram (EEG), electrocardiogram (EKG), treadmill and exercise equipment, pulmonary function equipment, operating tables, laboratory centrifuges, examination and treatment tables, and similar equipment.

2.3.2 Movable Nonmedical Equipment
This includes, but is not limited to, personal computer stations, patient room furnishings, food service trucks, case carts and distribution carts, and other portable equipment.

3 Equipment Requirements

*3.1 Major Technical Equipment
Major technical equipment shall include specialized equipment (medical or nonmedical) that is customarily installed by the manufacturer or vendor. It may require special structural designs, electromechanical requirements, or other considerations. Therefore, close coordination between owner, building designer, installer, construction contractors, and others shall be required.

3.2 Electronic Equipment

3.2.1 Protection
Special consideration shall be given to protecting computerized equipment such as multiphasic laboratory testing units, as well as computers, from power surges and spikes that might damage the equipment or programs.

3.2.2 Constant Power
Consideration shall also be given to the addition of a constant power source where loss of data input might compromise patient care.

4 Space Requirements

3.1 Fixed and Building Service Equipment
Space for accessing and servicing fixed and building service equipment shall be provided.

3.2 Movable Equipment
Facility planning and design shall consider the convenient and dedicated placement of equipment requiring floor space and mechanical connections and the voltage required for electrical connections where portable equipment is expected to be used. (See paragraph 1.4-1.3.1.2 for drawing requirements.)

> **APPENDIX**
>
> **A3.1** Examples of major technical equipment are X-ray and other imaging equipment, radiation therapy equipment, lithotripters, audiometry testing chambers, laundry equipment, computers, and similar items.

1.5 Planning, Design, and Construction

Appendix material, which appears in shaded boxes at the bottom of the page, is advisory only.

1 General Considerations

1.1 Applicability
The provisions of this chapter shall apply to all health facility projects.

1.2 Environment of Care Considerations
Facility construction, whether for freestanding buildings or expansion and/or renovation of existing buildings, can create conditions that are harmful to patients and staff. For that reason, health care facility planning, design, and construction activities shall include—in addition to consideration of space and operational needs—consideration of provisions for infection control, life safety, and protection of occupants during construction.

1.2.1 Infection Control Risk Assessment (ICRA)
During the planning phase of a project, after considering the facility's patient population and programs, the owner shall provide an infection control risk assessment. An ICRA is a determination of the potential risk of transmission of various air- and waterborne biological contaminants in the facility.

1.2.2 Owner Recommendations
Based on the ICRA, the owner shall provide the following:

1.2.2.1. Design recommendations.
Recommendations for design generated by the ICRA shall be provided for incorporation in the program.

1.2.2.2 Infection control risk mitigation recommendations (ICRMR).
Infection control risk mitigation recommendations shall describe the specific methods by which transmission of air- and waterborne biological contaminants will be avoided during the course of the construction project.

*1.3 Design Process and Implementation
Groups (stakeholders) affected by and integral to the design shall be included in the planning and implementation process. (See Section 1.2-2.1.2.6.)

2 Infection Control Risk Assessment Process

2.1 General

2.1.1 ICRA Panel
The ICRA shall be conducted by a panel with expertise in infection control, direct patient care, risk management, facility design, construction and construction phasing, ventilation, safety, and epidemiology.

2.1.2 Continuous Updates
The ICRA panel shall provide updated documentation of the risk assessment together with updated mitigation recommendations throughout planning, design, construction, and commissioning.

2.1.3 Monitoring
The owner shall also provide monitoring of the effectiveness of the applied ICRMR during the course of the project.

2.2 ICRA Considerations
The ICRA shall address, but not be limited to, the following:

APPENDIX

A1.3 Design Process and Implementation

a. To meet the objectives of this chapter, as well as those of Chapter 1.2, Environment of Care, health care organizations should develop an interdisciplinary design process to guide facility design. The intent of an interdisciplinary design process is to improve building performance by integrating design considerations from project inception. (Also see Section 1.2-A3.)

b. An interdisciplinary design team should be assembled as early as possible in the design process. The design team should include but not be limited to administrators, clinicians, infection control, safety officers, support staff, patient advocates/consumers, A/E consultants, and construction specialists. (Also see Section 1.2-A2.1.2.6.)

2.2.1 Design
Building design features, including the following, shall be addressed when developing the ICRA:

2.2.1.1 Number, location, and type of airborne infection isolation and protective environment rooms

2.2.1.2 Location(s) of special ventilation and filtration such as emergency department waiting and intake areas

2.2.1.3 Air-handling and ventilation needs in surgical services, airborne infection isolation and protective environment rooms, laboratories, local exhaust systems for hazardous agents, and other special areas

2.2.1.4 Water systems to limit Legionella sp. and waterborne opportunistic pathogens

*****2.2.1.5** Finishes and surfaces

2.2.2 Construction
When developing the ICRA, building and site areas anticipated to be affected by construction shall be addressed, including consideration of the following:

2.2.2.1 The impact of disrupting essential services to patients and employees

2.2.2.2 Determination of the specific hazards and protection levels for each

2.2.2.3 Location of patients by susceptibility to infection and definition of risks to each

2.2.2.4 Impact of potential outages or emergencies and protection of patients during planned or unplanned outages, movement of debris, traffic flow, cleanup, and testing and certification

2.2.2.5 Assessment of external as well as internal construction activities

2.2.2.6 Location of known hazards

2.3 Infection Control Risk Mitigation

2.3.1 ICRMR Preparation
The infection control risk mitigation recommendations shall be prepared by the ICRA panel and shall address, but not be limited to, the following:

2.3.1.1 Patient placement and relocation

2.3.1.2 Standards for barriers and other protective measures required to protect adjacent areas and susceptible patients from airborne contaminants

2.3.1.3 Temporary provisions or phasing for construction or modification of heating, ventilating, air conditioning, and water supply systems

2.3.1.4 Protection from demolition

2.3.1.5 Measures to be taken to train hospital staff, visitors, and construction personnel

2.3.2 Project Requirements
The owner shall ensure that construction-related infection control risk mitigation recommendations, as well as ICRA-generated design recommendations, are incorporated into the project requirements.

APPENDIX

A2.2.1.5 Finishes and surfaces
Preferred surface characteristics (of the ideal product) include the following:

a. Ease of maintenance/repair and cleanable
b. Does not support microbial growth
c. Nonporous—smooth
d. Sound absorption/acoustics, where applicable
e. Inflammable—Class I fire rating or better
f. Durable
g. Sustainable
h. Low VOC (no off-gassing)
i. Low smoke toxicity
j. Initial and life-cycle cost-effectiveness
k. Slip resistance—appropriate coefficient of friction
l. Ease of installation, demolition, and replacement
m. Non-problematic substrate and/or assemblies
n. Seamless
o. Resilient, impact resistant
p. Control of reflectivity/glare
q. Options for color, pattern, and texture
r. Non-toxic/non-allergenic

2.3.3 Infection Control Monitoring

The owner shall inspect the initial installation of the infection control measures and provide continuous monitoring of their effectiveness throughout the duration of the project.

2.3.3.1 This monitoring may be conducted by in-house infection control and safety staff or by independent outside consultants.

2.3.3.2 In either instance, provisions for monitoring shall include written procedures for emergency suspension of work and protective measures indicating the responsibilities and limitations of each party (owner, designer, constructor, and monitor).

3 Renovation

3.1 Phasing

Projects involving renovation of existing buildings shall include phasing to minimize disruption of existing patient services. This phasing is essential to ensure a safe environment in patient care areas.

3.1.1 Phasing Provisions

Phasing provisions shall include assurance for clean to dirty airflow, emergency procedures, criteria for interruption of protection, construction of roof surfaces, written notification of interruptions, and communication authority.

3.1.2 Noise and Vibration

Phasing plans shall include considerations of noise and vibration control that result from construction activities.

APPENDIX

A3.2 Ventilation of the Construction Zone

a. Airflow into the construction zone from occupied spaces should be maintained by means of a dedicated ventilation/exhaust system for the construction area.

b. Locations of exhaust discharge relative to existing fresh air intakes and filters, as well as the disconnection and sealing of existing air ducts, should be reviewed as required by the ICRA.

c. If the existing building system or a portion thereof is used to achieve this requirement, the system should be thoroughly cleaned prior to occupancy of the construction area.

---

*3.2 Isolation

During construction, renovation areas shall be isolated from occupied areas based on the ICRA.

3.3 Maintenance of Air Quality and Utilities

Existing air quality requirements and other utility requirements for occupied areas shall be maintained during any renovation or construction.

3.4 Nonconforming Conditions

It is not always financially feasible to renovate an entire existing structure in accordance with these Guidelines. Therefore, authorities having jurisdiction shall be permitted to grant approval to renovate portions of a structure if facility operation and patient safety in the renovated areas are not jeopardized by existing features of sections retained without complete corrective measures.

*4 Commissioning

Commissioning is a quality process used to achieve, validate, and document that facilities and component infrastructure systems are planned, constructed, installed, tested, and are capable of being operated and maintained in conformity with the design intent or performance expectations.

4.1 Mechanical Systems

Acceptance criteria for mechanical systems shall be specified.

4.1.1 Crucial ventilation specifications for air balance and filtration shall be verified before owner acceptance.

4.1.2 Areas requiring special ventilation (such as surgical services, protective environments, airborne infection isolation rooms, laboratories, and local exhaust systems for hazardous agents) shall be recognized as requiring mechanical systems that ensure infection control. Ventilation deficiencies shall not be accepted.

4.1.3 Acceptance criteria for local exhaust systems dealing with hazardous agents shall be specified and verified.

5 Record Drawings and Manuals

5.1 Drawings

5.1.1 Upon occupancy of the building or portion thereof, the owner shall be provided with a complete set of legible drawings showing construction, fixed equipment, and mechanical and electrical systems, as installed or built.

5.1.2 Drawings shall include a life safety plan for each floor reflecting NFPA 101 requirements.

5.2 Equipment Manuals

5.2.1 Upon completion of the contract, the owner shall be furnished with the following:

5.2.1.1 A complete set of manufacturers' operating, maintenance, and preventive maintenance instructions

5.2.1.2 Parts lists

5.2.1.3 Procurement information with numbers and a description for each piece of equipment

---

APPENDIX

A4 Commissioning

a. The commissioning process extends through all phases of a new construction or renovation project from conceptual design to occupancy and operations. Checks at each stage of the process should be made to ensure validation of performance to meet the owner's design requirements.

b. Commissioning should be performed by an entity that is independent from the installing contractor.

c. Total building commissioning. Historically, the term "commissioning" has referred to the process by which the heating, ventilation, and air conditioning (HVAC) system of a building was tested and balanced according to established standards prior to acceptance by the building owner. The HVAC commissioning did not include other building components that did not directly affect the performance of the HVAC systems. Today, the definition of commissioning is being expanded to total building commissioning (TBC). The fundamental objective of TBC is to create a process whereby the owner will be assured that all building and system components, not just the HVAC system, will function according to design intent, specifications, equipment manufacturers' data sheets, and operational criteria. Because all building systems are integrated and validated, the owner can expect benefits to include improved occupant comfort, energy savings, environmental conditions, system and equipment function, building operation and maintenance, and building occupants' productivity.

The TBC process should include a feedback mechanism that can be incorporated into the owner's postoccupancy evaluation process to enhance future facility designs.

Facility acceptance criteria should be based on the commissioning requirements specified in the contract documents. These criteria specify the tests, training, and reporting requirements necessary for the owner to validate that each building system complies with the performance standards of the basis of design and for final acceptance of the facility.

d. Systems and components to be included in TBC. Key systems and components that need to be tested and validated, at a minimum, during the TBC process include the design and operations of the HVAC, plumbing, electrical, emergency power, fire protection/suppression, telecommunications, nurse call, intrusion and other alarm devices, and medical gas systems, as well as specialty equipment.

Air balancing, pressure relationships, and exhaust criteria for mechanical systems should be clearly described and tested to create an environment of care that provides for infection control.

Areas requiring emergency power should be specified and tested.

Special plumbing systems should be certified to support the chemicals scheduled for use in them.

e. Areas to be included in commissioning. While all areas of the health care facility are included in the commissioning process, the following areas are of particular concern: critical and intensive care areas; surgical services; isolation rooms, including those used for airborne infection/pathogens; pharmacies, and other areas potentially containing hazardous substances.

f. A reference source for an existing HVAC commissioning process is ASHRAE Guideline 1, *The HVAC Commissioning Process*.

5.2.2 Operating staff shall be provided with instructions on how to properly operate systems and equipment.

5.2.3 Required information shall include energy ratings as needed for future conservation calculations.

5.3 Design Data

5.3.1 The owner shall be provided with complete design data for the facility, including the following:

5.3.1.1 Structural design loadings

5.3.1.2 Summary of heat loss assumption and calculations

5.3.1.3 Estimated water consumption

5.3.1.4 Medical gas outlet listing

5.3.1.5 List of applicable codes

5.3.1.6 Electric power requirements of installed equipment

5.3.2 All such data shall be supplied to facilitate future alterations, additions, and changes, including, but not limited to, energy audits and retrofit for energy conservation.

1.6 Common Requirements

Appendix material, which appears in shaded boxes at the bottom of the page, is advisory only.

1 General Considerations

1.1 Applicability
Except as modified elsewhere in this document, the provisions of this chapter shall apply to all health care facility projects.

2 Building Systems

2.1 Plumbing

2.1.1 General
Unless otherwise specified herein, all plumbing systems shall be designed and installed in accordance with the International Plumbing Code.

2.1.2 Plumbing and Other Piping Systems
2.1.2.1 Hot water systems. The following standards shall apply to hot water systems:

*(1) Capacity. The water-heating system shall have sufficient supply capacity at the temperatures and amounts indicated in the applicable table. Storage of water at higher temperatures shall be permitted.

(2) Hot water distribution systems serving patient/resident care areas shall be under constant recirculation to provide continuous hot water at each hot water outlet. Non-recirculated fixture branch piping shall not exceed 25 feet (7.62 meters) in length.

(3) Dead-end piping (risers with no flow, branches with no fixture) shall not be installed. In renovation projects, dead-end piping shall be removed. Empty risers, mains, and branches installed for future use shall be permitted.

*(4) Provisions shall be included in the domestic hot water system to limit the amount of Legionella bacteria and opportunistic waterborne pathogens.

2.1.2.2 Condensate drains

(1) Condensate drains for cooling coils shall be a type that may be cleaned as needed without disassembly. (Unless specifically required by local authorities, traps are not required for condensate drains.)

(2) An air gap shall be provided where condensate drains empty into building drains.

(3) Heater elements shall be provided for condensate lines in freezers or other areas where freezing may be a problem.

2.1.3 Plumbing Fixtures
The following standards shall apply to plumbing fixtures:

A2.1.2.1 (1) Water temperature is measured at the point of use or inlet to the equipment.

A2.1.2.1 (4) There are several ways to treat domestic water systems to kill Legionella and opportunistic waterborne pathogens. Complete removal of these organisms is not feasible, but methods to reduce the amount include hyperchlorination (free chlorine, chlorine dioxide, monochloramine), elevated hot water temperature, ozone injection, silver/copper ions, and ultraviolet light. Each of these options has advantages and disadvantages. While increasing the hot water supply temperature to 140°F (60°C) is typically considered the easiest option, the risk of scalding, especially to youth and the elderly, is significant. Additional consideration should be given to domestic water used in bone marrow transplant units. See CDC and ASHRAE Guideline 12, "Minimizing the Risk of Legionellosis Associated with Building Water Systems," for additional information. Another reference on this topic is "Legionella Control in Health Care Facilities," available from the American Society of Plumbing Engineers.

2.1.3.1 General

(1) Materials. The material used for plumbing fixtures shall be nonabsorptive and acid-resistant.

(2) Clearances. Water spouts used in lavatories and sinks shall have clearances adequate to avoid contaminating utensils and the contents of carafes, etc.

2.1.3.2 Hand-washing stations. General hand-washing stations used by medical and nursing staff, patients, and food handlers shall be trimmed with valves that can be operated without hands. Single-lever or wrist blade devices shall be permitted. Blade handles used for this purpose shall not exceed 4-1/2 inches (11.43 centimeters) in length.

2.1.3.3 Showers and tubs. Showers and tubs shall have nonslip walking surfaces.

2.1.3.4 Ice machines. Copper tubing shall be provided for supply connections to ice machines.

2.2 Heating, Ventilating, and Air-Conditioning (HVAC) Systems

2.2.1 Thermal Insulation and Acoustical Provisions
2.2.1.1 General. Insulation shall be provided within the building to conserve energy, protect personnel, prevent vapor condensation, and reduce noise.

(1) Vapor barrier. Insulation on cold surfaces shall include an exterior vapor barrier. (Material that will not absorb or transmit moisture will not require a separate vapor barrier.)

(2) Flame-spread rating. Insulation, including finishes and adhesives on the exterior surfaces of ducts, piping, and equipment, shall have a flame-spread rating of 25 or less and a smoke-developed rating of 50 or less as determined by an independent testing laboratory in accordance with NFPA 255.

(3) Renovation. Existing accessible insulation within areas of facilities to be modernized shall be inspected, repaired, and/or replaced, as appropriate.

2.2.1.2 Duct linings

(1) If duct lining is used, it shall be coated and sealed and shall meet ASTM C1071.

(2) These linings (including coatings, adhesives, and exterior surface insulation on pipes and ducts in spaces used as air supply plenums) shall have a flame-spread rating of 25 or less and a smoke-developed rating of 50 or less, as determined by an independent testing laboratory in accordance with NFPA 255.

(3) Duct linings exposed to air movement shall not be used in ducts serving operating rooms, delivery rooms, LDR rooms, nurseries, protective environment rooms, and critical care units. This requirement shall not apply to mixing boxes and sound attenuators that have special coverings over such lining.

(4) Duct lining shall not be installed within 15 feet (4.57 meters) downstream of humidifiers.

(5) Renovation. If existing lined ductwork is reworked in a renovation project, the liner seams and punctures shall be resealed.

2.2.2 HVAC Air Distribution
2.2.2.1 HVAC ductwork
(1) General

  (a) Air-handling duct systems shall be designed with accessibility for duct cleaning and shall meet the requirements of NFPA 90A.

  (b) When smoke partitions are required, heating, ventilating, and air conditioning zones shall be coordinated with compartmentation insofar as practical to minimize the need to penetrate fire and smoke partitions.

*(2) Duct humidifiers

  (a) If duct humidifiers are located upstream of the final filters, they shall be at least 15 feet (4.57 meters) upstream of the final filters.

(b) Ductwork with duct-mounted humidifiers shall have a means of water removal.

(c) An adjustable high-limit humidistat shall be located downstream of the humidifier to reduce the potential for condensation inside the duct.

(d) Humidifiers shall be connected to airflow proving switches that prevent humidification unless the required volume of airflow is present or high-limit humidistats are provided.

(e) All duct takeoffs shall be sufficiently downstream of the humidifier to ensure complete moisture absorption.

(f) Steam humidifiers shall be used. Reservoir-type water spray or evaporative pan humidifiers shall not be used.

(3) Fire and smoke dampers

(a) Fire and smoke dampers shall be constructed, located, and installed in accordance with the requirements of NFPA 101, 90A, and the specific damper's listing requirements.

(b) Fans, dampers, and detectors shall be interconnected so that damper activation will not damage ducts.

(c) Maintenance access shall be provided at all dampers.

(d) All damper locations shall be shown on design drawings.

APPENDIX

A2.2.2.1 (2) One way to achieve basic humidification may be by a steam-jacketed manifold-type humidifier with a condensate separator that delivers high-quality steam. Additional booster humidification (if required) should be provided by steam-jacketed humidifiers for each individually controlled area. Steam to be used for humidification may be generated in a separate steam generator. The steam generator feedwater may be supplied either from soft or reverse osmosis water. Provisions should be made for periodic cleaning.

(e) Dampers shall be activated in accordance with NFPA 90A. Installation of switching systems for restarting fans shall be permitted for fire department use in venting smoke after a fire has been controlled. Provisions to avoid possible damage to the system due to closed dampers shall be permitted.

(4) Construction requirements. Ducts that penetrate construction intended to protect against x-ray, magnetic, RFI, or other radiation shall not impair the effectiveness of the protection.

2.2.3 Steam and Hot Water Systems
2.2.3.1 Boilers

(1) Capacity. Boilers shall have the capacity, based upon the net ratings published by the Hydronics Institute or another acceptable national standard, to supply the normal heating, hot water, and steam requirements of all systems and equipment. Their number and arrangement shall accommodate facility needs despite the breakdown or routine maintenance of any one boiler. The capacity of the remaining boiler(s) (reserve capacity) shall be sufficient to provide hot water service for clinical, dietary, and patient or resident use; steam for sterilization and dietary purposes; and space heating for operating, delivery and birthing, labor, recovery, nurseries, and intensive care.

(2) Space heating requirements. Reserve capacity for facility space heating is not required in geographic areas where a design dry-bulb temperature of 25°F (-4°C) or more represents not less than 99 percent of the total hours in any one heating month as noted in the *ASHRAE Handbook— Fundamentals*, under the "Table for Climatic Conditions for the United States."

2.2.3.2 Boiler accessories. These, including feed pumps, heat-circulating pumps, condensate return pumps, fuel oil pumps, and waste heat boilers, shall be connected and installed to provide both normal and standby service.

2.3 Electrical Systems

2.3.1 Lighting
*2.3.1.1 General

(1) Recommended lighting levels for health care facilities developed by the Illuminating Engineering Society of North America (IES) shall be considered. Refer to the IES publication RP-29, *Lighting for Hospitals and Health Care Facilities.*

(2) As required by the functional program, special needs of the elderly shall be incorporated into the lighting design. Excessive contrast in lighting levels that makes effective sight adaptation difficult shall be minimized. Refer to IES publication RP-28, *Lighting and the Visual Environment for Senior Living.*

(3) Approaches to buildings and parking lots, and all occupied spaces within buildings, shall have fixtures that can be illuminated as necessary.

2.3.1.2 Emergency lighting. Light intensity of required emergency lighting shall generally comply with the IES recommendations.

2.3.1.3 Exit signs. Egress and exit lighting shall comply with NFPA 101.

APPENDIX

A2.3.1.1 Light intensity for staff and patient needs should generally comply with health care guidelines set forth in the IES publications referenced in Section 1.6-2.3.1.1. Consideration should be given to controlling intensity and/or wavelength to prevent harm to the patient's eyes (i.e., retina damage to premature infants and cataracts due to ultraviolet light).

Many procedures are available to satisfy lighting requirements, but the design should consider light quality as well as quantity for effectiveness and efficiency. While light levels in the IES publications are referenced herein, those publications include other useful guidance and recommendations which the designer is encouraged to follow.

2

Hospitals

2.1 General Hospitals

Appendix material, which appears in shaded boxes at the bottom of the page, is advisory only.

1 General Considerations

1.1 Applicability
The general hospital shall meet all the standards described herein. Deviations shall be described and justified in the functional program for specific approval by authorities having jurisdiction.

1.2 Functional Program
For each project, there shall be a functional program for the facility in accordance with Section 1.2-2.

1.2.1 Size and Layout
Department size and clear floor areas shall depend on program requirements and organization of services within the hospital. Combination or sharing of some functions shall be permitted provided the layout does not compromise safety standards and medical and nursing practices.

*1.2.2 Swing Beds
When the concept of swing beds is part of the functional program, care shall be taken to include requirements for all intended categories.

1.3 Site

*1.3.1 Parking
1.3.1.1 Each new facility, major addition, or major change in function shall have parking space to satisfy the needs of patients, personnel, and the public.

1.3.1.2 A formal parking study is desirable. In the absence of such a study, provide one space for each bed plus one space for each employee normally present on any single weekday shift. This ratio may be reduced in an area convenient to public transportation or public parking facilities, or where carpool or other arrangements to reduce traffic have been developed.

1.3.1.3 Additional parking may be required to accommodate outpatient and other services.

1.3.1.4 Separate and additional space shall be provided for service delivery vehicles and vehicles utilized for emergency patients.

2 Common Elements

2.1 General
The spaces included in this section are common to most hospital facilities and shall be required for a specific hospital unit or location when specified in the Guidelines text for that unit or location.

2.2 Patient Rooms or Care Areas

2.2.1 Toilet Rooms
Each patient shall have access to a toilet room without having to enter a general corridor area.

2.2.1.1 One toilet room shall serve no more than two patient rooms and no more than four beds.

2.2.1.2 The toilet room shall contain a water closet and a hand-washing station.

2.2.1.3 Toilet room doors shall swing outward or be double acting. Where local requirements permit, use of folding doors shall be permitted, provided adequate provisions are made for acoustical and visual privacy.

2.2.2 Patient Storage Locations
Each patient shall have within his or her room a separate wardrobe, locker, or closet suitable for hanging full-length garments and for storing personal effects.

2.3 Support Areas for Patient Care

2.3.1 Administrative Center or Nurse Station
2.3.1.1 This area shall have space for counters and storage and shall have convenient access to hand-washing stations.

2.3.1.2 This area may be combined with or include centers for reception and communication.

2.3.2 Documentation Area
Charting facilities shall have linear surface space adequate to ensure that staff and physicians can chart and have simultaneous access to information and communication systems.

2.3.3 Multipurpose Room
Multipurpose rooms are provided for staff, patients, and patients' families for patient conferences, reports, education, training sessions, and consultation.

2.3.3.1 These rooms shall be accessible to each nursing unit.

2.3.3.2 These rooms may be on other floors if convenient for regular use.

2.3.3.3 One such room shall be permitted to serve several nursing units and/or departments.

2.3.4 Medication Station
Medication shall be distributed from a medicine preparation room or unit, from a self-contained medicine dispensing unit, or by another approved system.

2.3.4.1 Medicine preparation room
(1) This room shall be under visual control of the nursing staff.

(2) This room shall contain a work counter, a hand-washing station, a lockable refrigerator, and locked storage for controlled drugs.

(3) When a medicine preparation room is to be used to store one or more self-contained medicine-dispensing units, the room shall be designed with adequate space to prepare medicines with the self-contained medicine-dispensing unit(s) present.

2.3.4.2 Self-contained medicine dispensing unit

(1) Location of a self-contained medicine dispensing unit shall be permitted at the nurse station, in the clean workroom, or in an alcove, provided the unit has adequate security for controlled drugs and adequate lighting to easily identify drugs.

(2) Convenient access to hand-washing stations shall be provided. (Standard cup-sinks provided in many self-contained units are not adequate for hand-washing.)

2.3.5 Nourishment Area
2.3.5.1 A nourishment area shall have a sink, work counter, refrigerator, storage cabinets, and equipment for hot and cold nourishment between scheduled meals. This area shall include space for trays and dishes used for nonscheduled meal service.

2.3.5.2 Provisions and space shall be included for separate temporary storage of unused and soiled dietary trays not picked up at mealtime.

2.3.5.3 Hand-washing stations shall be in or immediately accessible from the nourishment area.

2.3.6 Ice Machine
2.3.6.1 Ice-making equipment may be in the clean workroom/holding room or at the nourishment station.

2.3.6.2 Ice intended for human consumption shall be from self-dispensing ice makers.

2.3.7 Clean Workroom or Clean Supply Room
Such rooms shall be separate from and have no direct connection with soiled workrooms or soiled holding rooms.

2.3.7.1 Clean workroom. If the room is used for preparing patient care items, it shall contain a work counter, a hand-washing station, and storage facilities for clean and sterile supplies.

2.3.7.2 Clean supply room. If the room is used only for storage and holding as part of a system for distribution of clean and sterile materials, omission of the work counter and hand-washing station shall be permitted.

2.3.8 Soiled Workroom or Soiled Holding Room

Such rooms shall be separate from and have no direct connection with clean workrooms or clean supply rooms.

2.3.8.1 Soiled workrooms. These shall contain the following:

(1) A clinical sink (or equivalent flushing-rim fixture) and a hand-washing station. Both fixtures shall have a hot and cold mixing faucet.

(2) A work counter and space for separate covered containers for soiled linen and a variety of waste types.

2.3.8.2 Soiled holding rooms. Omission of the clinical sink and work counter shall be permitted in rooms used only for temporary holding of soiled material. If the flushing-rim clinical sink is not provided, facilities for cleaning bedpans shall be provided elsewhere.

2.3.9 Equipment and Supply Storage
2.3.9.1 Clean linen storage

(1) Location of the designated area within the clean workroom, a separate closet, or an approved distribution system on each floor shall be permitted.

(2) If a closed cart system is used, storage of clean linen carts in an alcove shall be permitted. This cart storage must be out of the path of normal traffic and under staff control.

2.3.9.2 Equipment storage room or alcove. Appropriate room(s) or alcove(s) shall be provided for storage of equipment necessary for patient care and as required by the functional program. Each unit shall provide sufficient storage area(s) located on the patient floor to keep its required corridor width free of all equipment and supplies, but not less than 10 square feet (0.93 square meters) per patient bed shall be provided.

2.3.9.3 Storage space for stretchers and wheelchairs. Space shall be provided in a strategic location, without restricting normal traffic.

2.3.9.4 Emergency equipment storage. Space shall be provided for emergency equipment that is under direct control of the nursing staff, such as a cardiopulmonary resuscitation (CPR) cart. This space shall be located in an area appropriate to the functional program but out of normal traffic.

2.3.10 Housekeeping Room
2.3.10.1 Housekeeping rooms shall be directly accessible from the unit or floor they serve and may serve more than one nursing unit on a floor.

2.3.10.2 In nursing locations, at least one housekeeping room per floor shall contain a service sink or floor receptor and provisions for storage of supplies and housekeeping equipment.

2.4 Support Areas for Staff

2.4.1 Staff Lounge Facilities
Lounge facilities shall be sized per the functional program but shall not be less than 100 square feet (9.29 square meters).

2.4.2 Staff Toilet Room(s)
These shall be conveniently located for staff use and may be unisex.

2.4.3 Staff Storage Facilities
2.4.3.1 Securable closets or cabinet compartments for the personal articles of nursing personnel shall be located in or near the nurse station. At a minimum, they shall be large enough for purses and billfolds.

2.4.3.2 If coat storage is provided, coats may be stored in closets or cabinets on each floor or in a central staff locker area.

3 Nursing Locations

3.1 Medical/Surgical Nursing Units
Each medical and surgical nursing unit shall include the following (see Sections 1.1-1.3.5 and 1.1-3 for waiver of standards where existing conditions make absolute compliance impractical):

Note: See other sections of this document for special care areas or units such as recovery rooms, critical care units, pediatric units, rehabilitation units, and skilled nursing care or other specialty units.

3.1.1 Typical Patient Rooms
Each patient room shall meet the following standards:

3.1.1.1 Capacity

(1) In new construction, the maximum number of beds per room shall be one unless the functional program demonstrates the necessity of a two-bed arrangement. Approval of a two-bed arrangement shall be obtained from the licensing authority.

(2) Where renovation work is undertaken and the present capacity is more than one patient, maximum room capacity shall be no more than the present capacity, with a maximum of four patients.

3.1.1.2 Space requirements. Minor encroachments, including columns and hand-washing stations, that do not interfere with functions may be ignored when determining space requirements for patient rooms.

*(1) Area. In new construction, patient rooms shall be constructed to meet the needs of the functional program and have a minimum of 100 square feet (9.29 square meters) of clear floor area per bed in multiple-bed rooms and 120 square feet (11.15

square meters) of clear floor area in single-bed rooms, exclusive of toilet rooms, closets, lockers, wardrobes, alcoves, or vestibules.

(2) Dimensions and clearances. The dimensions and arrangement of rooms shall be such that there is a minimum of 3 feet (91.44 centimeters) between the sides and foot of the bed and any wall or any other fixed obstruction. In multiple-bed rooms, a clearance of 4 feet (1.22 meters) shall be available at the foot of each bed to permit the passage of equipment and beds. (See "bed size" in the glossary.)

(3) Renovation. Where renovation work is undertaken, every effort shall be made to meet the above minimum standards. If it is not possible to meet the above minimum standards, the authorities having jurisdiction shall be permitted to grant approval to deviate from this requirement. In such cases, patient rooms shall have no less than 80 square feet (7.43 square meters) of clear floor area per bed in multiple-bed areas and 100 square feet (9.29 square meters) of clear floor area in single-bed rooms exclusive of the spaces previously noted in this section.

*3.1.1.3 Windows. Each patient room shall have a window in accordance with Section 2.1-8.2.2.5.

3.1.1.4 Patient privacy. In multiple-bed rooms, visual privacy from casual observation by other patients and visitors shall be provided for each patient. The design for privacy shall not restrict patient access to the entrance, hand-washing station, or toilet.

*3.1.1.5 Hand-washing stations. These shall be provided to serve each patient room.

(1) A hand-washing station shall be located in the toilet room.

(2) A hand-washing station shall be provided in the patient room in addition to that in the toilet room. This shall be located outside the patient's cubicle curtain and convenient to staff entering and leaving the room.

(3) A hand sanitation station in patient rooms utilizing waterless cleaners may be used in renovation

APPENDIX

A3.1.1.2 (1) In new construction, single patient rooms should be at least 12 feet (3.66 meters) wide by 13 feet (3.96 meters) deep (or approximately 160 square feet, or 14.86 square meters) exclusive of toilet rooms, closets, lockers, wardrobes, alcoves, or vestibules. These spaces should accommodate comfortable furniture for family members (one or two) without blocking access of staff members to patients. Efforts should be made to provide the patient with some control of the room environment.

A3.1.1.3 Windows are important for the psychological well-being of many patients, as well as for meeting fire safety code requirements. They are also essential for continued use of the area in the event of mechanical ventilation system failure.

A3.1.1.5 Where renovation work is undertaken, every effort should be made to meet this standard. Where space does not permit the installation of an additional hand-washing station in the patient room, or where it is technically infeasible, the authority having jurisdiction may grant approval of alternative forms of hand cleansing.

of existing facilities where existing conditions prohibit an additional hand-washing station.

3.1.1.6 Toilet rooms. Toilet rooms shall be provided in accordance with Section 2.1-2.2.1.

3.1.1.7 Patient storage locations. Patient storage shall be provided in accordance with Section 2.1-2.2.2.

*3.1.2 Patient/Family-Centered Care Rooms

3.1.3 Examination/Treatment Room(s)
Omission of such rooms shall be permitted if all patient rooms in the nursing unit are single-bed rooms.

3.1.3.1 Location. Centrally located examination and treatment room(s) shall be permitted to serve more than one nursing unit on the same floor.

3.1.3.2 Space requirements. Such rooms shall have a minimum floor area of 120 square feet (11.15 square meters).

3.1.3.3 Patient privacy. Provision shall be made to preserve patient privacy from observation from outside the exam room through an open door.

3.1.3.4 Facility requirements. The room shall contain a hand-washing station; storage facilities; and a desk, counter, or shelf space for writing.

3.1.4 Support Areas—General
3.1.4.1 The size and location of each support area shall depend on the numbers and types of beds served.

3.1.4.2 Location

(1) Provision for the support areas listed shall be in or readily available to each nursing unit.

(2) Each support area may be arranged and located to serve more than one nursing unit; however, unless otherwise noted, at least one such support area shall be provided on each nursing floor.

3.1.4.3 Identifiable spaces are required for each of the indicated functions. Where the words room or office are used, a separate, enclosed space for the one named function is intended; otherwise, the described area may be a specific space in another room or common area.

3.1.5 Support Areas for Medical/Surgical Nursing Units
*3.1.5.1 Administrative center(s) or nurse station(s). This area shall be provided in accordance with Section 2.1-2.3.1.

3.1.5.2 Documentation area. This area shall be provided on the unit in accordance with Section 2.1-2.3.2.

3.1.5.3 Nurse or supervisor office

*3.1.5.4 Multipurpose room(s). Room(s) shall be provided for patient conferences, reports, education, training sessions, and consultation in accordance with Section 2.1-2.3.3.

3.1.5.5 Hand-washing stations

(1) In nursing locations, hand-washing stations shall be conveniently accessible to the nurse station, medication station, and nourishment area.

APPENDIX

A3.1.2 Patient/Family-Centered Care Rooms
Where a facility contemplates patient/family-centered care rooms, the rooms should be constructed to meet the needs of the functional program.

a. Capacity. Patient/family-centered rooms should be single-bed rooms.

b. Area and dimensions. These rooms should have a minimum of 250 square feet (23.22 square meters) of clear floor area exclusive of family alcoves, toilet rooms, closets, lockers, wardrobes, vestibules, staff charting areas, or staff hand-washing stations, with a minimum clear dimension of 15 feet (4.57 meters).

c. Additional area. Additional areas should be provided at a minimum clear area of 30 square feet (2.79 square meters) per family member (permitted by the facility).

d. Environment of care. Consideration for a homelike atmosphere, furniture arrangements, and orientation to the patient bed and room windows should reflect the needs of the functional program.

A3.1.5.1 The station should permit visual observation of all traffic into the unit.

A3.1.5.4 Multipurpose rooms are used primarily for staff purposes and generally are not available for family or visitors. A waiting room convenient to the unit should be provided.

(2) If it is convenient to each, one hand-washing station shall be permitted to serve several areas.

3.1.5.6 Medication station. Provision shall be made for distribution of medications in accordance with Section 2.1-2.3.4.

3.1.5.7 Nourishment area. This area shall be provided in accordance with Section 2.1-2.3.5.

3.1.5.8 Ice machine. Each nursing unit shall have equipment to provide ice for treatments and nourishment. Ice-making equipment shall be provided in accordance with Section 2.1-2.3.6.

3.1.5.9 Patient bathing facilities

(1) Showers and bathtubs

   (a) Where individual bathing facilities are not provided in patient rooms, there shall be at least one shower and/or bathtub for each 12 beds without such facilities.

   (b) Each bathtub or shower shall be in an individual room or enclosure that provides privacy for bathing, drying, and dressing.

(2) Toilets. A toilet shall be provided within or directly accessible to each central bathing facility.

(3) Special bathing facilities, including space for attendant, shall be provided for patients on stretchers, carts, and wheelchairs at the ratio of one per 100 beds or a fraction thereof. These facilities may be on a separate floor if convenient for use.

3.1.5.10 Clean workroom or clean supply room. Such rooms shall be provided in accordance with Section 2.1-2.3.7.

3.1.5.11 Soiled workroom or soiled holding room. Such rooms shall be provided in accordance with Section 2.1-2.3.8.

APPENDIX

A3.1.5.13 A storage or bin space should be included for recyclable materials: white paper, mixed paper, cans, bottles, and cardboard.

3.1.5.12 Equipment and supply storage

(1) Clean linen storage. Each nursing unit shall contain a designated area for clean linen storage in accordance with Section 2.1-2.3.9.1.

(2) Equipment storage room or alcove. Appropriate room(s) or alcove(s) shall be provided in accordance with Section 2.1-2.3.9.2.

(3) Storage space for stretchers and wheelchairs. Space shall be provided in accordance with Section 2.1-2.3.9.3.

(4) Emergency equipment storage. Storage shall be provided for emergency equipment in accordance with Section 2.1-2.3.9.4.

*****3.1.5.13** Housekeeping room. One housekeeping room shall be provided for each nursing unit or nursing floor in accordance with Section 2.1-2.3.10.

Note: This housekeeping room may not be used for other departments and nursing units that require separate housekeeping rooms.

3.1.6 Support Areas for Staff
3.1.6.1 Staff lounge facilities. Lounge facilities shall be provided in accordance with Section 2.1-2.4.1.

3.1.6.2 Staff toilet room(s). Staff toilet rooms shall be provided in accordance with Section 2.1-2.4.2.

3.1.6.3 Staff storage facilities. Storage facilities for the personal use of staff shall be provided in accordance with Section 2.1-2.4.3.

3.1.7 Support Areas for Patients and Visitors
3.1.7.1 Visitor lounge. Each nursing unit shall have access to a lounge for visitors and family.

(1) This lounge shall be sized appropriately for the number of beds and/or nursing units served per the functional program.

(2) This lounge shall be conveniently located to the nursing unit(s) served.

(3) This lounge shall provide comfortable seating.

(4) This lounge shall be designed to minimize the impact of noise and activity on patient rooms and staff functions.

3.1.7.2 Toilet room(s). A toilet room(s) with hand-washing station shall be located convenient to multi-purpose room(s).

(1) Patient use. If the functional program calls for the toilet rooms(s) to be for patient use, it shall be designed/equipped for patient use.

(2) Public use. If called out in the functional program, the toilet room(s) serving the multipurpose rooms(s) may also be designated for public use.

3.2 Special Patient Care Areas

3.2.1 Applicability
As designated by the functional program, both airborne infection isolation and protective environment rooms may be required. Many facilities care for patients with an extreme susceptibility to infection (e.g., immunosuppressed patients with prolonged granulocytopenia, most notably bone marrow recipients, or solid-organ transplant recipients and patients with hematological malignancies who are receiving chemotherapy and are severely granulocytopenic). These rooms are not intended for use with patients diagnosed with HIV infection or AIDS, unless they are also severely granulocytopenic. Generally, protective environments are not needed in community hospitals, unless these facilities take care of these types of patients.

*3.2.2 Airborne Infection Isolation Room(s)
The airborne infection isolation room requirements contained in these Guidelines for particular areas throughout a facility should be predicated on an infection control risk assessment (ICRA) and based on the needs of specific community and patient populations served by an individual health care provider (see Glossary and Section 1.5–2.3).

3.2.2.1 Number. At least one airborne infection isolation room shall be provided in the hospital. The number of airborne infection isolation rooms for individual patient units shall be increased based upon an ICRA or by a multidisciplinary group designated for

that purpose. This process ensures a more accurate determination of environmentally safe and appropriate room types and spatial needs. Special ventilation requirements are found in Table 2.1-2.

3.2.2.2 Location. Airborne infection isolation rooms may be located within individual nursing units and used for normal acute care when not required for patients with airborne infectious diseases, or they may be grouped as a separate isolation unit.

3.2.2.3 Capacity. Each room shall contain only one bed.

3.2.2.4 Facility requirements. Each airborne infection isolation room shall comply with the acute care patient room section (Section 2.1–3.1.1) of this document as well as the following requirements:

(1) Each room shall have an area for hand-washing, gowning, and storage of clean and soiled materials located directly outside or immediately inside the entry door to the room.

(2) Construction requirements

(a) Airborne infection isolation room perimeter walls, ceiling, and floors, including penetrations, shall be sealed tightly so that air does not infiltrate the environment from the outside or from other spaces. (See Glossary.)

(b) Airborne infection isolation room(s) shall have self-closing devices on all room exit doors.

(3) Separate toilet, bathtub (or shower), and hand-washing stations shall be provided for each airborne infection isolation room.

*(4) Rooms shall have a permanently installed visual mechanism to constantly monitor the pressure

APPENDIX

A3.2.2 For additional information, refer to the Centers for Disease Control and Prevention (CDC) "Guidelines for Preventing the Transmission of Mycobacterium tuberculosis in Health Care Facilities" as they appear in the *Federal Register* dated October 28, 1994, and to the CDC "Guidelines for Environmental Infection Control in Health-Care Facilities," December 2003.

2006 Guidelines for Design and Construction of Health Care Facilities **43**

status of the room when occupied by patients with an airborne infectious disease. The mechanism shall continuously monitor the direction of the airflow.

*3.2.3 Protective Environment Room(s)
The differentiating factor between protective environment rooms and other patient rooms is the requirement for positive air pressure relative to adjoining spaces, with all supply air passing through high-efficiency particulate air (HEPA) filters with 99.97 percent efficiency for particles > 0.3 μm in diameter.

3.2.3.1 Applicability. When determined by an ICRA, special design considerations and ventilation to ensure the protection of patients who are highly susceptible to infection shall be required.

3.2.3.2 Functional program. The appropriate clinical staff shall be consulted regarding room type, and spatial needs to meet facility infection control requirements shall be incorporated into the functional program.

3.2.3.3 Number and location. The appropriate numbers and location of protective environment rooms shall be as required by the ICRA.

3.2.3.4 Capacity. Protective environment rooms shall contain only one bed.

3.2.3.5 Facility requirements. Protective environment rooms shall comply with Section 2.1-3.2.2. Special ventilation requirements are found in Table 2.1-2.

(1) Each protective environment room shall have an area for hand-washing, gowning, and storage of clean and soiled materials located directly outside or immediately inside the entry door to the room.

(2) Patient bathing and toilet facilities. Separate toilet, bathtub (or shower), and hand-washing stations shall be directly accessible from each protective environment room.

(3) Monitoring equipment. Rooms shall have a permanently installed visual mechanism to constantly monitor the pressure status of the room when occupied by patients requiring a protective environment. The mechanism shall continuously monitor the direction of the airflow.

(4) Construction requirements

(a) Protective environment room perimeter walls, ceiling, and floors, including penetrations, shall be sealed tightly so that air does not infiltrate the environment from the outside or from other spaces.

(b) Protective environment room(s) shall have self-closing devices on all room exit doors.

(5) Renovation. See references to protective environment rooms during renovation and construction in Section 1.5–2.2.

*3.2.3.6 Bone marrow transplant units. Rooms in allogeneic bone marrow transplant units shall be designed to meet specific patient needs.

3.2.4 Seclusion Room(s)

3.2.4.1 Applicability. If indicated by the functional program, the hospital shall provide one or more single-bed rooms for patients needing close supervision for medical and/or psychiatric care.

3.2.4.2 Location. These rooms may be part of the psychiatric unit described in Section 2.1-3.8.

3.2.4.3 Facility requirements. If the single-bed room(s) is part of the acute care nursing unit, the provisions of Section 2.1-3.8.2 shall apply, with the following exceptions:

(1) Each room shall be for single occupancy.

APPENDIX

A3.2.3.6 Bone marrow transplant facilities

General space and staffing requirements are critical for bone marrow transplant facilities. Patients in these units may be acutely aware of the surrounding environment, which is their life support system during the many weeks they are confined in an immuno-suppressed condition. Means of controlling unnecessary noise are important. At times, each patient may require individual privacy, although each is required to be under close staff supervision.

a. Location. Bone marrow transplant rooms should be located to have access within the hospital to out-of-unit diagnostic and treatment equipment, particularly radiation therapy equipment.

b. All bone marrow transplant-designated beds should be in exceptionally clean environments, which should consist of protective environment rooms equipped with HEPA filtration, preferably located close to each other.

c. A countertop with scrub sink and space for high-level disinfection procedures should be available outside the entrance to each patient room when located within the nursing unit or at each entrance to a dedicated bone marrow transplant room. A hand-washing station should be accessible near the entrance to each patient room within a dedicated bone marrow transplant unit.

d. Toilet and bathing facilities. Each bone marrow transplant patient room should have a private toilet room, which contains a water closet and a bathing facility, for the exclusive use of the patient. The patient should be able to enter the room directly without leaving the patient room or passing through the vestibule. The patient should also have a lavatory for the patient's exclusive use, located in the patient room or the private toilet room.

e. Patients should be housed in single-bed rooms with full-height partitions, sealed airtight to the structure to prevent cross-infections.

f. All surfaces, floors, walls, ceilings, doors, windows, and curtains in the patient room should be scrubbable.

g. Windows should be provided so that each patient may be cognizant of the outdoor environment. Windowsill height should not exceed 3 feet (0.91 meter) above the floor and should be above grade. All windows in the unit should be fixed sash and sealed to eliminate infiltration.

h. Viewing panels should be provided in doors or walls for nursing staff observation. Flame-retardant curtains or other means should be provided to cover windows and viewing panels when a patient requires visual privacy. Glazing should be safety glass, wire glass, or tempered clear plastic to reduce hazards from accidental breakage.

i. Nurse and emergency call systems. Each patient room should be provided with a nurse call system accessible at the bed, sitting area, and patient toilet room. An emergency call system should also be provided at each patient bed and toilet room to summon additional personnel from on-call rooms, consultation rooms, and staff lounges.

j. Facilities for administration of suction, compressed air, and oxygen should be provided at the bed.

k. Staff and visitor support areas. Each geographically distinct unit should provide appropriate space to support nurses' administrative activities, report/conference room activities, doctors' consultation, drug preparation and distribution, emergency equipment storage, and closed accessible waiting for family members.

(2) Each room shall be located to permit staff observation of the entrance, preferably adjacent to the nurse station.

(3) Each room shall be designed to minimize the potential for escape, concealment, injury, or suicide.

(4) If vision panels are used for observation of patients, the arrangement shall ensure patient privacy and prevent casual observation by visitors and other patients.

*3.2.5 Protected Units

3.3 Intermediate Care Units
Intermediate care units, sometimes referred to as step-down units, are routinely utilized in acute care hospitals for patients who require frequent monitoring of vital signs and/or nursing intervention that exceeds the level needed in a regular medical/surgical unit but is less than that provided in a critical care unit.

3.3.1 General
3.3.1.1 Classification. Intermediate care units can be progressive care units or specialty units such as cardiac, surgical (e.g., thoracic, vascular), neurosurgical/neurological monitoring, or chronic ventilator respiratory care units.

3.3.1.2 Applicability. These standards shall apply to adult beds designated to provide intermediate care, but not pediatric or neonatal intermediate care.

3.3.1.3 Location. In hospitals that provide intermediate care, beds shall be designated for this purpose. These

beds shall be permitted to constitute a separate unit or be a designated part of another unit.

3.3.1.4 Nurse management space. There shall be a separate physical area devoted to nursing management for the care of the intermediate patient.

3.3.2 Patient Rooms
The following shall apply to all intermediate care units unless otherwise noted.

3.3.2.1 Capacity
Maximum room capacity shall be four patients.

3.3.2.2 Space requirements. Minor encroachments, including columns and hand-washing stations, that do not interfere with functions may be ignored when determining space requirements for patient rooms.

(1) Area. In new construction, patient rooms shall be constructed to meet the needs of the functional program and have a minimum of 120 square feet (11.15 square meters) of clear floor area per bed in multiple-bed rooms and 150 square feet (13.94 square meters) of clear floor area for single-bed rooms, exclusive of toilet rooms, closets, lockers, wardrobes, alcoves, or vestibules.

(2) Clearances. In new construction, the dimensions and arrangement of rooms shall be such that there is a minimum clearance of 4 feet (1.22 meters) between the sides of the beds and other beds, walls, or fixed obstructions. A minimum clearance of 4 feet (1.22 meters) shall be available at the foot of each bed to permit the passage of equipment and beds.

(3) Renovation. Where renovation work is undertaken, every effort shall be made to meet these standards. If it is not possible to meet these minimum standards, the authorities having jurisdiction may grant approval to deviate from this requirement. In such cases, patient rooms shall have no less than 100 square feet (9.29 square meters) of clear floor area per bed in multiple-bed rooms and 120 square feet (11.15 square meters) of clear floor area in single-bed rooms.

3.3.2.3 Windows. Each patient room shall have a window in accordance with Section 2.1-8.2.2.5.

3.3.2.4 Patient privacy. In multiple-bed rooms, visual privacy shall be provided for each patient. The design for privacy shall not restrict patient access to the room entrance, lavatory, toilet, or room windows.

3.3.2.5 Nurse call systems. Nurse call systems for two-way voice communication shall be provided in accordance with Section 2.1-10.3.8. The call system for the unit shall include provisions for an emergency code resuscitation alarm to summon assistance from outside the intermediate care unit.

3.3.2.6 Hand-washing stations. These shall be provided to serve each patient room.

(1)   In new construction and renovation, a hand-washing station shall be provided in the patient room in addition to that in the toilet room.

(2)   The hand-washing station in the patient room shall be located outside the patient's cubicle curtain so it is convenient to staff entering and leaving the room.

3.3.2.7 Toilet rooms. Toilet rooms shall be provided in accordance with Section 2.1-2.2.1.

3.3.2.8 Bathing facilities. Patients shall have access to bathing facilities within their rooms or in a central bathing facility.

(1)   Each shower or bathtub in a central bathing facility shall be in an individual room or enclosure that provides privacy for bathing, drying, and dressing.

(2)   A water closet and lavatory in a separate enclosure shall be directly accessible to each central bathing facility.

3.3.2.9 Patient storage. Storage locations for patient use shall be provided in accordance with Section 2.1-2.2.2.

3.3.3 Airborne Infection Isolation Room

Access to at least one airborne infection isolation room shall be provided unless provided elsewhere in the facility. The number of airborne infection isolation rooms shall be determined on the basis of an infection control risk assessment (ICRA). Each room shall comply with the requirements of Section 2.1-3.2.2. Special ventilation requirements are found in Table 2.1-2.

3.3.4 Support Areas—General

3.3.4.1 Provision for the support areas listed below shall be in or readily available to each intermediate care unit.

3.3.4.2 The size and location of each staff support area shall depend upon the numbers and types of beds served.

3.3.4.3 Identifiable spaces are required for each of the indicated functions. Where the words "room" or "office" are used, a separate, enclosed space for the one named function is intended; otherwise, the described area may be a specific space in another room or common area.

3.3.4.4 Services shared with adjacent units shall be permitted.

3.3.5 Support Areas for Intermediate Care Units

3.3.5.1 Administrative center or nurse station

(1)   An administrative center or nurse station shall be provided in accordance with Section 2.1-2.3.1.

(2)   There shall be direct or remote visual observation between the administrative center or nurse station, staffed charting stations, and all patient beds in the unit.

3.3.5.2 Documentation area. This area shall be provided within the patient unit in accordance with Section 2.1-2.3.2.

3.3.5.3 Medication station. Provision shall be made for 24-hour distribution of medications in accordance with Section 2.1-2.3.4.

3.3.5.4 Hand-washing stations

(1)   In nursing locations, hand-washing stations shall be conveniently accessible to the nurse station, medication station, and nourishment area.

(2)   If it is convenient to each, one hand-washing station shall be permitted to serve several areas.

3.3.5.5 Nourishment area. There shall be a nourishment area with a work counter, a hand-washing station, a refrigerator, storage cabinets, and equipment for preparing and serving hot and cold nourishments between scheduled meals.

3.3.5.6 Ice machine. A self-dispensing ice machine shall be provided to supply ice for treatments and nourishment.

3.3.5.7 Clean workroom or clean supply room. This room shall be provided in accordance with Section 2.1-2.3.7.

3.3.5.8 Soiled workroom or soiled holding room. This room shall be provided in accordance with Section 2.1-2.3.8.

3.3.5.9 Equipment and supply storage

(1) Equipment storage room. An equipment storage room shall be provided for storage of equipment necessary for patient care.

    (a) This room shall be permitted to serve more than one unit.

    (b) Each unit shall provide sufficient storage area(s) located on the patient floor to keep its required corridor width free of all equipment and supplies, but not less than 20 square feet (1.86 square meters) per patient bed shall be provided.

(2) Emergency equipment storage. This shall be provided in accordance with Section 2.1-2.3.9.4.

3.3.5.10 Housekeeping room. This room shall be provided in accordance with Section 2.1-2.3.10.

3.3.6 Support Areas for Staff
3.3.6.1 Staff lounge facilities. Staff lounge facilities shall be provided in accordance with Section 2.1-2.4.1.

(1) The location of these facilities shall be convenient to the intermediate care unit.

(2) These facilities may be shared with other nursing unit(s).

3.3.6.2 Staff toilet room(s). These shall be provided in accordance with Section 2.1-2.4.2.

3.3.6.3 Staff storage facilities. Storage facilities for personal use of the staff shall be provided in accordance with Section 2.1-2.4.3.

3.4 Critical Care Units

3.4.1 General Considerations
3.4.1.1 Applicability

(1) The following standards are intended for typical critical care services. Design of critical care units shall comply with these standards and shall be appropriate to the needs of the functional program.

(2) Where specialized services are required, additions and/or modifications shall be made as necessary for efficient, safe, and effective patient care.

3.4.1.2 Environment of care. Critical care units require special space and equipment considerations for safe and effective patient care, staff functions, and family participation. Families and visitors to critical care units often wait for long periods, including overnight, under highly stressful situations. They tend to congregate at unit entries to be readily accessible to staff interaction. Clinical personnel perform in continously stressful circumstances over long hours. Often they cannot leave the critical care unit, necessitating space and services to accommodate their personal and staff group needs in close proximity to the unit. Design shall address such issues as privacy, atmosphere, and aesthetics for all involved in the care and comfort of patients in critical care units.

3.4.1.3 Functional program. Not every hospital will provide all types of critical care. Some hospitals may have a small combined unit; others may have separate, sophisticated units for highly specialized treatments. Critical care units shall comply in size, number, and type with these standards and with the functional program.

3.4.1.4 Unit location. The following shall apply to all types of critical care units unless otherwise noted.

(1) The location shall offer convenient access from the emergency, respiratory therapy, laboratory,

radiology, surgery, and other essential departments and services as defined by the functional program.

(2) The unit shall be located so that medical emergency resuscitation teams can respond promptly to emergency calls with minimum travel time.

(3) Space arrangement shall include provisions for access to emergency equipment from other departments.

(4) The location shall be arranged to eliminate the need for through traffic.

*3.4.1.5 Elevator considerations. In new construction, where elevator transport is required to move critically ill patients, the size of the cab, door width, and mechanisms and controls shall meet the specialized needs.

*3.4.2 Critical Care Units (General)
The following shall apply to all types of critical care units unless otherwise noted.

*3.4.2.1 Patient care areas

(1) Space requirements for new construction

 (a) Area. Each patient space (whether separate rooms, cubicles, or multiple-bed space) shall have a minimum of 200 square feet (18.58 square meters) of clear floor area with a minimum headwall width of 13 feet (3.96 meters) per bed, exclusive of anterooms, vestibules, toilet rooms, closets, lockers, wardrobes, and/or alcoves.

 (b) Clearances. Bed clearances for all adult and pediatric units shall be a minimum of 5 feet (1.52 meters) at the foot of the bed to the wall, 5 feet (1.52 meters) on the transfer side, 4 feet (1.22 meters) on the non-transfer side, and 8 feet (2.44 meters) between beds.

(2) Space requirements for renovation. In renovation of existing critical care units, every effort shall be made to meet the above minimum standards. If it is not possible to meet the above area standards, authorities having jurisdiction may grant approval to deviate from this requirement. In such cases, the following standards shall be met:

 (a) Separate rooms or cubicles for single patient use shall be no less than 150 square feet (13.94 square meters).

 (b) Multiple-bed space shall contain at least 150 square feet (13.94 square meters) of clear floor area per bed, exclusive of the spaces noted for new construction in Section 2.1-3.4.2.1 (1)(a).

(3) Windows. Each patient bed shall have visual access, other than skylights, to the outside environment, with not less than one outside window in each patient bed area, in accordance with Section 2.1-8.2.2.5.

(4) Privacy

 (a) When private rooms or cubicles are provided, view panels to the corridor shall be required with a means to ensure visual privacy.

 (b) Each patient bed area shall have space at each bedside for visitors and shall have provisions for visual privacy from casual observation by other patients and visitors.

*(5) Nurse call system

APPENDIX

A3.4.1.5 Transportation of patients to and from the critical care unit should ideally be separated from public corridors and visitor waiting areas.

A3.4.2 Provision should be made for rapid and easily accessible information exchange and communication within the unit and the hospital.

A3.4.2.1 In critical care units, the size of the patient care space should be determined by the intended functional use. The patient space in critical care units, especially those caring for surgical patients following major trauma or cardiovascular, transplant, or orthopedic procedures and those caring for medical patients simultaneously requiring ventilation, dialysis, and/or treatment with other large equipment (e.g., intra-aortic balloon pump) may be overwhelmed if designed to the absolute minimum clear floor area.

(a) Nurse call systems for two-way voice communication shall be provided in accordance with Section 2.1-10.3.8.

(b) The communication system for the unit shall include provisions for an emergency code resuscitation alarm to summon assistance from outside the critical care unit.

(6) Hand-washing stations

(a) Hand-washing stations shall be convenient to nurse stations and patient bed areas.

(b) There shall be at least one hand-washing station for every three beds in open plan areas and one in each patient room.

(c) The hand-washing station shall be located near the entrance to the patient cubicle or room, sized to minimize splashing water onto the floor, and equipped with hands-free operable controls.

(d) Where towel dispensers are provided, they shall operate so that dispensing requires only the towel to be touched.

(7) Construction requirements

(a) Doors

(i) Where only one door is provided to a bed space, it shall be at least 4 feet (1.22 meters) wide and arranged to minimize interference with movement of beds and large equipment.

(ii) Sliding doors shall not have floor tracks and shall have hardware or a breakaway feature that minimizes jamming possibilities.

APPENDIX

A3.4.2.1 (5). A staff emergency assistance system should be provided on the most accessible side of the bed. The system should annunciate at the nurse station with backup from another staffed area from which assistance can be summoned.

(iii) Where sliding doors are used for access to cubicles within a suite, a 3-foot-wide (91.44 centimeters) swinging door shall be permitted for personnel communication.

(b) Windows in renovation projects

(i) Clerestory windows with windowsills above the heights of adjacent ceilings may be used, provided they afford patients a view of the outside and are equipped with appropriate forms of glare and sun control.

(ii) Distance from the patient bed to the outside window shall not exceed 50 feet (15.24 meters).

(iii) Where partitioned cubicles are used, patients' view to outside windows shall be through no more than two separate clear vision panels.

(8) Design criteria for mechanical, electrical, and plumbing systems. The electrical, medical gas, heating, ventilation, and communication services shall support the needs of the patients and critical care team members under normal and emergency situations.

3.4.2.2 Airborne infection isolation room

(1) At least one airborne infection isolation room shall be provided, unless provided in another critical care unit. The number of airborne infection isolation rooms shall be determined based on an ICRA.

(2) Each room shall comply with the requirements of Section 2.1-3.2.2; however, the requirement for the bathtub (or shower) may be eliminated. Compact, modular toilet/sink combination units may replace the requirement for a "toilet room."

(3) Special ventilation requirements are found in Table 2.1-2.

3.4.2.3 Diagnostic, treatment, and service areas

(1) Special procedures room. This shall be provided if required by the functional program. It may be

located outside the critical care unit if conveniently accessible.

(2) The following shall be available. Provision of these services from the central departments or from satellite facilities shall be permitted as required by the functional program.

(a) Imaging facilities

(b) Respiratory therapy services

(c) Laboratory services

(d) Pharmacy services

3.4.2.4 Support areas for critical care units. The following shall be provided for all types of critical care units unless otherwise noted.

*(1) Administrative center or nurse station

(a) An administrative center or nurse station

shall be provided in accordance with Section 2.1-2.3.1.

(b) Visual observation. There shall be direct or remote visual observation between the administrative center, nurse station, or staffed charting stations and all patient beds in the critical care unit.

*(2) Documentation and information review spaces. Space shall be provided within the unit to accommodate the recording of patient information.

*(a) The documentation space shall be located within or adjacent to the patient bed space. It shall include countertop that will provide for a large flow sheet typical of critical care units and a computer monitor and keyboard. There shall be one documentation space with seating for each patient bed.

*(b) There shall be a specifically designated area within the unit for information review located to facilitate concentration.

APPENDIX

A3.4.2.4 (1). Patients should be visually observed at all times. This can be achieved in a variety of ways.

a. If a central station is chosen, it should be located to allow for complete visual control of all patient beds in the critical care unit. It should be designed to maximize efficiency in traffic patterns. Patients should be oriented so that they can see the nurse but cannot see the other patients. There should be an ability to communicate with the clerical staff without having to enter the central station.

b. If a central station is not chosen, the unit should be designed to provide visual contact between patient beds so that there can be constant visual contact between the nurse and patient.

A3.4.2.4 (2). The requirements for documenting patient information by providers have become substantial and continue to grow. A growing number of providers and others review patient records in critical care units. Confidentiality of patient information is important. Computers are increasingly used to meet these expectations.

a. Separate areas need to be designed for the unit secretary and staff charting. Planning should consider the potential volume of

staff (both medical and nursing) that could be present at any one time and translate that to adequate charting surfaces.

b. The secretarial area should be accessible to all. However, the charting areas may be somewhat isolated to facilitate concentration.

c. Storage for chart forms and supplies should be readily accessible.

d. Space for computer terminals and printer and conduit for computer hookup should be provided when automated information systems are in use or planned for the future.

e. Patient records should be readily accessible to clerical, nursing, and physician staff.

A3.4.2.4 (2)(a). Documentation space. The countertop area should be a minimum of 8 square feet (0.74 square meters). If a documentation space is to serve two patient beds, it should be a minimum of 10 square feet (0.93 square meter).

A3.4.2.4 (2)(b). Information review space. There should be a minimum of 8 square feet (0.74 square meters) of countertop and seating to accommodate two people for every five patient beds it serves.

*(3) Office space. Adequate office space for critical care medical and nursing management/administrative personnel shall be available immediately adjacent to the critical care unit. The offices shall be linked with the unit by telephone or an intercommunications system.

(4) Multipurpose room(s). Multipurpose room(s) shall be provided for staff, patients, and patients' families for patient conferences, reports, education, training sessions, and consultation. These rooms shall be accessible to each nursing unit.

*(5) Medication station. Provision shall be made for 24-hour distribution of medications in accordance with Section 2.1-2.3.4.

*(6) Patient monitoring equipment. Each unit shall contain equipment for continuous monitoring, with visual displays for each patient at the bedside

and at the nurse station. Monitors shall be located to permit easy viewing and access but shall not interfere with access to the patient.

(7) X-ray viewing facility. The unit shall have an x-ray viewing facility, which may be shared by more than one critical care unit provided direct access is available from each.

(8) Nourishment area. This area shall be provided in accordance with Section 2.1-2.3.5. It shall be immediately available within each critical care suite. More than one critical care unit shall be permitted to share this area provided direct access is available from each.

(9) Ice machine. This equipment shall be provided in accordance with Section 2.1-2.3.6.

(10) Clean workroom or clean supply room.

(a) This room shall be provided in accordance with Section 2.1-2.3.7.

(b) This room shall be immediately available in each critical care suite. More than one critical care unit shall be permitted to share a clean workroom or clean supply room provided direct access is available from each.

(11) Soiled workroom or soiled holding room.

(a) This room shall be provided in accordance with Section 2.1-2.3.8.

(b) It shall be immediately available in each critical care suite, but more than one critical care unit shall be permitted to share the room provided direct access is available from each.

(12) Equipment and supply storage

(a) Clean linen storage. This shall be provided in accordance with Section 2.1-2.3.9.1. This area shall be immediately available within each critical care suite. More than one critical care unit shall be permitted to share the room provided direct access is available from each.

*(b) Equipment storage room or alcove

(i) Appropriate room(s) or alcove(s) shall be provided in accordance with Section 2.1-2.3.9.2.

(ii) Each critical care unit shall have sufficient storage area(s) located on the patient floor to keep the required corridor width free of all equipment and supplies. No less than 20 square feet (1.86 square meters) per patient bed shall be provided for equipment storage.

(c) Wheelchair and stretcher storage. Space to store stretchers and wheelchairs shall be provided in accordance with Section 2.1-2.3.9.3.

(d) Emergency equipment storage. Space shall be provided in accordance with Section 2.1-2.3.9.4.

(13) Housekeeping room. A housekeeping room shall be provided within or immediately adjacent to the critical care unit.

(a) This room shall not be shared with other nursing units or departments.

(b) It shall contain a service sink or floor receptor and provisions for storage of supplies and housekeeping equipment.

3.4.2.5 Support areas for staff. The following shall be provided for all types of critical care units unless otherwise noted.

(1) Staff lounge(s) and toilet(s). The following may be located outside the unit if conveniently accessible.

(a) These shall be located so that staff may be recalled quickly to the patient area in emergencies.

(b) The lounge shall have telephone or intercom and emergency code alarm connections to the critical care unit it serves.

(c) If not provided elsewhere, provision for the storage of coats, etc., shall be made in this area.

(d) Adequate furnishings, equipment, and space for comfortable seating and the preparation and consumption of snacks and beverages shall be provided unless provisions have been made elsewhere.

(e) One lounge shall be permitted to serve adjacent critical care areas.

(2) Staff storage facilities. Facilities for personal use of staff shall be provided in accordance with Section 2.1-2.4.3.

(3) Staff accommodations. Sleeping and personal care accommodations shall be provided for staff on 24-hour, on-call work schedules.

3.4.2.6 Support areas for visitors
The following shall be provided and may be located outside the unit if conveniently accessible.

(1) Visitor waiting room

(a) This room shall be designed to accommodate the long stays and stressful conditions common to such spaces, including provisions for privacy, means to facilitate communications, and access to toilets.

(b) The locations and size shall be appropriate for the number of patients and units served, with a seating capacity of not less than one family member per patient bed.

3.4.3 Coronary Care Unit
Coronary patients have special needs. They are often fully aware of their surroundings but still need immediate and critical emergency care. In addition to the standards in Section 2.1-3.4.2, the following standards apply to the coronary critical care unit:

3.4.3.1 Each coronary patient shall have a separate room for acoustical and visual privacy.

3.4.3.2 Each coronary patient shall have access to a toilet in the room. Portable commodes shall be permitted in lieu of individual toilets, but provisions must be made for their storage, servicing, and odor control.

3.4.4 Combined Medical/Surgical Critical Care and Coronary Care

If medical/surgical and coronary critical care services are combined in one critical care unit, at least 50 percent of the beds shall be located in private rooms or cubicles.

3.4.5 Pediatric Critical Care

Critically ill pediatric patients have unique physical and psychological needs.

3.4.5.1 General

(1) Applicability. The standards previously set forth for a general critical care unit (Section 2.1-3.4.2) shall apply to a pediatric critical care unit.

(2) Functional program. If a facility has a specific pediatric critical care unit, the functional program shall include consideration for staffing, isolation, transportation, life support, and environmental systems.

3.4.5.2 Patient care areas. A pediatric critical care unit shall provide the following:

(1) Space requirements

(a) Space at each bedside for families and visitors in addition to the space provided for staff. The space provided for parental accommodations as defined by the functional program shall not limit or encroach upon the minimum clearance requirements for staff and medical equipment around the patient's bed station.

*(b) Sleeping space for parents who may be required to spend long hours with the patient. If the sleeping area is separate from the patient area, it shall be in communication with the critical care unit.

(2) Consultation/demonstration room within, or convenient to, the pediatric critical care unit for private discussions

(3) Storage facilities

*(a) Provisions for formula storage

(b) Separate storage cabinets or closets for toys and games

*(c) Equipment storage space. Space for equipment storage shall be provided in accordance with Section 2.1-2.3.9.2.

*3.4.5.3 Examination and treatment room(s)

3.4.6 Newborn Intensive Care Units

The following standards apply to the newborn intensive care unit (NICU):

3.4.6.1 Patient care areas

(1) Safety and security

*(a) All entries to the NICU shall be controlled. The family entrance and reception area shall be clearly identified. The reception area shall permit visual observation and contact with all traffic entering the unit.

(b) The NICU shall be designed as part of an overall safety program to protect the physical security of infants, parents, and staff and to minimize the risk of infant abduction.

APPENDIX

A3.4.5.2 (1)(b) Parent sleeping accommodations should be provided at the patient's bedside.

A3.4.5.2 (3)(a) Formula storage may be outside the unit but should be available for use at all times. The functional program should determine the location and size of formula storage.

A3.4.5.2 (3)(c) Space allowances for pediatric beds and cribs are greater than those for adult beds because of the variation in bed/crib sizes and the potential for change. The functional program may determine that general storage be provided in the pediatric critical care unit above the minimum required under Section 2.1-3.4.2.4 (12)(b).

A3.4.5.3 The number and location of examination/treatment rooms should be based on the functional program.

A3.4.6.1 (1)(a) There should be efficient access to the unit from the labor and delivery area and emergency department or other referral entry points.

(2) Space requirements

    (a) Each patient care space shall contain a minimum of 120 square feet (11.15 square meters) of clear floor area per bassinet excluding sinks and aisles.

    (b) There shall be an aisle adjacent to each infant care space with a minimum width of 4 feet (1.22 meters) in multiple-bed rooms. When single-patient rooms or fixed cubicle partitions are utilized in the design, there shall be an adjacent aisle of not less than 8 feet (2.44 meters) in clear and unobstructed width to permit the passage of equipment and personnel.

    (c) In multiple-bed rooms, there shall be a minimum of 8 feet (2.44 meters) between infant care beds.

(3) Viewing windows. When viewing windows are provided, provision shall be made to control casual viewing of infants.

(4) Privacy. Each patient care space shall be designed to allow privacy for the infant and family.

(5) Control station. A central area shall serve as a control station.

    (a) This area shall have space for counters and storage.

    (b) This area shall have convenient access to hand-washing stations.

    (c) It shall be permitted to be combined with or to include centers for reception and communication and patient monitoring.

(6) Hand-washing stations

    (a) In a multiple-bed room, every bed position shall be within 20 feet (6.10 meters) of a hands-free hand-washing station. Where an individual room concept is used, a hands-free hand-washing station shall be provided within each infant care room.

    (b) All hand-washing stations shall be large enough to contain splashing.

(7) Construction requirements

    (a) Noise control

        (i) Infant bed areas and the spaces opening onto them shall be designed to produce minimal background noise and to contain and absorb much of the transient noise that arises within the NICU.

        (ii) The combination of continuous background sound and transient sound in any patient care area shall not exceed an hourly Leq of 50 dB and an hourly L10 of 55 dB, both A-weighted slow response. The Lmax (transient sounds) shall not exceed 70 dB, A-weighted slow response.

    (b) Doors. At least one door to each patient room in the unit must be large enough in both width and height to accommodate portable x-ray and ultrasound equipment.

    (c) Ceilings

        (i) Ceilings shall be easily cleanable and nonfriable.

        (ii) Ceilings shall have a noise reduction coefficient (NRC) of at least 0.90.

        (iii) Ceiling construction shall limit passage of particles from above the ceiling plane into the clinical environment.

(8) Lighting

    (a) Provisions shall be made for indirect lighting and high-intensity lighting in the NICU.

    (b) Controls shall be provided to enable lighting to be adjusted over individual patient care spaces.

    (c) Darkening sufficient for transillumination shall be available when necessary.

(d) No direct ambient lighting shall be permitted in the infant care space, and any direct ambient lighting used outside the infant care area shall be located or framed to avoid a direct line of sight from any infant to the fixture. This does not exclude the use of direct procedure lighting.

(e) Lighting fixtures shall be easy to clean.

(f) At least one source of daylight shall be visible from newborn care areas.

> (i) External windows in infant care rooms shall be glazed with insulating glass to minimize heat gain or loss.
>
> (ii) External windows in infant care rooms shall be situated at least 2 feet (60.96 centimeters) away from any part of a baby's bed to minimize radiant heat loss from the baby.
>
> (iii) All external windows shall be equipped with easily cleaned shading devices that are neutral color or opaque to minimize color distortion from transmitted light.

3.4.6.2 Airborne infection isolation room. An airborne infection isolation room shall be required in at least one level of nursery care.

(1) The room shall be enclosed and separated from the nursery unit with provisions for observation of the infant from adjacent nurseries or control area(s).

(2) All airborne infection isolation rooms shall comply with the requirements of Section 2.1-3.2.2, except the requirements for separate toilet, bathtub, or shower.

APPENDIX

A3.4.6.4 (6) Whenever possible, supplies should flow through special supply entrances from external corridors so that penetration of the semi-sterile zone by non-nursery personnel is unnecessary.

A3.4.6.4 (7) Soiled materials should be sealed and stored in a soiled holding area until removed. This holding area should be located where there will be no need to pass back through the semi-sterile zone to remove the soiled materials.

3.4.6.3 Diagnostic, treatment, and service areas. Support space shall be accessible for respiratory therapy, blood gas lab, developmental therapy, social work, laboratory, pharmacy, radiology, and other ancillary services when these activities are routinely performed on the unit.

3.4.6.4 Support areas for newborn intensive care units

(1) Documentation area. Charting facilities shall have adequate linear surface space to ensure that staff and physicians may chart and have simultaneous access to information and communication systems.

(2) Nurse/supervisor office or station. This shall be provided in accordance with Section 2.1-3.4.2.4 (3).

(3) Multipurpose room(s) for staff, patients, and patients' families for patient conferences, reports, education, training sessions, and consultation.

> (a) These rooms must be accessible to each nursing unit. They may be on other floors if convenient for regular use.
>
> (b) One such room may serve several nursing units and/or departments.

(4) Medication station. A medication station shall be provided in accordance with Section 2.1-2.3.4.

(5) Lactation support space. Space shall be provided for lactation support and consultation in or immediately adjacent to the NICU. Provision shall be made, either within the room or conveniently located nearby, for hand-washing station, counter, refrigeration and freezing, storage for pump and attachments, and educational materials.

*(6) Clean workroom or clean supply room. This room shall be provided in accordance with Section 2.1-3.4.2.4 (10).

*(7) Soiled workroom or soiled holding room. This room shall be provided in accordance with Section 2.1-3.4.2.4 (11).

(8) Emergency equipment storage. Space for storage of emergency equipment shall be provided in accordance with Section 2.1-2.3.9.4.

(9) Housekeeping room. A housekeeping room shall be provided for the unit.

    (a) This room shall be directly accessible from the unit and dedicated for the exclusive use of the NICU.

    (b) This room shall contain a service sink or floor receptor and provisions for storage of supplies and housekeeping equipment.

3.4.6.5 Support areas for staff

(1) Staff lounge, storage facilities, and toilet. A lounge, locker room, and staff toilet shall be provided within or adjacent to the unit for staff use.

(2) Staff accommodations. Physician sleeping facilities with access to a toilet and shower. If not contained within the unit itself, the area shall have a telephone or intercom connection to the patient care area.

3.4.6.6 Support areas for patients and visitors

(1) Visitor waiting room. See Section 2.1-3.4.2.6.

(2) Parent/infant room(s). A room(s) shall be provided within the NICU that allow(s) parents and infants extended private time together.

    (a) The room(s) shall have direct, private access to sink and toilet facilities, communication linkage with the NICU staff, electrical and medical gas outlets as specified for other NICU beds, sleeping facilities for at least one parent, and sufficient space for the infant's bed and equipment.

    (b) The room(s) may be used for other purposes when they are not required for family use.

3.5 Postpartum Units
See Section 2.1-4.2.

3.6 Nurseries

3.6.1 General
Infants shall be housed in nurseries that comply with the standards in this section.

3.6.1.1 Location. All nurseries other than pediatric nurseries shall be convenient to the postpartum nursing unit and obstetrical facilities.

3.6.1.2 Layout

(1) The nurseries shall be located and arranged to preclude the need for unrelated pedestrian traffic.

(2) No nursery shall open directly onto another nursery.

3.6.2 Patient Care Areas (General)
The following standards shall apply to nurseries:

3.6.2.1 Space requirements. Enough space shall be provided for parents to stay 24 hours.

3.6.2.2 Viewing windows. Glazed observation windows to permit the viewing of infants from public areas, workrooms, and adjacent nurseries shall be provided.

3.6.2.3 Hand-washing station(s). At least one lavatory, equipped with a hands-free hand-washing facility, shall be provided for each eight or fewer infant stations.

3.6.2.4 Storage for infant supplies. Convenient, accessible storage for linens and infant supplies shall be provided at each nursery room.

3.6.3 Airborne Infection Isolation Room
An airborne infection isolation room shall be provided in or near at least one level of nursery care.

3.6.3.1 The room shall be enclosed and separated from the nursery unit with provisions for observation of the infant from adjacent nurseries or control area(s).

3.6.3.2 All airborne infection isolation rooms shall comply with the requirements of Section 2.1-3.2.2, except for separate toilet, bathtub, or shower.

3.6.4 Neonate Examination and Treatment Areas
Such areas, when required by the functional program, shall contain a work counter, storage facilities, and a hands-free hand-washing station.

3.6.5 Support Areas for Nurseries
The following standards shall apply to nurseries:

3.6.5.1 Documentation area. Charting facilities shall have linear surface space to ensure that staff and physicians may chart and have simultaneous access to information and communication systems.

*3.6.5.2 Workroom(s). Each nursery room shall be served by a connecting workroom.

(1) The workroom shall contain scrubbing and gowning facilities at the entrance for staff and housekeeping personnel, work counter, refrigerator, storage for supplies, and a hands-free hand-washing station.

(2) One workroom may serve more than one nursery room provided that required services are convenient to each.

(3) The workroom serving the full-term and continuing care nurseries may be omitted if equivalent work and storage areas and facilities, including those for scrubbing and gowning, are provided within that nursery. Space required for work areas located within the nursery is in addition to the area required for infant care.

(4) Provision shall be made for storage of emergency cart(s) and equipment out of traffic.

(5) Provision shall be made for the sanitary storage and disposal of soiled waste.

(6) Visual control shall be provided via borrowed lights and/or view panels between the staff work area and each nursery.

3.6.5.3 Lactation support room. A consultation/demonstration/breastfeeding or pump room shall be provided convenient to the nursery.

(1) Provision shall be made, either within the room or conveniently located nearby, for hand-washing station, counter, refrigeration and freezing, storage for pump and attachments, and educational materials.

(2) If conveniently located, this ancillary area shall be permitted to be shared for other purposes.

3.6.5.4 Neonate formula facilities

(1) Location. Where infant formula is prepared on-site, direct access from the formula preparation room to any nursery room is prohibited. The room may be located near the nursery or at other appropriate locations in the hospital.

(2) The formula preparation room shall include the following:

(a) Cleanup area for washing and sterilizing supplies. This area shall include a hand-washing station, facilities for bottle washing, a work counter, and sterilization equipment.

(b) Separate room for preparing infant formula. This room shall contain warming facilities, refrigerator, work counter, formula sterilizer, storage facilities, and a hand-washing station.

(c) Refrigerated storage and warming facilities for infant formula accessible for use by nursery personnel at all times.

(3) If a commercial infant formula is used, the separate cleanup and preparation rooms may be omitted. The storage and handling may be done in the nursery workroom or in another appropriate room that is conveniently accessible at all hours. The preparation area shall have a work counter, a hand-washing station, and storage facilities.

3.6.5.5 Soiled workroom or soiled holding room shall be provided in accordance with Section 2.1-2.3.8.

3.6.5.6 Housekeeping room

(1) A housekeeping/environmental services room shall be provided for the exclusive use of the

nursery unit. It shall be directly accessible from the unit.

(2) This room shall contain a service sink or floor receptor and provide for storage of supplies and housekeeping equipment.

3.6.6 Newborn Nursery
*3.6.6.1 Capacity. Each newborn nursery room shall contain no more than 16 infant stations. When a rooming-in program is used, the total number of bassinets in these units shall be permitted to be reduced, but the newborn nursery shall not be omitted in its entirety from any facility that includes delivery services.

3.6.6.2 Area. The minimum floor space shall be 24 square feet (2.23 square meters) per bassinet, exclusive of auxiliary work areas.

3.6.6.3 Baby-holding nursery. In postpartum and labor-delivery-recovery-postpartum (LDRP) units, a baby-holding nursery shall be permitted instead of a traditional nursery.

(1) The minimum floor area per bassinet, ventilation, electrical, and medical vacuum and gases shall be the same as that required for a full-term nursery.

(2) These holding nurseries shall be next to the nurse station on these units.

(3) The holding nursery shall be sized to accommodate the percentage of newborns who do not remain with their mothers during the postpartum stay.

3.6.7 Continuing Care Nursery
3.6.7.1 For hospitals that provide continuing care for infants requiring close observation (for example, low birth-weight babies who are not ill but require more hours of nursing than normal neonates), the minimum floor space shall be 50 square feet (4.65 square meters) per bassinet, exclusive of auxiliary work areas, with provisions for at least 4 feet (1.22 meters) between and at all sides of each bassinet.

3.6.7.2 The continuing care bassinets are permitted to be within the hospital's NICU in a defined location for these infants.

3.6.8 Pediatric Nursery
3.6.8.1 Capacity. To minimize the possibility of cross-infection, each nursery room serving pediatric patients shall contain no more than eight bassinets.

Note: Limitation on number of patients in a nursery room does not apply to the pediatric critical care unit.

3.6.8.2 Space requirements. Each bassinet shall have a minimum clear floor area of 40 square feet (3.72 square meters).

3.6.8.3 Facility requirements. Each room shall contain a hands-free hand-washing station, a nurse emergency call system, and a glazed viewing window for observing infants from public areas and workrooms.

*3.7 Pediatric and Adolescent Unit
The unit shall meet the following standards:

3.7.1 Patient Rooms
3.7.1.1 Capacity. Maximum room capacity shall be four patients.

3.7.1.2 Space requirements. The space requirements for pediatric patient beds shall be the same as for adult beds due to the size variation and the need to change from cribs to beds and vice-versa. See Section 2.1-3.1.1.2 for requirements.

*3.7.1.3 Family support requirements. Additional provisions for hygiene, toilets, sleeping, and personal belongings shall be made where the program indicates that parents will be allowed to remain with young children. (See Section 2.1-3.4.5 for pediatric critical care units and Section 2.1-3.6.6 for newborn nurseries.)

APPENDIX

A3.6.6.1 For facilities that use a rooming-in program in which all infants are returned to the nursery at night, a reduction in nursery size may not be practical.

A3.7 In view of their unique physical and developmental needs, pediatric and adolescent patients, to the extent their condition permits, should be grouped together in distinct units or distinct areas of general units separate from adults.

A3.7.1.3 Family support spaces, including family sleep rooms, pantry, toilets, showers, washers and dryers, and access to computers, phones, and copy machines, should be provided.

3.7.1.4 Window. Each patient room shall have a window in accordance with Section 2.1-8.2.2.5.

3.7.2 Airborne Infection Isolation Room(s)

3.7.2.1 At least one such room shall be provided in each pediatric unit. The total number of infection isolation rooms shall be determined by an ICRA.

3.7.2.2 Airborne infection isolation room(s) shall comply with the requirements of Section 2.1-3.2.2.

3.7.3 Examination/Treatment Rooms

An examination/treatment room shall be provided for pediatric and adolescent patients. A separate area for infant examination and treatment shall be permitted within the pediatric nursery workroom.

3.7.3.1 Space requirements. Examination/treatment rooms shall have a minimum floor area of 120 square feet (11.15 square meters).

3.7.3.2 Facility requirements. The room shall contain a hand-washing station; storage facilities; and a desk, counter, or shelf space for writing.

3.7.4 Support Areas for Pediatric/Adolescent Units

The staff support areas in the pediatric and adolescent nursing units shall conform to Sections 2.1-3.1.4 through 2.1-3.1.6 and shall also meet the following standards:

3.7.4.1 Multipurpose or individual room(s)

(1) These shall be provided within or adjacent to areas serving pediatric and adolescent patrons for dining, education, and developmentally appropriate play and recreation, with access and equipment for patients with physical restrictions.

(2) If the functional program requires, an individual room shall be provided to allow for confidential

parent/family comfort, consultation, and teaching.

(3) Insulation, isolation, and structural provisions shall minimize the transmission of impact noise through the floor, walls, or ceiling of the multipurpose room(s).

3.7.4.2 Formula facilities. Space for preparation and storage of infant formula shall be provided within the unit or other convenient location. Provisions shall be made for continuation of special formula that may have been prescribed for the infant prior to admission or readmission.

3.7.4.3 Clean and soiled workrooms. Separate clean and soiled workrooms or holding rooms shall be provided as described in Sections 2.1-2.3.7 and 2.1-2.3.8.

3.7.4.4 Equipment and supply storage

(1) Storage closets or cabinets shall be provided for toys, educational, and recreational equipment.

(2) Storage space shall be provided to permit exchange of cribs and adult beds.

(3) Provisions shall also be made for storage of equipment and supplies (including cots or recliners, extra linen, etc.) for parents who stay with the patient overnight.

3.7.5 Support Areas for Patients

3.7.5.1 Patient toilet room(s). Toilet room(s) with hand-washing station(s) in each room, in addition to those serving bed areas, shall be convenient to multipurpose room(s) and to each central bathing facility.

3.8 Psychiatric Nursing Unit

3.8.1 General

3.8.1.1 Psychiatric care in a medical unit. See Section 2.1-3.2.4 for psychiatric care in a medical unit.

3.8.1.2 Functional program. Provisions shall be made in the design for adapting the area for various types of medical and psychiatric therapies as described in the functional program.

*3.8.1.3 Environment of care. The facility shall provide a therapeutic environment appropriate for the planned treatment programs.

APPENDIX

A3.8.1.3 The facility should provide a therapeutic environment appropriate for the planned treatment programs. The environment should be characterized by a feeling of openness with emphasis on natural light. In every aspect of building design and maintenance it is essential to make determinations based on the potential risk to the specific patient population served.

*3.8.1.4 Security. Security appropriate for the planned treatment programs shall be provided.

3.8.1.5 Shared facilities. In no case shall adult and pediatric clients be mixed. This does not exclude sharing of nursing stations or support areas, as long as the separation and safety of the units can be maintained.

*3.8.2 Patient Rooms
See Section 2.3-2.1.1.

3.8.3 Seclusion Treatment Rooms
See Section 2.3-2.2.1.

3.8.4 Support Areas for Staff and Visitors
See Section 2.3-2.6.

3.9 In-Hospital Skilled Nursing Units
Many facilities have incorporated extended stay units for the medical/surgical department; these are often referred to as in-hospital skilled nursing units or facilities. These units should not be confused with long-term skilled nursing units found in Chapter 4.1 of these Guidelines. These extended stay unit beds are licensed hospital beds for patients requiring skilled nursing care as part of their recovery process. Many of these facilities are intended for elderly patients undergoing various levels of rehabilitation and recuperating stroke victims or brain trauma victims requiring rehabilitation.

3.9.1 General
3.9.1.1 Location

(1) The location of the unit shall provide convenient access to the Physical and Rehabilitation Medicine departments.

(2) Wherever possible, the unit shall be located to provide access to outdoor spaces that can be utilized for therapeutic purposes.

3.9.1.2 Layout. The unit shall be located to exclude unrelated traffic going through the unit to access other areas of the hospital.

APPENDIX

A3.8.1.4 A safe environment is critical; however, no environment can be entirely safe and free of risk. The majority of persons who attempt suicide suffer from a treatable mental disorder or a substance abuse disorder or both. Patients of inpatient psychiatric treatment facilities are considered at high risk for suicide; the environment should avoid physical hazards while maintaining a therapeutic environment. The built environment, no matter how well designed and constructed, cannot be relied upon as an absolute preventive measure. Staff awareness of their environment, latent risks of that environment, and the behavior risks and needs of the patients served in the environment are absolute necessities. Different organizations and different patient populations will require greater or lesser tolerance for risk.

a. Consideration should be given to visual control (including electronic surveillance) on nursing units of corridors, dining areas, and social areas such as dayrooms and activity areas. Hidden alcoves or blind corners or areas should be avoided.

b. The openness of the nurse station will be determined by the planned treatment program. Consideration should be given to patient privacy and also to staff safety.

A3.8.2 Patient Rooms. The guidelines noted in Sections 2.3-1 through 2.3-2.3.3 and Section 2.3-2.6 should apply, with the following exceptions:

a. The patient room size should meet the requirements in Section 2.1-3.1.1.2.

b. Adequate storage should meet the requirements in Section 2.1-2.2.2.

c. A desk or writing surface for patient use may be provided in each room, but this is not required.

d. A quiet room is not required on units of 12 beds or fewer unless required by the functional program.

e. The functional needs of the program should determine the need for a nurse call system. If a nurse call system is provided, it should meet the requirements of Section 2.1-10.3.8. However, provisions should be made for easy removal or covering of the call system.

f. Visual privacy in multi-bed rooms (e.g., cubicle curtains) is not required.

g. The functional needs of the program will determine the need for medical gas and/or vacuum systems. If a medical gas/vacuum system is provided, it should meet the requirements of Sections 2.1-10.1.4.1 and 2.1-10.1.2.1 (2). However, provisions should be made for easy removal and/or covering of the medical gas/vacuum system.

3.9.2 Patient Rooms
The basic requirements contained in Section 2.1-3.1.1 apply.

3.9.3 Treatment Areas
3.9.3.1 Physical rehabilitation room. When required by the functional program, a physical rehabilitation room shall be provided for the use of the skilled nursing unit if the unit is not located conveniently to the facility's physical and rehabilitation therapy departments. The room size and the equipment provided shall be adequate to provide the therapeutic milieu required by the facility's functional program.

3.9.4 Support Areas for In-Hospital Skilled Nursing Units
In addition to the support areas required under Sections 2.1-3.1.4 through 2.1-3.1.6, the following rooms and support elements shall be provided:

3.9.4.1 Storage for wheelchairs and walking aids. Additional storage spaces to accommodate the increase in wheelchair and walking aids used by this patient population shall be included in the design of the unit, with an additional square footage of 7 square feet (0.65 square meters) per bed.

3.9.5 Support Areas for Patients
3.9.5.1 Dining and recreation spaces

(1) Factors for determining space requirements. The space needed for dining and recreation shall be determined by considering the following:

    (a) The needs of patients who use adaptive equipment and mobility aids and receive assistance from support and service staff

    (b) The extent to which support programs shall be centralized or decentralized

    (c) The number of patients to be seated for dining at one time, as required by the functional program

(2) Space requirements. Nothing in these Guidelines is intended to restrict a facility from providing additional square footage per resident beyond what is required herein for dining rooms, activity areas, and similar spaces.

    (a) In new construction, the total area set aside for dining, patient lounges, and recreation shall be at least 25 square feet (2.32 square meters) per bed with a minimum total area of at least 225 square feet (20.90 square meters). At least 20 square feet (1.86 square meters) per bed shall be available for dining. Additional space may be required for outpatient day care programs.

    (b) For renovations, at least 14 square feet (1.30 square meters) per bed shall be available for dining. Additional space may be required for outpatient day care programs.

3.9.5.2 Private space. When required by the functional program, the unit shall contain private space for the use of individual patients, family, and caregivers to discuss the specific patient's needs or private family matters.

(1) This space shall have a minimum clear area of 250 square feet (23.23 square meters).

(2) This space is permitted to be considered part of the square footage per bed outlined in Section 2.1-3.9.5.2.

3.9.5.3 Patient grooming room. When required by the functional program, a room for patient grooming shall be provided.

(1) The minimum area shall not be part of the aggregate area under Section 2.1-3.9.5.2 and shall be as determined by the functional program.

(2) This room shall provide spaces for hair-washing station(s), hair clipping and hair styling, and other grooming needs.

(3) A hand-washing station, mirror, work counter(s), storage shelving, and sitting area(s) for patients shall be provided as part of the room.

3.9.6 Construction Requirements
3.9.6.1 Handrails

(1) Handrails located in accordance with ADA and all local, state, and federal requirements shall be installed on both sides of the patient use corridor. Where corridors are defined by walls, handrails shall be provided on both sides of all corridors normally used by patients.

(2) A minimum clearance of 1-1/2 inches (3.81 centimeters) shall be provided between the handrail and the wall.

(3) Rail ends shall be returned to the wall or floor.

4 Obstetrical Facilities

*4.1 General

4.1.1 Location and Layout
The obstetrical unit shall be located and designed to prohibit nonrelated traffic through the unit. When delivery and operating rooms are in the same suite, access and service arrangements shall be such that neither staff nor patients need to travel through one area to reach the other.

4.1.2 Newborn Nursery
A newborn nursery shall be provided. See Section 2.1-3.6.6.

4.1.3 Renovation
Except as permitted otherwise herein, existing facilities being renovated shall, as far as practicable, provide all the required support services.

4.2 Postpartum Unit

4.2.1 Postpartum Bedrooms
See Section 2.1-3.1.1.

4.2.2 Airborne Infection Isolation Room(s)
An airborne infection isolation room is not required for the obstetrical unit. Provisions for the care of the perinatal patient with an airborne infection shall be determined by an ICRA.

4.2.3 Examination/Treatment Room and/or Multipurpose Diagnostic Testing Room
4.2.3.1 Space requirements. This room shall have a minimum clear floor area of 120 square feet (11.15 square meters). When used as a multi-patient diagnostic testing room, a minimum clear floor area of 80 square feet (7.43 square meters) per patient shall be provided.

APPENDIX

A4.1 Obstetrical program models vary widely in their delivery methodologies. The models are essentially of three types. The following narrative describes the organizational framework of each model.

a. Traditional Model

Under the traditional model, labor, delivery, recovery, and postpartum occur in separate areas. The birthing woman is treated as the moving part. She is moved through these functional areas depending on the status of the birth process.

The functional areas are separate rooms consisting of the labor room, delivery room, recovery room, postpartum bedroom, and infant nurseries (levels determined by acuity).

b. Labor-Delivery-Recovery Model

All labor-delivery-recovery rooms (LDRs) are designed to accommodate the birthing process from labor through delivery and recovery of mother and baby. They are equipped to handle most complications, with the exception of cesarean sections.

The birthing woman moves only as a postpartum patient to her bedroom or to a cesarean section delivery room (surgical operative room) if delivery complications occur.

After the mother and baby are recovered in the LDR, they are transferred to a mother-baby care unit for postpartum stay.

c. Labor-Delivery-Recovery-Postpartum Model

Single-room maternity care in labor-delivery-recovery-postpartum rooms (LDRPs) adds a "P" to the LDR model. Room design and capability to handle most emergencies remain the same as the LDRs. However, the LDRP model eliminates a move to postpartum after delivery. LDRP uses one private room for labor, delivery, recovery, and postpartum stay.

Equipment is moved into the room as needed, rather than moving the patient to the equipped room. Certain deliveries are handled in a cesarean section delivery room (surgical operative room) should delivery complications occur.

4.2.3.2 Toilet room. An adjoining toilet room shall be provided for patient use.

4.2.4 Support Areas for the Postpartum Unit
The following support areas shall be provided for this unit.

4.2.4.1 A nurse station

4.2.4.2 Documentation area

4.2.4.3 A nurse office

4.2.4.4 Consultation/conference room(s)

4.2.4.5 Medication station. Provision shall be made for storage and distribution of drugs and routine medications. This may be done from a medicine preparation room or unit, from a self-contained medicine-dispensing unit, or by another system.

(1) Medicine preparation room or unit

    (a) If used, a medicine preparation room or unit shall be under visual control of nursing staff.

    (b) This room or unit shall contain a work counter, sink, refrigerator, and double-locked storage for controlled substances.

    (c) Convenient access to hand-washing stations shall be provided. (Standard cup-sinks provided in many self-contained units are not adequate for hand-washing.)

4.2.4.6 Nourishment area. A nourishment station shall be provided in accordance with Section 2.1-2.3.5.

4.2.4.7 Clean workroom or clean supply room. A clean workroom or clean supply room shall be provided in accordance with Section 2.1-2.3.7. A clean workroom is required if clean materials are assembled within the obstetrical suite prior to use.

4.2.4.8 Soiled workroom or soiled holding room. A soiled workroom or soiled holding room shall be provided for the exclusive use of the obstetrical suite in accordance with Section 2.1-2.3.8.

4.2.4.9 Equipment and supply storage

(1) Clean linen storage. This shall be provided in accordance with Section 2.1-2.3.9.1.

(2) Equipment storage room. Each unit shall provide sufficient storage area(s) on the patient floor to keep its required corridor width free of equipment and supplies.

    (a) This storage area shall be not less than 10 square feet (0.93 square meter) per postpartum room and 20 square feet (1.86 square meters) per each labor-delivery-recovery (LDR) or LDRP room.

    (b) This storage area shall be in addition to any storage in patient rooms.

(3) Storage space for stretchers and wheelchairs. Storage space shall be provided in accordance with Section 2.1-2.3.9.3.

(4) Emergency equipment storage. Storage shall be close to the nurse station.

4.2.4.10 Housekeeping room. A housekeeping room shall be provided for the exclusive use of the obstetrical suite in accordance with Section 2.1-2.3.10.

4.2.5 Support Areas for Staff
The following support areas shall be provided for this unit.

4.2.5.1 Staff lounge

4.2.5.2 Staff storage facilities. Lockable closets or cabinets for personal articles of staff shall be provided.

4.2.5.3 Staff toilet room

4.2.6 Support Areas for Patients and Visitors
The following support areas shall be provided for this unit.

4.2.6.1 Patient lounge. The patient lounge may be omitted if all rooms are single-bed rooms.

4.2.6.2 Patient bathing facilities

(1) Where bathing facilities are not provided in

patient rooms, there shall be at least one shower and/or bathtub for each six beds or fraction thereof.

(2) A toilet and hand-washing station shall be provided within or directly accessible to each bathing facility.

4.3 Cesarean/Delivery Suite

4.3.1 Labor Rooms
4.3.1.1 General

(1) Number. In facilities that have only one cesarean/delivery room, two labor rooms shall be provided.

(2) Access. Labor rooms shall have controlled access with doors that are arranged for observation from a nursing station.

4.3.1.2 Capacity. Where LDRs or LDRPs are not provided, a minimum of two labor beds shall be provided for each cesarean/delivery room.

4.3.1.3 Space requirements

(1) Each room shall be designed for either one or two beds, with a minimum clear area of 120 square feet (11.15 square meters) per bed.

(2) In renovation projects, labor room(s) (LDR or LDRP rooms may be substituted) shall have a minimum clear area of 100 square feet (9.29 square meters) per bed.

4.3.1.4 Windows. Windows in labor rooms, if provided, shall be located, draped, or otherwise arranged to preserve patient privacy from casual observation from outside the labor room.

4.3.1.5 Hand-washing station. Each labor room shall contain a hand-washing station.

4.3.1.6 Toilet room

(1) Each labor room shall have access to a toilet room.

(2) One toilet room may serve two labor rooms.

4.3.1.7 Bathing facilities. At least one shower (which

may be separate from the labor room if under staff control) for use of patients in labor shall be provided.

4.3.2 Delivery Room(s)
4.3.2.1 Space requirements. These shall have a minimum clear area of 300 square feet (27.87 square meters) exclusive of fixed cabinets and built-in shelves.

4.3.2.2 Emergency communication system. An emergency communication system shall be connected with the obstetrical suite control station.

4.3.3 Cesarean/Delivery Room(s)
4.3.3.1 Number. There shall be a minimum of one such room in every obstetrical unit.

4.3.3.2 Space requirements. These shall have a minimum clear floor area of 360 square feet (33.45 square meters) with a minimum dimension of 16 feet (4.88 meters) exclusive of built-in shelves or cabinets.

4.3.4 Infant Resuscitation Space
4.3.4.1 Location. Infant resuscitation shall be provided within cesarean/delivery room(s) and delivery rooms or in a separate but immediately accessible room.

4.3.4.2 Space requirements

(1) Space in delivery rooms. A minimum clear floor area of 40 square feet (3.72 square meters) shall be provided for the infant resuscitation space in addition to the required area of each delivery or cesarean/delivery room.

(2) Space in a separate room. Infant resuscitation space provided in a separate but immediately accessible room shall have a minimum clear floor area of 150 square feet (13.94 square meters).

4.3.4.3 Electrical outlets. Six single or three duplex electrical outlets shall be provided for the infant in addition to the facilities required for the mother.

4.3.5 Recovery Room(s)
LDR or LDRP rooms, when located within or adjacent to the cesarean/delivery suite, may be substituted.

4.3.5.1 Capacity. Recovery rooms shall contain at least two beds.

4.3.5.2 Support areas for recovery rooms

(1) Nurse station and documentation area. Recovery room shall have a nurse station with charting facilities located to permit visual control of all beds.

(2) Hand-washing station. Each room shall include a hand-washing station.

(3) Medication dispensing facilities. Each room shall include facilities for dispensing medicine.

(4) Clinical sink. A clinical sink with bedpan flushing device shall be available.

(5) Equipment and supply storage. Storage for supplies and equipment shall be available.

4.3.5.3 Support areas for families

(1) When required by the functional program, there shall be enough space for baby and crib and a chair for the support person. There shall be the ability to maintain visual privacy for the new family.

4.3.6 Support Areas for the Cesarean/Delivery Suite
4.3.6.1 General. Individual rooms shall be provided as indicated in the following standards; otherwise, alcoves or other open spaces that do not interfere with traffic may be used.

4.3.6.2 Areas solely for the cesarean/delivery suite. The following support areas shall be provided:

(1) A control/nurse station. This shall be located to restrict unauthorized traffic into the suite.

(2) Soiled workroom or soiled holding room. This room shall be provided in accordance with Section 2.1-2.3.8.

(3) Fluid waste disposal

APPENDIX

A4.3.6.3 (5) High-speed autoclaves should only be used in an emergency situation (e.g., a dropped instrument and no sterile replacement readily available).

4.3.6.3 Areas permitted to be shared. The following support areas shall be permitted to be shared with the surgical facilities in accordance with the functional program. Where shared, areas shall be arranged to avoid direct traffic between the delivery and operating rooms.

(1) A supervisor's office or station

(2) Medication station. A drug distribution station with hand-washing stations and provisions for controlled storage, preparation, and distribution of medication shall be provided. A self-contained medication dispensing unit in accordance with Section 2.1-2.3.4 may be utilized instead.

(3) Scrub facilities for cesarean/delivery rooms

    (a) Two scrub positions shall be provided adjacent to the entrance to each cesarean/delivery room.

    (b) Scrub facilities shall be arranged to minimize any splatter on nearby personnel or supply carts.

    (c) In new construction, view windows shall be provided at scrub stations to permit the observation of room interiors.

(4) Anesthesia workroom. An anesthesia workroom for cleaning, testing, and storing anesthesia equipment shall be provided. It shall contain a work counter, sink, and provisions for separation of clean and soiled items.

*(5) Sterilization facilities. Sterilization facilities with high-speed sterilizers shall be located convenient to all cesarean/delivery rooms. Sterilization facilities shall be separate from the delivery area and adjacent to clean assembly.

(6) Clean workroom or clean supply room

    (a) Clean workroom. A clean workroom shall be provided if clean materials are assembled within the obstetrical suite prior to use. It shall contain a work counter, hand-washing station, and space for storage of supplies.

(b) Clean supply room. Provision of a clean supply room shall be permitted when the functional program defines a system for the storage and distribution of clean and sterile supplies. See (7)(a) just below for sterile storage.

(7) Equipment and supply storage. Storage room(s) shall be provided for equipment and supplies used in the obstetrical suite. These shall include the following:

(a) A clean sterile storage area readily available to the delivery room. The size shall be based on level of usage, functions provided, and supplies from the hospital central distribution area.

(b) Medical gas storage facilities. See Section 2.1-5.3.5.14 (3).

(c) An area for storing stretchers out of the path of normal traffic

(8) Housekeeping room. Housekeeping room with a floor receptacle or service sink and storage space for housekeeping supplies and equipment.

4.3.7 Support Areas for Staff

The following support areas shall be permitted to be shared with the surgical facilities in accordance with the functional program. Where shared, areas shall be arranged to avoid direct traffic between the delivery and operating rooms.

4.3.7.1 Lounge and toilet facilities. Lounge and toilet facilities for obstetrical staff convenient to delivery, labor, and recovery areas. The toilet room shall contain hand-washing stations.

4.3.7.2 Staff change areas

(1) The clothing change area(s) shall be laid out to encourage one-way traffic and eliminate cross-traffic between clean and contaminated personnel.

(2) The area(s) shall contain lockers, showers, toilets, hand-washing stations, and space for donning and disposing scrub suits and booties.

4.3.7.3 Support person change areas. Change areas, designed as described above, shall be provided for male and female support persons.

4.3.7.4 Staff accommodations. An on-call room(s) shall be provided for physician and/or staff. It may be located elsewhere in the facility.

4.3.8 Support Areas for Visitors

The following support areas shall be permitted to be shared with the surgical facilities in accordance with the functional program.

4.3.8.1 Waiting room. A waiting room, with toilets, telephones, and provisions for drinking water shall be conveniently located. The toilet room shall contain hand-washing stations.

4.4 LDR and LDRP Rooms

When required by the functional program, delivery procedures in accordance with birthing concepts may be performed in the LDR or LDRP rooms.

4.4.1 Location

LDR room(s) may be located in a separate LDR suite or as part of the cesarean/delivery suite. The postpartum unit may contain LDRP rooms.

4.4.2 Capacity

Each LDR or LDRP room shall be for single occupancy.

4.4.3 Space Requirements

*4.4.3.1 New construction. These rooms shall have a minimum clear floor area of 300 square feet (27.87 square meters) with a minimum dimension of 13 feet (3.96 meters), exclusive of toilet room, closet, alcove, or vestibules.

(1) Where required by the functional program, there shall be enough space for a crib and reclining chair for a support person.

(2) An area within the room but distinct from the

> **APPENDIX**
>
> **A4.4.3.1** A minimum dimension of 15 feet (4.57 meters) is preferable to accommodate the equipment and staff needed for complex deliveries.

mother's area shall be provided for infant stabilization and resuscitation.

4.4.3.2 Renovation. When renovation work is undertaken, every effort shall be made to meet the above minimum standards. If it is not possible to meet the above square-foot standards, existing LDR or LDRP rooms shall be permitted to have a minimum clear area of 200 square feet (18.58 square meters).

4.4.4 Patient Privacy
Windows or doors within a normal sightline that would permit observation into the room shall be arranged or draped as necessary for patient privacy.

4.4.5 Hand-Washing Stations
Each room shall be equipped with hand-washing stations. (Hand-washing stations with hands-free operation are acceptable for scrubbing.)

4.4.6 Patient Bathroom
Each LDR or LDRP room shall have direct access to a private toilet with shower or tub.

4.4.7 Medical Gas Outlets
4.4.7.1 See Table 2.1-5 for medical gas outlet requirements.

4.4.7.2 These outlets shall be located in the room so they are accessible to the mother's delivery area and infant resuscitation area.

4.4.8 Finishes
Finishes shall be selected to facilitate cleaning and to resist strong detergents.

4.4.9 Lighting
Portable examination lights shall be permitted, but must be immediately accessible.

5 Diagnostic and Treatment Locations

*5.1 Emergency Service

5.1.1 General
*5.1.1.1 Definition
Levels of emergency care range from initial emergency management to definitive emergency care.

APPENDIX

A5.1 Surge Capacity
In preparation for the emergence of highly infectious patients, hospitals should have the capacity to handle a surge of up to ten or a fourfold increase above the current emergency department capacity for such patients.

a. This preparation should include the provision of adjacent space for triage and management of infectious patients.

b. Utility upgrades for these areas (oxygen, water, electrical) should be considered.

c. The area should provide for depressurization to help control aerosolized infectious particles with 100 percent exhaust capability. If 100 percent exhaust cannot be achieved, appropriate proven technology should be utilized to reduce airborne particles by > 95 percent. If patient care areas are to be utilized in the hospital to house these patients, the route to the patient care unit should minimize the potential for cross-contamination. Existing smoke control areas could be utilized to meet the ventilation requirements. Air-handling systems should be designed to provide required pressure differentials. Written protocols must be developed to ensure proper performance of the means to accomplish the intended goals. DHHS, the Office of Emergency Preparedness, will have more up-to-date information.

A5.1.1.1 Classification of emergency departments/ services/trauma centers
Basic aspects of previous Level I-IV emergency department/ services classifications are still recognizable in current criteria statements but have evolved substantially to address changes in practice, needs, and technologies. The following publications are especially useful references for understanding and listing current refined and expanded requirements:

American College of Surgeons. "Trauma Center Descriptions and Their Roles in a Trauma System," chapter 2 in *Resources for Optimal Care of the Injured Patient* (ACS, 1999). This reference provides detailed descriptions of Level I–Level IV trauma centers. (www.facs.org)

Riggs, Leonard M., Jr., ed. *Emergency Department Design* (American College of Emergency Physicians, 1993). The author discusses planning for various levels of treatment acuity. (www.acep.org)

(1) Initial emergency management is care provided to stabilize a victim's condition and to minimize potential for further injury during transport to an appropriate service. Patients may be brought to the "nearest hospital," which may or may not have all required services for definitive emergency management. In those cases, it is important that the hospital be able to assess and stabilize emergent illnesses and injuries and arrange for appropriate transfer.

(2) Emergency care may range from the suturing of lacerations to full-scale emergency medical procedures. Facilities that include personnel and equipment for definitive emergency care provide for 24-hour service and complete emergency care leading to discharge to the patient's home or direct admission to the appropriate hospital.

5.1.1.2 Applicability. The extent and type of emergency service to be provided depends on community needs and the availability of other services in the area.

(1) While initial emergency management shall be available at every hospital, full-scale definitive emergency services may be impractical and/or an unnecessary duplication.

(2) All services need adequate equipment and 24-hour staffing to ensure no delay in essential treatment.

5.1.1.3 Requirements

(1) The following standards are intended only as minimums. Additional facilities, as needed, shall be as required to satisfy the functional program.

(2) Provisions for facilities to provide non-emergency treatment of outpatients are covered in Chapter 3.2.

5.1.2 Initial Emergency Management
5.1.2.1 General

(1) At a minimum, each hospital shall have provisions for emergency treatment for staff, employees, and visitors, as well as for persons who may be unaware of or unable to immediately reach services in other facilities. This is not only for patients with minor illnesses or injuries that may

require minimal care but also for persons with severe illness and injuries who must receive immediate emergency care and assistance prior to transport to other facilities.

(2) Provisions for initial emergency management shall include the following:

5.1.2.2 Entrance. A well-marked, illuminated, and covered entrance shall be provided at grade level. The emergency vehicle entry cover shall provide shelter for both the patient and the emergency medical crew during transfer from an emergency vehicle into the building.

5.1.2.3 Reception, triage, and control station. This shall be located to permit staff observation and control of access to treatment area, pedestrian and ambulance entrances, and public waiting area.

5.1.2.4 Communication system. Communication hookups to the Poison Control Center and regional emergency medical service (EMS) system.

5.1.2.5 A treatment room

(1) Space requirements

(a) This shall have not less than 120 square feet (11.15 square meters) of clear area, exclusive of toilets, waiting area, and storage.

(b) The treatment room may have additional space and provisions for several patients with cubicle curtains for privacy. Multiple-bed treatment rooms shall provide a minimum of 80 square feet (7.43 square meters) per patient cubicle.

(2) Facility requirements. Each treatment room shall contain an examination light, work counter, hand-washing stations, medical equipment, cabinets, medication storage, adequate electrical outlets above floor level, and counter space for writing.

5.1.2.6 Airborne infection control. At least one airborne infection isolation room shall be provided as described in Table 2.1-2 and Sections 2.1-3.2.2.2, 2.1-3.2.2.4 (2)(a) and (b), and 3.2.2.4 (4). The need for additional airborne infection isolation rooms or for protective environment rooms as described in Section 2.1-3.2.3 shall be determined by an ICRA.

5.1.2.7 Equipment and supply storage. Storage for general medical/surgical emergency supplies, medications, and equipment such as ventilator, defibrillator, splints, etc. This shall be located out of traffic and under staff control.

5.1.2.8 Waiting room. Provisions for reception, control, and public waiting. These shall include a public toilet with hand-washing station(s) and a telephone.

5.1.2.9 Patient toilet. A patient toilet room with hand-washing station(s). This shall be convenient to the treatment room(s).

*5.1.3 Definitive Emergency Care
5.1.3.1 General. Where 24-hour emergency service is to be provided, the type, size, and number of the services shall be as defined in the functional program. As a minimum, the following shall be provided:

5.1.3.2 Emergency access. Paved emergency access to permit discharge of patients from automobiles and ambulances and temporary parking convenient to the entrance shall be provided.

5.1.3.3 Entrance. A well-marked, illuminated, and covered entrance shall be provided at grade level.

(1) This shall provide direct access from public roads for ambulance and vehicle traffic.

(2) Entrance and driveway shall be clearly marked.

(3) If a raised platform is used for ambulance discharge, a ramp shall be provided for pedestrian and wheelchair access.

*5.1.3.4 Reception, triage, and control station

(1) Reception, triage, and control station shall be located to permit staff observation and control of access to treatment area, pedestrian and ambulance entrances, and public waiting area. (See Table 2.1-5.)

(2) The triage area requires special consideration. As the point of entry and assessment for patients with undiagnosed and untreated airborne infections, the triage area shall be designed and ventilated to reduce exposure of staff, patients, and families to airborne infectious diseases. (See Table 2.1-2.)

5.1.3.5 Communications center. The communications center shall be convenient to the nursing station and have radio, telephone, and intercommunication systems. (See Section 2.1-8.1.3.)

5.1.3.6 Public waiting area

APPENDIX

A5.1.3 Fast-Track Area
A separate fast-track area when annual emergency department visits exceed 20,000–30,000 visits should be considered. This area should include space for registration, discharge, triage, and waiting, as well as a physician/nurse work station. Storage areas for supplies and medication should be included. A separate treatment/procedure room of 120 square feet (11.15 square meters) of clear floor space should be provided. Examination/treatment areas should be 100 square feet (9.29 square meters) of clear floor space, with hand-washing stations, vacuum, oxygen, and air outlets, and examination lights. At least one treatment/examination room should be designated for pelvic examinations.

A5.1.3.4 The design of the emergency department is critical, particularly at the main public access point, to ensure that emergency medical staff and hospital security personnel maintain control of

access at all times. In the event of a disaster, terrorist event, or infectious disease outbreak, the emergency service must remain under the control of the hospital and limit contamination to ensure its continued availability as a resource.

a. Efforts will be made to separate patients waiting for triage in a secure area with appropriate ventilation that is clearly visible from the triage station. This area will be separate from the post-triage waiting area to limit the spread of contamination and/or contagion.

b. Although the triage station must have unobstructed visibility of the waiting area to permit observation of patients waiting for treatment, a reception and control or security function must be provided to monitor the main entrance to the department and all public areas. Public access points to the treatment area shall be minimal in number, and under direct observation by the reception and control or security function.

(1) This shall have toilet facilities, drinking fountains, and telephones.

(2) If so determined by the hospital ICRA, the emergency department waiting area shall require special measures to reduce the risk of airborne infection transmission. These measures may include enhanced general ventilation and air disinfection similar to inpatient requirements for airborne infection isolation rooms. See the CDC "Guidelines for Preventing the Transmission of Mycobacterium tuberculosis in Health Care Facilities."

5.1.3.7 Diagnostic, treatment, and service areas

(1) Examination and treatment room(s)

(a) Space requirements. Each examination room shall have a minimum clear floor area of 120 square feet (11.15 square meters), exclusive of fixed casework.

(b) Facility requirements. Each examination room shall contain work counter(s); cabinets; hand-washing stations; supply storage facilities; examination lights; a desk, counter, or shelf space for writing; and a vision panel adjacent to and/or in the door.

(c) Renovation. Where renovation work is undertaken, every effort shall be made to meet these minimum standards. In such cases, each room shall have a minimum clear area of 100 square feet (9.29 square meters), exclusive of fixed or wall-mounted cabinets and built-in shelves.

(d) Treatment cubicles

(i) Where treatment cubicles are in open multiple-bed areas, each cubicle shall have a minimum of 80 square feet (7.43 square meters) of clear floor space and shall be separated from adjoining cubicles by curtains.

(ii) Hand-washing stations shall be provided for each four treatment cubicles or major fraction thereof in multiple-bed areas.

(e) For oxygen and vacuum, see Table 2.1-5.

(f) Treatment/examination rooms used for pelvic exams shall allow for the foot of the examination table to face away from the door.

*(2) Trauma/cardiac rooms for emergency procedures, including emergency surgery

(a) Space requirements

(i) Each room shall have at least 250 square feet (23.23 square meters) of clear floor space.

(ii) Additional space with cubicle curtains for privacy may be provided to accommodate more than one patient at a time in the trauma room.

(b) Facility requirements. The room shall contain cabinets and emergency supply shelves, x-ray film illuminators, examination lights, and counter space for writing.

(c) Patient monitoring. Provisions shall be made for monitoring the patients.

(d) Supply storage. Storage shall be provided for immediate access to attire used for universal precautions.

(e) Door width. Doorways leading from the ambulance entrance to the cardiac trauma room shall be a minimum of 5 feet (1.52 meters) wide to simultaneously accommodate stretchers, equipment, and personnel.

(f) Renovation. In renovation projects, every effort shall be made to have existing cardiac/trauma rooms meet the above minimum standards. If it is not possible to meet the above square-foot standards, the authorities having jurisdiction may grant approval to deviate from this requirement. In such cases, these rooms shall

APPENDIX

A5.1.3.7 (2) Access should be convenient to the ambulance entrance.

be no less than a clear area of 240 square feet (22.30 square meters), and doorways leading from the ambulance entrance to the room may be 4 feet (1.22 meters) wide.

(3) Provisions for orthopedic and cast work. These may be in separate room(s) or in the trauma room.

    (a) Space requirements. The clear floor space for this area shall be dependent on the functional

APPENDIX

A5.1.3.7 (4) When advanced imaging technologies such as CT are available, the emergency department should have convenient access.

A5.1.3.7 (5) Decontamination area on the exterior perimeter
a. Ideally 150 feet (45.72 meters) from the ambulance entrance (if required by the constraints of the structures involved, this may be no less than 30 feet (9.14 meters) from the ambulance entrance).

b. At a location where no windows or doors abut the defined area or where all doors are securable from the outside and all windows are capable of being shuttered.

c. Boundaries shall be defined on the paved ground surface with a yellow paint line and the word "DECON" painted within these boundaries.

d. At least two shower heads, temperature-controlled and separated by at least 6 feet (1.83 meters); a separate spigot for attachment of a hose.

e. Semipermanent or portable/collapsible structures (curtains, tents, etc.) that will provide shelter from the environment, privacy, and some containment of the contaminant/infectious agent.

f. Secured access to the hospital telephone system and a duplex electrical outlet for each two shower heads and no closer than 4 feet (1.22 meters) to any shower.

g. Exterior lighting to maximize visibility; appropriate for wet/shower facilities.

h. Negative airflow and ventilation system on the hospital perimeter wall but drawing air within the confines of the decontamination structure; exhausted directly to the outdoors, no less than 50 feet (15.24 meters) away from the decontamination site with no recirculation of air. This system shall be defunctionalized when the decontamination structure is not in use.

i. Water runoff shall be contained and disposed of safely to ensure that it does not enter community drainage systems. This shall be accomplished either by graded floor structures leading to a drain with a collection system separate from that of the hospital or by the use of plastic pools or specialized decontamination stretchers.

Decontamination room within the facility
a. Separate, independent, secured external entrance adjacent to the ambulance entrance, but no less than 30 feet (9.14 meters) distant; lighted and protected from the environment in the same way as the ambulance entrance; a yellow painted boundary line 3 feet (0.91 meter) from each side of the door and extending 6 feet (1.83 meters) from the hospital wall; the word "DECON" painted within these boundaries.

b. Internal entrance to a corridor within the emergency area.

c. It shall have spatial requirements and the medical support services of a standard emergency area airborne infection isolation room, with air externally exhausted separate from the hospital system. It shall contain a work counter, hand-washing station with hands-free controls, an area for personnel gowning, and a storage area for supplies, as well as equipment for the decontamination process.

d. Ceiling, wall, and floor finishes shall be smooth, nonporous, scrubbable, nonadsorptive, nonperforated, capable of withstanding cleaning with and exposure to harsh chemicals, nonslip, and without crevices or seams. Floors shall be self-coving to a height of 6 inches (15.24 centimeters). The surface of the floor shall be self-finished and require no protective coating for maintenance.

e. Two hospital telephones; two duplex electrical outlets, secured appropriately for a wet environment.

f. At least two hand-held shower heads, temperature-controlled; curtains or other devices to allow patient privacy, to the extent possible.

g. Appropriately heated and air-cooled for a room with an external door and very high relative humidity.

h. Water drainage must be contained and disposed of safely to ensure that it does not enter the hospital or community drainage systems. There should be a "saddle" at the floor of the door buck to prevent efflux.

i. A certified physicist or other qualified expert representing the owner or the state agency shall specify the type, location, and amount of radiation protection to be installed in accordance with final approved department layout and the functional program. These specifications shall be incorporated into the plans.

j. The decontamination area may function as an isolation room or a patient hygiene room under routine departmental function.

program and the procedures and equipment accommodated here.

(b) Plaster trap. If a sink is used for the disposal of plaster of paris, a plaster trap shall be provided.

(c) Equipment and supply storage. They shall include storage for splints and other orthopedic supplies, traction hooks, x-ray film illuminators, and examination lights.

*(4) Diagnostic service areas. Convenient access to radiology and laboratory services shall be provided.

*(5) Decontamination area

(a) Location. In new construction, a decontamination room shall be provided with an outside entry door as far as practical from the closest other entrance. The internal door of this room shall open into a corridor of the emergency department, swing into the room, and be lockable against ingress from the corridor.

(b) Space requirements. The room shall provide a minimum of 80 square feet (7.43 square meters) clear floor area.

(c) Facility requirements

(i) The room shall be equipped with two hand-held shower heads with temperature

controls and dedicated holding tank with floor drain.

(ii) Portable or hard-piped oxygen shall be provided. Portable suction shall also be available.

(d) Construction requirements. The room shall have all smooth, nonporous, scrubbable, nonadsorptive, nonperforated surfaces. Fixtures shall be acid resistant. The floor of the decontamination room shall be self-coving to a height of 6 inches (15.24 centimeters).

(e) This section does not preclude decontamination capability at other locations or entrances immediately adjacent to the emergency department.

*(6) Pediatric care

5.1.3.8 Special patient care areas

(1) Airborne infection isolation room. At least one airborne infection isolation room shall be provided as described in Table 2.1-2 and Sections 2.1-3.2.2.2, 3.2.2.4 (2)(a) and (b), and 3.2.2.4 (4). The need for additional airborne infection isolation rooms or for protective environment rooms as described in Section 2.1-3.2.3 shall be determined by an ICRA.

A5.1.3.7 (6) Pediatric treatment rooms. Provisions for the treatment of pediatric cases in dedicated pediatric room(s) within the unit should be provided. The quantity of dedicated rooms should depend on the census of the particular institution.

a. This area should include space for registration, discharge, triage, waiting, and a playroom. Pediatric designated rooms should be adjacent to a family waiting area and toilet. An area for the nurse station and physician station, storage for supplies and medication, and one to two isolation rooms should also be included.

b. Each examination/treatment room should have 100 square feet (9.29 square meters) of clear floor space, with a separate procedure/trauma room of 120 square feet (11.15 square meters) of

clear floor space. Each of these rooms should have hand-washing stations; vacuum, oxygen, and air outlets; examination lights; and wall/column-mounted ophthalmoscopes/otoscopes.

Where possible, rooms should be sized larger than 120 square feet (11.15 square meters) of clear area (exclusive of casework) to accommodate the additional equipment and escorts that accompany pediatric cases.

c. Particular attention should be paid to the soundproofing of these treatment rooms.

d. At least one room for pelvic examinations should be included.

e. X-ray illuminators should be available.

*(2) Observation units

    (a) Each patient bed area shall have space at each bedside for visitors, and provision for visual privacy from casual observation by other patients and visitors.

    (b) Hand-washing stations. Hand-washing stations shall be provided for each four treatment cubicles or major fraction thereof. Hand-washing stations shall be convenient to nurse stations and patient bed areas.

    (c) Toilet room. One toilet room shall be provided for each eight treatment cubicles or major fraction thereof.

    (d) Shower room. One shower room shall be provided for each sixteen treatment cubicles or major fraction thereof; the shower room and toilet room may be combined into the same room.

    (e) Nourishment area. A nourishment station that may be shared shall be provided. It shall include a sink, work counter, refrigerator, storage cabinets, and equipment for hot and cold nourishment between scheduled meals.

(3) Secure holding room. When required by the functional program, there shall be a secure holding room. This room shall be designed to prevent injury to patients.

    (a) All finishes, light fixtures, vents and diffusers, and sprinklers shall be tamper resistant.

    (b) There shall not be any electrical outlets, medical gas outlets, or similar devices.

    (c) There shall be no sharp corners, edges, or protrusions, and the walls shall be free of objects or accessories of any kind.

    (d) Patient room doors shall swing out and shall have hardware on the exterior side only. Doors shall have an electric strike that is tied into the fire alarm.

5.1.3.9 Support areas for definitive emergency management facilities

(1) Administrative center or nurse station for staff work and charting.

    (a) These areas shall have space for counters, cabinets, and medication storage, and shall have convenient access to hand-washing stations.

    (b) They are permitted to be combined with or include centers for reception and communication or poison control.

APPENDIX

A5.1.3.8 (2) Observation/holding units for patients requiring observation up to 23 hours or admission to an inpatient unit should be located separately but near the main emergency department. The size will depend upon the function (observation and/or holding), patient acuity mix, and projected utilization.

a. As defined by the functional plan, this area should consist of a centralized nurse station; 100 square feet (9.29 square meters) of clear floor space for each cubicle, with vacuum, oxygen, and air outlets, monitoring space, and nurse call buttons.

b. A patient bathroom should be provided.

c. Storage space for medical and dietary supplies should be included.

d. X-ray illuminators should be available.

A5.1.3.9 (2) A security station and/or system should be located to maximize visibility of the treatment areas, waiting areas, and key entrance sites.

a. The system should include visual monitoring devices installed both internally in the emergency department as well as externally at entrance sites and parking lots.

b. Special requirements for a security station should include accommodation for hospital security staff, local police officers, and monitoring equipment.

c. Design consideration should include installation of silent alarms, panic buttons, and intercom systems, and physical barriers such as doors to patient entry areas.

d. The security monitoring system should be included on the hospital's emergency power backup system.

(c) Nursing stations decentralized near clusters of treatment rooms are permitted.

(d) Where feasible, visual observation of all traffic into the unit and of all patients shall be provided from the nursing station.

*(2) Security station. Where dictated by local needs, a security system shall be located near the emergency entrances and triage/reception area.

(3) Poison control center and EMS communications center. If provided, they shall be permitted to be part of the staff work and charting area.

(4) Scrub stations. Scrub stations located in or adjacent and convenient to each trauma and/or orthopedic room.

(5) Provisions for disposal of solid and liquid waste. This may be a clinical sink with bedpan flushing device within the soiled workroom.

(6) Clean workroom or clean supply room. A clean workroom or clean supply room shall be provided in accordance with Section 2.1-2.3.7. If the area serves children, additional storage shall be provided to accommodate supplies and equipment in the range of sizes required for pediatrics.

*(7) Soiled workroom or soiled holding room. A soiled workroom or soiled holding room shall be provided in accordance with Section 2.1-2.3.8 for the exclusive use of the emergency service.

(8) Equipment and supply storage

(a) Wheelchair and stretcher storage. Storage for wheelchairs and stretchers for arriving patients shall be located out of traffic with convenient access from emergency entrances.

(b) Emergency equipment storage. Sufficient space shall be provided for emergency equipment (e.g., a CPR cart, pumps, ventilators, patient monitoring equipment, and portable x-ray unit) in accordance with Section 2.1-2.3.9.4.

(9) Housekeeping room. A housekeeping room shall be directly accessible from the unit and shall contain a service sink or floor receptor and provisions for storage of supplies and housekeeping equipment.

5.1.3.10 Support areas for staff

(1) Staff lounge. Convenient and private access to staff toilets, lounge, and lockers shall be provided.

(2) Staff storage facilities. Securable closets or cabinet compartments shall be provided for the personal effects of emergency service personnel in accordance with Section 2.1 2.4.3.

*5.1.3.11 Support areas for patients

*(1) Bereavement room

(2) Patient toilet room. A minimum of one patient toilet room per eight treatment rooms or fraction thereof shall be provided, with hand-washing station(s) in each toilet room.

5.2 Freestanding Emergency Service

5.2.1 Definition
Freestanding emergency service shall mean an extension of an existing hospital emergency department that is physically separate from the main hospital emergency department and that is intended to provide comprehensive emergency service. A service that does not provide 24-hour-a-day, seven-day-a-week operation

> **APPENDIX**
>
> **A5.1.3.9 (7)** Disposal space for regulated medical waste (e.g., gauzes/linens soaked with body fluids) should be separate from routine disposal space.
>
> **A5.1.3.11** Other space considerations. Provision of a patient hygiene room with shower and toilet facilities should be considered.
>
> **A5.1.3.11 (1)** At least one bereavement room should be provided. This room should be accessible from both the emergency treatment corridor and the emergency waiting area. This room should be comfortable enough to provide respite to the bereaved family and should be equipped with a sound transmission coefficient equivalent to 65 for the walls and 45 for the floors and ceiling.

or that is not capable of providing basic services as defined for hospital emergency departments shall not be classified as a freestanding emergency service and shall be described under other portions of this document.

5.2.1.1 Physically separate from the main hospital means not located on the same campus.

5.2.2 Facility Requirements

Except as noted in the following sections, the requirements for freestanding emergency service shall be the same as for hospital emergency service as described in Section 2.1-5.1.

5.2.2.1 General. See Section 2.1-5.1.1.

5.2.2.2 Initial emergency management. See Section 2.1-5.1.2.

5.2.2.3 Definitive emergency care. See Section 2.1-5.1.3.

5.2.2.4 Support areas. See Sections 2.1-5.1.3.9 through 2.1-5.1.3.11.

APPENDIX

A5.3 Surgery

a. The size and location of the surgical procedure rooms shall be determined by the level of care to be provided. The levels of care as defined by the American College of Surgeons are as follows:

Class A: Provides for minor surgical procedures performed under topical, local, or regional anesthesia without pre-operative sedation. Excluded are intravenous, spinal, and epidural routes; these methods are appropriate for Class B and Class C facilities.

Class B: Provides for minor or major surgical procedures performed in conjunction with oral, parenteral, or intravenous sedation or under analgesic or dissociative drugs.

Class C: Provides for major surgical procedures that require general or regional block anesthesia and support of vital bodily functions.

b. When invasive procedures are performed on patients known or suspected to have pulmonary tuberculosis, these procedures should not be performed in the operating suite. They should be performed in a room meeting airborne infection isolation room ventilation requirements or in a space using local exhaust ventilation. If the procedure must be performed in the operating suite, see the "CDC Guidelines for Preventing the Transmission of Mycobacterium Tuberculosis in Health Care Facilities."

5.2.3 Additional Requirements

The freestanding emergency service shall have the following capabilities and/or functions within the facility:

5.2.3.1 Diagnostic and treatment areas

(1) Diagnostic imaging. This shall include radiography and fluoroscopy.

(2) Observation beds. At least one of these shall have full cardiac monitoring.

(3) Laboratory. These facilities shall accommodate those functions described in Section 2.1-5.11.

5.2.3.2 Service areas

(1) Pharmacy

(2) Provision for serving patient and staff meals shall be provided. A kitchen or a satellite serving facility shall be permitted.

(3) Support services and functions shall include housekeeping, laundry, general stores, maintenance and plant operations, and security.

*5.3 Surgery

5.3.1 Surgical Suites

Note: Additions to, and adaptations of, the following elements shall be made for the special procedure operating rooms found in larger facilities.

5.3.1.1 Size. The number of operating rooms and recovery beds and the sizes of the support areas shall be based on the expected surgical workload.

5.3.1.2 Layout

(1) The surgical suite shall be located and arranged to prevent nonrelated traffic through the suite.

(2) The clinical practice setting shall be designed to facilitate movement of patients and personnel into, through, and out of defined areas within the surgical suite. Signs shall clearly indicate the surgical attire required.

(3) An operating room suite design with a sterile core shall provide for no cross-traffic of staff and supplies from the soiled/decontaminated areas to the sterile/clean areas. The use of facilities outside the operating room for soiled/decontaminated processing and clean assembly and sterile processing shall be designed to move the flow of goods and personnel from dirty to clean/sterile without compromising universal precautions or aseptic techniques in both departments.

(4) The surgical suite shall be divided into three designated areas—unrestricted, semirestricted, and restricted—defined by the physical activities performed in each area.

   (a) Unrestricted area

      (i) The unrestricted area includes a central control point established to monitor the entrance of patients, personnel, and materials.

      (ii) Street clothes are permitted in this area and traffic is not limited.

   (b) Semirestricted area

      (i) The semirestricted area includes the peripheral support areas of the surgical suite. It has storage areas for clean and sterile supplies, work areas for storage and processing of instruments, and corridors leading to the restricted areas of the surgical suite.

      (ii) Traffic in this area is limited to authorized personnel and patients. Personnel are required to wear surgical attire and cover all head and facial hair.

   (c) Restricted area

      (i) The restricted area includes operating and procedure rooms, the clean core, and scrub sink areas.

      (ii) Surgical attire and hair coverings are required. Masks are required where open sterile supplies or scrubbed persons may be located.

5.3.1.3 Provision of outpatient surgery. In the functional program, the size, location, and configuration of the surgical suite and support areas shall reflect the projected volume of outpatients. This may be achieved by designing either an outpatient surgery facility or a combined inpatient/outpatient surgical suite.

(1) Hospital surgical suite. Where outpatient surgery is provided in the surgical suite of the hospital facility, it shall comply with the requirements for outpatient surgery in Chapter 3.7, Outpatient Surgical Facility.

(2) Separate hospital unit or outpatient surgical facility. Where outpatient surgery and post-anesthetic care is provided in a separate unit of the hospital facility or in a separate outpatient surgical facility, it shall comply with the requirements for outpatient surgery in Chapter 3.7.

5.3.2 Operating and Procedure Rooms
5.3.2.1 General operating room(s)

(1) New construction

   (a) Space requirements. Each room shall have a minimum clear area of 400 square feet (37.16 square meters) exclusive of fixed or wall-mounted cabinets and built-in shelves, with a minimum of 20 feet (6.10 meters) clear dimension between fixed cabinets and built-in shelves.

   (b) Communication system. Each room shall have a system for emergency communication with the surgical suite control station.

   (c) X-ray viewers. X-ray film viewers for handling at least four films simultaneously or digital image viewers shall be provided.

   (d) Construction requirements. Operating room perimeter walls, ceiling, and floors, including penetrations, shall be sealed. (See Glossary.)

*(2) Renovation. Where renovation work is undertaken, every effort shall be made to meet the above minimum standards. If it is not possible to meet the above square-footage standards, each room shall have a minimum clear area of 360 square feet (33.45 square meters), exclusive of fixed or wall-mounted cabinets and built-in shelves, with a minimum of 18 feet (5.49 meters) clear dimension between fixed cabinets and built-in shelves.

5.3.2.2 Room(s) for cardiovascular, orthopedic, neurological, and other special procedures that require additional personnel and/or large equipment

(1) Space requirements. When included, these room(s) shall have, in addition to the above requirements for general operating rooms, a minimum clear area of 600 square feet (55.74 square meters), with a minimum of 20 feet (6.10 meters) clear dimension exclusive of fixed or wall-mounted cabinets and built-in shelves.

(2) Pump room. Where open-heart surgery is performed, an additional room in the restricted area of the surgical suite, preferably adjoining this operating room, shall be designated as a pump room where extra corporeal pump(s), supplies, and accessories are stored and serviced.

(3) Equipment storage rooms. Where complex orthopedic and neurosurgical surgery is performed, additional rooms shall be in the restricted area of the surgical suite, preferably adjoining the specialty operating rooms, which shall be designated as equipment storage rooms for the large equipment used to support these procedures.

(4) Plumbing and electrical connections. Appropriate plumbing and electrical connections shall be

APPENDIX

A5.3.2.1 (2) The functional program may require additional clear space, plumbing, and mechanical facilities to accommodate special functions in one or more of these rooms. When existing functioning operating rooms are modified, and it is impractical to increase the square footage because of walls or structural members, the operating room may continue in use when requested by the hospital.

provided in the cardiovascular, orthopedic, neurosurgical, pump, and storage rooms.

(5) Renovation. Where renovation work is undertaken, every effort shall be made to meet the above minimum standards. If it is not possible to meet the above square-footage standards, the following standards shall be met:

(a) Orthopedic surgical rooms shall have a minimum clear area of 360 square feet (33.45 square meters), with a minimum dimension of 18 feet (5.49 meters).

(b) Rooms for cardiovascular, neurological, and other special procedures shall have a minimum clear area of 400 square feet (37.16 square meters).

5.3.2.3 Additional requirements for orthopedic surgery

(1) Equipment storage. Where included, this room shall, in addition to the above requirements, have enclosed storage space for splints and traction equipment. Storage may be outside the operating room but must be conveniently located.

(2) Plaster trap. If a sink is used for the disposal of plaster of paris, a plaster trap shall be provided.

5.3.2.4 Room(s) for surgical cystoscopic and other endourologic procedures

(1) Space requirements

(a) This room shall have a minimum clear area of 350 square feet (32.52 square meters) exclusive of fixed or wall-mounted cabinets and built-in shelves, with a minimum of 15 feet (4.57 meters) clear dimension between fixed cabinets and built-in shelves.

(b) In renovation projects, rooms for surgical cystoscopy shall be permitted to have a minimum clear area of 250 square feet (23.23 square meters).

(2) X-ray viewer. X-ray viewing capability to accommodate at least four films simultaneously shall be provided.

5.3.2.5 Endoscopy suite. See Chapter 3.9, Gastrointestinal Endoscopy Facilities.

5.3.3 Pre- and Postoperative Holding Areas
5.3.3.1 Preoperative patient holding area(s). In facilities with two or more operating rooms, areas shall be provided to accommodate stretcher patients as well as sitting space for ambulatory patients.

(1) Location. These areas shall be under the direct visual control of the nursing staff and may be part of the recovery suite to achieve maximum flexibility in managing surgical caseloads.

(2) Space requirements. Each stretcher station shall be a minimum of 80 square feet (7.43 square meters) exclusive of general circulation space through the ward and shall have a minimum clearance of 4 feet (1.22 meters) on the sides of the stretchers and the foot of the stretchers.

(3) Patient privacy. Provisions such as cubicle curtains shall be made for patient privacy.

(4) Provisions shall be made for the isolation of infectious patients.

(5) An airborne infection isolation room is not required in a preoperative holding area. Provisions for the recovery of a potentially infectious patient with an airborne infection shall be determined by an ICRA.

*****5.3.3.2** Post-anesthetic care units (PACUs)

(1) Space requirements. The design shall provide a minimum of 80 square feet (7.43 square meters) for each patient bed, exclusive of general circulation space within the PACU, with a space for additional equipment described in the functional program and for clearance of at least 5 feet (1.52 meters) between patient beds and 4 feet (1.22 meters) between patient bedsides and adjacent walls.

(2) Layout. In new construction, at least one door to the recovery room shall provide access directly from the surgical suite without crossing public hospital corridors.

(3) Patient privacy. Provisions for patient privacy such as cubicle curtains shall be made.

(4) Facility requirements. Each PACU shall contain a medication station; hand-washing stations; nurse station with charting facilities; clinical sink; provisions for bedpan cleaning; and storage space for stretchers, supplies, and equipment.

(a) Hand-washing station(s). At least one hand-washing station with hands-free or wrist blade-operable controls shall be available for every four beds, uniformly distributed to provide equal access from each bed.

(b) Staff toilet. A staff toilet shall be located within the working area to maintain staff availability to patients.

(5) Provisions shall be made for the isolation of infectious patients.

(6) An airborne infection isolation room (AIIR) is not required in a PACU. Provisions for the recovery of a potentially infectious patient with an airborne infection shall be determined by an ICRA.

5.3.3.3 Phase II recovery. Where outpatient surgeries are to be part of the surgical suite, and where outpatients receive Class B or Class C sedation, a separate Phase II or step-down recovery room shall be provided.

(1) Layout. In new construction, at least one door shall access the PACU without crossing unrestricted corridors of the hospital.

(2) Space requirements

(a) The design shall provide a minimum of 50 square feet (4.65 square meters) for each patient in a lounge chair, with space for additional equipment described in the functional

APPENDIX

A5.3.3.2 Separate and additional recovery space may be necessary to accommodate patients. If children receive care, recovery space should be provided for pediatric patients and the layout of the surgical suite should facilitate the presence of parents in the PACU.

program and for clearance of 4 feet (1.22 meters) on the sides of the lounge chairs and the foot of the lounge chairs.

(b) A minimum clear floor area of 100 square feet (9.29 square meters) shall be provided in single-bed rooms.

(3) Patient privacy. Provisions for patient privacy such as cubicle curtains shall be made.

(4) Facility requirements. The room shall contain hand-washing stations, a nurse station with charting facilities, clinical sink, provision for bedpan cleaning, and storage space for supplies and equipment.

(a) Hand-washing stations

(i) A hand-washing station shall be provided in each room.

(ii) At least one hand-washing station with hands-free operable controls shall be provided for every four lounge chairs, uniformly distributed to provide equal access from each lounge chair.

(b) Toilet rooms

(i) Staff toilet. A staff toilet shall be provided with direct access to the working area to maintain staff availability to patients.

(ii) Patient toilet. A patient toilet shall be provided with direct access to the Phase II recovery unit for the exclusive use of patients.

(5) Provisions shall be made for the isolation of infectious patients.

(6) An airborne infection isolation room is not required in a Phase II recovery area. Provisions for the recovery of a potentially infectious patient with an airborne infection shall be determined by an ICRA.

5.3.4 Diagnostic and Treatment Locations

5.3.4.1 Examination provisions. Provisions shall be made for patient examination, interviews, preparation, testing, and obtaining vital signs of patients for outpatient surgery.

5.3.4.2 Area for preparation and examination of frozen sections. This area may be part of the general laboratory if immediate results are obtainable without unnecessary delay in the completion of surgery.

5.3.5 Support Areas for the Surgical Suite

Support areas, except for the enclosed soiled workroom mentioned in Section 2.1-5.3.5.10 and the housekeeping room in Section 2.1-5.3.5.14, may be shared with the obstetrical facilities in accordance with the functional program. Support areas, where shared with delivery rooms, shall be designed to avoid the passing of patients or staff between the operating room and the delivery room areas. The following shall be provided:

5.3.5.1 A control station. This shall be located to permit visual observation of all traffic into the suite.

5.3.5.2 A supervisor office or station. The number of offices, stations, and teaching areas in the surgical suite shall depend upon the functional program.

5.3.5.3 Documentation area. The dictation and report preparation area may be accessible from the lounge area.

5.3.5.4 Scrub facilities. Two scrub positions shall be provided near the entrance to each operating room.

(1) Two scrub positions may serve two operating rooms if both positions are adjacent to the entrance of each operating room.

(2) Scrub facilities shall be arranged to minimize incidental splatter on nearby personnel, medical equipment, or supply carts.

(3) In new construction, view windows at scrub stations permitting observation of room interiors shall be provided.

(4) The scrub sinks shall be recessed into an alcove out of the main traffic areas. The alcove shall be

located off the semirestricted or restricted areas of the surgical suite.

5.3.5.5 Medication station. Provision shall be made for storage and distribution of drugs and routine medications in accordance with Section 2.1-2.3.4.

5.3.5.6 Ice machine. An ice machine shall be provided in accordance with Section 2.1-2.3.6.

5.3.5.7 Patient holding area. In facilities with two or more operating rooms, an area shall be provided to accommodate stretcher patients waiting for surgery. This holding area shall be under the visual control of the nursing staff.

5.3.5.8 A substerile service areas(s). This area acts as a service area between two or more operating or procedure rooms. Other facilities for processing and sterilizing reusable instruments, etc., are typically located in another hospital department, such as central services.

(1) It shall be equipped with a flash sterilizer, warming cabinet, sterile supply storage area, and hand-washing station with hands-free controls.

(2) A sterilizing facility(ies) with high-speed sterilizer(s) or other sterilizing equipment for immediate or emergency use shall be grouped to service several operating rooms for convenient, efficient use.

(3) A work space and hand-washing station shall be provided if required by the functional program.

5.3.5.9 Clean workroom or clean supply room. Soiled and clean workrooms or holding rooms shall be separated. The clean workroom or supply room shall not be used for food preparation.

(1) Storage space for sterile and clean supplies shall be sized to meet the functional program. The space shall be moisture and temperature controlled and free from cross-traffic.

(2) Clean workroom. A clean workroom shall be provided when clean materials are assembled within the surgical suite prior to use or following the decontamination cycle.

(a) It shall contain a work counter, a hand-washing station, storage facilities for clean supplies, and a space to package reusable items.

(b) The storage for sterile supplies must be separated from this space.

(3) Clean supply room. If the room is used only for storage and holding as part of a system for distribution of clean and sterile supply materials, the work counter and hand-washing station may be omitted.

5.3.5.10 Soiled workroom or holding room. Soiled and clean workrooms or holding rooms shall be separated.

(1) An enclosed soiled workroom (or soiled holding room that is part of a system for the collection and disposal of soiled material) shall be provided for the exclusive use of the surgical suite.

(2) The room shall be located in the restricted area.

(3) The soiled workroom shall contain a flushing-rim clinical sink or equivalent flushing-rim fixture, a hand-washing station, a work counter, and space for waste receptacles and soiled linen receptacles. Rooms used only for temporary holding of soiled material may omit the flushing-rim clinical sink and work counters. However, if the flushing-rim clinical sink is omitted, other provisions for disposal of liquid waste shall be provided.

(4) The room shall not have direct connection with operating rooms or other sterile activity rooms.

5.3.5.11 Anesthesia workroom. An anesthesia workroom for cleaning, testing, and storing anesthesia equipment.

(1) This room shall contain work counter(s) and sink(s) and racks for cylinders.

(2) Provisions shall be made for separate storage of clean and soiled items.

(3) In new construction, depending on the functional and space programs, the anesthesia workroom shall provide space for anesthesia case carts and other anesthesia equipment.

5.3.5.12 Storage for blood, organs, and pathological specimens

(1) Provisions for refrigerated blood bank storage that meets the standards of the American Blood Banking Association shall be provided.

(2) Storage for harvested organs. Where applicable, refrigeration facilities for harvested organs shall be provided.

5.3.5.13 Storage for pathological specimens. Provisions for storage of pathological specimens prior to transfer to pathology section shall be provided.

5.3.5.14 Equipment and supply storage

*(1) Storage room(s) shall be provided for equipment and supplies used in the surgical suite. Each surgical suite shall provide sufficient storage area to keep its required corridor width free of equipment and supplies, but not less than 150 square feet (13.94 square meters) or 50 square feet (4.65 square meters) per operating room, whichever is greater.

(2) Storage areas shall be provided for portable x-ray equipment, stretchers, fracture tables, warming devices, auxiliary lamps, etc. These areas shall be out of corridors and traffic.

(3) Medical gas storage. Main storage of medical gases may be outside or inside the facility in accordance with NFPA 99. Provision shall be made for additional separate storage of reserve gas cylinders necessary to complete at least one day's procedures.

5.3.5.15 Housekeeping facilities. Housekeeping facilities shall be provided for the exclusive use of the surgical suite. They shall be directly accessible from the suite and shall contain a service sink or floor receptor and

provisions for storage of supplies and housekeeping equipment.

5.3.6 Support Areas for Staff
5.3.6.1 Staff lounge and toilet facilities

(1) Separate or combined lounges shall be provided for male and female staff.

(2) Lounge(s) shall be designed to minimize the need to leave the suite and to provide convenient access to the recovery room.

5.3.6.2 Staff clothing change areas. Appropriate areas shall be provided for male and female personnel (orderlies, technicians, nurses, and doctors) working within the surgical suite.

(1) The areas shall contain lockers, showers, toilets, hand-washing stations, and space for donning surgical attire.

(2) These areas shall be arranged to encourage a one-way traffic pattern so that personnel entering from outside the surgical suite can change and move directly into the surgical suite.

5.3.7 Support Areas for Patients
5.3.7.1 Patient clothing change areas. If the functional program defines outpatient surgery as part of the surgical suite, a separate area shall be provided where outpatients and same-day admission patients may change from street clothing into hospital gowns and be prepared for surgery.

(1) It shall include a waiting room, locker(s), toilet(s), and clothing change or gowning area.

(2) Where private holding room(s) or cubicle(s) are provided, a separate change area is not required.

5.4 Interventional Imaging Facilities

5.4.1 Cardiac Catheterization Lab (Cardiology)
5.4.1.1 Location. The cardiac catheterization lab is normally a separate suite, but location in the imaging suite shall be permitted provided the appropriate sterile environment is provided. See Section 2.1-5.5.7.

APPENDIX

5.3.5.14 (1) Equipment storage room(s) for equipment and supplies used in the surgical suite should be strategically located and sized for convenient access and utilization. In larger surgical suites, storage spaces should be located for ready access to specialty rooms.

5.4.1.2 Space requirements

(1) Procedure rooms

    (a) The number of procedure rooms shall be based on expected utilization.

    (b) The procedure room shall be a minimum of 400 square feet (37.16 square meters) exclusive of fixed cabinets and shelves.

(2) Prep, holding, and recovery rooms. The size of the prep, holding, and recovery areas shall be based on expected utilization.

5.4.1.3 Electrophysiology labs. If electrophysiology labs are also provided in accordance with the approved functional program, these labs may be located within and integral to the catheterization suite or located in a separate functional area proximate to the cardiac care unit.

5.4.1.4 Support areas for the cardiac catheterization lab

(1) Scrub facilities. Scrub facilities with hands-free operable controls shall be provided adjacent to the entrance of procedure rooms, and shall be arranged to minimize incidental splatter on nearby personnel, medical equipment, or supplies.

(2) Patient prep, holding, and recovery area or room. A patient preparation, holding, and recovery area or room shall be provided and arranged to provide visual observation before and after the procedure.

(3) Control room or area. A control room or area shall be provided and shall be large enough to contain and provide for the efficient functioning of the x-ray and image recording equipment. A view window permitting full view of the patient from the control console shall be provided.

(4) Electrical equipment room. An equipment room or enclosure large enough to contain x-ray transformers, power modules, and associated electronics and electrical gear shall be provided.

(5) Viewing room. A viewing room shall be available for use by the cardiac catheterization suite.

(6) Clean workroom or clean supply room. A clean workroom or clean supply room shall be provided in accordance with Section 2.1-2.3.7.

(7) Soiled workroom or soiled holding room. A soiled workroom shall be provided in accordance with Section 2.1-2.3.8.

(8) Film file room. Film file room shall be available for use by the cardiac catheterization suite.

(9) Housekeeping closet. A housekeeping closet shall be provided in accordance with Section 2.1-2.3.10.

5.4.1.5 Support areas for staff

(1) Staff clothing change area(s). Staff change area(s) shall be provided and arranged to ensure a traffic pattern so that personnel can enter from outside the suite, change their clothing, and move directly into the cardiac catheterization suite.

5.5 Imaging Suite

5.5.1 General
*5.5.1.1 Functional program. Equipment and space shall be as necessary to accommodate the functional program. The imaging department provides diagnostic procedures. An imaging department commonly includes fluoroscopy, radiography, mammography, tomography, computerized tomography scanning, ultrasound, magnetic resonance, angiography, and similar techniques.

*5.5.1.2 Layout. Beds and stretchers shall have ready

APPENDIX

A5.5.1.1 Space layouts should be developed in compliance with manufacturer's recommendations because area requirements may vary from machine to machine. Since technology changes frequently and from manufacturer to manufacturer, rooms can be sized larger to allow upgrading of equipment over time.

A5.5.1.2 Particular attention should be paid to the management of outpatients for preparation, holding, and observation. The emergency, surgery, cystoscopy, and outpatient clinics should be accessible to the imaging suite. Imaging should be located on the ground floor, if practical, because of equipment ceiling height requirements, close proximity to electrical services, and expansion considerations.

access to and from other departments of the institution.

5.5.1.3 Radiation protection. Most imaging requires radiation protection. A certified physicist or other qualified expert representing the owner or appropriate state agency shall specify the type, location, and amount of radiation protection to be installed in accordance with the final approved department layout and equipment selections.

(1) Where protected alcoves with view windows are required, a minimum of 1 foot 6 inches (45.72 centimeters) shall be provided between the view window and the outside partition edge.

(2) Radiation protection requirements shall be incorporated into the specifications and the building plans.

5.5.1.4 Construction requirements

(1) Floor. Floor shall be adequate to meet load requirements.

(2) Ceiling. A lay-in type ceiling shall be permitted to be considered for ease of installation, service, and remodeling.

5.5.2 Angiography
5.5.2.1 General

*(1) Space requirements. Space shall be provided as necessary to accommodate the functional program.

(2) Provision shall be made within the facility for extended post-procedure observation of outpatients.

5.5.2.2 Control room. A control room shall be provided as necessary to accommodate the functional program. A view window shall be provided to permit full view of the patient.

*5.5.2.3 Viewing area. A viewing area shall be provided.

5.5.2.4 Scrub facilities. A scrub sink located outside the staff entry to the procedure room shall be provided for use by staff.

5.5.2.5 Equipment storage. Storage for portable equipment and catheters shall be provided.

*5.5.2.6 Patient holding area. A patient holding area shall be provided.

5.5.3 Computerized Tomography (CT) Scanning
5.5.3.1 Space requirements. CT scan rooms shall be as required to accommodate the equipment.

5.5.3.2 Control room. A control room shall be provided that is designed to accommodate the computer and other controls for the equipment.

(1) A view window shall be provided to permit full view of the patient.

(2) The angle between the control and equipment centroid shall permit the control operator to see the patient's head.

(3) The control room shall be located to allow convenient film processing.

5.5.3.4 Patient toilet. A patient toilet shall be provided. It shall be convenient to the procedure room and, if directly accessible to the scan room, arranged so a patient can leave the toilet without having to reenter the scan room.

5.5.4 Diagnostic X-Ray
*5.5.4.1 Space requirements. Radiography rooms shall be of a size to accommodate the functional program.

*5.5.4.2 Tomography, radiography/fluoroscopy rooms

(1) Separate toilets with hand-washing stations shall be provided with direct access from each fluoroscopic room so that a patient can leave the toilet without having to reenter the fluoroscopic room.

(2) Rooms used only occasionally for fluoroscopic procedures shall be permitted to use nearby patient toilets if they are located for immediate access.

*5.5.4.3 Mammography rooms

5.5.4.4 Shielded control alcoves

(1) Each x-ray room shall include a shielded control alcove. This area shall be provided with a view window designed to provide full view of the examination table and the patient at all times, including full view of the patient when the table is in the tilt position or the chest x-ray is in use.

(2) For mammography machines with built-in shielding for the operator, the alcove shall be permitted to be omitted when approved by the certified physicist or state radiation protection agency.

5.5.5 Magnetic Resonance Imaging (MRI)
5.5.5.1 Space requirements

(1) Space shall be provided as necessary to accommodate the functional program.

(2) The MRI room shall be permitted to range from 325 square feet (30.19 square meters) to 620 square feet (57.60 square meters), depending on the vendor and magnet strength.

5.5.5.2 Layout. When spectroscopy is provided, caution shall be exercised in locating it in relation to the magnetic fringe fields.

*5.5.5.3 Control room. A control room shall be provided with full view of the MRI.

*5.5.5.4 Patient holding area. A patient holding area shall be provided.

*5.5.5.5 Computer room. A computer room shall be provided.

*5.5.5.6 Darkroom. A darkroom shall be provided.

*5.5.5.7 Cryogen storage. Cryogen storage shall be provided.

5.5.5.8 Equipment installation requirements

*(1) Power conditioning shall be provided.

*(2) Magnetic shielding shall be provided.

(3) For super-conducting MRI, cryogen venting and emergency exhaust must be provided in accordance with the original equipment manufacturer's specifications.

5.5.6 Ultrasound
5.5.6.1 Space requirements. Space shall be provided as necessary to accommodate the functional program.

5.5.6.2 Patient toilet. A patient toilet, accessible from the procedure room, shall be provided.

APPENDIX

A5.5.4.3 Mammography rooms should be a minimum of 100 square feet (9.29 square meters).

A5.5.5.3 Control rooms should be a minimum of 100 square feet (9.29 square meters), but may be larger depending on the vendor and magnet size.

A5.5.5.4 When patient holding areas are provided, they should be located near the MRI unit and should be large enough to accommodate stretcher(s).

A5.5.5.5 A computer room may range from 150 square feet (13.94 square meters) to 380 square feet (35.30 square meters) depending on the vendor and magnet strength. Self-contained air conditioning supplement is normally required.

A5.5.5.6 A darkroom may be required for loading cassettes and shall be located near the control room. This darkroom shall be outside the 10-gauss field.

A5.5.5.7 Cryogen storage may be required in areas where service to replenish supplies is not readily available. When provided, space should be a minimum of 50 square feet (4.65 square meters) to accommodate two large dewars of cryogen.

A5.5.5.8 (1) Power conditioning and voltage regulation equipment as well as direct current (DC) may be required.

5.5.7 Cardiac Catheterization Lab (Cardiology)
The cardiac catheterization lab is normally a separate suite (see Section 2.1-5.4.1) but location within the imaging suite shall be permitted provided the appropriate sterile environment is provided. Combination with angiography shall be permitted in low usage situations.

5.5.8 Support Areas for the Imaging Suite
The following spaces are common to the imaging department and are minimum requirements unless stated otherwise:

5.5.8.1 Control desk and reception area

5.5.8.2 Offices for radiologist(s) and assistant(s). Offices shall include provisions for viewing, individual consultation, and charting of film.

5.5.8.3 Hand-washing stations

(1) Hand-washing stations shall be provided within each procedure room unless the room is used only for routine screening such as chest x-rays where the patient is not physically handled by the staff.

(2) Hand-washing stations shall be provided convenient to the MRI room, but need not be within the room.

5.5.8.4 Consultation area. An appropriate area for individual consultation with referring clinicians shall be provided.

5.5.8.5 Patient holding area. A convenient holding area under staff control shall be provided to accommodate inpatients on stretchers or beds.

5.5.8.6 Clerical offices/spaces. Office space shall be provided as necessary for the functional program.

5.5.8.7 Film processing room

(1) If film systems are used, a darkroom shall be provided for processing film unless the processing equipment normally used does not require a darkroom for loading and transfer. When daylight processing is used, the darkroom shall be permitted to be minimal for emergency and special uses.

(2) Film processing shall be located convenient to the procedure rooms and to the quality control area.

5.5.8.8 Quality control area. An area or room shall be provided near the processor for viewing film immediately after it is processed. All view boxes shall be illuminated to provide light of the same color value and intensity for appropriate comparison of several adjacent films.

5.5.8.9 Contrast media preparation

(1) If contrast media are used, this area shall include a sink, counter, and storage to allow for mixing of contrast media.

(2) One preparation room, if conveniently located, shall be permitted to serve any number of rooms.

(3) Where pre-prepared media are used, this area shall be permitted to be omitted, but storage shall be provided for the media.

5.5.8.10 Cleanup facilities. Provisions for cleanup shall be located within the suite for convenient access and use.

(1) The facilities shall include service sink or floor receptacle as well as storage space for equipment and supplies.

(2) If automatic film processors are used, a receptacle of adequate size with hot and cold water for cleaning the processor racks shall be provided.

5.5.8.11 Clean storage. Provision shall be made for the storage of clean supplies and linens. If conveniently located, storage shall be permitted to be shared with another department.

5.5.8.12 Soiled holding. Provision shall be made for soiled holding. Separate provisions for contaminated handling and holding shall be made. Hand-washing stations shall be provided.

5.5.8.13 Film storage

(1) Film storage (active). A room with cabinet or shelves for filing patient film for immediate retrieval shall be provided.

(2) Film storage (inactive). A room or area for inactive film storage shall be provided. It shall be permitted to be outside the imaging suite, but must be under imaging's administrative control and properly secured to protect films against loss or damage.

(3) Storage for unexposed film. If film systems are used, storage facilities for unexposed film shall include protection of film against exposure or damage and shall not be warmer than the air of adjacent occupied spaces.

5.5.8.14 Medication storage. Provision shall be made for locked storage of medications and drugs.

5.5.9 Support Areas for Staff

The following spaces are common to the imaging department and are minimum requirements unless stated otherwise:

5.5.9.1 Staff lounge. Staff lounge with lockers shall be permitted to be outside the suite but shall be convenient for staff use.

5.5.9.2 Staff toilets. Toilets shall be permitted to be outside the suite but shall be convenient for staff use. In suites of three or more procedure rooms, toilets internal to the suite shall be provided.

5.5.10 Support Areas for Patients

The following spaces are common to the imaging department and are minimum requirements unless stated otherwise:

5.5.10.1 Patient waiting area

(1) The area shall be out of traffic, under staff control, and shall have seating capacity in accordance with the functional program.

(2) If the suite is routinely used for outpatients and inpatients at the same time, separate waiting areas shall be provided with screening for visual privacy between them.

(3) If so determined by an ICRA, the diagnostic imaging waiting area shall require special measures to reduce the risk of airborne infection transmission. These measures shall include enhanced general ventilation and air disinfection techniques similar to inpatient requirements for airborne infection isolation rooms (see Table 2.1-2). See the "CDC Guidelines for Preventing the Transmission of Mycobacterium Tuberculosis in Health Care Facilities."

5.5.10.2 Patient toilet rooms. Toilet rooms with hand-washing stations convenient to the waiting rooms and equipped with an emergency call system shall be provided.

5.5.10.3 Patient dressing rooms. Dressing rooms shall be provided convenient to the waiting areas and x-ray rooms. Each room shall include a seat or bench, mirror, and provisions for hanging patients' clothing and securing valuables.

5.6 Nuclear Medicine

5.6.1 General

*5.6.1.1 Space requirements.** Space shall be provided as necessary to accommodate the functional program. Where the functional program calls for it, nuclear medicine procedure room(s) shall accommodate the equipment specified in the functional program, a stretcher, exercise equipment (treadmill and/or bicycle), and staff work space.

APPENDIX

A5.6.1.1 Nuclear medicine may include positron emission tomography, which is not common to most facilities. It requires specialized planning for equipment.

5.6.1.2 Radiation protection requirements. A certified physicist or other qualified expert representing the owner or state agency shall specify the type, location, and amount of radiation protection to be installed in accordance with final approved department layout and equipment selection. These specifications shall be incorporated into the plans.

5.6.1.3 Construction requirements. Provision for wiring raceways, ducts, or conduits shall be made in floors, walls, and ceilings. Ceiling-mounted equipment shall have properly designed rigid support structures located above the finished ceiling.

5.6.2 Radiopharmacy

If radiopharmaceutical preparation is performed on-site, an area adequate to house a radiopharmacy shall be provided with appropriate shielding.

5.6.2.1 Space requirements

(1) This area shall include adequate space for storage of radionuclides, chemicals for preparation, dose calibrators, and record-keeping.

(2) If pre-prepared materials are used, storage and calculation area may be considerably smaller than that for on-site preparation.

(3) Space shall provide adequately for dose calibration, quality assurance, and record-keeping.

5.6.2.2 Radiation protection requirements. The area may still require shielding from other portions of the facilities.

5.6.2.3 Construction requirements

(1) Floors and walls shall be constructed of easily decontaminated materials.

(2) Vents and traps for radioactive gases shall be provided if such are used.

APPENDIX

A5.6.3 Positron Emission Tomography (PET) Facilities
Space requirements
a. Space should be provided as necessary to accommodate the functional program. PET scanning is generally used in experimental settings and requires space for a scanner and for a cyclotron.

b. Scanner room. The scanner room should be a minimum of 300 square feet (27.87 square meters).

c. Cyclotron room. Where a cyclotron room is required, it should be a minimum of 225 square feet (20.90 square meters) with a 16-square-foot (1.47 square meters) space safe for storage of parts that may need to cool down for a year or more.

Laboratory facilities
a. Both a hot (radioactive) lab and a cold (nonradioactive) lab may be required, each a minimum of 250 square feet (23.23 square meters).

b. A blood lab of a minimum of 80 square feet (7.43 square meters) should be provided.

Facility requirements
a. Patient holding area. A patient holding area to accommodate two stretchers should be provided.

b. Gas storage area. A gas storage area large enough to accommodate bottles of gas should be provided. Each gas will be piped individually and may go to the cyclotron or to the lab.

Construction requirements
Radiation protection. Significant radiation protection may be required, since the cyclotron may generate high radiation.

Ventilation requirements
a. Ventilation adequate for the occupancy is required. Compressed air may be required to pressurize a water circulation system.

b. Special ventilation systems together with monitors, sensors, and alarm systems may be required to vent gases and chemicals.

c. The heating, ventilating, and air conditioning system will require particular attention; highest pressures should be in coldest (radiation) areas and exhaust should be in hottest (radiation) areas. Redundancy may be important.

Plumbing requirements
The cyclotron is water cooled with de-ionized water. A heat exchanger and connection to a compressor or connection to chilled water may be required. A redundant plumbing system connected to a holding tank may be required to prevent accidental leakage of contaminated water into the regular plumbing system.

(3) Hoods for pharmaceutical preparation shall meet applicable standards.

*5.6.3 Positron Emission Tomography (PET)

5.6.4 Nuclear Medicine Area

The nuclear medicine area, when operated separately from the imaging department, shall include the following:

5.6.4.1 Space requirements. Space shall be adequate to permit entry of stretchers and beds and able to accommodate imaging equipment, electronic consoles, and if present, computer terminals.

5.6.4.2 A control desk and reception area

5.6.4.3 Hand-washing stations. These shall be provided within each procedure room.

*5.6.4.4 Dose administration area. A dose administration area as specified by the functional program shall be provided, located near the preparation area. Since as much as several hours may elapse for a dose to take effect, the area shall provide for visual privacy from other areas.

5.6.4.5 Support areas for the nuclear medicine area

(1) Consultation area. A consultation area with view boxes illuminated to provide light of the same color value and intensity for appropriate comparison of several adjacent films shall be provided. Space shall be provided for computer access and display terminals if such are included in the program.

(2) Patient holding area

    (a) A holding area for patients on stretchers or beds shall be provided out of traffic and under control of staff.

    (b) Combination of this area with the dose administration area shall be permitted provided there is visual privacy between the areas.

(3) Offices

    (a) Medical staff offices. Offices for physicians and assistants shall be provided and equipped for individual consultation, viewing, and charting of film.

    (b) Other staff offices. Clerical offices and spaces shall be provided as necessary for the program to function.

*(4) Darkroom. If film processing is used, an on-site darkroom shall be provided for film processing.

(5) Computer room. When the functional program requires a centralized computer area, it shall be a separate room with access terminals available within the imaging rooms.

(6) A soiled workroom or holding room

    (a) Soiled workroom. It shall contain a hand-washing station and a clinical sink (or equivalent flushing-rim fixtures).

    (b) Soiled holding room. If the room is used for temporary holding of soiled materials, omission of the clinical sink shall be permitted.

(7) Equipment and supply storage

    (a) Film storage. Inactive film storage under departmental administrative control and properly secured to protect film against loss or damage shall be provided and can be off site.

    (b) Clean linen storage. A storage area for clean linen with a hand-washing station.

APPENDIX

A5.6.4.4 Because patients in this area may be held for long periods of time, the design of the area should incorporate such features as comfortable seating, varied lighting, an entertainment center, music headphones, and availability of reading materials.

A5.6.4.5 (4) The darkroom should contain protective storage facilities for unexposed film that guard the film against exposure or damage.

(8) Housekeeping rooms. Provisions for cleanup shall be located within the suite for convenient access and use. Cleanup facilities shall include service sink or floor receptacle as well as storage space for housekeeping equipment and supplies.

5.6.4.6 Support areas for staff

(1) Staff toilet(s). These shall be provided convenient to the nuclear medicine laboratory.

5.6.4.7 Support areas for patients

(1) Patient waiting areas. Waiting areas shall be provided out of traffic, under staff control, and with seating capacity in accordance with the functional program. If the department is routinely used for outpatients and inpatients at the same time, separate waiting areas shall be provided with screening or visual privacy between the waiting areas.

(2) Patient dressing rooms

(a) These shall be convenient to the waiting area and procedure rooms.

(b) Each dressing room shall include a seat or bench, a mirror, and provisions for hanging patients' clothing and securing valuables.

(3) Patient toilet rooms. Toilet rooms reserved for

APPENDIX

A5.6.5.1 Equipment manufacturers' recommendations should be sought and followed, since space requirements may vary from one machine to another and one manufacturer to another.

a. The radiotherapy suite may contain electron beam therapy or radiation therapy or both.

b. Although not recommended, a simulation room may be omitted in small linear accelerator facilities where other positioning geometry is provided.

A5.6.5.1 (2) Minimum size should be 260 square feet (24.15 square meters) for the simulator room; 680 square feet (63.17 square meters), including the maze, for accelerator rooms; and 450 square feet (41.81 square meters) for cobalt rooms.

nuclear medicine patients shall be provided convenient to waiting and procedure rooms.

5.6.5 Radiotherapy Suite
*5.6.5.1 Space requirements

(1) Rooms and spaces shall be provided as necessary to accommodate the functional program.

*(2) Simulator, accelerator, and cobalt rooms shall be sized to accommodate the equipment and patient access on a stretcher, medical staff access to the equipment and patient, and service access.

5.6.5.2 Radiation protection requirements. Cobalt, linear accelerators, and simulation rooms require radiation protection.

(1) Layouts shall be designed to prevent the escape of radioactive particles.

(2) Openings into the room, including doors, ductwork, vents, and electrical raceways and conduits, shall be baffled to prevent direct exposure to other areas of the facility.

(3) A certified physicist representing the owner or appropriate state agency shall specify the type, location, and amount of protection to be installed in accordance with final approved department layout and equipment selection. The architect shall incorporate these specifications into the hospital building plans.

5.6.5.3 Construction requirements

(1) Flooring shall be adequate to meet load requirements for equipment, patients, and personnel.

(2) Provision for wiring raceways, ducts, or conduit shall be made in floors and ceilings.

(3) Ceiling-mounted equipment shall have properly designed rigid support structures located above the finished ceiling.

5.6.5.4 Support areas for the radiotherapy suite. The following areas shall be provided. Sharing of these areas between the radiotherapy suite and other areas shall be permitted if required by the functional program:

(1) Exam rooms for each treatment room. These shall be as specified by the functional program.

  (a) Each exam room shall be a minimum of 100 square feet (9.29 square meters).

  (b) Each exam room shall be equipped with a hand-washing station.

(2) A stretcher hold area

  (a) This shall be located adjacent to the treatment rooms, screened for privacy, and combined with a seating area for outpatients.

  (b) The size of the area will be dependent on the program for outpatients and inpatients.

(3) Patient gowning area

  (a) Safe storage for valuables and clothing shall be provided.

  (b) At least one space should be large enough for staff-assisted dressing.

(4) Business office and/or reception/control area

(5) Darkroom. This shall be convenient to the treatment room(s) and the quality control area.

  (a) Where daylight processing is used, the darkroom may be minimal for emergency use.

  (b) If automatic film processors are used, a receptacle of adequate size with hot and cold water for cleaning the processor racks shall be provided either in the darkroom or nearby.

(6) Film file area

(7) Film storage area for unprocessed film.

(8) Housekeeping room. This shall be equipped with service sink or floor receptor and large enough for equipment or supplies storage.

5.6.5.5 Optional support areas for the radiotherapy suite. The following areas may be required by the functional program:

(1) Offices

  (a) Oncologist's office (may be combined with consultation room)

  (b) Physicist's office (may be combined with treatment planning)

(2) Treatment planning and record room

(3) Consultation room

(4) Quality control area. This shall have view boxes illuminated to provide light of consistent color value and intensity.

(5) Computer control area. This is normally located just outside the entry to the treatment room(s).

(6) Dosimetry equipment area

(7) Hypothermia room (may be combined with an exam room)

(8) Workstation/nutrition station

5.6.5.6 Additional support areas for linear accelerator

(1) Mold room with exhaust hood and hand-washing station

(2) Block room with storage. The block room may be combined with the mold room.

5.6.5.7 Additional support areas for cobalt room

(1) Hot lab

5.7 Rehabilitation Therapy Department

5.7.1 General
Rehabilitation therapy is primarily for restoration of body functions and may contain one or several categories of services.

5.7.1.1 If a formal rehabilitation therapy service is included in a project, the facilities and equipment shall be as necessary to accommodate the functional program.

5.7.1.2 Where two or more rehabilitation services are included, facilities and equipment may be shared as appropriate.

5.7.2 Physical Therapy
If physical therapy is part of the service, at least the following shall be provided:

5.7.2.1 Individual treatment area(s) with privacy screens or curtains. Each such space shall have not less than 70 square feet (6.51 square meters) of clear floor area.

5.7.2.2 Exercise area and facilities

5.7.2.3 Provision for additional therapies. If required by the functional program, provisions for thermotherapy, diathermy, ultrasonics, and hydrotherapy shall be made.

5.7.2.4 Hand-washing stations

(1)   Hand-washing stations for staff shall be located either within or at each treatment space.

(2)   Each treatment room shall have at least one hand-washing station.

5.7.2.5 Support areas for physical therapy

(1)   Soiled material storage. Separate storage for soiled linen, towels, and supplies shall be provided.

(2)   Equipment and supply storage

   (a)   Clean linen and towel storage

   (b)   Storage for equipment and supplies

5.7.2.6 Support areas for patients. If required by the functional program, patient dressing areas, showers, and lockers shall be provided. They shall be accessible and usable by the disabled.

APPENDIX

A5.7.3.2 The facilities should be similar to a residential environment.

5.7.3 Occupational Therapy
If occupational therapy is part of the service, at least the following shall be provided:

5.7.3.1 Work areas and counters. These shall be suitable for wheelchair access.

*__5.7.3.2__ Teaching area. An area for teaching daily living activities shall be provided. It shall contain an area for a bed, kitchen counter with appliances and sink, a bathroom, and a table and chair.

5.7.3.3 Hand-washing stations

5.7.3.4 Equipment and supply storage

5.7.4 Prosthetics and Orthotics
If prosthetics and orthotics are part of the service, at least the following shall be provided:

5.7.4.1 Workspace for technicians

5.7.4.2 Space for evaluation and fitting. This shall have provision for privacy.

5.7.4.3 Space for equipment, supplies, and storage

5.7.5 Speech and Hearing Services
If speech and hearing services are offered, at least the following shall be provided:

5.7.5.1 Space for evaluation and treatment

5.7.5.2 Space for equipment and storage

5.7.6 Support Areas for the Rehabilitation Therapy Department
Each rehabilitation therapy department shall include the following, which may be shared or provided as separate units for each service:

5.7.6.1 Reception and control station(s). This shall permit visual control of waiting and activities areas and may be combined with office and clerical space.

5.7.6.2 Office and clerical space. Provision shall be made for filing and retrieval of patient records.

5.7.6.3 Multipurpose room. Access to a demonstration/ conference room shall be provided.

5.7.6.4 Wheelchair and stretcher storage. Space(s) shall be provided for storing wheelchairs and stretchers out of traffic while patients are using the services. These spaces may be separate from the service area but must be conveniently located.

5.7.6.5 Housekeeping room. A conveniently accessible housekeeping room and service sink for housekeeping use shall be provided.

5.7.7 Support Areas for Staff

Each rehabilitation therapy department shall include the following, which may be shared or provided as separate units for each service:

5.7.7.1 Convenient access to toilets

5.7.7.2 Locking closets or cabinets shall be provided within the vicinity of each work area for securing staff personal effects.

5.7.8 Support Areas for Patients

Each rehabilitation therapy department shall include the following, which may be shared or provided as separate units for each service:

5.7.8.1 Patient waiting area(s). These shall be located out of traffic with provision for wheelchairs.

5.7.8.2 Patient toilets with hand-washing stations accessible to wheelchair patients.

5.8 Respiratory Therapy Service

The type and extent of respiratory therapy service in different institutions vary greatly. In some, therapy is delivered in large sophisticated units, centralized in a specific area; in others, basic services are provided only at patients' bedsides. If respiratory service is provided, the following elements shall be provided as a minimum, in addition to those elements stipulated in Sections 2.1-5.7.6.1 and 5.7.6.2 and 2.1-5.7.7.1 and 5.7.7.2:

5.8.1 Locations for Cough-Inducing and Aerosol-Generating Procedures

5.8.1.1 All cough-inducing procedures performed on patients who may have infectious Mycobacterium tuberculosis shall be performed in rooms using local exhaust ventilation devices (e.g., booths or special enclosures that have discharge HEPA filters and exhaust directly to the outside).

5.8.1.2 If a ventilated booth is used, the air exchange rate within the booth shall be at least 12 air changes per hour, with a minimum exhaust flow rate of 50 cfm and differential pressure of 0.01" w.c. (2.5 Pa).

5.8.1.3 These procedures may also be performed in a room that meets the ventilation requirements for airborne infection control. See Table 2.1-2 for airborne infection isolation room ventilation requirements.

5.8.2 Outpatient Testing and Demonstration

If respiratory services such as testing and demonstration for outpatients are part of the program, additional facilities and equipment shall be provided as necessary for the appropriate function of the service, including but not limited to the following:

5.8.2.1 A reception and control station

5.8.2.2 Room(s) for patient education and demonstration

5.8.2.3 Patient waiting area with provision for wheelchairs

5.8.2.4 Patient toilets and hand-washing stations

5.8.3 Space and Utilities for Cleaning and Disinfecting Equipment

5.8.3.1 The space for receiving and cleaning soiled materials shall be physically separated from the space for storage of clean equipment and supplies.

5.8.3.2 Appropriate local exhaust ventilation shall be provided if glutaraldehyde or other noxious disinfectants are used in the cleaning process.

5.8.4 Storage for Equipment and Supplies

5.9 Renal Dialysis Unit (Acute and Chronic)

5.9.1 General

5.9.1.1 Functional program. Equipment and space shall be provided as necessary to meet the functional program, which may include treatment for acute (inpatient) and chronic cases, home treatment, and kidney dialyzer reuse facilities.

5.9.1.2 Location

(1) The location shall offer convenient access for outpatients. Accessibility to the unit from parking and public transportation shall be a consideration.

(2) Inpatient services are permitted in critical care units and designated areas in the hospital with appropriate utilities.

5.9.2 Treatment Area

5.9.2.1 Layout. The treatment area shall be permitted to be an open area and shall be separate from administrative and waiting areas.

5.9.2.2 Space requirements

(1) Area. Individual patient treatment areas shall contain at least 80 square feet (7.43 square meters), exclusive of general circulation space within the ward.

(2) Clearance. There shall be at least a 4-foot (1.22 meters) space between beds and/or lounge chairs.

5.9.2.3 Privacy. The open unit shall be designed to provide privacy for each patient.

5.9.2.4 Nurse station(s). These shall be located within the dialysis treatment area and designed to provide visual observation of all patient stations.

5.9.2.5 Hand-washing stations

(1) Hand-washing stations shall be convenient to the nurse station and patient treatment areas.

(2) There shall be at least one hand-washing station serving no more than four stations.

(3) The hand-washing stations shall be uniformly distributed to provide equal access from each patient station.

5.9.2.6 Patient toilet. A patient toilet with hand-washing stations shall be provided.

5.9.2.7 Stat laboratory

(1) If a stat laboratory for blood and urinalysis is provided, the stat laboratory shall contain a hand-washing station, work counters, storage spaces, an undercounter refrigerator for specimens, and a cup sink.

(2) An area for the phlebotomists' use shall be provided adjacent to the laboratory.

(3) A pass-through for specimens shall be provided between the patient toilet room and the laboratory.

5.9.2.8 Private treatment area. If home training is provided in the unit, a private treatment area shall be provided.

(1) A private treatment area of at least 120 square feet (11.15 square meters) shall be provided for patients who are being trained to use dialysis equipment at home.

(2) This room shall contain a counter, hand-washing stations, and a separate drain for fluid disposal.

5.9.2.9 Airborne infection isolation room(s). The number of and need for required airborne infection isolation rooms shall be determined by an ICRA. When required, the airborne infection isolation room(s) shall comply with the requirements of Section 2.1-3.2.2.

5.9.3 Examination Room
An examination room with hand-washing stations and writing surface shall be provided with at least 100 square feet (9.29 square meters).

5.9.4 Support Areas for the Renal Dialysis Unit
5.9.4.1 Administrative space. Office and clinical workspace shall be available for administrative services.

5.9.4.2 Medication dispensing station. If required by the functional program, there shall be a medication dispensing station for the dialysis center.

(1) A work counter and hand-washing stations shall be included in this area.

(2) Provisions shall be made for the controlled storage, preparation, distribution, and refrigeration of medications.

5.9.4.3 Nourishment station. If a nourishment station for the dialysis service is provided, it shall contain a hand-washing station, a work counter, a refrigerator, storage cabinets, a water-dispensing unit separate from the hand-washing station, and equipment for serving nourishments as required. The nourishment station shall be located away from the treatment area to prevent the risk of cross-contamination.

5.9.4.4 Dialyzer reprocessing room. If dialyzers are reused, a reprocessing room sized to perform the functions required shall be provided.

(1) This room shall include a one-way flow of materials from soiled to clean.

(2) This room shall include provisions for refrigeration for temporary storage of dialyzers, decontamination/cleaning areas, sinks, processors, computer processors and label printers, a packaging area, and dialyzer storage cabinets.

5.9.4.5 Mixing room and delivery system. Each facility using a central batch delivery system shall provide, either on the premises or through written arrangements, individual delivery systems for the treatment of any patient requiring special dialysis solutions. The mixing room shall include a sink, storage space, and holding tanks.

5.9.4.6 Water treatment equipment room. The water treatment equipment shall be located in an enclosed room.

5.9.4.7 Equipment repair room. If required by the functional program, an equipment repair and breakdown room shall be equipped with a hand-washing station, deep service sink, work counter, and storage cabinet.

5.9.4.8 Clean workroom or supply room. A clean workroom shall be provided. Soiled and clean workrooms or holding rooms shall be separated and have no direct connection.

(1) Clean workroom. If the room is used for preparing patient care items, it shall contain a work counter, a hand-washing station, and storage facilities for clean and sterile supplies.

(2) Clean supply room. If the room is used only for storage and holding as part of a system for distri-

bution of clean and sterile materials, the work counter and hand-washing station may be omitted.

5.9.4.9 Soiled workroom. A soiled workroom shall be provided and contain a flushing-rim sink, hand-washing station, work counter, storage cabinets, waste receptacles, and a soiled linen receptacle.

5.9.4.10 Equipment and supply storage

(1) Clean linen storage. A clean linen storage area shall be provided. It may be within the clean workroom, a separate closet, or an approved distribution system. If a closed cart system is used, storage may be in an alcove. It must be out of the path of normal traffic and under staff control.

(2) Supply areas/carts. Supply areas or supply carts shall be provided.

(3) Stretcher/wheelchair storage. If stretchers are provided, storage space shall be available for wheelchairs and stretchers, out of direct line of traffic.

5.9.4.11 Environmental services closet. An environmental services closet shall be provided adjacent to and for the exclusive use of the unit.

(1) The closet shall contain a floor receptor or service sink and storage space for housekeeping supplies and equipment.

(2) Water supply and drain connection for testing machines shall be provided.

5.9.5 Support Areas for Staff
Appropriate staff clothing change areas and lounge shall be available for male and female personnel. The areas shall contain lockers, shower, toilet, and hand-washing stations.

5.9.6 Support Areas for Patients
5.9.6.1 Patient support provisions. A waiting room, toilet room with hand-washing stations, source of drinking water, public telephone, and seating accommodations for waiting periods shall be available or accessible to the dialysis unit.

5.9.6.2 Patient storage. Storage for patients' belongings shall be provided.

5.9.7 Diagnostic Areas

5.9.7.1 Laboratory space. If required by the functional program, a laboratory space, including counters, sinks, cabinets, label machines, computers, and hand-washing sinks, shall be provided to accommodate processing of blood draws and urine samples.

5.9.8 Construction Requirements

*5.9.8.1 Piping. Design consideration shall be given to the disposal of liquid waste from the dialyzing process to prevent odor and backflow.

*5.9.8.2 Temperature/humidity control

*5.10 Hyperbaric Suite

APPENDIX

A5.9.8.1 All installed reverse osmosis water and dialysis solution piping should be accessible.

A5.9.8.2 Due to the nature of the dialyzing process and the nature of the patient's illness, the temperature should be maintained at 72° to 78°F (22° to 26°C) with a relative humidity level of 30 to 60 percent.

A5.10 Hyperbaric Suite
Applicability
These guidelines should apply to hyperbaric facilities designated for clinical hyperbaric oxygen therapy, including hospital-affiliated and freestanding facilities.

General Facility Requirements
Hyperbaric chambers should be constructed in conformance with applicable construction codes (ASME PVHO-1, Safety Standard for Pressure Vessels for Human Occupancy) and carry a "U" stamp.

The facility should be constructed to comply with applicable local, state, and national construction codes governing the type of occupancy (health care, commercial, other) housing the hyperbaric chamber(s).

When a hyperbaric suite/clinic is provided, it should meet the requirements of Chapter 20, NFPA 99, and Chapter 12, NFPA 101.

Multiplace (NFPA Class "A" Chamber) Facilities
Emergency exit requirements
a. The facility housing a Class A chamber should be designed to allow rapid or emergency removal of patients and staff.

b. In the case of multiple Class A chambers installed in a single setting or a Class A chamber that contains multiple compartments, the rapid or emergency removal of a patient or personnel from one chamber/compartment should not restrict in any way the rapid and simultaneous removal of patients or personnel from all other chambers or compartments.

c. A minimum of two exits should be provided for the chamber room unless a single exit opens directly to a primary evacuation hallway.

Space requirements
The space required to house Class A chambers and supporting equipment should be defined by NFPA 99, Chapter 20 and the equipment manufacturer, but in any case should not be less than the following:

a. Minimum clearances around a (Class A) hyperbaric chamber should be as follows:

b. Chamber entry should be designed for gurney/stretcher access: 10 feet (3.04 meters).

c. Entries designed for wheeled gurneys should be provided with access ramps that are flush with the chamber entry doorway.

d. Chambers that utilize fixed internal stretcher frames and transfer gurneys should be designed to allow immediate removal of the patient upon chamber depressurization.

e. Chamber man lock entries or compartments utilizing circular entry hatchways: 4 feet (1.21 meters).

f. The chamber should have a minimum of 4 feet (1.21 meters) of clearance all the way around the chamber, except as specified with regard to entry areas.

g. If the chamber control console is immediately adjacent to the chamber, a minimum passageway of 4 feet (1.21 meters) should be provided between the control console and any obstruction.

Monoplace (Class B) Facilities
Emergency exit requirements
a. In the case of multiple Class B chambers installed in a single setting, the rapid or emergency removal of a patient from one chamber should not restrict in any way the rapid and simultaneous removal of patients from all other chambers.

b. A minimum of two exits should be provided for the chamber room unless a single exit opens directly to a primary evacuation hallway.

c. Exit doorways should have a minimum opening of 46 inches. (1.16 meters)

Space requirements

The space required to house Class B chambers and supporting equipment should be defined by the equipment manufacturer, but in any case should not be less than the following:

The space housing Class B chambers should conform to NFPA 99, Chapter 20 requirements.

Minimum clearances between individual (Class B) hyperbaric chambers should be as follows:

a. Chamber and side wall, 18 inches (45.72 centimeters). Exception: If any chamber controls, ventilation valves, or other operator-adjustable devices are located on or under the chamber adjacent to the side wall, minimum clearance should be 36 inches (91.44 centimeters).

b. Between control side of two chambers, 48 inches (1.21 meters).

c. Between back side of two chambers, 24 inches (60.96 centimeters)

d. A minimum passage of 14 inches (35.56 centimeters) should be provided at the foot end of each chamber. An oxygen shut-off valve should be provided for each chamber and should be unobstructed by the chamber and located as to be immediately accessible to the chamber operator.

e. A minimum space of 102 inches (2.59 meters) should be available at the head end of the chamber to allow for the safe insertion and removal of the patient from the chamber.

f. Any electrical service outlets located within 10 feet of the Class B chamber entrance should be sited no less than 3 feet (0.91 meter) above floor level.

Support Areas

The following support areas should be provided for the hyperbaric facility. If the hyperbaric facility is included as an integral portion of another service such as a wound care department, support areas may be shared:

Support areas for the hyperbaric suite

a. Reception/control desk

b. Patient waiting area. The waiting area should be large enough to accommodate the clinical program and chamber mix if also used as a holding area. The area should be out of traffic, under staff control, and should have seating capacity in accordance with the functional program. When the hyperbaric suite is routinely used for outpatients and inpatients at the same time, separate waiting areas should be provided with screening for visual privacy between the waiting areas. Patient waiting areas may be omitted for two or fewer Class B hyperbaric chamber units.

c. Holding area. The area should be out of traffic flow from the chamber and should not obstruct access to the exits. A holding area under staff control should accommodate inpatients on stretchers or beds. Stretcher patients should be out of the direct line of normal traffic. The patient holding area may be omitted for two or less individual hyperbaric chamber units.

d. Consultation/treatment rooms. Appropriate room for individual consultation and treatment with referring clinicians should be provided.

e. Patient record storage area. An area should be provided that is out of traffic flow and under staff control. This can be in the clinical area or located at the reception/control desk.

f. Hand-washing stations. A lavatory equipped for hand-washing with hands-free operable controls should be located in the room where the hyperbaric chambers are located.

g. Compressor room. This area should be large enough to house the chamber compressors, accumulator tanks, fire suppression system and their ability to meet the requirements of NFPA 99, Chapter 20. The reserve breathing gases could also be housed here if it is in close proximity to the chamber room.

h. Soiled holding area. A soiled holding room should be provided with waste receptacles and soiled linen receptacles.

i. Equipment and supply storage

Clean supply and linen storage. A clean storage space should be provided for clean supplies and linens. Hand-washing fixtures should be provided with hands-free operable controls. When a separate storage room is provided, it may be shared with another department.

Gas cylinder room. This room should be large enough to accommodate the storage of enough (H) cylinders and manifolds for the reserve breathing gases required for chamber operations. The minimum room size should be able to house eight (H) cylinders and two gas manifolds, consisting of at least two (H) cylinders on each manifold.

j. Housekeeping room. The housekeeping room should contain a floor receptor or service sink and storage space for housekeeping supplies and equipment, and should be located nearby.

Support areas for staff

Toilets with hand-washing fixtures with hands-free operable controls may be outside the suite but should be convenient for staff use.

Support areas for patients

a. Patient dressing rooms. Dressing rooms for outpatients should be provided and should include a seat or bench, mirror, and provisions for hanging patients' clothing and for securing valuables. At least one dressing room should be provided to accommodate wheelchair patients.

b. Patient toilet rooms. Toilet rooms should be provided with hand-washing fixtures with hands-free operable controls with direct access from the hyperbaric suite.

5.11 Laboratory Suite

5.11.1 General

5.11.1.1 Type. Laboratory facilities shall be provided for the performance of tests in hematology, clinical chemistry, urinalysis, microbiology, anatomic pathology, cytology, and blood banking to meet the workload described in the functional program.

5.11.1.2 Location. Certain procedures may be performed on-site or provided through a contractual arrangement with a laboratory service acceptable to the authority having local jurisdiction.

(1) Provisions shall be made for the following procedures to be performed on-site: blood counts, urinalysis, blood glucose, electrolytes, blood urea and nitrogen (BUN), coagulation, transfusions (type and cross-match capability), and stat gram stains.

(2) Provisions shall be included for specimen collection and processing.

5.11.1.3 Equipment requirements. The functional program shall describe the type and location of all special equipment that is to be wired, plumbed, or plugged in, and the utilities required to operate each.

Note: Refer to NFPA code requirements applicable to hospital laboratories, including standards clarifying that hospital units do not necessarily have the same fire safety requirements as commercial chemical laboratories.

5.11.2 Facility Requirements
The following physical facilities shall be provided within the hospital:

5.11.2.1 Work areas

(1) Laboratory work counter(s) with space for microscopes, appropriate chemical analyzer(s), incubator(s), centrifuge(s), biosafety hoods, etc. shall be provided.

(2) Work areas shall include sinks with water and access to vacuum, gases, and air, and electrical services as needed.

5.11.2.2 Hand-washing stations. These shall be located within 25 feet (7.62 meters) of each workstation and within each room with a workstation.

5.11.2.3 Design considerations

(1) Chemical safety provisions. These shall include emergency shower, eye-flushing devices, and appropriate storage for flammable liquids, etc.

(2) Terminal sterilization provisions. Facilities and equipment shall be provided for terminal sterilization of contaminated specimens before transport (autoclave or electric oven). (Terminal sterilization is not required for specimens that are incinerated on-site.)

(3) Radioactive material-handling provisions. If radioactive materials are employed, facilities for long-term storage and disposal of these materials shall be provided. No special provisions shall normally be required for body waste products from most patients receiving low-level isotope diagnostic material. Requirements of authorities having jurisdiction shall be verified.

5.11.2.4 Support areas for the laboratory suite

(1) Administrative areas. These shall include offices as well as space for clerical work, filing, and record maintenance.

(2) Refrigerated blood storage facilities. A refrigerator to store blood for transfusions shall be equipped with temperature-monitoring and alarm signals.

*(3) Storage facilities for reagents, standards, supplies, and stained specimen microscope slides, etc. These shall include refrigeration. Such facilities shall conform to applicable NFPA standards.

(4) A specimen collection facility. This facility may be located outside the laboratory suite.

(a) The blood collection area shall have a work counter, space for patient seating, and hand-washing stations.

(b) The urine and feces collection facility shall be equipped with a water closet and hand-washing station.

5.11.2.5 Support areas for staff. Lounge, locker, and toilet facilities shall be conveniently located for male and female laboratory staff. Location of these areas outside the laboratory area and sharing of these areas with other departments shall be permitted.

5.12 Morgue

5.12.1 Location
These facilities shall be accessible through an exterior entrance and shall be located to avoid the need for transporting bodies through public areas.

*5.12.2 Autopsy Facilities
If autopsies are performed in the hospital, the following elements shall be provided:

5.12.2.1 Refrigerated facilities for body holding. Body-holding refrigerators shall be equipped with temperature-monitoring and alarm signals.

5.12.2.2 An autopsy room. This shall contain the following:

(1) A work counter with a hand-washing station

(2) A storage space for supplies, equipment, and specimens

(3) An autopsy table

(4) A deep sink for washing specimens

5.12.2.3 Housekeeping facilities. A housekeeping service sink or receptor shall be provided for cleanup and housekeeping.

5.12.3 Body-Holding Room
If autopsies are performed outside the facility, a well-ventilated, temperature-controlled body-holding room shall be provided.

6 Service Areas

6.1 Pharmacy

6.1.1 General
6.1.1.1 Functional program. The size and type of services to be provided in the pharmacy will depend upon the type of drug distribution system used, number of patients to be served, and extent of shared or purchased services. These factors shall be described in the functional program.

6.1.1.2 Location. The pharmacy room or suite shall be located for convenient access, staff control, and security.

6.1.1.3 Facility requirements

(1) Facilities and equipment shall be as necessary to accommodate the functional program. (Satellite facilities, if provided, shall include those items required by the program.)

(2) As a minimum, the following elements shall be provided:

6.1.2 Dispensing Facilities
6.1.2.1 A room or area for receiving, breakout, and inventory control of materials used in the pharmacy

6.1.2.2 Work counters and space for automated and manual dispensing activities

***6.1.2.3** An extemporaneous compounding area. This shall include a sink and sufficient counter space for drug preparation.

6.1.2.4 An area for reviewing and recording

6.1.2.5 An area for temporary storage, exchange, and restocking of carts

> **APPENDIX**
>
> **A5.12.2** Autopsy rooms should be equipped with downdraft local exhaust ventilation.
>
> **A6.1.2.3** Floor drainage may also be required, depending on the extent of compounding conducted.

6.1.2.6 Security provisions for drugs and personnel in the dispensing counter area, if one is provided

6.1.3 Manufacturing Facilities

6.1.3.1 A bulk compounding area

6.1.3.2 Provisions for packaging and labeling

6.1.3.3 A quality-control area

6.1.4 Storage

Cabinets, shelves, and/or separate rooms or closets shall be provided.

6.1.4.1 Bulk storage

6.1.4.2 Active storage

6.1.4.3 Refrigerated storage

6.1.4.4 Storage for volatile fluids and alcohol. This shall be constructed according to applicable fire safety codes for the substances involved.

6.1.4.5 Storage for narcotics and controlled drugs. Secure storage shall be provided for narcotics and controlled drugs

6.1.4.6 Equipment and supply storage. Storage shall be provided for general supplies and equipment not in use.

6.1.5 Support Areas for the Pharmacy

6.1.5.1 Patient information. Provision shall be made for cross-checking medication and drug profiles of individual patients.

6.1.5.2 Pharmacological information. Poison control, reaction data, and drug information centers

6.1.5.3 Office. A separate room or area shall be provided for office functions. This room shall include space to accommodate a desk, filing capabilities, communication equipment, and reference materials.

APPENDIX

A6.2.1.1 Consideration may also be required for meals to VIP suites and for cafeterias for staff, ambulatory patients, and visitors, as well as providing for nourishments and snacks between scheduled meal service.

6.1.5.4 Provisions for patient counseling and instruction. A room separate from the pharmacy shall be permitted to meet this requirement.

6.1.5.5 A room for education and training. A multipurpose room shared with other departments shall be permitted to serve this purpose.

6.1.5.6 Outpatient consultation/education area. If the functional program requires dispensing of medication to outpatients, an area for consultation and patient education shall be provided.

6.1.5.7 Hand-washing stations. Hand-washing stations shall be provided within each separate room where open medication is prepared for administration.

6.1.5.8 Sterile work area. If intravenous (IV) solutions are prepared in the pharmacy, a sterile work area with a laminar-flow workstation designed for product protection shall be provided. The laminar-flow workstation shall include a nonhydroscopic filter rated at 99.97 percent (HEPA), as tested by dioctyl-phtalate (DOP) tests, and have a visible pressure gauge for detection of filter leaks or defects.

6.1.5.9 Additional equipment and supply storage. If unit dose procedure is used, additional space and equipment for supplies, packaging, labeling, and storage, as well as for the carts.

6.1.6 Support Areas for Staff

6.1.6.1 Staff toilet. Convenient access to toilet shall be provided.

6.1.6.2 Staff storage. Convenient access to locker shall be provided.

6.2 Dietary Facilities

6.2.1 General

*6.2.1.1 Applicability. Food service facilities shall provide food service for staff, visitors, inpatients, and outpatients in accordance with the functional program.

6.2.1.2 Location. Patient food preparation areas shall be located adjacent to delivery, interior transportation, and storage facilities.

6.2.1.3 Standards. Food service facilities and equipment shall conform to these standards and to the standards of the National Sanitation Foundation and other applicable codes.

6.2.1.4 Construction requirements. Finishes in the dietary facility shall be selected to ensure cleanability and the maintenance of sanitary conditions.

6.2.2 Functional Elements

If on-site conventional food service preparation is used, the following shall be provided, in size and number appropriate for the functional program:

6.2.2.1 Receiving/control stations. An area for receiving and control of incoming dietary supplies shall be provided.

(1) This area shall be separated from the general receiving area

(2) It shall contain a control station and a breakout area for loading, uncrating, and weighing supplies.

6.2.2.2 Hand-washing stations. Hands-free operable hand-washing stations shall be conveniently accessible at locations throughout the unit.

6.2.2.3 Food preparation work spaces

(1) Work spaces shall be provided for food preparation, cooking, and baking. These areas shall be as close as possible to the user (i.e., tray assembly and dining).

(2) Additional spaces shall be provided for thawing and portioning.

6.2.2.4 Assembly and distribution. A patient tray assembly area shall be close to the food preparation and distribution areas.

6.2.2.5 Food service carts

(1) A cart distribution system shall be provided, with spaces for storage, loading, distribution, receiving, and sanitizing of the food service carts.

(2) The cart traffic shall be designed to eliminate any danger of cross-circulation between outgoing food carts and incoming, soiled carts, and the cleaning and sanitizing process. Cart circulation shall not be through food processing areas.

6.2.2.6 Dining area. Dining space(s) shall be provided for ambulatory patients, staff, and visitors. These spaces shall be separate from the food preparation and distribution areas.

6.2.2.7 Area for receiving, scraping, and sorting soiled tableware. This shall be adjacent to ware-washing and separate from food preparation areas.

6.2.2.8 Ware-washing facilities

(1) These shall be designed to prevent contamination of clean wares with soiled wares through cross-traffic.

(2) The clean wares shall be transferred for storage or use in the dining area without having to pass through food preparation areas.

6.2.2.9 Pot-washing facilities

(1) These shall include multi-compartmented sinks of adequate size for the intended use, convenient to the using service.

(2) Supplemental heat for hot water to clean pots and pans shall be by booster heater, steam jet, or other appropriate means.

(3) Mobile carts or other provisions shall be made for drying and storing pots and pans.

6.2.2.10 Facilities for commissary or contract services from other areas

(1) Provision shall be made to protect food delivered to ensure freshness, retain hot and cold, and avoid contamination. If delivery is from outside sources, protection against weather shall be provided.

(2) Provision shall be made for thorough cleaning and sanitizing of equipment to avoid mixing soiled and clean equipment.

6.2.2.11 Vending services. If vending devices are used for unscheduled meals, a separate room shall be provided that can be accessed without having to enter the main dining area.

(1) The vending room shall contain coin-operated machines, bill changers, a hand-washing station, and a sitting area.

(2) Facilities for servicing and sanitizing the machines shall be provided as part of the facility's food service program.

6.2.3 Support Areas for Dietary Facilities
6.2.3.1 Office spaces. Offices for the use of the food service manager shall be provided. In smaller facilities, this space may be located in an area that is part of the food preparation area.

6.2.3.2 Equipment

(1) Mechanical devices shall be heavy-duty, suitable for use intended, and easily cleaned.

(2) Where equipment is movable, heavy-duty locking casters shall be provided. If equipment is to have fixed utility connections, the equipment shall not be equipped with casters.

(3) Walk-in coolers, refrigerators, and freezers shall be insulated at floor as well as at walls and top.

(4) Coolers, refrigerators, and freezers shall be thermostatically controlled to maintain desired temperature settings in increments of 2 degrees or less.

   (a) Coolers and refrigerators shall be capable of maintaining a temperature down to freezing.

   (b) Freezers shall be capable of maintaining a temperature of 20 degrees below 0° F.

   (c) Interior temperatures shall be indicated digitally so as to be visible from the exterior. Controls shall include audible and visible high and low temperature alarm. Time of alarm shall be automatically recorded.

(5) Walk-in units

   (a) These may be lockable from outside but must have release mechanism for exit from inside at all times.

   (b) Interior shall be lighted.

   (c) All shelving shall be corrosion resistant, easily cleaned, and constructed and anchored to support a loading of at least 100 pounds per linear foot.

(6) Cooking equipment. All cooking equipment shall be equipped with automatic shutoff devices to prevent excessive heat buildup.

(7) Ice-making equipment

   (a) This equipment shall be convenient for service and easily cleaned.

   (b) It shall be provided for both drinks and food products (self-dispensing equipment) and for general use (storage-bin type equipment).

(8) Construction requirements. Under-counter conduits, piping, and drains shall be arranged to not interfere with cleaning of the equipment or of the floor below.

6.2.3.3 Equipment and supply storage

(1) General. Storage spaces shall be convenient to the receiving area and accessible without traveling through the food preparation area.

(2) Food storage

   (a) Storage spaces for bulk, refrigerated, and frozen foods shall be provided. Provision shall be made for storage of a minimum of four days' supplies.

   (b) Food storage components shall be grouped for convenient access to the receiving and food preparation areas.

   (c) All food shall be stored clear of the floor. Lowest shelf shall be not less than 12 inches (30.48 centimeters) above the floor or shall be closed in and sealed tight for ease of cleaning.

(3) Additional storage rooms. These shall be provided as necessary for the storage of cooking wares, extra trays, flatware, plastic and paper products, and portable equipment.

(4) Cleaning supplies storage. A separate storage room shall be provided for the storage of nonfood items such as cleaning supplies that might contaminate edibles.

6.2.3.4 Housekeeping rooms

(1) These shall be provided for the exclusive use of the dietary department and shall contain a floor sink and space for mops, pails, and supplies.

(2) Where hot water or steam is used for general cleaning, additional space within the room shall be provided for the storage of hoses and nozzles.

6.2.4 Support Areas for Staff
6.2.4.1 Toilets, lockers, and lounges. Toilets, lockers and lounge facilities shall be convenient to the dietary department. These facilities shall be permitted to be shared with adjacent services provided they are adequately sized.

6.3 Central Services
The following shall be provided:

6.3.1 Soiled and Clean Work Areas
The soiled and clean work areas shall be physically separated.

6.3.1.1 Soiled workroom

(1) This room shall be physically separated from all other areas of the department.

(2) Work space shall be provided to handle the cleaning and initial sterilization/disinfection of all medical/surgical instruments and equipment. Work tables, sinks, flush-type devices, and washer/sterilizer decontaminators shall be provided.

(3) Pass-through doors and washer/sterilizer deconta-

minators shall deliver into clean processing area/workrooms.

***6.3.1.2** Clean assembly/workroom. This workroom shall contain hand-washing stations, work space, and equipment for terminal sterilizing of medical and surgical equipment and supplies.

6.3.2 Equipment and Supply Storage Areas
6.3.2.1 Clean/sterile medical/surgical supplies

(1) A room for breakdown shall be provided for manufacturers' clean/sterile supplies. The clean processing area shall not be in this area but in an adjacent space.

(2) Storage for packs, etc., shall include provisions for ventilation, humidity, and temperature control.

6.3.2.2 Storage room for patient care and distribution carts. This area shall be adjacent and easily available to clean and sterile storage and close to the main distribution point to keep traffic to a minimum and ease work flow.

6.3.3 Support Areas for Staff
6.3.3.1 Administrative/changing room. If required by the functional program, this room shall be separate from all other areas and provide for staff to change from street clothes into work attire.

6.3.3.2 Staff accommodations. Lockers, hand-washing

APPENDIX

A6.3.1.2 Sterilization room. This room is used exclusively for the inspection, assembly, and packaging of medical/surgical supplies and equipment for sterilization.

a. Access to the sterilization room should be restricted.

b. This room should contain Hi-Vacuum or gravity steam sterilizers and sterilization equipment to accommodate heat-sensitive equipment (ETO sterilizer) and ETO aerators.

c. It should contain worktables, counters, a hand-washing station, ultrasonic storage facilities for backup supplies and instrumentation, and a drying cabinet or equipment.

d. The area should be spacious enough to hold sterilizer carts for loading of prepared supplies for sterilization.

station, and showers shall be made available within the immediate vicinity of the department.

6.4 Linen Services

6.4.1 General
Each facility shall have provisions for storing and processing of clean and soiled linen for appropriate patient care. Processing may be done within the facility, in a separate building on- or off-site, or in a commercial or shared laundry.

6.4.2 Internal Linen Processing
Facilities and equipment shall be as required for cost-effective operation as described in the functional program. At a minimum, the following elements shall be provided:

6.4.2.1 Soiled linen holding room. A separate room shall be provided for receiving and holding soiled linen until ready for pickup or processing.

6.4.2.2 Clean linen storage. A central clean linen storage and issuing room(s) shall be provided in addition to the linen storage required at individual patient units.

6.4.2.3 Cart storage area(s). These shall be provided for separate parking of clean- and soiled-linen carts out of traffic.

6.4.2.4 A clean linen inspection and mending room or area. If not provided elsewhere, a clean linen inspection, delinting, folding, assembly, and packaging area shall be provided as part of the linen services.

(1) Mending shall be provided for in the linen services department.

(2) A space for tables, shelving, and storage shall be provided.

6.4.2.5 Hand-washing stations. These shall be provided in each area where unbagged, soiled linen is handled.

APPENDIX

A6.4.4.3 This may require a capacity for processing a seven-day supply in a 40-hour week.

6.4.3 Additional Areas for Outside Laundry Services
If linen is processed outside the building, provisions shall also be made for:

6.4.3.1 Service entrance. A service entrance, protected from inclement weather, shall be provided for loading and unloading of linen.

6.4.3.2 Control station. A control station shall be provided for pickup and receiving.

6.4.4 On-Site Laundry Facility
If linen is processed in a laundry facility that is part of the project (within or as a separate building), the following shall be provided in addition to the requirements for internal processing facilities in Section 2.1-6.4.2.

6.4.4.1 Layout. Equipment shall be arranged to permit an orderly work flow and minimize cross-traffic that might mix clean and soiled operations.

6.4.4.2 Control and distribution room. A receiving, holding, and sorting room shall be provided for control and distribution of soiled linen. Discharge from soiled linen chutes shall be received in a separate room adjacent to it.

*6.4.4.3 Laundry processing room. This shall have commercial or industrial-type equipment that can process at least a seven-day supply within the regular scheduled work week.

6.4.4.4 Hand-washing stations. Employee hand-washing stations shall be provided in each room where clean or soiled linen is processed and handled.

6.4.4.5 Storage for laundry supplies

6.4.4.6 Staff support locations. Conveniently accessible staff lockers, showers, and lounge shall be provided.

6.4.5 Linen Chutes
If provided, these shall meet or exceed the following standards:

6.4.5.1 Standards

(1) Service openings to chutes shall comply with NFPA 101.

(2) Chutes shall meet the provisions described in NFPA 82.

(3) Chute discharge into collection rooms shall comply with NFPA 101.

6.4.5.2 Dimensions. The minimum cross-sectional dimension of gravity chutes shall be 2 feet (60.96 centimeters).

6.5 Materials Management

6.5.1 Receiving
The following shall be provided:

6.5.1.1 Off-street unloading facilities

6.5.1.2 Receiving area
Adequate receiving areas shall be provided to accommodate delivery trucks and other vehicles.

*(1) Location

(a) Dock areas shall be segregaged from other occupied building areas and located so that noise and odors from operation will not adversely affect building occupants.

(b) The receiving area shall be convenient to service elevators and other internal corridor systems.

(c) Receiving areas shall be segregated from waste staging and other outgoing materials-handling functions.

(2) Space requirements

(a) Adequate space shall be provided to enable breakdown, sorting, and staging of incoming materials and supplies.

(b) Balers and other devices shall be located to capture packaging for recycling or return to manufacturer or deliverer.

(c) In facilities with centralized warehousing, adequate space shall be provided at receiving points to permit the staging of reusable

transport containers for supplies moving from central warehouses to individual receiving sites.

6.5.2 General Stores
In addition to supply facilities in individual departments, a central storage area shall be provided.

6.5.2.1 General
General stores may be located in a separate building on site with provisions for protection against inclement weather during transfer of supplies. The following shall be provided:

6.5.2.2 General storage room(s)

(1) Location. Location of storage in separate, concentrated areas within the institution or in one or more individual buildings on site shall be permitted. Off-site location for a portion of this storage shall be permitted.

(2) Space requirements. General storage room(s) with a total area of not less than 20 square feet (1.86 square meters) per inpatient bed shall be provided.

6.5.2.3 Additional storage areas for outpatient facilities

(1) Location. Location of additional storage areas in combination with and in addition to the general stores, or in a central area within the outpatient department, shall be permitted. Off-site location for a portion of this storage shall also be permitted.

(2) Space requirements. Additional storage areas for outpatient facilities shall be provided in an amount not less than 5 percent of the total area of those facilities.

6.5.3 Waste Management
*6.5.3.1 Collection and storage. Waste collection and storage locations shall be determined by the facility as a component of the functional program.

APPENDIX

A6.5.1.2 (1) The receiving area should be located to promote the safe, secure, and efficient movement of arriving materials without compromising patient areas.

(1) Location

   (a) The location of compactors, balers, sharps, and recycling container staging at docks or other waste removal areas shall be stipulated by the functional program.

   (b) Red bag waste shall be staged in enclosed and secured areas. Biohazardous and environmentally hazardous materials, including mercury, nuclear reagent waste, and other regulated waste types, shall be segregated and secured.

(2) Space requirements

   (a) The functional program shall stipulate the categories and volumes of waste for disposal and the methods of handling and disposal of waste.

   (b) The functional program shall outline the space requirements, including centralized waste collection and storage spaces. Size of spaces shall be based upon the volume of projected waste and length of anticipated storage.

(3) Regulated waste storage spaces

   (a) If provided, regulated medical waste or infectious waste storage spaces shall have a floor drain, cleanable floor and wall surfaces, lighting, and exhaust ventilation, and should be safe from weather, animals and unauthorized entry.

   (b) Refrigeration requirements for such storage facilities shall comply with state and/or local regulations.

6.5.3.2 Refuse chutes. If provided, these shall meet or exceed the following standards:

(1) Chutes shall meet the provisions described in NFPA 82.

(2) Service openings to chutes shall comply with NFPA 101.

(3) Chute discharge into collection rooms shall comply with NFPA 101.

(4) The minimum cross-sectional dimension of gravity chutes shall be 2 feet (60.96 centimeters).

Note: See Section 2.1-9.3 for text on waste processing.

6.6 Environmental Services

6.6.1 Facilities for Cleaning and Sanitizing Carts
Facilities shall be provided to clean and sanitize carts

APPENDIX

A6.5.3.1 Collection and storage. The underlying framework of waste management comprises waste minimization and segregation. Facilities should seek both to minimize all components of each waste stream and to separate different components of the total waste stream. At a minimum, the functional program should include consideration of regular trash, medical/infectious waste, hazardous waste, and low-level radioactive waste.

The program should address the development of effective collection, transport, pest control, and storage systems; waste management and contingency planning; protection of the health and safety of workers; and proper siting of all on-site waste treatment technologies.

Optimizing waste management has programmatic and space impacts throughout the facility at points where waste is generated, collected, and staged for disposal. For facilities or municipalities with recycling programs in place, particular consideration should be given to sorting and staging areas. The following elements are examples that may be considered:

a. Building should include adequate space to accommodate bins/carts for appropriate waste segregation such as recyclables, infectious waste, sharps, etc. Corridors and materials handling systems should be designed to achieve an efficient movement of waste from points of generation to storage or treatment while minimizing the risk to personnel.

b. Dedicated storage and flow space and cleaning/sanitation facilities should facilitate reuse of items such as medical products, food service items, and the like to eliminate disposables and reduce waste.

c. Space should be included for autoclaves, shredders, and other technologies for processing medical waste prior to removals to landfill. Secure storage should be provided for staging fluorescent lamps for recycling.

serving the central service department, dietary facilities, and linen services. These facilities shall be permitted to be centralized or departmentalized.

6.6.2 Housekeeping Rooms
In addition to the housekeeping rooms required in certain departments, sufficient housekeeping rooms shall be provided throughout the facility to maintain a clean and sanitary environment.

6.6.2.1 Number. There shall not be fewer than one housekeeping room for each floor.

6.6.2.2 Facility requirements. Each shall contain a floor receptor or service sink and storage space for house-keeping equipment and supplies.

6.7 Engineering Services and Maintenance

6.7.1 General
Sufficient space shall be included in all mechanical and electrical equipment rooms for proper maintenance of equipment. Provisions shall also be made for removal and replacement of equipment. The following shall be provided:

6.7.2 Equipment Locations
Room(s) or separate building(s) shall be provided for boilers, mechanical, and electrical equipment, except:

6.7.2.1 Rooftop air conditioning and ventilation equipment installed in weatherproof housings

6.7.2.2 Standby generators where the engine and appropriate accessories (i.e., batteries) are properly heated and enclosed in a weatherproof housing

6.7.2.3 Cooling towers and heat rejection equipment

6.7.2.4 Electrical transformers and switchgear where required to serve the facility and where installed in a weatherproof housing

6.7.2.5 Medical gas parks and equipment

6.7.2.6 Air-cooled chillers where installed in a weather-proof housing

6.7.2.7 Trash compactors and incinerators

6.7.2.8 Site lighting, post indicator valves, and other equipment normally installed on the exterior of the building

6.7.3 Engineer's Office
This shall have file space and provisions for protected storage of facility drawings, records, manuals, etc.

6.7.4 General Maintenance Shop(s)
These shall be provided to accommodate repair and maintenance requirements.

6.7.5 Medical Equipment Shop
A separate area or room shall be provided specifically for storage, repair, and testing of electronic and other medical equipment. The amount of space and type of utilities will vary with the type of equipment involved and types of outside contracts used, as specified in the functional program.

6.7.6 Equipment and Supply Storage
6.7.6.1 Supply storage

(1) A storage room shall be provided for building maintenance supplies.

(2) Storage for solvents and flammable liquids shall comply with applicable NFPA codes.

6.7.6.2 Outdoor equipment storage. Yard equipment and supply storage areas shall be provided. These shall be located so that equipment may be moved directly to the exterior without interference with other work.

7 Administrative and Public Areas

7.1 Public Areas
The following shall be provided:

7.1.1 Entrance
This shall be at grade level, sheltered from inclement weather, and accessible to the disabled.

7.1.2 Lobby
This shall include:

7.1.2.1 A counter or desk for reception and information

7.1.2.2 Public waiting area(s)

7.1.2.3 Public toilet facilities

7.1.2.4 Public telephones

7.1.2.5 Provisions for drinking water

7.1.3 Public Waiting Areas

All public waiting areas serving more than 15 people shall include toilet room(s) equipped with hand-washing stations. These toilet rooms shall be located near the waiting areas and may serve more than one such area.

7.2 Administrative and Related Support Areas

The following shall be provided:

7.2.1 Admissions Area

If required by the functional program for initial admission of inpatients, the area shall include:

7.2.1.1 A separate waiting area for patients and accompanying persons

7.2.1.2 A work counter or desk for staff

7.2.1.3 Wheelchair storage. A storage area for wheelchairs shall be provided out of the path of normal traffic.

7.2.2 Interview Space(s)

These shall include provisions for private interviews relating to social service, credit, and admissions.

7.2.3 General or Individual Office(s)

These shall be provided for business transactions, medical and financial records, and administrative and professional staff.

7.2.4 Multipurpose Room(s)

These shall be provided for conferences, meetings, and health education purposes, and shall include provi-

---

APPENDIX

A8.1.2.1 NFPA 101 generally covers fire/safety requirements only, whereas the building codes also apply to structural elements. The fire/safety items of NFPA 101 would take precedence over other codes in case of conflict. Appropriate application of each would minimize problems.

---

sions for the use of visual aids. Several services shall be permitted to share one multipurpose room.

7.2.5 Medical Records

Rooms, areas, or offices for the following personnel and/or functions shall be provided:

7.2.5.1 Medical records administrator/technician

7.2.5.2 Review and dictation

7.2.5.3 Sorting, recording, or microfilming records

7.2.5.4 Record storage

7.2.6 Equipment and Supply Storage

Storage shall be provided for office equipment and supplies.

7.2.7 Support Areas for Employees and Volunteers

Lockers, lounges, toilets, etc. shall be provided for employees and volunteers. These shall be in addition to, and separate from, those required for medical staff and the public.

8 Construction Standards

8.1 Design and Construction, including Fire-Resistant Standards

8.1.1 Building Codes

8.1.1.1 General. Every building and portion thereof shall be designed and constructed to sustain all live and dead loads, including seismic and other environmental forces, in accordance with accepted engineering practices and standards as prescribed by local jurisdiction or the International Building Code or NFPA 5000, Building Construction and Safety Code. (See Sections 1.1-1.3.2 through 1.1-1.3.4.)

8.1.1.2 Freestanding buildings. Separate freestanding buildings for the boiler plant, laundry, shops, general storage, or other nonpatient contact areas shall be built in accordance with applicable building codes for such occupancy.

8.1.2 Construction Requirements

*8.1.2.1 General. Construction shall comply with the applicable requirements of NFPA 101, the standards contained herein, and the requirements of authorities having jurisdiction. If there are no applicable local codes, the International Building Code or NFPA 5000 shall be used (see Section 1.1-7).

8.1.2.2 Fire prevention/protection measures. Compartmentation, exits, fire alarms, automatic extinguishing systems, and other fire prevention and fire protection measures, including those within existing facilities, shall comply with NFPA 101, with the following stipulation. The Fire-Safety Evaluation System (FSES) is permitted, subject to AHJ approval, in new construction and renovation. (The FSES is intended as an evaluation tool for fire safety only.) See Section 1.1-7 for exceptions.

Note: For most projects it is essential that third-party reimbursement requirements also be followed. Verify where these may be in excess of standards in these Guidelines.

8.1.2.3 Interior finishes. Interior finishing materials shall comply with the flame-spread limitations and the smoke-production limitations indicated in NFPA 101. This requirement does not apply to minor quantities of wood or other trim (see NFPA 101) or to wall covering less than 4 mil thick applied over a noncombustible base.

8.1.2.4 Insulation materials. Building insulation materials, unless sealed on all sides and edges with noncombustible material, shall have a flame-spread rating of 25 or less and a smoke-developed rating of 150 or less when tested in accordance with NFPA 255.

8.1.3 Provisions for Disasters
See also Section 1.1-5.

8.1.3.1 General

(1) Unless specifically approved, hospitals shall not be built in areas subject to damage or inaccessibility due to natural floods.

(2) Where facilities may be subject to wind or water hazards, provision shall be made to ensure continuous operation.

8.1.3.2 Emergency communication system. An emer-

gency-radio communication system shall be provided in each facility.

(1) This system shall operate independently of the building's service and emergency power systems during emergencies.

(2) The system shall have frequency capabilities to communicate with state emergency communication networks.

(3) Additional communication capabilities are required of facilities containing a formal community emergency-trauma service or other specialty services (such as regional pediatric critical care units) that utilize staffed patient transport units.

8.2 General Standards for Details and Finishes

8.2.1 General
8.2.1.1 New construction. Details and finishes in new construction projects, including additions and alterations, shall comply with the following standards (see Section 1.1-3 concerning existing facilities where total compliance is structurally impractical).

*__8.2.1.2__ Renovation. If approved by the authorities having jurisdiction, retained portions of existing facilities that are not required to be totally modernized due to financial or other hardships shall be permitted, as a minimum, to comply with applicable requirements of the Existing Health Care Occupancies Section of NFPA 101.

8.2.2 Details
8.2.2.1 Corridor width

(1) In outpatient suites and in areas not commonly used for patient bed or stretcher transportation, reduction of corridor width to 5 feet (1.52 meters) shall be permitted.

(2) Location of items such as drinking fountains, telephone booths, vending machines, and portable

---

APPENDIX

A8.2.1.2 A plan of correction for these portions of existing facilities should be developed and implemented.

equipment shall not restrict corridor traffic or reduce the corridor width below the minimum standard.

8.2.2.2 Ceiling height. The minimum ceiling height shall be 7 feet 10 inches (2.39 meters), with the following exceptions:

(1) Corridors, storage rooms, toilet rooms, etc. Ceilings in these spaces shall be not less than 7 feet 8 inches (2.34 meters) in height. Ceiling heights in small, normally unoccupied spaces may be reduced.

(2) Rooms with ceiling-mounted equipment/light fixtures. Ceilings in radiographic, operating, and delivery rooms, and other rooms containing ceiling-mounted equipment or ceiling-mounted surgical light fixtures, shall be of sufficient height to accommodate the equipment or fixtures and their normal movement.

(3) Seclusion treatment rooms. These rooms shall have a minimum ceiling height of 9 feet (2.74 meters).

(4) Boiler rooms. Boiler rooms shall have ceiling clearances not less than 2 feet 6 inches (76.20 centimeters) above the main boiler header and connecting piping.

(5) Clearances

(a) Suspended tracks, rails, and pipes located in the traffic path for patients in beds and/or on stretchers, including those in inpatient service areas, shall be not less than 7 feet (2.13 meters) above the floor. Clearances in other areas may be 6 feet 8 inches (2.03 meters).

(b) Where existing structures make the above ceiling clearance impractical, clearances shall be as required to avoid injury to individuals up to 6 feet 4 inches (1.93 meters) tall.

8.2.2.3 Doors

(1) Door type

(a) All doors between corridors, rooms, or spaces subject to occupancy, except elevator doors, shall be of the swing type.

(b) Manual or automatic sliding doors may be exempt from this standard where fire and other emergency exiting requirements are not compromised and where cleanliness of surfaces can be maintained.

(2) Door size

(a) General. Where used in these Guidelines, door width and height shall be the nominal dimension of the door leaf, ignoring projections of frame and stops. **Note:** Although these standards are intended to accommodate access by patients and patient equipment, size of office furniture, etc., shall also be considered.

(b) Inpatient bedrooms

(i) New construction. The minimum door size for inpatient bedrooms in new work shall be 3 feet 8 inches (1.12 meters) wide and 7 feet (2.13 meters) high to provide clearance for movement of beds and other equipment.

(ii) Renovation. Existing doors of not less than 2 feet 10 inches (86.36 centimeters) wide may be considered for acceptance where function is not adversely affected and replacement is impractical.

(c) Rooms for stretchers/wheelchairs. Doors to other rooms used for stretchers (including hospital wheeled-bed stretchers) and/or wheelchairs shall have a minimum width of 2 feet 10 inches (86.36 centimeters).

(3) Door swing. Doors, except those to spaces such as small closets not subject to occupancy, shall not swing into corridors in a manner that might obstruct traffic flow or reduce the required corridor width. (Large walk-in-type closets are considered inhabitable spaces.)

(4) Door hardware

(a) Patient bathing/toilet facilities

(i) Rooms that contain bathtubs, sitz baths, showers, and/or water closets for inpatient use shall be equipped with doors and hardware permitting emergency access from the outside.

(ii) When such rooms have only one opening or are small, the doors shall open outward or in a manner that will avoid pressing a patient who may have collapsed within the room.

(iii) Similar considerations may be desirable for certain outpatient services.

(b) Patient toilet rooms in psychiatric units. If required by the functional program, design of door hardware on patient toilet rooms in psychiatric nursing units shall be permitted to allow staff to control access.

8.2.2.4 Thresholds and expansion joints

(1) Thresholds and expansion joint covers shall be flush with the floor surface to facilitate the use of wheelchairs and carts.

(2) Expansion and seismic joints shall be constructed to restrict the passage of smoke.

8.2.2.5 Windows

(1) Operable windows. Operable windows are not required in patient rooms. If operable windows are provided in patient rooms or suites, operation of such windows shall be restricted to inhibit possible escape or suicide.

8.2.2.6 Insect screens. Windows and outer doors that frequently may be left open shall be equipped with insect screens.

8.2.2.7 Glazing materials

Note: Provisions of this section concern safety from hazards of breakage. NFPA 101 contains additional requirements for glazing in exit corridors, etc., especially in buildings without sprinkler systems.

(1) Safety glass; wired glass; or plastic, break-resistant material that creates no dangerous cutting edges when broken shall be used in the following:

(a) Glass doors, lights, sidelights, borrowed lights, and windows located within 12 inches (30.48 centimeters) of a door jamb (with a bottom-frame height of less than 5 feet or 1.52 meters above the finished floor)

(b) Wall openings in active areas such as recreation and exercise rooms, unless otherwise required for fire safety

(2) Safety glass—tempered or plastic glazing materials shall be used for the following:

(a) Shower doors and bath enclosures

(b) Interior windows and doors, including those in pediatric and psychiatric unit corridors

(3) Flame-spread ratings. Plastic and similar materials used for glazing shall comply with the flame-spread ratings of NFPA 101.

(4) Renovation. In renovation projects, only glazing within 1 foot 6 inches (45.72 centimeters) of the floor must be changed to safety glass, wire glass, or plastic, break-resistant material.

8.2.2.8 Hand-washing stations

(1) Fittings. Location and arrangement of fittings for hand-washing stations shall permit their proper use and operation. Particular care shall be given to the clearances required for blade-type operating handles.

(2) Mirrors. Mirrors shall not be installed at hand-washing stations in food preparation areas, nurseries, clean and sterile supply areas, scrub sinks, or other areas where asepsis control would be lessened by hair combing.

(3) Provisions for hand drying

(a) Provisions for hand drying shall be included at all hand-washing stations except scrub sinks.

(b) These provisions shall be paper or cloth units enclosed to protect against dust or soil and to ensure single-unit dispensing. Hot air dryers shall be permitted provided that installation precludes possible contamination by recirculation of air.

(4) Anchoring. Lavatories and hand-washing stations shall be securely anchored to withstand an applied vertical load of not less than 250 pounds (113.4 kilograms) on the fixture front.

8.2.2.9 Grab bars. Grab bars shall be provided in all patient toilets, showers, bathtubs, and sitz baths at a wall clearance of 1-1/2 inches (3.81 centimeters). Bars, including those that are part of such fixtures as soap dishes, shall be sufficiently anchored to sustain a concentrated load of 250 pounds (113.40 kilograms).

8.2.2.10 Radiation protection

(1) Radiation protection requirements for x-ray and gamma ray installations shall conform with NCRP Report Nos. 33 and 49 and all applicable local requirements. Testing is to be coordinated with local authorities to prevent duplication of test observations or construction inspections.

(2) Provision shall be made for testing completed installations before use. All defects shall be corrected before approval.

8.2.2.11 Noise control

(1) Recreation rooms, exercise rooms, equipment rooms, and similar spaces where impact noises may be generated shall not be located directly over patient bed areas or delivery and operating suites, unless special provisions are made to minimize such noise.

(2) The noise reduction criteria shown in Table 2.1-1 shall apply to partitions, floors, and ceiling construction in patient areas.

8.2.2.12 Temperature control. Rooms containing heat-producing equipment, such as boiler or heater rooms or laundries, shall be insulated and ventilated to prevent the floor surface above and/or the adjacent walls of occupied areas from exceeding a temperature of 10°F (6°C) above ambient room temperature.

8.2.3 Finishes
8.2.3.1 Noncombustible or flame-retardant materials

(1) Cubicle curtains and draperies shall be noncombustible or flame-retardant and shall pass both the large- and small-scale tests of NFPA 701 when applicable.

(2) Materials and certain plastics known to produce noxious gases when burned shall not be used for mattresses, upholstery, and other items insofar as practical.

8.2.3.2 Floors

(1) Floor materials shall be easily cleanable and appropriately wear-resistant for the location.

   (a) Floors in areas used for food preparation or food assembly shall be water-resistant.

   (b) Floor surfaces, including tile joints, shall be resistant to food acids.

   (c) In all areas subject to frequent wet-cleaning methods, floor materials shall not be physically affected by germicidal cleaning solutions.

(2) Floors subject to traffic while wet (such as shower and bath areas, kitchens, and similar work areas) shall have a nonslip surface.

(3) In new construction or major renovation work, the floors and wall bases of all operating rooms and any delivery rooms used for cesarean sections shall be monolithic and joint free.

(4) The floors and wall bases of kitchens, soiled workrooms, and other areas subject to frequent wet cleaning shall also be homogenous, but may have tightly sealed joints.

(5) Floors in areas and rooms in which flammable anesthetic agents are stored or administered shall comply with NFPA 99.

8.2.3.3 Walls

(1) Wall finishes. Wall finishes shall be washable. In the vicinity of plumbing fixtures, wall finishes shall be smooth and water-resistant.

(2) Dietary and food preparation areas. In these areas, wall construction, finish, and trim, including the joints between the walls and the floors, shall be free of insect- and rodent-harboring spaces.

(3) Operating rooms, cesarean delivery rooms, isolation rooms, and sterile processing rooms. In these rooms, wall finishes shall be free of fissures, open joints, or crevices that may retain or permit passage of dirt particles.

8.2.3.4 Ceilings

(1) Ceilings, including exposed structure in areas normally occupied by patients or staff in food preparation and food storage areas, shall be cleanable with routine housekeeping equipment. Acoustic and lay-in ceiling, where used, shall not interfere with infection control.

(2) In dietary areas and in other areas where dust fall-out may present a problem, suspended ceilings shall be provided.

(3) Semirestricted areas

   (a) Ceiling finishes in semirestricted areas such as airborne infection isolation rooms, protective environment rooms, clean corridors, central sterile supply spaces, specialized radiographic rooms, and minor surgical procedure rooms shall be smooth, scrubbable, nonabsorptive, nonperforated, capable of withstanding cleaning with chemicals, and without crevices that can harbor mold and bacterial growth.

   (b) If lay-in ceiling is provided, it shall be gasketed or clipped down to prevent the passage of particles from the cavity above the ceiling plane into the semirestricted environment. Perforated, tegular, serrated cut, or highly textured tiles are not acceptable.

(4) Restricted areas. Ceiling finishes in restricted areas such as operating rooms shall be monolithic, scrubbable, and capable of withstanding chemicals. Cracks or perforations in these ceilings are not allowed.

8.2.3.5 Penetrations. Floors and walls penetrated by pipes, ducts, and conduits shall be tightly sealed to minimize entry of rodents and insects. Joints of structural elements shall be similarly sealed.

8.2.3.6 Psychiatric patient locations. In psychiatric patient rooms, toilets, and seclusion rooms, the ceiling and air distribution devices, lighting fixtures, sprinkler heads, and other appurtenances shall be of a tamper-resistant type.

8.2.3.7 Protective isolation locations. Rooms used for protective isolation and anterooms adjacent to rooms used for protective isolation shall have seamless flooring with integral coved base.

9 Special Systems

9.1 General

9.1.1 Testing
9.1.1.1 Prior to acceptance of the facility, all special systems shall be tested and operated to demonstrate to the owner or his designated representative that the installation and performance of these systems conform to design intent.

9.1.1.2 Test results shall be documented for maintenance files.

9.1.2 Documentation
9.1.2.1 Upon completion of the special systems equipment installation contract, the owner shall be furnished with a complete set of manufacturers' operating, maintenance, and preventive maintenance instructions, a parts lists, and complete procurement information including equipment numbers and descriptions.

9.1.2.2 Operating staff persons shall also be provided with written instructions for proper operation of systems and equipment. Required information shall include all safety or code ratings as needed.

9.1.3 Insulation

Insulation shall be provided surrounding special system equipment to conserve energy, protect personnel, and reduce noise.

9.2 Elevators

9.2.1 General

All hospitals having patient facilities (such as bedrooms, dining rooms, or recreation areas) or critical services (such as operating, delivery, diagnostic, or therapeutic areas) located on other than the grade-level entrance floor shall have electric or hydraulic elevators.

9.2.2 Number

In the absence of an engineered traffic study, the following guidelines for number of elevators shall apply:

9.2.2.1 At least two hospital-type elevators shall be installed where 1 to 59 patient beds are located on any floor other than the main entrance floor.

9.2.2.2 At least two hospital-type elevators shall be installed where 60 to 200 patient beds are located on floors other than the main entrance floor, or where the major inpatient services are located on a floor other than those containing patient beds. (Reduction in elevator service shall be permitted for those floors providing only partial inpatient services.)

9.2.2.3 At least three hospital-type elevators shall be installed where 201 to 350 patient beds are located on floors other than the main entrance floor, or where the major inpatient services are located on a floor other than those containing patient beds. (Reduction in elevator service shall be permitted for those floors providing only partial inpatient services.)

9.2.2.4 For hospitals with more than 350 beds, the number of elevators shall be determined from a study

APPENDIX

A9.2.3.2 Elevator car doors should have a clear opening of not less than 4.5 feet (1.37 meters).

A9.2.5.2 This is so the light control feature will be overridden or disengaged should it encounter smoke at any landing.

of the hospital plan and the expected vertical transportation requirements.

9.2.3 Dimensions and Clearances

9.2.3.1 Hospital-type elevator cars shall have inside dimensions that accommodate a patient bed with attendants. Cars shall be at least 5 feet 8 inches (1.73 meters) wide by 9 feet (2.74 meters) deep.

***9.2.3.2** Car doors shall have a clear opening of not less than 4 feet (1.22 meters) wide and 7 feet (2.13 meters) high.

9.2.3.3 In renovations, an increase in the size of existing elevators shall not be required if the elevators can accommodate patient beds used in the facility.

9.2.3.4 Additional elevators installed for visitors and material handling shall be permitted to be smaller than noted above, within restrictions set by standards for disabled access.

9.2.4 Leveling Device

Elevators shall be equipped with a two-way automatic level-maintaining device with an accuracy of ± 1/4 inch (± 6.35 millimeters).

9.2.5 Elevator Controls

9.2.5.1 Each elevator, except those for material handling, shall be equipped with an independent keyed switch for staff use for bypassing all landing button calls and responding to car button calls only.

***9.2.5.2** Elevator call buttons and controls shall not be activated by heat or smoke. Light beams, if used for operating door reopening devices without touch, shall be used in combination with door-edge safety devices and shall be interconnected with a system of smoke detectors.

9.2.6 Installation and Testing

9.2.6.1 Standards. Installation and testing of elevators shall comply with ANSI/ASME A17.1 for new construction and ANSI/ASME A17.3 for existing facilities. (See ASCE/SEI 7 for seismic design and control systems requirements for elevators.)

9.2.6.2 Documentation. Field inspections and tests shall be made and the owner shall be furnished with written certification stating that the installation meets the requirements set forth in this section as well as all applicable safety regulations and codes.

9.3 Waste Processing

For waste collection and storage and refuse chute requirements, see Section 2.1-6.5.3.

9.3.1 Waste Treatment and Disposal

*9.3.1.1 Incineration. On-site hospital incinerators shall comply with federal, state, and local regulatory and environmental requirements. The design and construction of incinerators shall comply with NFPA 82.

9.3.1.2 Other technologies. Types of non-incineration waste treatment technology(ies) shall be determined by the facility in conjunction with environmental, economic, and regulatory considerations. The functional program shall describe waste treatment technology components.

(1) Location

    (a) Safe transfer routes, distances from waste sources, temporary storage requirements, and space requirements for treatment equipment shall be considered in determining the location for a non-incineration technology.

    (b) The location of the technology shall not cause traffic problems as waste is brought in and out.

    (c) Odor, noise, and the visual impact of medical waste operations on patients, visitors, public access, and security shall be considered.

(2) Space requirements. These shall be determined by the equipment requirements, including associated area for opening waste entry doors, access to control panels, space for hydraulic lifts, conveyors, and operational clearances. Mobile or portable units, trailer-mounted units, underground installations, or all-weather enclosed shelters at an outdoor site may also be used, subject to local regulatory approvals.

(3) Ventilation. Exhaust vents, if any, from the treatment technology shall be located a minimum of

25 feet (7.62 meters) from inlets to HVAC systems. If the technology involves heat dissipation, sufficient cooling and ventilation shall be provided.

9.3.2 Nuclear Waste Disposal

See Code of Federal Regulations, Title X, parts 20 and 35, concerning the handling and disposal of nuclear materials in health care facilities.

10 Building Systems

10.1 Plumbing

10.1.1 General

Unless otherwise specified herein, all plumbing systems shall be designed and installed in accordance with the International Plumbing Code.

10.1.2 Plumbing and Other Piping Systems

10.1.2.1 General piping and valves

(1) All piping, except control-line tubing, shall be identified.

APPENDIX

A9.3.1.1 The EPA has identified medical waste incineration as a significant contributor to air pollution worldwide.

a. Health care facilities should seek to minimize incineration of medical waste, consistent with local and state regulations and public health goals.

b. When incinerators are used, consideration should be given to the recovery of waste heat from on-site incinerators used to dispose of large amounts of waste materials. Incinerators should be designed in a manner fully consistent with protection of public and environmental health, both on-site and off-site, and in compliance with federal, state, and local statutes and regulations. Toward this end, permit applications for incinerators and modifications thereof should be supported by Environmental Assessments and/or Environmental Impact Statements (EISs) and/or Health Risk Assessments (HRAs) as may be required by regulatory agencies. Except as noted below, such assessments should utilize standard U.S. EPA methods, specifically those set forth in U.S. EPA guidelines, and should be fully consistent with U.S. EPA guidelines for health risk assessment. Under some circumstances, however, regulatory agencies having jurisdiction over a particular project may require use of alternative methods.

(2) All valves shall be tagged, and a valve schedule shall be provided to the facility owner for permanent record and reference.

(3) No plumbing piping shall be exposed overhead or on walls where possible accumulation of dust or soil may create a cleaning problem or where leaks would create a potential for food contamination.

10.1.2.2 Hemodialysis/hemoperfusion piping

(1) In new construction and renovation in any hospital where hemodialysis or hemoperfusion is routinely performed, a separate water supply and a drainage facility that does not interfere with hand-washing shall be provided.

(2) When the functional program includes hemodialysis, continuously circulated filtered cold water shall be provided. Piping shall be in accordance with AAMI RD6.2.

10.1.2.3 Potable water supply systems

(1) Capacity. Systems shall be designed to supply water at sufficient pressure to operate all fixtures and equipment during maximum demand. Supply capacity for hot- and cold-water piping shall be determined on the basis of fixture units, using recognized engineering standards. When the ratio of plumbing fixtures to occupants is proportionally more than required by the building occupancy and is in excess of 1,000 plumbing fixture units, a diversity factor shall be permitted.

(2) Valves. Each water service main, branch main, riser, and branch to a group of fixtures shall have valves.

  (a) Stop valves shall be provided for each fixture.

  (b) Appropriate panels for access shall be provided at all valves where required.

(3) Backflow prevention

  (a) Systems shall be protected against cross-connection in accordance with American Water Works Association (AWWA) Recommended

Practice for Backflow Prevention and Cross-Connection Control.

  (b) Vacuum breakers or backflow prevention devices shall be installed on hose bibs and supply nozzles used for connection of hoses or tubing in laboratories, housekeeping sinks, bedpan-flushing attachments, autopsy tables, etc.

(4) Bedpan-flushing devices. Bedpan-flushing devices (may be cold water) shall be provided in each inpatient toilet room; however, installation is optional in psychiatric and alcohol-abuse units where patients are ambulatory.

(5) Potable water storage. Potable water storage vessels (hot and cold) not intended for constant use shall not be installed.

(6) Emergency eyewash and showers shall comply with ANSI Z358.1.

10.1.2.4 Hot water systems. See Section 1.6-2.1.2.1.

10.1.2.5 Drainage systems

(1) Piping

  (a) Drain lines from sinks used for acid waste disposal shall be made of acid-resistant material.

  (b) Drain lines serving some types of automatic blood-cell counters shall be of carefully selected material that will eliminate potential for undesirable chemical reactions (and/or explosions) between sodium azide wastes and copper, lead, brass, solder, etc.

  (c) Insofar as possible, drainage piping shall not be installed within the ceiling or exposed in operating and delivery rooms, nurseries, food preparation centers, food-serving facilities, food storage areas, central services, electronic data processing areas, electric closets, and other sensitive areas. Where exposed overhead drain piping in these areas is unavoidable, special provisions shall be made to protect the space below from leakage, condensation, or dust particles.

(2) Floor drains

(a) Floor drains shall not be installed in operating and delivery rooms.

*(b) If a floor drain is installed in cystoscopy, it shall contain a nonsplash, horizontal-flow flushing bowl beneath the drain plate.

(c) Dietary area floor drains and/or floor sinks

(i) Type. These shall be of a type that can be easily cleaned by removing the cover. Removable stainless steel mesh shall be provided in addition to grilled drain covers to prevent entry of large particles of waste that might cause stoppages.

(ii) Location. Floor drains or floor sinks shall be provided at all "wet" equipment (as ice machines) and as required for wet cleaning of floors. Location of floor drains and floor sinks shall be coordinated to avoid conditions where locations of equipment make removal of covers for cleaning difficult.

(3) Autopsy table drain systems. Drain systems for autopsy tables shall be designed to positively avoid splatter or overflow onto floors or back siphonage and for easy cleaning and trap flushing.

(4) Sewers. Building sewers shall discharge into community sewerage. Where such a system is not available, the facility shall treat its sewage in accordance with local and state regulations.

(5) Kitchen grease traps

(a) Grease traps shall be of capacity required.

(b) Grease traps shall be located and arranged to permit easy access without the need to enter food preparation or storage areas.

(c) Grease traps shall be accessible from outside the building without need to interrupt any services.

(6) Plaster traps. Where plaster traps are used, provisions shall be made for appropriate access and cleaning.

10.1.2.6 Condensate drains. See Section 1.6-2.1.2.2.

10.1.3 Plumbing Fixtures
In addition to the requirements of Section 1.6-2.1.3, the following standards shall apply to plumbing fixtures in a general hospital:

10.1.3.1 Clinical sinks

(1) Clinical sinks shall be trimmed with valves that can be operated without hands. Single-lever or wrist blade devices shall be permitted. Handles on clinical sinks shall be at least 6 inches (15.24 centimeters) long.

(2) Clinical sinks shall have an integral trap wherein the upper portion of the water trap provides a visible seal.

10.1.3.2 Scrub sinks. Freestanding scrub sinks and lavatories used for scrubbing in procedure rooms shall be trimmed with foot, knee, or ultrasonic controls; single-lever wrist blades are not permitted.

10.1.4 Medical Gas and Vacuum Systems
10.1.4.1 Medical gas systems. The installation, testing, and certification of nonflammable medical gas and air systems shall comply with the requirements of NFPA 99. (See Table 2.1-5 for rooms requiring station outlets.)

APPENDIX

A10.1.2.5 (2)(b) Floor drains in cystoscopy operating rooms have been shown to disseminate a heavily contaminated spray during flushing. Unless flushed regularly with large amounts of fluid, the trap tends to dry out and permit passage of gases, vapors, odors, insects, and vermin directly into the operating room.

For new construction, if the users insist on a floor drain, the drain plate should be located away from the operative site, and should be over a frequently flushed nonsplash, horizontal-flow type of bowl, preferably with a closed system of drainage. Alternative methods include (a) an aspirator/trap installed in a wall connected to the collecting trough of the operating table by a closed, disposable tube system, or (b) a closed system using portable collecting vessels. (See NFPA 99.)

10.1.4.2 Vacuum systems

(1) Clinical vacuum system installations shall be in accordance with NFPA 99. (See Table 2.1-5 for rooms that require station outlets.)

(2) The vacuum discharge shall be located at least 25 feet from all outside air intakes, doors, and operable windows.

10.2 Heating, Ventilating, and Air-Conditioning (HVAC) Systems

*10.2.1 General
*10.2.1.1 Mechanical system design

(1) Efficiency. The mechanical system shall be designed for overall efficiency and appropriate life-cycle cost. Details for cost-effective implementation of design features are interrelated and too numerous (as well as too basic) to list individually.

   (a) Recognized engineering procedures shall be followed for the most economical and effec-

tive results. A well-designed system can generally achieve energy efficiency at minimal additional cost and simultaneously provide improved patient comfort.

   (b) Different geographic areas may have climatic and use conditions that favor one system over another in terms of overall cost and efficiency.

   (c) In no case shall patient care or safety be sacrificed for conservation.

   (d) Insofar as practical, the facility shall include provisions for recovery of waste cooling and heating energy (ventilation, exhaust, water and steam discharge, cooling towers, incinerators, etc.).

   (e) Use of recognized energy-saving mechanisms such as variable-air-volume (VAV) systems, load shedding, programmed controls for unoccupied periods (nights and weekends, etc.), and use of natural ventilation shall be considered, site and climatic conditions permitting.

   (f) Facility design considerations shall include site, building mass, orientation, configuration, fenestration, and other features relative to passive and active energy systems.

(2) Air-handling systems

   *(a) These shall be designed with an economizer cycle where appropriate to use outside air. (Use of mechanically circulated outside air does not reduce need for filtration.)

   (b) VAV systems. The energy-saving potential of variable-air-volume systems is recognized, and the standards herein are intended to maximize appropriate use of those systems. Any system used for occupied areas shall include provisions to avoid air stagnation in interior spaces where thermostat demands are met by temperatures of surrounding areas.

   (c) Noncentral air-handling systems (i.e., individual room units used for heating and cooling

---

APPENDIX

A10.2.1 Remodeling and work in existing facilities may present special problems. As practicality and funding permit, existing insulation, weather stripping, etc., should be brought up to standard for maximum economy and efficiency. Consideration should be given to additional work that may be needed to achieve this.

A10.2.1.1 Protection of HVAC systems against chemical, biological, and radiological attack should be considered. System design features that should be evaluated include protection of outside air intakes, location of return air grilles, and types of filtration. The following documents provide additional information regarding these issues:

a. "Guidance for Protecting Building Environments from Airborne Chemical, Biological, or Radiological Attacks," Department of Health and Human Services/Centers for Disease Control and Prevention/National Institute for Occupational Safety and Health, May 2002.

b. "Protecting Buildings and their Occupants from Airborne Hazards" (draft), Army Corps of Engineers, TI 853-01, October 2001.

A10.2.1.1 (2)(a) It may be practical in many areas to reduce or shut down mechanical ventilation under appropriate climatic and patient care conditions and to use open windows for ventilation.

purposes, such as fan-coil units, heat pump units, etc.). These units may be used as recirculating units only. All outdoor air requirements shall be met by a separate central air-handling system with proper filtration, as noted in Table 2.1-3.

(3) Vibration isolators. Mechanical equipment, ductwork, and piping shall be mounted on vibration isolators as required to prevent unacceptable structure-borne vibration.

(4) System valves. Supply and return mains and risers for cooling, heating, and steam systems shall be equipped with valves to isolate the various sections of each system. Each piece of equipment shall have valves at the supply and return ends.

(5) Renovation. If system modifications affect greater than 10 percent of the system capacity, designers shall utilize pre-renovation water/air flow rate measurements to verify that sufficient capacity is available and that renovations have not adversely affected flow rates in non-renovated areas.

*10.2.1.2 Ventilation and space conditioning requirements. All rooms and areas used for patient care shall have provisions for ventilation.

(1) Ventilation rates. The ventilation systems shall be designed and balanced, as a minimum, according to the requirements shown in Table 2.1-2 and the applicable notes. The ventilation rates shown in Table 2.1-2 do not preclude the use of higher, more appropriate rates.

(2) Air change rates. Air supply and exhaust in rooms for which no minimum total air change rate is noted may vary down to zero in response to room load. For rooms listed in Table 2.1-2, where VAV systems are used, minimum total air change shall be within limits noted.

(3) Temperature and humidity. Space temperature and relative humidity shall be as indicated in Table 2.1-2.

(4) Air movement direction. To maintain asepsis control, airflow supply and exhaust shall generally be controlled to ensure movement of air from "clean" to "less clean" areas, especially in critical areas.

(5) Although natural ventilation for nonsensitive areas and patient rooms (via operable windows) shall be permitted, mechanical ventilation shall be considered for all rooms and areas in the facility.

10.2.1.3 Testing and documentation

(1) Upon completion of the equipment installation contract, the owner shall be furnished with a complete set of manufacturers' operating, maintenance, and preventive maintenance instructions, parts lists, and complete procurement information, including equipment numbers and descriptions. Required information shall include energy ratings as needed for future conservation calculations.

(2) Operating staff persons shall also be provided with written instructions for proper operation of systems and equipment.

10.2.2 Requirements for Specific Locations

10.2.2.1 Airborne infection isolation rooms. The infectious disease isolation room is used for isolating the airborne spread of infectious diseases, such as measles, varicella, or tuberculosis.

(1) The design of airborne infection isolation rooms (AIIRs) shall be permitted to include provisions for normal patient care during periods not requiring isolation precautions.

(2) Use of supplemental recirculating devices shall be permitted in the patient room to increase the equivalent room air exchanges; however, such recirculating devices do not provide outside air

---

APPENDIX

A10.2.1.2 Owing to potential operational problems for the ultraviolet germicidal irradiation (UVGI) lamps, and the fact that the effectiveness of UVGI is dependent on the airflow pattern in the room, use of UVGI may be considered as a supplement to the ventilation system design, rather than the main control mechanism. The ACH of the room should therefore be set as if no UVGI system is installed.

requirements. Recirculation of air within individual isolation rooms shall be permitted if HEPA filters are used.

(3) Rooms with reversible airflow provisions for the purpose of switching between protective environment and AII functions are not acceptable.

10.2.2.2 Protective environment rooms. The protective environment (PE) room is used to protect the patient from common environmental airborne infectious microbes (i.e., Aspergillus spores).

(1) These special ventilation areas shall be designed to provide directed airflow from the cleanest patient care area to less clean areas.

(2) These rooms shall be protected with HEPA filters at 99.97 percent efficiency for a 0.3 μm sized particle in the supply airstream. These interrupting filters protect patient rooms from maintenance-derived release of environmental microbes from the ventilation system components. Recirculation HEPA filters can be used to increase the equivalent room air exchanges.

(3) Constant volume airflow is required for consistent ventilation for the protected environment.

(4) If the facility determines that airborne infection isolation is necessary for protective environment patients, an anteroom shall be provided.

(5) Rooms with reversible airflow provisions for the purpose of switching between protective environment and airborne infection isolation functions are not acceptable.

10.2.2.3 Psychiatric patient areas. Special consideration shall be given to the type of heating and cooling units, ventilation outlets, and appurtenances installed in patient-occupied areas of psychiatric units. The following shall apply:

(1) All air grilles and diffusers shall be of a type that prohibits the insertion of foreign objects. All exposed fasteners shall be tamper-resistant.

(2) All convector or HVAC enclosures exposed in the room shall be constructed with rounded corners and shall have enclosures fastened with tamper-resistant screws.

(3) HVAC equipment shall be of a type that minimizes the need for maintenance within the room.

APPENDIX

A10.2.2.4 (3)(a) Operating and delivery room ventilation

a. The operating and delivery room ventilation systems should operate at all times to maintain the air movement relationship to adjacent areas. The cleanliness of the spaces is compromised when the ventilation system is shut down. For example, airflow from a less clean space such as the corridor can occur, and standing water can accumulate in the ventilation system (near humidifiers or cooling coils).

b. The recommended air change rate in an operating room is 20 to 25 air changes per hour (ACH) for ceiling heights between 9 feet (2.74 meters) and 12 feet (3.66 meters).

c. The system should provide a single directional flow regime, with both high and low exhaust locations.

d. A face velocity of around 25 to 35 fpm (0.13 to 0.18 m/s) is sufficient from the non-aspirating diffuser array provided the array size itself is set correctly. The non-aspirating diffuser array size

should be set appropriately such that it covers at least the area footprint of the table plus a reasonable margin around it. In the cited study, this margin is 21 inches (53.34 centimeters) on the short side and 12 inches (25.40 centimeters) on the long side.

Note: The above conclusions were derived from studies conducted by the National Institutes of Health: Farhad Memarzadeh and Andrew P. Manning, "Comparison of Operating Room Ventilation Systems in the Protection of the Surgical Site" (ASHRAE Transactions 2002, Vol. 108, pt. 2) and Farhad Memarzadeh and Zheng Jiang, "Effect of Operation Room Geometry and Ventilation System Parameter Variations on the Protection of the Surgical Site" (IAQ 2004).

e. If additional diffusers are required, they may be located outside this central diffuser array. Up to 30 percent of the central diffuser array may be allocated to non-diffuser items (medical gas columns, lights, etc.).

10.2.2.4 Operating and delivery rooms

(1) Air supply

    (a) In new construction and major renovation work, air supply for operating and delivery rooms shall be from non-aspirating ceiling diffusers with a face velocity in the range of 25 to 35 fpm (0.13 to 0.18 m/s), located at the ceiling above the center of the work area. Return air shall be near the floor level, at a minimum. Return air shall be permitted high on the walls, in addition to the low returns.

    (b) Each operating and delivery room shall have at least two return-air inlets located as far from each other as practical.

    (c) Turbulence and other factors of air movement shall be considered to minimize the fall of particulates onto sterile surfaces.

(2) Temperature. Temperature shall be individually controlled for each operating and delivery room.

(3) Ventilation rates

    *(a) Operating and delivery room ventilation systems shall operate at all times, except during maintenance and conditions requiring shutdown by the building's fire alarm system.

    (b) During unoccupied hours, operating and delivery room air change rates may be reduced, provided the positive room pressure is maintained as required in Table 2.1-2.

(4) Standards for special procedures. Where extraordinary procedures, such as organ transplants, justify special designs, installation shall properly meet performance needs as determined by applicable standards. These special designs should be reviewed on a case-by-case basis.

10.2.2.5 Cough-inducing procedure rooms. Rooms used for sputum induction, aerosolized pentamadine treatments, or other cough-inducing procedures shall meet the requirements of Table 2.1-2 for airborne infection isolation rooms. If booths are used, refer to Section 2.1-5.8.1.

10.2.2.6 Anesthesia storage rooms. The ventilation system for anesthesia storage rooms shall conform to the requirements of NFPA 99, including the gravity option. Mechanically operated air systems are optional in these rooms.

10.2.2.7 ETO sterilizer space. The ventilation system for the space that houses ethylene oxide (ETO) sterilizers shall be designed as follows:

(1) A dedicated (not connected to a return air or other exhaust system) exhaust system shall be provided. Refer to 29 CFR Part 1910.1047.

(2) All source areas shall be exhausted, including the sterilizer equipment room, service/aeration areas, and the space above the sterilizer door, as well as the aerator.

    (a) If the ETO cylinders are not located in a well-ventilated, unoccupied equipment space, an exhaust hood shall be provided over the cylinders.

    (b) The relief valve shall be terminated in a well-ventilated, unoccupied equipment space or outside the building.

    (c) If the floor drain to which the sterilizer(s) discharges is not located in a well-ventilated, unoccupied equipment space, an exhaust drain cap shall be provided (coordinate with local codes).

(3) General airflow shall be away from the sterilizer operator(s).

(4) A dedicated exhaust duct system for ETO shall be provided. The exhaust outlet to the outside shall be at least 25 feet (7.62 meters) away from any air intake.

(5) An audible and visual alarm shall activate in the sterilizer work area, and in a 24-hour staffed location, upon loss of airflow in the exhaust system.

10.2.2.8 Food preparation centers

(1) Exhaust hoods handling grease-laden vapors in food preparation centers shall comply with NFPA 96.

(2) All hoods over cooking ranges shall be equipped with grease filters, fire-extinguishing systems, and heat-actuated fan controls.

(3) Cleanout openings shall be provided every 20 feet (6.10 meters) and at changes in direction in the horizontal exhaust duct systems serving these hoods. Horizontal runs of ducts serving range hoods shall be kept to a minimum.

(4) Food preparation centers shall have ventilation systems whose air supply mechanisms are interfaced appropriately with exhaust hood controls or relief vents so that exfiltration or infiltration to or from exit corridors does not compromise the exit corridor restrictions of NFPA 90A or the pressure requirements of NFPA 96.

10.2.2.9 Fuel-fired equipment rooms. Rooms with fuel-fired equipment shall be provided with sufficient outdoor air to maintain equipment combustion rates and to limit workstation temperatures.

10.2.3 Thermal Insulation and Acoustical Provisions
See Section 1.6-2.2.1.

10.2.4 HVAC Air Distribution
10.2.4.1 Return air systems. For patient care areas, return air shall be via ducted systems.

10.2.4.2 HVAC ductwork. See Section 1.6-2.2.2.1.

> ### APPENDIX
>
> **A10.2.4.3 (2)** Acceptable concentrations of anesthetizing agents are unknown at this time. The absence of specific data makes it difficult to set specific standards. However, any scavenging system should be designed to remove as much of the gas as possible from the room environment. It is assumed that anesthetizing equipment will be selected and maintained to minimize leakage and contamination of room air. See Industrial Ventilation: A Manual of Recommended Practice, published by the American Conference of Governmental Industrial Hygienists (www.acgih.org), for additional information.

10.2.4.3 Exhaust systems

(1) General

(a) To enhance the efficiency of recovery devices required for energy conservation, combined exhaust systems shall be permitted.

(b) Local exhaust systems shall be used whenever possible in place of dilution ventilation to reduce exposure to hazardous gases, vapors, fumes, or mists.

(c) Fans serving exhaust systems shall be located at the discharge end and shall be readily serviceable.

(d) Airborne infection isolation rooms shall not be served by exhaust systems incorporating a heat wheel.

*(2) Anesthesia scavenging systems

(a) Each space routinely used for administering inhalation anesthesia and inhalation analgesia shall be served by a scavenging system to vent waste gases.

(b) When anesthesia scavenging systems are required, air supply shall be at or near the ceiling. Return or exhaust air inlets shall be near the floor level.

(c) If a vacuum system is used, the gas-collecting system shall be arranged so it does not disturb patients' respiratory systems.

(d) Gases from the scavenging system shall be exhausted directly to the outside. The anesthesia evacuation system may be combined with the room exhaust system, provided the part used for anesthesia gas scavenging exhausts directly to the outside and is not part of the recirculation system.

(e) Scavenging systems are not required for areas where gases are used only occasionally, such as the emergency department, offices for routine dental work, etc.

10.2.4.4 Air outlets and inlets

*(1) Fresh air intakes

(a) Fresh air intakes shall be located at least 25 feet (7.62 meters) from exhaust outlets of ventilating systems, combustion vents (including those serving rooftop air handling equipment), medical-surgical vacuum systems, plumbing vents, or areas that may collect vehicular exhaust or other noxious fumes. (Prevailing winds and/or proximity to other structures may require greater clearances.)

(b) Plumbing vents that terminate at a level above the top of the air intake may be located as close as 10 feet (3.05 meters).

(c) The bottom of outdoor air intakes serving central systems shall be as high as practical, but at least 6 feet (1.83 meters) above ground level, or, if installed above the roof, 3 feet (91.44 centimeters) above roof level.

(2) Relief air. Relief air is exempt from the 25-foot (7.62-meter) separation requirement. Relief air is defined as air that otherwise could be returned (recirculated) to an air handling unit from the occupied space, but is being discharged to the outdoors to maintain building pressure, such as during outside air economizer operation.

(3) Gravity exhaust. Where conditions permit, gravity exhaust shall be permitted for nonpatient areas such as boiler rooms, central storage, etc.

(4) Construction requirements. The bottoms of air distribution devices (supply/return/exhaust) shall be at least 3 inches (7.62 centimeters) above the floor.

10.2.4.5 Ventilation hoods

(1) Exhaust hoods and safety cabinets

(a) Hoods and safety cabinets may be used for normal exhaust of a space providing minimum air change rates are maintained.

(b) If air change standards in Table 2.1-2 do not provide sufficient air for proper operation of exhaust hoods and safety cabinets (when in use), supplementary makeup air (filtered and preheated) shall be provided around these units to maintain the required airflow direction and exhaust velocity. Use of makeup air will avoid dependence upon infiltration from outdoor and/or from contaminated areas.

(c) Makeup systems for hoods shall be arranged to minimize "short circuiting" of air and to avoid reduction in air velocity at the point of contaminant capture.

(2) Laboratory fume hoods. Laboratory fume hoods shall meet the following standards:

(a) General standards

(i) An average face velocity of at least 75 feet per minute (0.38 meters per second)

(ii) Connection to an exhaust system to the outside that is separate from the building exhaust system

(iii) Location of an exhaust fan at the discharge end of the system

(iv) Inclusion of an exhaust duct system of noncombustible corrosion-resistant material as needed to meet the planned usage of the hood

(b) Special standards for use with strong oxidants

(i) Fume hoods and their associated equipment in the air stream intended for use with perchloric acid and other strong oxidants shall be constructed of stainless steel or other material consistent with special exposures.

APPENDIX

A10.2.4.4 (1) Requirements to minimize cross-contamination between fresh air intakes and various exhaust outlets may be determined by engineering modeling or calculations performed in accordance with the *ASHRAE Handbook—Fundamentals.*

(ii) These hoods and equipment shall be provided with a water wash and drain system to permit periodic flushing of duct and hood.

(iii) Electrical equipment intended for installation within such ducts shall be designed and constructed to resist penetration by water. Lubricants and seals shall not contain organic materials.

(iv) When perchloric acid or other strong oxidants are only transferred from one container to another, standard laboratory fume hoods and the associated equipment may be used in lieu of stainless steel construction.

(c) Special standards for use with infectious or radioactive materials. In new construction and major renovation work, each hood used to process infectious or radioactive materials shall meet the following requirements:

(i) Each hood shall have a minimum face velocity of 90 to 110 feet per minute (0.45 to 0.56 meters per second) with suitable pressure-independent air-modulating devices and alarms to alert staff of fan shutdown or loss of airflow.

(ii) Each shall also have filters with a 99.97 percent efficiency (based on the DOP test method) in the exhaust stream and be designed and equipped to permit the safe removal, disposal, and replacement of contaminated filters. Filters shall be as close to the hood as practical to minimize duct contamination.

(iii) Fume hoods intended for use with radioactive isotopes shall be constructed of stainless steel or other material suitable for the particular exposure and shall comply with NFPA 801, Facilities for Handling Radioactive Materials. **Note:** Radioactive isotopes used for injections, etc., without probability of airborne particulates or gases may be processed in a clean-workbench-type hood where acceptable to the Nuclear Regulatory Commission.

10.2.5 HVAC Filters
10.2.5.1 Filter efficiencies

(1) All central ventilation or air conditioning systems shall be equipped with filters with efficiencies equal to, or greater than, those specified in Table 2.1-3.

(2) Noncentral air-handling systems shall be equipped with permanent (cleanable) or replaceable filters with a minimum efficiency of MERV 3 (68 percent weight arrestance).

(3) Filter efficiencies, tested in accordance with ASHRAE 52.1, shall be average.

10.2.5.2 Filter bed location. Where two filter beds are required, filter bed no. 1 shall be located upstream of the air conditioning equipment and filter bed no. 2 shall be downstream of any fan or blowers.

10.2.5.3 Filter frames. Filter frames shall be durable and proportioned to provide an airtight fit with the enclosing ductwork. All joints between filter segments and enclosing ductwork shall have gaskets or seals to provide a positive seal against air leakage.

10.2.5.4 Filter housing blank-off panels. Filter housing blank-off panels shall be permanently attached to the frame, constructed of rigid materials, and have sealing surfaces equal to or greater than the filter media installed in the filter frame.

10.2.5.5 Filter manometers. A manometer shall be installed across each filter bed having a required efficiency of 75 percent or more, including hoods requiring HEPA filters. Provisions shall be made to allow access to the manometer for field testing.

10.2.6 Steam and Hot Water Systems
See Section 1.6-2.2.3.

10.3 Electrical Systems

10.3.1 General
10.3.1.1 Applicable standards

(1) All electrical material and equipment, including conductors, controls, and signaling devices, shall be installed in compliance with applicable sections of NFPA 70 and NFPA 99.

(2) All electrical material and equipment shall be listed as complying with available standards of listing agencies or other similar established standards where such standards are required.

(3) Field labeling of equipment and materials shall be permitted only when provided by a nationally recognized testing laboratory that has been certified by the Occupational Safety and Health Administration (OSHA) for that referenced standard.

10.3.1.2 Testing and documentation. The electrical installations, including alarm, nurse call, and communication systems, shall be tested to demonstrate that equipment installation and operation is appropriate and functional. A written record of performance tests on special electrical systems and equipment shall show compliance with applicable codes and standards.

10.3.2 Electrical Requirements for Specific Hospital Locations
10.3.2.1 Inhalation anesthetizing locations. At inhalation anesthetizing locations, all electrical equipment and devices, receptacles, and wiring shall comply with applicable sections of NFPA 99 and NFPA 70.

10.3.3 Electrical Distribution and Transmission
10.3.3.1 Switchboards

(1) Location

    (a) Main switchboards shall be located in an area separate from plumbing and mechanical equipment and shall be accessible to authorized persons only.

    (b) Switchboards shall be convenient for use, readily accessible for maintenance, and away from traffic lanes.

    (c) Switchboards shall be located in a dry, ventilated space free of corrosive or explosive fumes, gases, or any flammable material.

(2) Overload protective devices. These shall operate properly in ambient room temperatures.

10.3.3.2 Panelboards

(1) Panelboards serving critical branch, equipment system, or normal system loads shall be located on the same floor as the loads to be served.

(2) Location of panelboards serving life safety branch loads on the floor above or the floor below the loads to be served shall be permitted.

(3) New panelboards shall not be located in public access corridors.

10.3.3.3 Ground-fault circuit interrupters

(1) Ground-fault circuit interrupters (GFCIs) shall comply with NFPA 70.

(2) When ground-fault circuit interrupters are used in critical areas, provisions shall be made to ensure that other essential equipment is not affected by activation of one interrupter.

10.3.4 Power Generating and Storing Equipment
10.3.4.1 Emergency electrical service

(1) Emergency power shall be provided for in accordance with NFPA 99, NFPA 101, and NFPA 110.

(2) Where stored fuel is required, storage capacity shall permit continuous operation for at least 4 hours.

10.3.5 Lighting
10.3.5.1 General. See Section 1.6-2.3.1.1.

10.3.5.2 Lighting for specific locations in the hospital

(1) Patient rooms. Patient rooms shall have general lighting and night lighting.

    (a) A reading light shall be provided for each patient.

        (i) Reading light controls shall be accessible to the patient(s) without the patient having to get out of bed.

(ii) Incandescent and halogen light sources that produce heat shall be avoided to prevent burns to the patient and/or bed linen.

(iii) Unless specifically designed to protect the space below, the light source shall be covered by a diffuser or lens.

(iv) Flexible light arms, if used, shall be mechanically controlled to prevent the lamp from contacting the bed linen.

(b) At least one night light fixture in each patient room shall be controlled at the room entrance.

(c) Lighting for coronary and intensive care bed areas shall permit staff observation of the patient while minimizing glare.

(2) Nursing unit corridors. Corridors in nursing units shall have general illumination with provisions for reducing light levels at night.

(3) Exam/treatment/trauma rooms. A portable or fixed examination light shall be provided for examination, treatment, and trauma rooms.

(4) Operating and delivery rooms. Operating and delivery rooms shall have general lighting in addition to special lighting units provided at surgical and obstetrical tables. General lighting and special lighting shall be on separate circuits.

10.3.5.3 Emergency lighting. See Section 1.6-2.3.1.2.

10.3.5.4 Exit signs. See Section 1.6-2.3.1.3.

10.3.6 Equipment

10.3.6.1 X-ray equipment

APPENDIX

A10.3.6.2 Special attention should be paid to safety hazards associated with equipment cabling. Every attempt should be made to minimize these hazards, where practical.

A10.3.6.3 Refer to NFPA 99 for a description of the essential electrical system.

(1) Fixed and mobile x-ray equipment installations shall conform to articles 517 and 660 of NFPA 70.

(2) The x-ray film illuminator unit or units for displaying at least two films simultaneously shall be installed in each operating room, specified emergency treatment rooms, and x-ray viewing room of the radiology department. All illuminator units within one space or room shall have lighting of uniform intensity and color value.

*10.3.6.2 Special electrical equipment. Special equipment is identified in the sections on critical care units, newborn nurseries, pediatric and adolescent unit, psychiatric nursing unit, obstetrical suite, surgical suites, emergency service, imaging suite, nuclear medicine, laboratory suite, rehabilitation therapy department, renal dialysis unit, respiratory therapy service, morgue, pharmacy, dietary facilities, administrative and public areas, medical records, central services, general stores, and linen services. These sections shall be consulted to ensure compatibility between programmatically defined equipment needs and appropriate power and other electrical connection needs.

*10.3.6.3 Hand-washing stations and scrub sinks. If operation of a scrub sink or a hand-washing station in critical care areas, emergency departments, labor and delivery, and surgical suites is dependent on the building electrical service, it shall be connected to the essential electrical system.

10.3.7 Receptacles

10.3.7.1 Receptacles in corridors

(1) Duplex-grounded receptacles for general use shall be installed approximately 50 feet (15.24 meters) apart in all corridors and within 25 feet (7.62 meters) of corridor ends.

(2) Receptacles in pediatric and psychiatric unit corridors shall be of the tamper-resistant type.

(3) Special receptacles marked for x-ray use shall be installed in corridors of patient areas so that mobile equipment may be used anywhere within a patient room using a cord length of 50 feet (15.24 meters) or less. If the same mobile x-ray unit is used in operating rooms and in nursing

areas, receptacles for x-ray use shall permit the use of one plug in all locations. Where capacitive discharge or battery-powered x-ray units are used, special x-ray receptacles are not required.

10.3.7.2 Receptacles in patient care areas

(1) Patient rooms. Each patient room shall have duplex-grounded receptacles.

  (a) There shall be one at each side of the head of each bed; one for television, if used; one on every other wall; and one for each motorized bed.

  (b) Receptacles may be omitted from exterior walls where construction or room configuration makes installation impractical.

(2) Intermediate care rooms. These shall have at least four duplex outlets per bed. The outlets shall be arranged to provide two duplex outlets on each side of the head of the bed.

(3) Critical care areas. As defined by NFPA 99 and NFPA 70, including pediatric and newborn intensive care units, critical care areas shall have at least seven duplex outlets at the head of each bed, crib, or bassinet. Approximately 50 percent of critical care outlets shall be connected to emergency system power and be so labeled.

(4) Nurseries. Nurseries shall have at least two duplex-grounded receptacles for each bassinet.

(5) LDRP rooms. LDRP rooms shall have receptacles as required for patient rooms (Section 2.1-10.3.7.2 (1)); in addition, the bassinet shall have receptacles as required for nursery bassinets (Section 2.1-10.3.7.2 (4)).

(6) Trauma and resuscitation rooms. These shall have eight duplex outlets located convenient to the head of each bed.

(7) Emergency department. Examination and treatment rooms in the emergency department shall have a minimum of six duplex outlets located convenient to the head of each bed. Approximately 50 percent of emergency care outlets shall be connected to emergency system power and be so labeled.

(8) Each general care examination and treatment table and each work table shall have access to two duplex receptacles.

(9) Operating and delivery rooms

  (a) Each operating and delivery room shall have at least six receptacles convenient to the head of the procedure table.

  (b) Each operating room shall have at least 16 simplex or eight duplex receptacles. Where mobile x-ray, laser, or other equipment requiring special electrical configurations is used, additional receptacles distinctively marked for x-ray or laser use shall be provided.

(10) Renal dialysis units

  (a) For renal dialysis units, two duplex receptacles shall be on each side of a patient bed or lounge chair.

  (b) One duplex receptacle on each side of the bed shall be connected to emergency power.

10.3.7.3 Emergency system receptacles. Electrical receptacle cover plates or electrical receptacles supplied from the emergency systems shall be distinctively colored or marked for identification. If color is used for identification purposes, the same color shall be used throughout the facility.

10.3.8 Call Systems

10.3.8.1 General. Alternate technologies shall be permitted for emergency or nurse call systems. If radio frequency systems are utilized, consideration shall be given to electromagnetic compatibility between internal and external sources.

10.3.8.2 Patient room call station. In patient areas, each patient room shall be served by at least one calling station for two-way voice communication.

(1) Each bed shall be provided with a call device. Two call devices serving adjacent beds may be served by one calling station.

(2) Signal location

    (a) Calls shall activate a visible signal in the corridor at the patient's door, in the clean workroom, in the soiled workroom, in medication, charting, clean linen storage, nourishment, equipment storage, and examination/treatment room(s) and at the nursing station of the nursing unit.

    (b) In multi-corridor nursing units, additional visible signals shall be installed at corridor intersections.

    (c) In rooms containing two or more calling stations, indicating lights shall be provided at each station.

(3) Nurse call systems at each calling station shall be equipped with an indicating light that remains lighted as long as the voice circuit is operating.

10.3.8.3 Emergency call system

(1) The emergency call shall be designed so that a signal activated at a patient's call station will initiate a visible and audible signal that can be turned off only at the patient call station and that is distinct from the regular nurse call signal.

(2) The emergency call shall activate an annunciator panel at the nurse station, a visible signal in the corridor at the patient's door, and at other areas defined by the functional program.

(3) Specific locations in the hospital

    (a) Patient toilet and bathing facilities. A nurse emergency call system shall be provided at each inpatient toilet, bath, sitz bath, and shower room. A nurse emergency call shall be accessible to a collapsed patient lying on the floor. Inclusion of a pull cord will satisfy this standard.

    (b) Outpatient and treatment areas. Provisions for emergency calls shall be provided in outpatient and treatment areas where patients may be subject to incapacitation.

    (c) Imaging suite. Patient toilet rooms within the imaging suite shall be equipped with a nurse emergency call.

    (d) Renal dialysis units. Toilet rooms in renal dialysis units shall be served by an emergency call. The call shall activate a signal at the nurses' station.

10.3.8.4 Limited call system. In areas such as critical care, recovery, pre-op, and emergency, where patients are under constant visual surveillance, the nurse call may be limited to the following:

(1) A bedside button or station that activates a signal readily seen at the control station to summon additional assistance (see Section 2.1-10.3.8.5)

(2) An emergency code resuscitation alarm to summon medical assistance from the code team

10.3.8.5 Staff emergency assistance system

(1) Location of call system. An emergency assistance system for staff to summon additional assistance shall be provided in each operating, delivery, recovery, emergency examination, treatment, and intermediate care area, and in critical care units, nurseries, special procedure rooms, cardiac catheterization rooms, stress-test areas, triage, outpatient surgery, admission and discharge areas, and areas for psychiatric patients, including seclusion and security rooms, anterooms and toilet rooms serving them, communal toilet and bathing facility rooms, and dining, activity, therapy, exam, and treatment rooms.

(2) Location of annunciator. This system shall annunciate visibly and audibly in the clean workroom, in the soiled workroom, in medication, charting, clean linen storage, nourishment, equipment storage, and examination/treatment room(s) if provided, and at the nursing station of the nursing unit, with backup to another staffed area from which assistance can be summoned.

10.3.8.6 Emergency resuscitation alarm. In critical care units, recovery, and pre-op, the call system shall include provisions for an emergency code resuscitation alarm to summon assistance from outside the unit.

10.3.8.7 Alarm in psychiatric units. A nurse call is not required in psychiatric nursing units, but if one is included the following shall apply:

(1) Provisions shall be made for easy removal or for covering of call button outlets.

(2) In psychiatric nursing units, all hardware shall have tamper-resistant fasteners.

10.4 Telecommunications and Information Systems

10.4.1 Locations for terminating telecommunications and information system devices shall be provided.

10.4.2 A room shall be provided for central equipment locations. Special air conditioning and voltage regulation shall be provided when recommended by the manufacturer.

10.4.3 All patient care-related telecommunications and information systems shall be powered from the essential electrical system.

10.5 Electronic Safety and Security

10.5.1 Electronic Surveillance Systems
Electronic surveillance systems include but are not limited to patient elopement systems, door access/control systems, video/audio monitoring systems, patient location systems, and infant abduction prevention systems.

10.5.1.1 Electronic surveillance systems are not required, but if provided for the safety of the patients, any devices in patient areas need to be mounted so they are unobtrusive and in a tamper-resistant enclosure.

10.5.1.2 Electronic surveillance system monitoring devices need to be located so they are not readily observable by the general public or patients.

10.5.1.3 If installed, electronic surveillance systems shall receive power from the emergency electrical system in the event of a disruption of normal electrical power.

10.5.2 Fire Alarm System
All health care facilities shall be provided with a fire alarm system in accordance with NFPA 101 and NFPA 72.

Table 2.1-1
Sound Transmission Limitations in General Hospitals

	Airborne sound transmission class (STC)[1]	
	Partitions	Floors
New construction[2]		
Patient room to patient room	45	40
Public space to patient room[3]	55	40
Service areas to patient room[4]	65	45
Patient room access corridor[5]	45	45
Exam room to exam room	45	--
Exam room to public space	45	--
Toilet room to public space	45	--
Consultation rooms/conference rooms to public space	45	--
Consultation rooms/conference rooms to patient rooms	45	--
Staff lounges to patient rooms	45	--
Existing construction[2]		
Patient room to patient room	35	40
Public space to patient room[3]	40	40
Service areas to patient room[4]	45	45

[1] Sound transmission class (STC) shall be determined by tests in accordance with methods set forth in ASTM E90 and ASTM E413. Where partitions do not extend to the structure above, sound transmission through ceilings and composite STC performance must be considered.

[2] Treatment rooms shall be treated the same as patient rooms.

[3] Public space includes corridors (except patient room access corridors), lobbies, dining rooms, recreation rooms, and similar space.

[4] Service areas for the purposes of this table include kitchens, elevators, elevator machine rooms, laundries, garages, maintenance rooms, boiler and mechanical equipment rooms, and similar spaces of high noise. Mechanical equipment located on the same floor or above patient rooms, offices, nurses stations, and similar occupied space shall be effectively isolated from the floor.

[5] Patient room access corridors contain composite walls with doors/windows and have direct access to patient rooms.

Table 2.1-2

Ventilation Requirements for Areas Affecting Patient Care in Hospitals and Outpatient Facilities[1]

Area designation	Air movement relationship to adjacent area[2]	Minimum air changes of outdoor air per hour[3]	Minimum total air changes per hour[4, 5]	All air exhausted directly to outdoors[6]	Recirculated by means of room units[7]	Relative humidity[8] (%)	Design temperature[9] (degrees F/C)
NURSING UNITS							
Patient room	–	2	6[10]	–	–	–	70-75 (21–24)
Toilet room	In	–	10	Yes	–	–	–
Newborn nursery suite	–	2	6	–	No	30-60	72-78 (22-26)
Protective environment room[11]	Out	2	12	–	No	–	75 (24)
Airborne infection isolation room[11]	In	2	12	Yes[12]	No	–	75 (24)
Isolation alcove or anteroom	In/Out	–	10	Yes	No	–	–
Patient corridor	–	–	2	–	–	–	–
OBSTETRICAL FACILITIES							
Delivery room[13]	Out	3	15	–	No	30-60	68-73 (20–23)
Labor/delivery/recovery	–	2	6[10]	–	–	–	70-75 (21–24)
Labor/delivery/recovery/postpartum	–	2	6[10]	–	–	–	70-75 (21–24)
EMERGENCY, SURGERY, AND CRITICAL CARE							
Operating/surgical cystoscopic rooms[11, 13]	Out	3	15	–	No	30-60	68-73 (20–23)[14]
Recovery room[13]	–	2	6	–	No	30-60	70-75 (21-24)
Critical and intensive care	–	2	6	–	No	30-60	70-75 (21-24)
Intermediate care	–	2	6[10]	–	–	–	70-75 (21-24)
Newborn intensive care	–	2	6	–	No	30-60	72-78 (22-26)
Treatment room[15]	–	–	6	–	–	–	75 (24)
Trauma room[15]	Out	3	15	–	No	30-60	70-75 (21-24)
Bronchoscopy[11]	In	2	12	Yes	No	30-60	68-73 (20–23)
Triage	In	2	12	Yes[16]	–	–	70-75 (21-24)
ER waiting rooms	In	2	12	Yes[12, 16]	–	–	70-75 (21-24)
Procedure room	Out	3	15	–	No	30-60	70-75 (21-24)
Laser eye room	Out	3	15	–	No	30-60	70-75 (21-24)
X-ray (surgical/critical care and catheterization)	Out	3	15	–	No	30-60	70-75 (21-24)
Anesthesia gas storage	In	–	8	Yes	–	–	–
SUPPORT AREAS							
Medication room	Out	–	4	–	–	–	–
Clean workroom or clean holding	Out	–	4	–	–	–	–
Soiled workroom or soiled holding	In	–	10	Yes	No	–	–
DIAGNOSTIC AND TREATMENT AREAS							
Examination room	–	–	6	–	–	–	75 (24)
Treatment room	–	–	6	–	–	–	75 (24)
Physical therapy and hydrotherapy	In	–	6	–	–	–	75 (24)
Gastrointestinal endoscopy room	–	2	6	–	No	30-60	68-73 (20–23)
Endoscopic instrument processing room[17]	In	–	10	Yes	No	–	–
Imaging[18]							
X-ray (diagnostic & treatment)	–	–	6	–	–	–	75 (24)
Darkroom	In	–	10	Yes	No	–	–
Imaging waiting rooms	In	2	12	Yes[12, 16]	–	–	70-75 (21-24)
Laboratory[19]							
General[18]	–	–	6	–	–	–	75 (24)
Biochemistry[18]	In	–	6	Yes	No	–	75 (24)
Cytology	In	–	6	Yes	No	–	75 (24)
Glass washing	In	–	10	Yes	–	–	–

Table 2.1-2 (continued)
Ventilation Requirements for Areas Affecting Patient Care in Hospitals and Outpatient Facilities[1]

Area designation	Air movement relationship to adjacent area[2]	Minimum air changes of outdoor air per hour[3]	Minimum total air changes per hour[4, 5]	All air exhausted directly to outdoors[6]	Recirculated by means of room units[7]	Relative humidity[8] (%)	Design temperature[9] (degrees F/C)
Histology	In	—	6	Yes	No	—	75 (24)
Microbiology[18]	In	—	6	Yes	No	—	75 (24)
Nuclear medicine	In	—	6	Yes	No	—	75 (24)
Pathology	In	—	6	Yes	No	—	75 (24)
Serology	In	—	6	Yes	No	—	75 (24)
Sterilizing	In	—	10	Yes	—	—	—
Autopsy room[11]	In	—	12	Yes	No	—	—
Nonrefrigerated body-holding room	In	—	10	Yes	—	—	70 (21)
SERVICE AREAS							
Pharmacy	Out	—	4	—	—	—	—
Food preparation center	—	—	10	—	No	—	—
Warewashing	In	—	10	Yes	No	—	—
Dietary day storage	In	—	2	—	—	—	—
Laundry, general	—	—	10	Yes	—	—	—
Soiled linen (sorting and storage)	In	—	10	Yes	No	—	—
Clean linen storage	Out	—	2	—	—	—	—
Soiled linen and trash chute room	In	—	10	Yes	No	—	—
Bedpan room	In	—	10	Yes	—	—	—
Bathroom	In	—	10	—	—	—	75 (24)
Housekeeping room	In	—	10	Yes	No	—	—
STERILIZING AND SUPPLY							
ETO-sterilizer room	In	—	10	Yes	No	30-60	75 (24)
Sterilizer equipment room	In	—	10	Yes	—	—	—
Central medical and surgical supply							
Soiled or decontamination room	In	—	6	Yes	No	—	68-73 (20–23)
Clean workroom	Out	—	4	—	No	30-60	75 (24)
Sterile storage	Out	—	4	—	—	(Max) 70	—

[1] The ventilation rates in this table cover ventilation for comfort, as well as for asepsis and odor control in areas of acute care hospitals that directly affect patient care and are determined based on healthcare facilities being predominantly "No Smoking" facilities. Where smoking may be allowed, ventilation rates will need adjustment. Areas where specific ventilation rates are not given in the table shall be ventilated in accordance with ASHRAE Standard 62, *Ventilation for Acceptable Indoor Air Quality*, and *ASHRAE Handbook—HVAC Applications*. Specialized patient care areas, including organ transplant units, burn units, specialty procedure rooms, etc., shall have additional ventilation provisions for air quality control as may be appropriate. OSHA standards and/or NIOSH criteria require special ventilation requirements for employee health and safety within health care facilities.

[2] Design of the ventilation system shall provide air movement which is generally from clean to less clean areas. If any form of variable air volume or load shedding system is used for energy conservation, it must not compromise the corridor-to-room pressure balancing relationships or the minimum air changes required by the table.

[3] To satisfy exhaust needs, replacement air from the outside is necessary. Table 2.1-2 does not attempt to describe specific amounts of outside air to be supplied to individual spaces except for certain areas such as those listed. Distribution of the outside air, added to the system to balance required exhaust, shall be as required by good engineering practice. Minimum outside air quantities shall remain constant while the system is in operation. In variable volume systems, the minimum outside air setting on the air-handling unit shall be calculated using the ASHRAE 62 method.

[4] Number of air changes may be reduced when the room is unoccupied if provisions are made to ensure that the number of air changes indicated is reestablished any time the space is being utilized. Adjustments shall include provisions so that the direction of air movement shall remain the same when the number of air changes is reduced. Areas not indicated as having continuous directional control may have ventilation systems shut down when space is unoccupied and ventilation is not otherwise needed, if the maximum infiltration or exfiltration permitted in Note 2 is not exceeded and if adjacent pressure balancing relationships are not compromised. Air quantity calculations must account for filter loading such that the indicated air change rates are provided up until the time of filter change-out. The minimum total air change requirements for Table 2.1-2 shall be based on the supply air quantity in positive pressure rooms, and the exhaust air quantity in negative pressure rooms.

[5] Air change requirements indicated are minimum values. Higher values should be used when required to maintain indicated room conditions (temperature and humidity), based on the cooling load of the space (lights, equipment, people, exterior walls and windows, etc.).

Table 2.1-2 (continued)

Ventilation Requirements for Areas Affecting Patient Care in Hospitals and Outpatient Facilities[1]

[6] Air from areas with contamination and/or odor problems shall be exhausted to the outside and not recirculated to other areas. Note that individual circumstances may require special consideration for air exhaust to the outside, e.g., in intensive care units in which patients with pulmonary infection are treated, and rooms for burn patients.

[*7] Recirculating room HVAC units refers to those local units that are used primarily for heating and cooling of air, and not disinfection of air. Because of cleaning difficulty and potential for buildup of contamination, recirculating room units shall not be used in areas marked "No." However, for airborne infection control, air may be recirculated within individual isolation rooms if HEPA filters are used. Isolation and intensive care unit rooms may be ventilated by reheat induction units in which only the primary air supplied from a central system passes through the reheat unit. Gravity-type heating or cooling units such as radiators or convectors shall not be used in operating rooms and other special care areas. See footnote A7 (at the bottom of the page) for a description of recirculation units to be used in isolation rooms.

[8] The ranges listed are the minimum and maximum limits where control is specifically needed. The maximum and minimum limits are not intended to be independent of a space's associated temperature. The humidity is expected to be at the higher end of the range when the temperature is also at the higher end, and vice versa. See Figure 2.1-1 for a graphic representation of the indicated changes on a psychrometric chart. Shaded area is acceptable range.

[9] Where temperature ranges are indicated, the systems shall be capable of maintaining the rooms at any point within the range during normal operation. A single figure indicates a heating or cooling capacity of at least the indicated temperature. This is usually applicable when patients may be undressed and require a warmer environment. Nothing in these guidelines shall be construed as precluding the use of temperatures lower than those noted when the patients' comfort and medical conditions make lower temperatures desirable. Unoccupied areas such as storage rooms shall have temperatures appropriate for the function intended.

[10] Total air changes per room for patient rooms, intermediate care, labor/delivery/recovery rooms, and labor/delivery/recovery/postpartum rooms may be reduced to 4 when supplemental heating and/or cooling systems (radiant heating and cooling, baseboard heating, etc.) are used.

[*11] Differential pressure shall be a minimum of 0.01" water gauge (2.5 Pa). If alarms are installed, allowances shall be made to prevent nuisance alarms of monitoring devices.

[12] If it is not practical to exhaust the air from the airborne infection isolation room to the outside, the air may be returned through HEPA filters to the air-handling system exclusively serving the isolation room.

[13] National Institute for Occupational Safety and Health (NIOSH) Criteria Documents regarding Occupational Exposure to Waste Anesthetic Gases and Vapors, and Control of Occupational Exposure to Nitrous Oxide indicate a need for both local

exhaust (scavenging) systems and general ventilation of the areas in which the respective gases are utilized.

[14] Some surgeons may require room temperatures that are outside of the indicated range. All operating room design conditions shall be developed in consultation with surgeons, anesthesiologists, and nursing staff.

[15] The term trauma room as used here is the operating room space in the emergency department or other trauma reception area that is used for emergency surgery. The first aid room and/or "emergency room" used for initial treatment of accident victims may be ventilated as noted for the "treatment room." Treatment rooms used for bronchoscopy shall be treated as bronchoscopy rooms. Treatment rooms used for cryosurgery procedures with nitrous oxide shall contain provisions for exhausting waste gases.

[16] In a ventilation system that recirculates air, HEPA filters can be used in lieu of exhausting the air from these spaces to the outside. In this application, the return air shall be passed through the HEPA filters before it is introduced into any other spaces.

[17] The endoscopic instrument processing room is a room adjacent to the gastrointestinal endoscopy room that is used for cleaning endoscopic equipment and instruments.

[18] When required, appropriate hoods and exhaust devices for the removal of noxious gases or chemical vapors shall be provided (see Section 2.1-10.2.4.5. (2) and NFPA 99).

[19] The air movement relationships for laboratories apply between laboratory and adjacent non-laboratory spaces. Reference DHHS publication "Biosafety in Microbiological and Biomedical Laboratories" (CDC and NIH) on the CDC Web site.

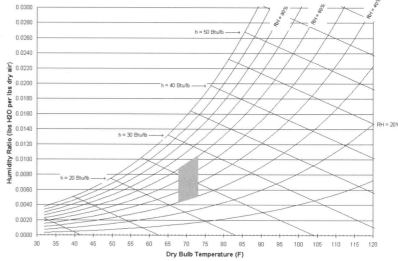

Psychrometric Chart

[A7] Recirculating devices with HEPA filters may have potential uses in existing facilities as interim, supplemental environmental controls to meet requirements for the control of airborne infectious agents. Limitations in design must be recognized. The design of either portable or fixed systems should prevent stagnation and short circuiting of airflow. The supply and exhaust locations should direct clean air to areas where health care workers are likely to work, across the infectious source, and then to

the exhaust, so that the health care worker is not in position between the infectious source and the exhaust location. The design of such systems should also allow for easy access for scheduled preventative maintenance and cleaning.

[A11] The verification of airflow direction can include a simple visual method such as smoke trail, ball-in-tube, or flutterstrip. These devices will require a minimum differential air pressure to indicate airflow direction.

Table 2.1-3
Filter Efficiencies for Central Ventilation and Air Conditioning Systems in General Hospitals

Area designation	No. filter beds	Filter bed no. 1 (MERV, %)	Filter bed no. 2 (MERV, %)
All areas for inpatient care, treatment, and diagnosis, and those areas providing direct service or clean supplies such as sterile and clean processing, etc.	2	8 (30%)	14 (90%)
Protective environment room	2	8 (30%)	17 (99.97%)
Laboratories	1	13 (80%)	—
Administrative, bulk storage, soiled holding areas, food preparation areas, and laundries	1	8 (30%)	—

Notes
1. Additional roughing or prefilters should be considered to reduce maintenance required for filters with efficiency higher than 75 percent.
2. MERV = minimum efficiency rating value. MERVs are based on ASHRAE 52.2.
3. The filtration efficiency ratings are based on average dust spot efficiency per ASHRAE 52.1.

Table 2.1-4
Hot Water Use—General Hospital

	Clinical	Dietary	Laundry
Liters per hour per bed[1]	11.9	7.2	7.6
Gallons per hour per bed[1]	3	2	2
Temperature (°C)	41-49[2]	49[3]	71[4]
Temperature (°F)	105-120[2]	120[3]	160[4]

[1] Quantities indicated for design demand of hot water are for general reference minimums and shall not substitute for accepted engineering design procedures using actual number and types of fixtures to be installed. Design will also be affected by temperatures of cold water used for mixing, length of run and insulation relative to heat loss, etc. As an example, total quantity of hot water needed will be less when temperature available at the outlet is very nearly that of the source tank and the cold water used for tempering is relatively warm.

[2] The range represents the maximum and minimum allowable temperatures.

[3] Provisions shall be made to provide 180°F (82°C) rinse water at warewasher (may be by separate booster) unless a chemical rinse is provided.

[4] Provisions shall be made to provide 160°F (71°C) hot water at the laundry equipment when needed. (This may be by steam jet or separate booster heater.) However, it is emphasized that this does not imply that all water used would be at this temperature. Water temperatures required for acceptable laundry results will vary according to type of cycle, time of operation, and formula of soap and bleach as well as type and degree of soil. Lower temperatures may be adequate for most procedures in many facilities, but the higher 160°F (71°C) should be available when needed for special conditions.

Table 2.1-5
Station Outlets for Oxygen, Vacuum (Suction), and Medical Air Systems in Hospitals[1]

Section	Location	Oxygen	Vacuum	Medical Air
2.1-3.1.1	Patient rooms (medical and surgical)	1/bed	1/bed	—
2.1-3.1.3	Examination/treatment (medical, surgical, and postpartum care)	1/room	1/room	—
2.1-3.2.2/3.2.3	Airborne infection isolation/protective environment rooms	1/bed	1/bed	—
2.1-3.2.4	Seclusion room (medical, surgical, and postpartum)	1/bed	1/bed	—
2.1-3.3	Intermediate care	2/bed	2/bed	1/bed
2.1-3.4.2	Critical care (general)	3/bed	3/bed	1/bed
2.1-3.4.2.2	Airborne infection isolation	3/bed	3/bed	1/bed
2.1-3.4.3	Coronary critical care	3/bed	2/bed	1/bed
2.1-3.4.5	Pediatric critical care	3/bed	3/bed	1/bed
2.1-3.4.6	Newborn intensive care	3/bassinet	3/bassinet	3/bassinet
2.1-3.6.6	Newborn nursery (full-term)	1/4 bassinets[2]	1/4 bassinets[2]	1/4 bassinets[2]
2.1-3.6.8	Pediatric nursery	1/bassinet	1/bassinet	1/bassinet
2.1-3.7.1	Pediatric and adolescent	1/bed	1/bed	1/bed
2.1-3.8.2	Psychiatric patient rooms	—	—	—
2.1-3.8.3	Seclusion treatment room	—	—	—
2.1-5.3.2.1	General operating room	2/room	3/room	—
2.1-5.3.2.2	Cardio, ortho, neurological	2/room	3/room	—
2.1-5.3.2.3	Orthopedic surgery	2/room	3/room	—
2.1-5.3.2.4	Surgical cysto and endo	1/room	3/room	—
2.1-5.3.3.2	Post-anesthesia care unit	1/bed	3/bed	1/bed
2.1-5.3.3.3	Phase II recovery[3]	1/bed	3/bed	—
2.1-5.3.5.11	Anesthesia workroom	1 per workstation	—	1 per workstation
2.1-4.2.1	Postpartum bedroom	1/bed	1/bed	—
2.1-4.3.1	Labor room	1/room	1/room	1/room
2.1-4.3.2/4.3.3	Cesarean/delivery room	2/room	3/room	1/room
2.1-4.3.4	Infant resuscitation space[4]	1/bassinet	1/bassinet	1/bassinet
2.1-4.3.5	OB recovery room	1/bed	3/bed	1/room
2.1-4.4	Labor/delivery/recovery (LDR)	1/bed	1/bed	—
2.1-4.4	Labor/delivery/recovery/postpartum (LDRP)	1/bed	1/bed	—
2.1-5.1.2.5	Initial emergency management	1/bed	1/bed	—
2.1-5.1.3.4	Triage area (definitive emergency care)	1/station	1/station	—
2.1-5.1.3.7 (1)	Definitive emergency care exam/treatment rooms	1/bed	1/bed	1/bed
2.1-5.1.3.8 (2)	Definitive emergency care observation unit	1/bed	1/bed	—
2.1-5.1.3.7 (1)	Trauma/cardiac room(s)	2/bed	3/bed	1/bed
2.1-5.1.3.7 (3)	Orthopedic and cast room	1/room	1/room	—
2.1-5.5.5	MRI	1/room	1/room	1/room
2.1-5.4.1	Cardiac catheterization lab	2/bed	2/bed	2/bed
2.1-5.12.2.2	Autopsy room	—	1 per workstation	—

[1] For any area or room not described above, the facility clinical staff shall determine outlet requirements after consultation with the authority having jurisdiction.

[2] Four bassinets may share one outlet that is accessible to each bassinet.

[3] If the Phase II recovery area is a separate area from the PACU, only one vacuum per bed or station shall be required.

[4] When infant resuscitation takes place in a room such as cesarean section/delivery or LDRP, then the infant resuscitation services must be provided in that room in addition to the minimum service required for the mother.

2.2 Small Inpatient Primary Care Hospitals

Appendix material, which appears in shaded boxes at the bottom of the page, is advisory only.

*1 General Considerations

1.1 Applicability
The small inpatient primary care hospital shall meet the general standards described herein. Such facilities shall also meet the general standards outlined in the referenced ambulatory care facilities chapters in these Guidelines.

1.2 Functional Program
The functional program shall describe the various components planned for the facility and how they will interface with each other.

1.2.1 Size and Layout
Department sizes and clear floor areas depend on program requirements and organization of services within the facility. As required by community needs, combination or sharing of some functions shall be permitted, provided the layout does not compromise safety standards and medical nursing practices.

1.2.2 Swing Beds
When the concept of swing beds is part of the functional program, care shall be taken to include requirements for all intended categories.

1.2.3 Transfer and Service Agreements
All necessary transfer and service agreements with secondary or tertiary care hospitals shall be included in the functional program.

1.3 Site

1.3.1 Transfer Support Features
1.3.1.1 Part of the facility's transfer agreements with higher care hospital providers shall include use of helicopter and/or ambulance services to ensure the timely transfer to a tertiary care center of patients presenting to the emergency room of the primary care inpatient center.

1.3.1.2 Helicopter pad and ambulance ports shall be located close to the emergency suite and the designated patient rooms holding patients requiring transfer to a tertiary care center for treatment after stabilization.

1.3.1.3 Where appropriate, features such as garages, landing pads, approaches, lighting, and fencing required to meet state and local regulations that govern the placement, safety features, and elements required to accommodate helicopter and ambulance services shall be provided.

1.3.2 Parking
1.3.2.1 Each new facility, major addition, or major change in function shall be provided with parking

---

APPENDIX

*A1 Since the early 1990s, the health care community has been looking at traditional hospital models (and nursing homes built under the Hill-Burton hospital model) and their delivery of care roles as established in the 1947 Hill-Burton Act. The Kellogg Foundation Report titled "Hospital Community Benefits Standards," published in the early 1990s, stated that to eliminate identified health disparities, all primary care providers should become more community responsive in their orientation and develop coalitions with local health departments, community health centers, and the communities they serve.

The purpose of the small inpatient primary care hospital is to provide a community-focused, short-term overnight stay environment designed to provide primary care to patient populations within a designated rural or underserved community based on the federal standard metropolitan statistical area (SMSA) and defined under the Code of Federal Regulations 42 CFR 5.1.

The concept of the model is to allow an adaptable facility that can meet the needs of the community it serves. It is intended to serve as a stand-alone overnight facility (stays of 96 hours or less), to provide for outpatient treatment modalities, and to serve as a small inpatient primary care center or as a satellite of an existing hospital in a rural or designated underserved population area. These facilities may be attached to and operated as part of a local health department complex or an ambulatory surgery treatment center; in fact, this is encouraged. There must be transfer, service, and reciprocity agreements with general hospitals and tertiary care hospitals as a prerequisite for using this model.

spaces to satisfy the needs of the patient population, personnel, and public.

1.3.2.2 In the absence of a formal parking study, provide one space for each bed plus one space for each employee normally present on any single weekday shift.

1.3.2.3 Additional parking may be required to accommodate other services.

1.3.2.4 Separate and additional space shall be provided for service delivery vehicles, vehicles utilized for emergency services, and mobile transportable units.

2 Nursing Unit

2.1 General

2.1.1 Size
2.1.1.1 A single nursing unit shall be provided for the small inpatient primary care facility. The number of patient rooms contained in the unit shall be as determined by the functional program but shall not exceed 25 beds per unit.

2.1.1.2 An additional unit may be incorporated into the design of the facility based on a demographic analysis and the facility's demonstrated ability to provide adequate support services for the additional beds.

2.1.2 Multiple Modalities
The unit shall be designed to accommodate multiple patient modalities, with adequate support areas to accomplish the modalities referenced in the functional program.

2.1.3 Facility Requirements
Each nursing unit shall include the following:

APPENDIX

A2.2.2.1 In new construction, single-patient rooms should be at least 12 feet (3.65 meters) wide by 13 feet (3.96 meters) deep (approximately 160 square feet or 14.86 square meters) exclusive of toilet rooms, closets, lockers, wardrobes, alcoves, or vestibules. These spaces should accommodate comfortable furniture for one or two family members without blocking staff member access to patients. Efforts should be made to provide the patient with some control of the room environment.

2.2 Typical Patient Rooms

2.2.1 Capacity
2.2.1.1 New construction. In new construction, the maximum number of beds per room shall be one unless the functional program demonstrates the necessity of a two-bed arrangement. Approval of a two-bed arrangement shall be obtained from the licensing authority.

2.2.1.2 Renovation. Where renovation work is undertaken and the present capacity is more than one patient, maximum room capacity shall be no more than the present capacity, with a maximum of four patients.

2.2.2 Space Requirements
Minor encroachments, including columns and handwashing stations, that do not interfere with functions may be ignored when determining space requirements for patient rooms.

*2.2.2.1 Area. In new construction, patient rooms shall be constructed to meet the needs of the functional program and have a minimum of 100 square feet (9.29 square meters) of clear floor area per bed in multiple-bed rooms and 120 square feet (11.15 square meters) of clear floor area in single-bed rooms, exclusive of toilet rooms, closets, lockers, wardrobes, alcoves, or vestibules.

2.2.2.2 Dimensions and clearances. The dimensions and arrangement of rooms shall be such that there is a minimum of 3 feet (91.44 centimeters) between the sides and foot of the bed and any wall or any other fixed obstruction. In multiple-bed rooms, a clearance of 4 feet (1.22 meters) shall be available at the foot of each bed to permit the passage of equipment and beds.

2.2.2.3 Renovation. Where renovation work is undertaken, every effort shall be made to meet the above minimum standards. If it is not possible to meet the above minimum standards, the authorities having jurisdiction may grant approval to deviate from this requirement. In such cases, patient rooms shall have no less than 80 square feet (7.43 square meters) of clear floor area per bed in multiple-bed areas and 100 square feet (9.29 square meters) of clear floor area in single-bed rooms, exclusive of the spaces previously noted in this section.

2.2.3 Windows

Each patient room shall have a window in accordance with Section 2.1-8.2.2.5.

2.2.4 Patient Privacy

Visual privacy from casual observation by other patients and visitors shall be provided. Design for privacy shall not restrict patient access to any area of the room.

2.2.5 Hand-Washing Stations

A hand-washing station for the exclusive use of the staff shall be provided to serve each patient room and shall be placed outside the patient toilet room.

2.2.6 Toilet Rooms and Bathing Facilities

A patient toilet room shall be provided and shall contain a water closet, hand-washing station, and shower. The door to the patient toilet shall swing outward or be double acting.

2.2.7 Patient Storage Locations

Each patient shall have within his or her room a separate wardrobe, locker, or closet suitable for hanging full-length garments and for storing personal effects.

2.2.8 Family/Caregiver Accommodations

2.2.8.1 Areas for overnight stay for patient's significant other or for the patient's selected family caregiver shall be provided.

2.2.8.2 Adequate spaces for sitting, lounging, and visiting shall be provided to meet the needs outlined in the functional program.

2.3 Special Patient Care Areas

2.3.1 Airborne Infection Isolation Room

If the functional program requires a dedicated airborne infection isolation room, it shall meet the criteria established in Section 2.1-3.2.2.

2.3.2 Protective Environment Room

If the functional program requires a protective environment room, it shall meet the criteria established in Section 2.1-3.2.3.

2.3.3 Seclusion Room

If the functional program requires a seclusion room, it shall meet the criteria established in Section 2.3-2.2.1.

2.3.4 Critical Care Rooms

The patient rooms described in this section shall have the capability of serving as temporary critical care patient rooms in the event a patient arrives at the facility in need of stabilization and monitoring prior to transfer to a tertiary care facility. These rooms are intended for temporary care of patients needing transportation to an intensive care setting in a higher level facility, not for active critical care treatment. These rooms shall also be capable of serving the needs of patients requiring hospice and ventilator care.

2.3.5 LDR/LDRP Rooms

When an obstetrical patient presents herself to the small inpatient primary care center, arrangements for transfer of the patient to a tertiary care center with maternity programs shall be made. However, in the event the transfer cannot be accomplished in a timely manner, the small inpatient primary care center shall include the following:

2.3.5.1 The small inpatient primary care center shall have patient rooms with the capability of serving as labor/delivery/recovery or labor/delivery/recovery/postpartum (LDR/LDRP) rooms in the event that an obstetrical patient enters arrives at the facility in need of such services. These rooms shall have a second patient station with electrical, medical gas, and vacuum services to accommodate infant resuscitation needs.

2.3.5.2 If LDR/LDRP functions are programmed for a small inpatient primary care center, a storage area with a minimum of 100 square feet (9.29 square meters) per LDR bed shall be provided for the storage of case carts, delivery equipment, and bassinets.

2.4 Support Areas—General

2.4.1 The size and location of each support area shall depend on the numbers and types of modalities served.

2.4.2 Location

Provision for the support areas listed shall be readily available in each nursing unit.

2.4.3 Identifiable spaces are required for each of the indicated functions.

2.5 Support Areas for Nursing Unit(s)

2.5.1 Administrative Center or Nurse Station

2.5.1.1 Location. This area shall be located to control access to the nursing unit and serve as a security checkpoint for visitors and vendors entering the nursing unit. It shall have direct visual access to the entrance to the unit.

2.5.1.2 Facility requirements

(1) This area shall have space for counters and storage.

(2) This area shall have convenient access to hand-washing facilities.

(2) This area may be combined with or include centers for reception and communication.

2.5.2 Documentation Area

Charting facilities shall have linear surface space to ensure that staff and physicians can chart and have simultaneous access to information and communication systems.

2.5.3 Nurse or Supervisor Office

2.5.4 Hand-Washing Stations

2.5.4.1 Hand-washing stations shall be conveniently accessible to the nurse station, medication station, and nourishment area.

2.5.4.2. If it is convenient to each, one hand-washing station shall be permitted to serve several areas.

2.5.5 Medication Station

Provisions shall be made for the distribution of medications. This may be done from a medicine preparation room or unit, from a self contained-medicine dispensing unit, or by another approved system.

2.5.5.1 Medicine preparation room

(1) This room shall be under visual control of the nursing staff.

(2) This room shall contain a work counter, a hand-washing station, a lockable refrigerator, and locked storage for controlled drugs.

(3) When a medicine preparation room is to be used to store one or more self-contained medicine-dispensing units, the room shall be designed with adequate space to prepare medicines with the self-contained medicine-dispensing unit(s) present.

2.5.5.2 Self-contained medicine dispensing unit

(1) Location of a self-contained medicine dispensing unit shall be permitted at the nurse station, in the clean workroom, or in an alcove, provided the unit has adequate security for controlled drugs and adequate lighting to easily identify drugs.

(2) Convenient access to hand-washing stations shall be provided. (Standard cup sinks provided in many self-contained units are not adequate for hand-washing.)

2.5.6 Nourishment Area

2.5.6.1 A nourishment area shall have a sink, work counter, refrigerator, storage cabinets, and equipment for hot and cold nourishment. This area shall include space for trays and dishes used for nonscheduled meal service.

2.5.6.2 Provisions and space shall be included for separate temporary storage of unused and soiled dietary trays not picked up at mealtime.

2.5.6.3 Hand-washing stations shall be in or immediately accessible from the nourishment area.

2.5.7 Ice Machines

Each nursing unit shall have equipment to provide ice for treatments and nourishment.

2.5.7.1 Ice-making equipment may be in the clean workroom or the nourishment room.

2.5.7.2 Ice intended for human consumption shall be provided in the nourishment station and shall be served from self-dispensing ice makers.

2.5.8 Clean Workroom or Clean Supply Room

Such rooms shall be separate from and have no direct connection with soiled workrooms or soiled holding rooms.

2.5.8.1 Clean workroom. If the room is used for preparing patient care items, it shall contain a work counter, a hand-washing station, and storage facilities for clean and sterile supplies.

2.5.8.2 Clean supply room. If the room is used only for storage and holding as part of a system for distribution of clean and sterile materials, omission of the work counter and hand-washing station shall be permitted.

2.5.9 Soiled Workroom or Soiled Holding Room

Such rooms shall be separate from and have no direct connection with clean workrooms or clean supply rooms.

2.5.9.1 Soiled workroom. These shall contain the following:

(1) A clinical sink (or equivalent flushing-rim fixture) and a hand-washing station. Both fixtures shall have a hot and cold mixing faucet.

(2) A work counter and space for separate covered containers for soiled linen and a variety of waste types.

2.5.9.2 Soiled holding room. Omission of the clinical sink and work counter shall be permitted in rooms used only for temporary holding of soiled material. If the flushing-rim clinical sink is not provided, facilities for cleaning bedpans shall be provided in the patient toilet rooms.

2.5.10 Equipment and Supply Storage

2.5.10.1 Clean linen storage. Each nursing unit shall contain a designated area for clean linen storage.

(1) Location of this area within the clean workroom, a separate closet or alcove, or an approved distribution system shall be permitted.

(2) If a closed cart system is used, storage in an alcove shall be permitted. This cart storage shall be out of the path of normal traffic, under staff control, and protected from contamination.

2.5.10.2 Equipment storage room or alcove. A room or alcove shall be provided in each nursing unit appropriate for the storage of equipment necessary for patient care and as required by the functional program. Each unit shall provide sufficient storage areas located on the patient floor to keep its required corridor width free of all equipment and supplies, but not less than 10 square feet (0.93 square meters) per patient bed shall be provided.

2.5.10.3 Emergency equipment storage. Space shall be provided for emergency equipment that is under direct control of the nursing staff, such as a cardiopulmonary resuscitation (CPR) cart. This space shall be located in an area appropriate to the functional program, but out of normal traffic.

2.5.11 Housekeeping Room

A housekeeping room shall be provided for each nursing unit.

2.5.11.1 The room shall contain a service sink or floor receptor.

2.5.11.2 Provisions for storage of supplies and housekeeping equipment shall be made within the room.

2.6 Support Areas for Staff

2.6.1 Staff Lounge

2.6.1.1 Size. Facilities provided for staff shall be programmatically sized but not less than 100 square feet (9.29 square meters) in area.

2.6.1.2 Location. These facilities shall be located as close as possible to the centralized nurse station or, if the nurse station is decentralized, in close proximity to the work core of the nursing unit.

2.6.2 Staff Toilet Rooms

Toilet rooms for the exclusive use of staff shall be conveniently located in the unit.

2.6.3 Staff Storage Locations

Securable lockers, closets, and cabinet compartments for the personal articles of staff shall be located in or near the nurse station and staff lounge.

2.7 Support Areas for Patients

2.7.1 Patient Toilet Rooms

In addition to those serving bed areas, patient toilet rooms shall be conveniently located to multipurpose rooms. Patient toilet rooms located within the multi-purpose rooms may also be designated for public use.

3 Diagnostic and Treatment Locations

As dictated by the functional program and community needs (and agreements with tertiary care centers), the following elements shall be provided for clinical services:

3.1 Examination and Treatment Rooms

3.1.1 General Purpose Examination Rooms
General purpose examination rooms for medical, obstetrical, and similar functions shall be provided.

3.1.1.1 Space requirements

(1) Area. These rooms shall have a minimum clear floor area of 80 square feet (7.43 square meters) excluding vestibules, toilets, and closets.

(2) Clearances. Room arrangement shall permit a minimum clearance of 2 feet 8 inches (81.28 centimeters) around the examination table.

3.1.1.2 Hand-washing station. A hand-washing sink shall be provided.

3.1.1.3 Documentation space. A counter or shelf space for writing shall be provided.

3.1.2 Special Purpose Examination Rooms
Rooms for special clinics such as eye, ear, nose, and throat examinations shall be designed and outfitted to accommodate the procedures and the equipment used.

3.1.2.1 Hand-washing station. A hand-washing station shall be provided.

3.1.2.2 Documentation space. A counter or shelf space for writing shall be provided.

3.1.3 Treatment Rooms
3.1.3.1 Space requirements. Rooms for minor surgical and cast procedures shall have a minimum floor area of 120 square feet (11.15 square meters) excluding vestibule, toilet, and closets. The minimum room dimension shall be 10 feet (3.05 meters) clear.

3.1.3.2 Hand-washing station. A hand-washing station shall be provided.

3.1.3.3 Documentation space. A counter or shelf for writing shall be provided.

3.1.4 Observation Rooms
3.1.4.1 Location. Rooms for the isolation of suspect or disturbed patients shall be convenient to a nurse or control station. This is to permit close observation of patients and to minimize the possibility that patients can hide, escape, injure themselves, or commit suicide.

3.1.4.2 Space requirements. These rooms shall have a minimum floor area of 80 square feet (7.43 square meters).

3.1.4.3 Modification of an examination room to accommodate this function shall be permitted.

3.1.4.4 Toilet room. A toilet room with hand-washing station shall be immediately accessible.

3.1.5 Support Areas for Examination and Treatment Rooms
3.1.5.1 Work station. A work station shall be provided.

(1) The work station shall have a counter, communication system, space for supplies, and provisions for charting.

(2) If a fully integrated electronic information management system is planned, the following shall be provided:

(a) A centralized work station controlling all ingress and egress to the unit

(b) Additional alcoves or spaces within individual rooms to accommodate the information technology equipment needed to accomplish the integration

3.1.5.2 Medication station. This may be part of the work station.

(1) This shall include a work counter, hand-washing station, lockable refrigerator, and locked storage for controlled drugs. (Standard cup sinks in

many self-contained units are not adequate for hand-washing.)

(2) If a self-contained medicine dispensing unit is provided, it may be located at the work station, in the clean workroom, or in an alcove, provided the unit has adequate security for controlled drugs and adequate lighting to easily identify drugs.

3.1.5.3 Sterilizing facilities. A system for sterilizing equipment and supplies shall be provided. Sterilizing procedures may be done on or off site as long as the off-site location is monitored by the facility regularly and meets the facility's infection control criteria for sterilizing locations and transportation and handling methods for sterilized supplies. Disposable supplies may be used to satisfy the facility's needs.

3.1.5.4 Clean storage. A separate room or closet for storing clean and sterile supplies shall be provided. This storage shall be in addition to that provided by cabinets and shelves.

3.1.5.5 Soiled workroom or soiled holding room. Such rooms shall be separate from and have no direct connection with clean workrooms or clean supply rooms.

(1) Soiled workrooms. These shall contain the following:

  (a) A clinical sink (or equivalent flushing-rim fixture) and a hand-washing station. Both fixtures shall have a hot and cold mixing faucet.

  (b) A work counter and space for separate covered containers for soiled linen and a variety of waste types

(2) Soiled holding rooms. Omission of the clinical sink and work counter shall be permitted in rooms used only for temporary holding of soiled material. If the flushing-rim clinical sink is not provided, facilities for cleaning bedpans shall be provided elsewhere.

3.1.5.6 Wheelchair storage. Wheelchair storage spaces shall be out of the line of traffic.

3.2 Emergency Facilities

Emergency facilities for the small inpatient primary care center shall meet the criteria established for Section 2.1-5.2, Freestanding Emergency Service.

3.3 Surgical Facilities

Surgical procedures that occur in these facilities shall be limited to types that can be performed and supported in an ambulatory surgical setting.

3.3.1 Surgical facilities for the small inpatient primary care center shall meet the criteria established for Sections 2, 3, 5, and 6 of Chapter 3.7, Outpatient Surgical Facilities.

3.3.2 Such facilities shall meet all criteria established under Chapter 18 of NFPA 101, Life Safety Code.

3.4 Imaging Facilities

Facilities for basic diagnostic procedures shall be provided, including the following:

*3.4.1 Radiography Rooms

Radiography rooms shall be of a size to accommodate the functional program.

3.4.2 Support Areas for Imaging Facilities

3.4.2.1 Viewing and administrative areas shall be provided.

3.4.2.2 Film processing facilities shall be provided. (If part of a picture archiving and communication system (PACS), film processing may be retained for emergency use and film development for special cases.)

3.4.2.3 Storage facilities shall be provided for film and equipment.

3.4.3 Support Areas for Staff and Patients

3.4.3.1 Toilet rooms with hand-washing stations accessible to dressing rooms, work stations, and fluoroscopy rooms shall be provided.

APPENDIX

A3.4.1 Radiography rooms should be a minimum of 180 square feet (7.43 square meters). (Dedicated chest X-ray rooms may be smaller.)

3.4.3.2 Dressing rooms or booths shall be as required for services provided, with convenient toilet access.

3.5 Laboratory

Facilities shall be provided within the outpatient department or through an effective contract arrangement with a tertiary care center, for hematology, clinical chemistry, urinalysis, cytology, pathology, and bacteriology. If these services are provided on contract, the following support spaces shall be provided in the facility:

3.5.1 Stat Laboratory

3.5.1.1 A laboratory room with work counters, storage shelving and cabinets, vented flammable storage units, hand-washing station, and vacuum, gas, and electrical services shall be provided.

3.5.1.2 Blood storage facilities meeting the Clinical Laboratory Improvement Act standards for blood banks shall be provided.

3.5.2 Specimen Collection

Specimen collection facilities with pass-through toilet for collection of urine and solid samples, blood-drawing cubicles, adequate seating spaces, storage spaces for specimen collection supplies, and work counters for the preparation, labeling, and storage of specimens awaiting pick-up shall be provided.

3.6 Telemedicine Facilities

If the facility has telemedicine agreements with tertiary care centers, the following support areas for the mobile transportable units, staff, and patients shall be provided:

3.6.1 Reception and Waiting

3.6.1.1 Size. A reception and waiting area for patients and visitors shall be sized according to program needs.

3.6.1.2 Toilets. The area shall be equipped with public and staff toilets.

3.6.2 Staging Area

A staging area for privacy isolation of inpatients awaiting diagnostic treatment shall be provided.

3.6.2.1 Location. The staging area shall be located in a triage area near the patient corridor but separate from the corridor to ensure proper isolation and privacy.

3.6.2.2 Facility requirements

(1)   The staging area shall contain hand-washing stations equipped with hands-free operable controls.

(2)   Ventilation in the staging area shall provide negative air pressure to the surrounding areas.

3.6.3 Consultation Rooms

Rooms shall be provided for staff viewing and consultation with the tertiary care specialist.

3.6.3.1 Privacy and confidentiality of patients records and discussions shall be considered when designing these rooms.

3.6.3.2 Consultation rooms shall be provided at a ratio of one room per mobile transportable unit access port.

3.6.4 Support Areas for Telemedicine Facilities

In facilities where telemedicine is contemplated, adequate spaces to support the telemedicine functions shall be planned in conjunction with information technology spaces. Satellite linkages, communication and viewing rooms and consoles, consultation spaces, electronic interview rooms, and satellite hookups shall be considered when planning the spaces.

3.6.5 Support Areas for Patients

Outpatient clothing change and waiting areas shall be provided. Separate areas shall be provided for male and female patients to change from street clothing into hospital gowns and to wait for procedures.

3.6.5.1 These areas shall include lockers and clothing change or gowning area(s). Provisions for visual and sound privacy shall be made in these spaces.

3.6.5.2 A toilet for patient use shall be provided.

3.6.6 Mobile Transportable Unit Facility Requirements
3.6.6.1 Access ports

(1)   A weather enclosure to protect the transportable unit and patient from the elements shall be a main consideration when considering placement and enclosure of these spaces.

(2) One or more ports shall be provided for use by the facility and the tertiary care center, as required by the functional program and identified community needs.

3.6.6.2 Connection to special life safety needs. The mobile transportable unit shall be integrated with all of the facility's life safety systems, including connection to the facility's fire alarm, sprinkler, security, and exiting systems.

3.7 Additional Diagnostic and Treatment Facilities
Additional diagnostic and treatment facilities for the small inpatient primary care center shall meet the criteria established in the following sections of these Guidelines:
Section 3.1-7.2.3.1, Cough-Inducing and Aerosol-Generating Procedures
Section 3.1-6, Special Systems
Section 3.1-7, Building Systems
Chapter 3.4, Freestanding Outpatient Diagnostic and Treatment Facilities
Chapter 3.9, Gastrointestinal Endoscopy Facilities

If mobile units are used to provide these services, refer to Chapter 3.12, Mobile, Transportable, and Relocatable Units.

4 Service Areas

4.1 Materials Management

4.1.1 Waste Management
4.1.1.1 Collection and storage. Space and facilities shall be provided for the sanitary storage of waste.

4.1.1.2 Refuse chutes. If trash chutes are used, they shall comply with NFPA 82.

Note: See Section 2.2-7.1 for text on waste processing.

4.2 Environmental Services

4.2.1 Housekeeping Rooms
At a minimum, one housekeeping room per support unit or suite shall be provided. These rooms shall contain a sink and storage spaces for clean supplies and cleaning equipment.

4.3 Engineering Services and Maintenance
The following shall be provided:

4.3.1 Equipment Rooms
Equipment rooms for boilers, mechanical equipment, and electrical equipment shall have a minimum clearance around the equipment of 2 feet 6 inches (76.20 centimeters) for ease of maintenance.

4.3.2 Storage Rooms
Storage rooms shall be provided for supplies and equipment.

5 Administrative and Public Areas

5.1 Public Areas
These shall be conveniently accessible to persons with disabilities and include the following:

5.1.1 Entrance
The entrance to the small inpatient primary care center shall be located at grade level and be able to accommodate wheelchairs.

5.1.2 Reception
A reception and information counter or desk shall be located to control the entrance to the facility and to monitor visitors and arriving patients.

5.1.3 Public Waiting Spaces

5.1.4 Public Toilets

5.1.5 Public Telephones

5.1.6 Provisions for Drinking Water

5.1.7 Enclosed Vending Area

5.1.8 Wheelchair Storage Areas
These shall be provided out of the path of traffic.

5.2 Administrative Areas

5.2.1 Interview Spaces
Spaces shall be provided for private interviews related to social services, credit, patient intake, and so on. These spaces shall be designed for confidentiality and privacy.

5.2.2 General and Individual Offices

5.2.2.1 Offices shall be provided for business transactions, medical records, and administrative and professional staff.

5.2.2.2 General clerical spaces or rooms for typing, photocopying, filing, and other clerical work shall be provided. These shall be separated from the public areas for confidentiality.

5.2.3 Multipurpose Rooms

Multipurpose rooms equipped for visual aids shall be provided for conferences, training, meetings, health education programs, and community outreach activities.

5.2.4 Equipment and Supply Storage

Facilities shall be provided for storage of general supplies and equipment needed for continuing operation.

5.2.5 Employee Storage Locations

Storage spaces with locking drawers or cabinets shall be provided for the personal effects of the staff. Such storage shall be near individual work stations and under staff control.

6 Construction Standards

6.1 Building Codes

The diagnostic and treatment locations, service areas, and administrative and public areas in this chapter shall be permitted to fall under the business occupancy provisions of the applicable life safety and building codes if they are separated from the inpatient portion of the facility by two-hour construction.

6.2 General Standards for Details and Finishes

The required minimum corridor width for inpatient facilities (8 feet or 2.44 meters) shall apply to all areas where patients are housed and receive treatment.

7 Special Systems
7.1 General
Section 2.1-9 and related schedules shall apply to this chapter.

7.2 Waste Processing

Facilities shall be provided for the disposal of waste. If incinerators are used, they shall comply with NFPA 82 and all local air pollution regulations.

Note: For waste collection and storage and refuse chute requirements, see Section 2.2-6.1.1.

8 Building Systems

8.1 Plumbing

8.1.1 Hemodialysis and Hemoperfusion Piping
8.1.1.1 In facilities where hemodialysis and hemoperfusion are routinely performed, there shall be separate water supply and drainage facilities that do not interfere with required staff, visitors, and patient hand-washing functions.

8.1.1.2 If perfusion or dialysis occurs at the patient bedside, a separate outlet for de-ionized water and drainage of effluent shall be provided at the patient bedside. It shall be located to prevent contact with electrical outlets and equipment and from potential water droplet contamination of the patient, staff, and visitors.

8.2 Heating, Ventilating, and Air-Conditioning (HVAC) Systems
Section 2.1-10.2 and related schedules shall apply to this chapter.

8.3 Electrical Systems
Section 2.1-10.3 and related schedules shall apply to this chapter.

8.4 Security Systems
Consideration shall be given in the design of these facilities for active and passive security systems. Locking arrangements, security alarms, and monitoring devices shall be placed carefully and shall not interfere with the life and safety features necessary to operate and maintain a healthy and functional environment.

2.3 Psychiatric Hospitals

Appendix material, which appears in shaded boxes at the bottom of the page, is advisory only.

1 General Considerations

1.1 Applicability
This section covers a psychiatric hospital intended for the care and treatment of inpatients and outpatients who do not require acute medical/surgical care services. See Section 2.1-3.8 for psychiatric units within acute care hospitals.

1.2 Functional Program
See Section 1.2-2.

1.3 Shared Services
Where the psychiatric facility is part of another facility, services such as dietary, storage, pharmacy, and laundry should be shared insofar as practical. In some cases, all ancillary service requirements will be met by the principal facility. In other cases, programmatic concerns and requirements may dictate separate services.

1.4 Swing Beds
Change to the occupancy of a group of rooms within the facility shall be permitted to accommodate different patient groups based on age, sex, security level, or treatment programs.

*1.5 Environment of Care

1.5.1 Therapeutic Environment
The facility shall provide a therapeutic environment appropriate for the planned treatment programs.

1.5.2 Security
The design shall provide the level of security appropriate for the planned treatment programs.

1.5.3 Details and Finishes and Equipment
Special design considerations for injury and suicide prevention shall be given to details, finishes, and equipment as specified in Sections 2.3-6.2 and 2.3-8.

1.6 Site

1.6.1 Parking
In the absence of a formal parking study, the facility shall provide at least one space for each employee normally present during one weekday shift plus one space for every five beds, or a total of 1.5 spaces per patient. This ratio may be reduced when justified by availability of convenient public transportation and public parking. Additional parking may be required for outpatients or other services.

APPENDIX

A1.5 Environment of Care
A safe environment is critical; however, no environment can be entirely safe and free of risk. The majority of persons who attempt suicide suffer from a treatable mental disorder or a substance abuse disorder or both. Patients of inpatient psychiatric treatment facilities are considered at high risk for suicide; the environment should avoid physical hazards while maintaining a therapeutic environment. The built environment, no matter how well it is designed and constructed, cannot be relied upon as an absolute preventive measure. Staff awareness of their environment, the latent risks of that environment, and the behavior risks and needs of the patients served in the environment are absolute necessities. Different organizations and different patient populations will require greater or lesser tolerance for risk.

a. The facility should provide a therapeutic environment appropriate for the planned treatment programs. The environment should be characterized by a feeling of openness with emphasis on natural light. In every aspect of building design and maintenance it is essential to make determinations based on the potential risk to the specific patient population served.

b. Consideration should be given to visual control (including electronic surveillance) of nursing unit corridors, dining areas, and social areas such as dayrooms and activity areas. Hidden alcoves or blind corners or areas should be avoided.

c. The openness of the nurse station will depend on the planned treatment program. Consideration should be given to patient privacy and also to staff safety.

2 Nursing Locations

2.1 General Psychiatric Nursing Unit

Each nursing unit shall include the following (see Sections 1.1-1.3.5 and 1.1-3 for exceptions to standards where existing conditions make absolute compliance impractical).

2.1.1 Typical Psychiatric Patient Rooms

Each patient room shall meet the following standards:

2.1.1.1 Capacity. Maximum room capacity shall be two patients.

2.1.1.2 Space requirements. Minor encroachments, including columns and hand-washing stations, that do not interfere with functions may be ignored when determining space requirements for patient rooms.

(1) Patient room areas, exclusive of toilet rooms, closets, lockers, wardrobes, alcoves, or vestibules, shall be at least 100 square feet (9.29 square meters) for single-bed rooms and 80 square feet (7.43 square meters) per bed for multiple-bed rooms.

(2) The areas noted herein are intended as minimums and do not prohibit use of larger rooms where required by the functional program.

2.1.1.3 Windows. Each patient room shall have a window in accordance with Section 2.1-8.2.2.5.

2.1.1.4 Desk. There shall be a desk or writing surface in each room for patient use.

2.1.1.5 Patient toilet rooms

(1) Each patient shall have access to a toilet room without having to enter the general corridor area. (This direct access requirement may be disregarded if it conflicts with the supervision of patients as required by the functional program.)

> **APPENDIX**
>
> **A2.1.3** Outdoor areas are not required; however, if patient care programs require them to be provided, they should be arranged to prevent confused residents from wandering outside of designated resident areas.

(2) One toilet room shall serve no more than four beds and no more than two patient rooms.

(3) The toilet room shall contain a water closet and a hand-washing station.

(4) The door to the toilet room shall swing outward or be double-acting.

2.1.1.6 Patient storage locations

(1) Each patient shall have within his or her room a separate wardrobe, locker, or closet suitable for hanging full-length garments and for storing personal effects.

(2) Adequate storage shall be available for a daily change of clothes for seven days.

2.1.2 Security Rooms

Security rooms may be included if required by the functional program.

2.1.2.1 Security rooms shall be single-bed rooms designed to minimize potential for escape, hiding, injury to self or others, or suicide. Access to toilets, showers, and wardrobes shall be restricted.

2.1.2.2 Security rooms may be centralized on one unit or decentralized among units.

*2.1.3 Outdoor Areas

2.2 Special Patient Care Areas

2.2.1 Seclusion Room

The seclusion treatment room is intended for short-term occupancy. Within the psychiatric nursing unit, this space provides for patients requiring security and protection.

2.2.1.1 Capacity

(1) Each room shall be for only one patient.

(2) There shall be at least one seclusion room for each 24 beds or fraction thereof on each psychiatric unit.

(3) If a facility has more than one psychiatric nursing unit, the number of seclusion rooms shall be a function of the total number of psychiatric beds in the facility.

2.2.1.2 Location

(1) The room(s) shall be located for direct nursing staff supervision.

(2) Seclusion rooms may be grouped together.

2.2.1.3 Space requirements

(1) Seclusion treatment rooms shall have an area of at least 60 square feet (5.57 square meters) with a minimum wall length of 7 feet (2.13 meters) and a maximum wall length of 11 feet (3.35 meters).

(2) Where restraint beds are required by the functional program, 80 square feet (7.43 square meters) shall be required.

2.2.1.4 Layout. Seclusion treatment rooms shall be accessed by an anteroom or vestibule that also provides access to a toilet room. The doors to the anteroom and the toilet room shall be a minimum of 3 feet 8 inches (1.12 meters) wide.

2.2.1.5 Details and finishes. Seclusion treatment rooms shall be constructed to prevent patient hiding, escape, injury, or suicide.

(1) Fire rating of materials

   (a) Where the interior of the seclusion treatment room is padded with combustible materials, these materials shall be of a type acceptable to the local authority having jurisdiction.

   (b) The room area, including floor, walls, ceilings, and all openings, shall be protected with not less than one-hour-rated construction.

(2) Seclusion treatment rooms shall not contain outside corners or edges.

(3) Doors

   (a) The entrance door to the seclusion room shall swing out.

   (b) Doors shall be 3 feet 8 inches (1.12 meters) wide and shall permit staff observation of the patient through a vision panel, while also maintaining provisions for patient privacy.

(4) Minimum ceiling height shall be 9 feet (2.74 meters).

(5) Electrical switches and receptacles are prohibited within the seclusion room.

2.2.2 Airborne Infection Isolation Room(s)

2.2.2.1 Number. The need for and number of required airborne infection isolation rooms in the psychiatric hospital shall be determined by an ICRA.

2.2.2.2 Where required, the airborne infection isolation room(s) shall comply with the general requirements of Section 2.1-3.2.2.

2.3 Child Psychiatric Unit

Child psychiatric unit patient areas shall be separate and distinct from any adult psychiatric unit patient areas. The standards of Sections 2.3-2.1, 2.3-2.2.1 and 2.2.2, and 2.3-2.6 shall be applied to child units with the following exceptions:

2.3.1 Patient Rooms

2.3.1.1 Capacity. Maximum room capacity shall be four children.

2.3.1.2 Space requirements. Patient room areas (with beds or cribs) shall be at least 100 square feet (9.29 square meters) for single-bed rooms; 80 square feet (7.43 square meters) per bed and 60 square feet (5.57 square meters) per crib in multiple-bed rooms.

2.3.1.3 Storage. Storage space shall be provided for toys, equipment, extra cribs and beds, and cots or recliners for parents who may stay overnight.

2.3.2 Activity Areas

2.3.2.1 Space requirements

(1) The combined area for social activities shall be 35 square feet (3.25 square meters) per patient.

(2) The total area for social activities and dining space shall be a minimum of 50 square feet (4.65 square meters) per patient.

(3) If a separate dining space is provided, it shall be a minimum of 15 square feet (1.39 square meters) per patient.

*2.3.3 Outdoor Areas

2.4 Geriatric, Alzheimer's, and Other Dementia Unit
The standards of Sections 2.3-2.1, 2.3-2.2.1 and 2.2.2, and 2.3-2.6 shall be applied to geriatric units with the following exceptions:

2.4.1 Patient Rooms
2.4.1.1 Space requirements. Patient room areas shall be at least 120 square feet (11.15 square meters) in single-bed rooms and 200 square feet (18.58 square meters) in multiple-bed rooms.

2.4.1.2 Linen storage. Each patient bedroom shall have storage for extra blankets, pillows, and linen.

2.4.1.3 Doors. Doors to patient rooms shall be a minimum of 3 feet 8 inches wide (1.12 meters).

2.4.1.4 Nurse call system

(1) A nurse call system shall be provided in accordance with the standards in Section 2.1-10.3.8.

(2) Provisions shall be made for easy removal of or for covering call button outlets.

(3) Call cords or strings in excess of 6 inches (15.24 centimeters) shall not be permitted.

2.4.2 Support Areas for Geriatric, Alzheimer's, and Other Dementia Units
2.4.2.1 Social spaces. The standards of Section 2.3-2.9.1 shall apply for social spaces, except that the combined area for social activities shall be 30 square

APPENDIX

A2.3.3 Outdoor areas should be protected to allow children to have easy access to secure outdoor areas for play and therapy in facilities where length of stay is two weeks or greater.

feet (2.79 square meters) per patient.

2.4.2.2 Bathing facilities. Patients shall have access to at least one bathtub in each nursing unit.

2.4.2.3 Wheelchair storage. Storage space for wheelchairs shall be provided in the nursing unit.

2.5 Forensic Psychiatric Unit

2.5.1 General
The standards of Sections 2.3-2.1, 2.3-2.2.1 and 2.2.2, and 2.3-2.6 shall apply to forensic units.

2.5.2 Forensic Unit Requirements
2.5.2.1 Forensic units shall have security vestibules or sally ports at the unit entrance.

2.5.2.2 Specialized program requirements may indicate the need for additional treatment areas, police and courtroom space, and security considerations.

2.5.2.3 Areas for children, juveniles, and adolescents shall be separated from adult areas.

2.6 Support Areas—General

2.6.1 Location
2.6.1.1 Provision for the support areas listed shall be located in or readily available to each nursing unit unless otherwise noted.

2.6.1.2 Each support area may be arranged and located to serve more than one nursing unit; however, unless otherwise noted, at least one such support area shall be provided on each nursing floor.

2.6.2 Where the words room or office are used, a separate, enclosed space for the one named function is intended; otherwise, the described area may be a specific space in another room or common area.

2.7 Support Areas for Psychiatric Nursing Units

2.7.1 Administrative Center or Nurse Station

2.7.2 Documentation Area
A separate charting area with provisions for acoustical and patient file privacy shall be provided.

2.7.3 Office(s) for Staff

2.7.4 Multipurpose Room(s)

Location of these spaces either within the psychiatric unit or immediately accessible to it shall be permitted unless otherwise dictated by the functional program.

2.7.4.1 Visitor room. A visitor room for patients to meet with friends or family with a minimum floor space of 100 square feet (9.29 square meters).

2.7.4.2 Quiet room. A quiet room shall be provided for a patient who needs to be alone for a short period of time but does not require a seclusion room.

(1) A minimum of 80 square feet (7.43 square meters) shall be provided.

(2) The visitor room may serve this purpose.

2.7.4.3 Consultation room(s)

(1) Separate consultation room(s), with minimum floor space of 100 square feet (9.29 square meters) each, shall be provided at a room-to-bed ratio of one consultation room for each 12 psychiatric beds.

(2) The room(s) shall be designed for acoustical and visual privacy and constructed to achieve a level of voice privacy of 50 STC (which in terms of vocal privacy means some loud or raised speech is heard only by straining, but is not intelligible).

(3) The visitor room may serve as a consultation room.

2.7.4.4 Conference room. A conference and treatment planning room shall be provided for use by the psychiatric unit. This room may be combined with the charting room.

2.7.4.5 Space for group therapy. This may be combined with the quiet space noted in Section 2.3-2.9.1 when the unit accommodates not more than 12 patients and when at least 225 square feet (20.90 square meters) of enclosed private space is available for group therapy activities.

2.7.5 Hand-Washing Stations
See Section 2.1-3.1.5.5.

2.7.6 Medication Station
See Section 2.1-2.3.4.

2.7.7 Nourishment Area
Food service within the unit may be one or a combination of the following:

2.7.7.1 A nourishment station

2.7.7.2 A kitchenette designed for patient use with staff control of heating and cooking devices

2.7.7.3 A kitchen service within the unit that includes a hand-washing station, storage space, refrigerator, and facilities for meal preparation

2.7.8 Ice Machine
See Section 2.1-2.3.6.

2.7.9 Clean Workroom or Clean Supply Room
See Section 2.1-2.3.7.

2.7.10 Soiled Workroom
See Section 2.1-2.3.8.

2.7.11 Equipment and Supply Storage
Location of these areas either within the psychiatric units or immediately accessible to them shall be permitted unless otherwise dictated by the functional program.

2.7.11.1 Clean linen storage. See Section 2.1-3.1.5.12 (1).

2.7.11.2 Wheelchair storage space. Storage space for wheelchairs may be outside the psychiatric unit, provided that provisions are made for convenient access as needed for disabled patients.

2.7.11.3 Emergency equipment storage. Space shall be provided for emergency equipment that is under direct control of the nursing staff, such as a CPR cart.

(1) This space shall be in close proximity to a nurse station.

(2) The space may serve more than one unit.

2.7.11.4 Administrative supplies storage

2.7.12 Housekeeping Room
Location of this room either in or immediately accessible to the nursing unit shall be permitted unless otherwise dictated by the functional program. See Section 2.1-3.1.5.13.

2.8 Support Areas for Staff

2.8.1 Staff Lounge Facilities

2.8.2 Staff Toilet Room(s)

2.8.3 Staff Storage Locations
Securable closets or cabinet compartments for the personal effects of nursing personnel shall be conveniently located to the duty station. At a minimum, these shall be large enough for purses and billfolds.

2.9 Support Areas for Patients

2.9.1 Social Spaces
2.9.1.1 At least two separate social spaces, one appropriate for noisy activities and one for quiet activities, shall be provided.

2.9.1.2 Space requirements

(1) The combined area shall be at least 25 square feet (2.32 square meters) per patient with at least 120 square feet (11.15 square meters) for each of the two spaces.

(2) This space may be shared by dining activities if an additional 15 square feet (1.39 square meters) per patient is added; otherwise, 20 square feet (1.86 square meters) per patient shall be provided for dining.

2.9.1.3 Dining facilities may be located off the nursing unit in a central area.

2.9.2 Patient Bathing Facilities
2.9.2.1 A bathtub or shower shall be provided for each six beds not otherwise served by bathing facilities within the patient rooms.

2.9.2.2 Bathing facilities shall be designed and located for patient convenience and privacy.

2.9.3 Patient Laundry Facilities
Patient laundry facilities with an automatic washer and dryer shall be provided.

2.9.4 Patient Storage Facilities
A staff-controlled, secured storage area shall be provided for patients' effects determined potentially harmful (e.g., razors, nail files, cigarette lighters, etc.).

3 Diagnostic and Treatment Locations

3.1 Examination and Treatment Room(s)

3.1.1 Location
These shall be permitted to serve several nursing units and may be on a different floor if conveniently located for routine use.

3.1.1.2 Space requirements. Examination rooms shall have a minimum floor area of 120 square feet (11.15 square meters), excluding space for vestibule, toilets, and closets.

3.1.1.3 Facility requirements. The room shall contain a hand-washing station; storage facilities; and a desk, counter, or shelf space for writing.

3.2 Imaging Suite
Radiology services are not required to be provided within a psychiatric hospital. If they are provided, the radiology suite shall comply with Section 2.1-5.5.

3.3 Nuclear Medicine
Nuclear medicine services are not required to be provided within a psychiatric hospital. If they are provided, the nuclear medicine area shall comply with Section 2.1-5.6.

3.4 Rehabilitation Therapy Department

3.4.1 General
Rehabilitation therapy in a psychiatric hospital is primarily for the diagnosis and treatment of mental functions but may also seek to address physical functions in varying degrees. It may contain one or several categories of services.

3.4.1.1 If a formal rehabilitative therapy service is included in a project, the facilities and equipment shall be as necessary to accommodate the functional program.

3.4.1.2 Where two or more rehabilitative services are included, facilities and equipment may be shared as appropriate.

3.4.2 Physical Therapy

An individual's physical health can have a direct effect on his or her mental health. Therefore, physical therapy may be desirable in a psychiatric hospital, especially for long-term care patients and elderly patients. If physical therapy is included in the functional program, the following shall be provided.

3.4.2.1 Individual treatment area(s)

(1) Privacy. Each area shall have privacy screens or curtains.

(2) Each such space shall have not less than 60 square feet (5.57 square meters) of clear floor area.

3.4.2.2 Exercise area and facilities

3.4.2.3 Provision for additional therapies. If required by the functional program, provisions for thermotherapy, diathermy, ultrasonics, and hydrotherapy shall be made.

3.4.2.4 Hand-washing stations

(1) Hand-washing stations for staff shall be available either within or at each treatment space.

(2) One hand-washing station may serve several treatment stations.

3.4.2.5 Support areas for physical therapy

(1) Soiled material storage. Separate storage for soiled linen, towels, and supplies shall be provided.

(2) Equipment and supply storage

    (a) Clean linen and towel storage

    (b) Storage for equipment and supplies

3.4.2.6 Support areas for patients. Dressing areas, showers, and lockers for outpatients shall be provided.

3.4.3 Occupational Therapy

Occupational therapy may include such activities as woodworking, leather tooling, art, needlework, painting, sewing, metalwork, and ceramics. The following shall be provided:

3.4.3.1 Work areas and counters

(1) These shall be suitable for wheelchair access.

(2) Work areas shall be sized for one therapy group at a time.

3.4.3.2 Other facilities

*(1) A separate room or alcove shall be provided for a kiln.

*(2) Display areas shall be provided.

3.4.3.3 Hand-washing stations

3.4.3.4 Equipment and supply storage

(1) Storage shall be provided for supplies and equipment.

(2) Secured storage shall be provided for potentially harmful supplies and equipment.

3.4.3.5 Electrical switching. Remote electrical switching shall be provided for potentially harmful equipment.

3.4.4 Vocational Therapy

Vocational therapy assists patients in the development and maintenance of productive work and interaction skills through the use of work tasks. These activities may occur in an industrial therapy workshop in another department or outdoors. If vocational therapy

---

APPENDIX

A3.4.3.2 (1) Exposure to some art materials, such as solvents and ceramic glazes, is associated with adverse health effects. Such risks should be controlled by adopting methods recommended in appropriate instructional manuals.

A3.4.3.2 (2) Display areas for patients' work, such as shelves or wall surfaces, should be provided.

is included in the functional program, the following shall be provided:

3.4.4.1 Work areas

(1) These shall be suitable for wheelchair access.

(2) Group work areas shall be sized for one therapy group at a time.

3.4.4.2 Hand-washing stations. These shall be provided if required by the functional program.

3.4.4.3 Equipment and supply storage

(1) Storage for supplies and equipment shall be provided.

(2) Secured storage for potentially harmful supplies and equipment shall be provided.

3.4.4.4 Electrical switching. Remote electrical switching shall be provided for potentially harmful equipment.

3.4.5 Recreation Therapy
Recreation therapy assists patients in the development and maintenance of community living skills through the use of leisure-time activity tasks. These activities may occur in a recreation therapy department, in specialized facilities (e.g., gymnasium), multipurpose space in other areas (e.g., the nursing unit), or outdoors. If recreation therapy is included in the functional program, the following shall be provided:

3.4.5.1 Activity areas. Activity areas shall be suitable for wheelchair access.

3.4.5.2 Hand-washing stations. These shall be provided if required by the functional program.

3.4.5.3 Equipment and supply storage

(1) Storage for supplies and equipment shall be provided.

(2) Secured storage for potentially harmful supplies and equipment shall be provided.

3.4.5.4 Electrical switching. Remote electrical switching shall be provided for potentially harmful equipment.

3.4.6 Education Therapy
Education therapy may be a program requirement, especially for children and adolescents. If education therapy is part of the functional program, the following shall be provided.

3.4.6.1 Classroom with student desks with 30 square feet (2.79 square meters) per desk and at least 150 square feet (13.94 square meters) per classroom shall be provided.

3.4.6.2 Desk and lockable storage for the teacher shall be provided.

3.4.6.3 Storage for supplies, equipment, and books shall be provided.

3.4.7 Support Areas for Rehabilitative Therapy Departments
Each rehabilitative therapy department shall include the following, which may be shared or provided as separate units for each service.

3.4.7.1 Reception and control station(s)

(1) If reception and control station(s) are required by the functional program, provision shall be made for visual control of waiting and activity areas.

(2) Reception and control stations may be combined with office and clerical space.

3.4.7.2 Patient waiting area(s)

(1) Location. Patient waiting area(s) shall be located out of traffic, with provision for wheelchairs.

(2) Omission of the waiting area shall be permitted if it is not required by the functional program. (Patient waiting time for rehabilitation therapy should be minimized in a psychiatric hospital.)

3.4.7.3 Office and clerical space. Provision shall be made for filing and retrieval of patient records.

3.4.7.4 Multipurpose room. Access to a demonstration/conference room shall be provided.

3.4.7.5 Housekeeping room. A conveniently accessible

housekeeping room and service sink for housekeeping use shall be provided.

3.4.8 Support Areas for Staff

3.4.8.1 Convenient access to toilets and lockers shall be provided.

3.4.8.2 A secured area or cabinet shall be provided within the vicinity of each work area for securing staff personal effects.

3.4.9 Support Areas for Patients

Patient toilets with hand-washing stations that are accessible to wheelchair patients shall be provided.

3.5 Laboratory Suite

3.5.1 Laboratory Requirements

Required laboratory tests may be performed on-site or provided through a contractual arrangement with a laboratory service.

3.5.1.1 Provisions shall be made for the following procedures to be performed on-site: urinalysis, blood glucose, and electrolytes.

3.5.1.2 Provisions shall also be made for specimen collection and processing.

3.5.2 Facility Requirements

Minimum facilities on-site shall include a defined area with a laboratory lab counter, sink with water, refrigerated storage, storage for equipment and supplies, clerical area, and record storage.

4 Service Areas

4.1 Pharmacy

As described in the functional program, the size and type of facilities and equipment to be provided in the pharmacy shall depend on the type of patients and illnesses treated, type of drug distribution system used, number of patients to be served, and extent of shared or purchased services.

4.1.1 Pharmacy Room or Suite

4.1.1.1 Location. The pharmacy room or suite shall be located for convenient access, staff control, and security.

4.1.1.2 Facility requirements. It shall include provisions for procurement, storage, distribution, and recording of drugs and other pharmacy products.

4.1.2 Satellite Facilities

Satellite facilities, if provided, shall include those items required by the functional program.

4.2 Dietary Facilities

See Section 2.1-6.2.

4.3 Central Services

If only primary medical care is provided, central services may not be required or may be provided by countertop sterilizing/cleaning equipment. If decontamination and sterilization are required on-site, a full central services area shall be provided (see Section 2.1-6.3).

4.4 Linen Services

See Section 2.1-6.4.

4.5 Materials Management

4.5.1 General Stores

4.5.1.1 Location. Location of storage in separate, concentrated areas within the institution or in one or more individual buildings on-site shall be permitted. A portion of this storage may be provided off-site.

4.5.1.2 Space requirements. General storage room(s) with a total area of not less than 4 square feet (0.37 square meters) per inpatient bed shall be provided.

4.5.2 Waste Management

See Section 2.1-6.5.3. (See Section 2.1-9.3 for text on waste processing.)

4.6 Environmental Services

4.6.1 Facilities for Cleaning and Sanitizing Carts

See Section 2.1-6.6.1.

4.6.2 Housekeeping Room

See Section 2.1-6.6.2.

4.7 Engineering Services and Maintenance

See Section 2.1-6.7.

5 Administrative and Public Areas

See Section 2.1-7.

5.1 Medical Records
See Section 2.1-7.2.5.

5.2 Employee Facilities
See Section 2.1-7.2.7.

6 Construction Standards

6.1 Design and Construction, Including Fire-Resistant Standards
See Section 2.1-8.1.

6.2 General Standards for Details and Finishes

6.2.1 General
Details and finishes shall comply with Section 2.1-8.2 except as shown in this section. Special design consideration shall be given to injury and suicide prevention as discussed here:

6.2.2 Details
6.2.2.1 Doors

(1) Door width. The minimum door width for patient use access in new work shall be at least 3 feet (91.44 centimeters).

(2) Door swings. Door swings for private patient bathrooms or shower areas shall swing out to allow for staff emergency access.

(3) Door closers

    (a) Door closers are to be avoided unless required.

    (b) Door closer devices, if required on the patient room door, shall be mounted on the public side of the door rather than the private patient side of the door.

    (c) Ideally, the door closer (if required) should be within view of a nurse or staff workstation.

(4) Door hinges

    (a) Door hinges shall be designed to minimize points for hanging (i.e., cut hinge type).

    (b) Door hinges used shall be consistent with the level of care for the patient.

(5) Door lever handles. These shall point downward when in the latched position.

(6) Fasteners. All hardware shall have tamper-resistant fasteners.

*6.2.2.2 Windows. All glazing (both interior and exterior), borrow lights, and glass mirrors shall be fabricated with laminated safety glass or protected by polycarbonate, laminate, or safety screens.

6.2.2.3 Furniture

(1) Clothing rods or hooks, if present, shall be designed to minimize the opportunity for residents to cause injury.

(2) Furniture shall be constructed to withstand physical abuse.

(3) Drawer pulls shall be of the recessed type to eliminate the possibility of use as a tie-off point.

6.2.2.4 Bathroom hardware and accessories. Special design considerations for injury and suicide prevention shall be given to shower, bath, toilet, and sink hardware and accessories, including grab bars and toilet paper holders.

(1) Grab bars

    (a) ADA- or ANSI-compliant grab bars are required in 10 percent of the private/semi-private patient toilet rooms. The remaining rooms are not required to have grab bars.

    (b) Grab bars in patient toilet rooms for fully ambulatory patients shall be removable.

APPENDIX

A6.2.2.2 The use of drapery is discouraged.

(c) Where grab bars are provided, the space between the bar and the wall shall be filled to prevent a cord being tied around it for hanging.

(d) Bars, including those that are part of such fixtures as soap dishes, shall be sufficiently anchored to sustain a concentrated load of 250 pounds (113.4 kilograms).

(2) The following are not permitted:

(a) Towel bars

(b) Shower curtain rods

(c) Lever handles

6.2.3 Finishes
6.2.3.1 Ceilings

(1) In private patient bathrooms, the ceiling shall be of the tamper-resistive type or of sufficient height to prevent patient access. Ceiling systems of a non-secured (non-clipped down) lay-in ceiling tile design are not permitted.

(2) In patient bedrooms where acoustical ceilings are permitted by the functional program, the ceiling shall be secured or of sufficient height to prevent patient access.

(3) In private patient bathrooms, any plumbing, piping, ductwork, or other potentially hazardous elements shall be concealed above a ceiling.

(4) In patient bedrooms and bathrooms, ceiling access panels shall be secured or of sufficient height to prevent patient access.

(5) In patient bedrooms and bathrooms, ventilation grilles shall be secured and have small perforations to eliminate their use as a tie-off point or shall be of sufficient height to prevent patient access.

6.2.3.2 Sprinkler heads and other protrusions

(1) In unsupervised patient areas, sprinkler heads shall be recessed or of a design to minimize patient access.

(2) In private patient bathrooms, air distribution devices, lighting fixtures, sprinkler heads, and other appurtenances shall be of the tamper-resistant type.

7 Special Systems

7.1 General

7.1.1 Testing
7.1.1.1 Prior to acceptance of the facility, all special systems shall be tested and operated to demonstrate to the owner or his designated representative that the installation and performance of these systems conform to design intent.

7.1.1.2 Test results shall be documented for maintenance files.

7.1.2 Documentation
7.1.2.1 Upon completion of the special systems equipment installation contract, the owner shall be furnished with a complete set of manufacturers' operating, maintenance, and preventive maintenance instructions, parts lists, and complete procurement information including equipment numbers and descriptions.

7.1.2.2 Operating staff persons shall also be provided with written instructions for proper operation of systems and equipment. Required information shall include all safety or code ratings as needed.

7.1.3 Insulation
Insulation shall be provided surrounding special systems equipment to conserve energy, protect personnel, and reduce noise.

7.2 Elevators

7.2.1 General
All buildings with patient facilities (such as bedrooms, dining rooms, or recreation areas) or services (such as diagnostic or therapeutic areas) located on other than the main entrance floor shall have electric or hydraulic elevators.

7.2.2 Leveling Device
Elevators shall be equipped with a two-way automatic level-maintaining device with an accuracy of ±1/4 inch (±6.35 millimeters).

7.2.3 Elevator Controls

7.2.3.1 Each elevator, except those for material handling, shall be equipped with an independent keyed switch for staff use for bypassing all landing button calls and responding to car button calls only.

*7.2.3.2 Elevator call buttons shall be key controlled if required by the functional program, and controls shall not be activated by heat or smoke. Light beams, if used for operating door reopening devices without touch, shall be used in combination with door-edge safety devices and shall be interconnected with a system of smoke detectors.

7.2.4 Installation and Testing

7.2.4.1 Standards. Installation and testing of elevators shall comply with ANSI/ASME A17.1 for new construction and ANSI/ASME A17.3 for existing facilities. (See ASCE 7-93 for seismic design and control systems requirements for elevators.)

7.2.4.2 Documentation. Field inspections and tests shall be made and the owner shall be furnished with written certification stating that the installation meets the requirements set forth in this section as well as all applicable safety regulations and codes.

7.3 Waste Processing

See Section 2.1-9.3. (See Section 2.1-6.5.3 for text on waste management.)

8 Building Systems

8.1 Plumbing

8.1.1 General

Unless otherwise specified herein, all plumbing systems shall be designed and installed in accordance with the chapters in the International Plumbing Code that area applicable for this occupancy.

8.1.2 Plumbing and Other Piping Systems

8.1.2.1 General piping and valves. See Section 2.1-10.1.2.1.

8.1.2.2 Potable water supply systems. See Section 2.1-10.1.2.3.

8.1.2.3 Hot water systems. See Section 1.6-2.1.2.1.

8.1.2.4 Drainage systems. See Section 2.1-10.1.2.5.

8.1.2.5 Condensate drains. See Section 1.6-2.1.2.2.

8.1.2.6 Plumbing in food preparation and storage areas. See Section 2.1-10.1.2.5.

8.1.3 Plumbing Fixtures

8.1.3.1 See Sections 1.6-2.1.3 and 2.1-10.1.3.

8.1.3.2 Special design considerations for injury and suicide prevention shall be given to shower, bath, toilet, and sink plumbing fixtures. Shower heads shall be of flush-mounted design to minimize hanging appendages.

8.1.4 Medical Gas and Vacuum Systems

8.1.4.1 Installation, testing, and certification of nonflammable medical gas and air systems. See Section 2.1-10.1.4.1.

8.1.4.2 Clinical vacuum systems. See Section 2.1-10.1.4.2.

8.2 Heating, Ventilating, and Air-Conditioning (HVAC) Systems

8.2.1 General

8.2.1.1 Mechanical system design

*(1) Efficiency. The mechanical system shall be designed for overall efficiency and appropriate life-cycle cost. Details for cost-effective implementation of design features are interrelated and too numerous (as well as too basic) to list individually.

   (a) Recognized engineering procedures shall be followed for the most economical and effective results.

(b) In no case shall patient care or safety be sacrificed for conservation.

(c) Insofar as practical, the facility shall include provisions for recovery of waste cooling and heating energy (ventilation, exhaust, water and steam discharge, cooling towers, incinerators, etc.).

*(d) Use of recognized energy-saving mechanisms such as variable-air-volume (VAV) systems, load shedding, programmed controls for unoccupied periods (nights and weekends, etc.), and natural ventilation shall be considered, site and climatic conditions permitting.

(e) Facility design considerations shall include site, building mass, orientation, configuration, fenestration, and other features relative to passive and active energy systems.

(2) Air-handling systems

(a) These shall be designed with an economizer cycle where appropriate to use outside air. (Use of mechanically circulated outside air does not reduce need for filtration.)

(b) VAV systems. The energy-saving potential of variable air volume systems is recognized, and these standards are intended to maximize appropriate use of such systems. Any system used for occupied areas shall include provisions to avoid air stagnation in interior spaces where thermostat demands are met by temperatures of surrounding areas.

(c) Noncentral air-handling systems (i.e., individual room units that are used for heating and cooling purposes, such as fan-coil units, heat pump units, etc.). These units may be used as recirculating units only. All outdoor requirements shall be met by a separate central air-handling system with the proper filtration, as noted in Table 2.1-3.

(3) Vibration isolators. Mechanical equipment, ductwork, and piping shall be mounted on vibration

isolators as required to prevent unacceptable structure-borne vibration.

(4) System valves. Supply and return mains and risers for cooling, heating, and steam systems shall be equipped with valves to isolate the various sections of each system. Each piece of equipment shall have valves at the supply and return ends.

(5) Renovation. If system modifications affect greater than 10 percent of the system capacity, designers shall utilize pre-renovation water/air flow rate measurements in the affected zones to verify that sufficient capacity is available and that renovations have not adversely affected flow rates in non-renovated areas.

8.2.1.2 Ventilation and space conditioning requirements. All rooms and areas used for patient care shall have provisions for ventilation.

(1) Ventilation rates. The ventilation systems shall be designed and balanced, as a minimum, according to the requirements shown in Table 2.1-2 and its applicable notes. The ventilation rates shown in Table 2.1-2 do not preclude the use of higher, more appropriate rates.

(2) Air change rates. Air supply and exhaust in rooms for which no minimum total air change rate is noted may vary down to zero in response to room load. For rooms listed in Table 2.1-2, where VAV systems are used, minimum total air change shall be within limits noted.

(3) Temperature and humidity levels. Space temperature and relative humidity shall be as indicated in Table 2.1-2.

8.2.1.3 Documentation

(1) Upon completion of the equipment installation contract, the owner shall be furnished with a complete

APPENDIX

A8.2.1.1 (1)(d) Systems with excessive installation and/or maintenance costs that negate long-range energy savings should be avoided.

set of manufacturers' operating, maintenance, and preventive maintenance instructions, parts lists, and complete procurement information, including equipment numbers and descriptions. Required information shall include energy ratings as needed for future conservation calculations.

(2) Operating staff persons shall also be provided with written instructions for proper operation of systems and equipment.

8.2.2 Requirements for Specific Locations

8.2.2.1 Patient-occupied areas. Special consideration shall be given to the type of heating and cooling units, ventilation outlets, and appurtenances installed in patient-occupied areas of the psychiatric hospital. The following shall apply:

(1) All air grilles and diffusers shall be of a type that prohibits the insertion of foreign objects. All exposed fasteners shall be tamper-resistant.

(2) All convector or HVAC enclosures exposed in the room shall be constructed with rounded corners and shall have enclosures fastened with tamper-resistant screws.

(3) HVAC equipment shall be of a type that minimizes the need for maintenance within the room.

8.2.2.2 Cough-inducing procedure rooms. Rooms used for sputum induction, aerosolized pentamidine treatments, and other cough-inducing procedures shall meet the requirements of Table 2.1-2 for airborne infection isolation rooms. If booths are used, refer to Section 2.1-5.8.1.

8.2.2.3 Food preparation centers

(1) Exhaust hoods handling grease-laden vapors in food preparation centers shall comply with NFPA 96.

(2) All hoods over cooking ranges shall be equipped

A8.2.4.2 (2) See *Industrial Ventilation: A Manual of Recommended Practice*, published by the American Conference of Governmental Industrial Hygienists (www.acgih.org), for additional information.

with grease filters, fire-extinguishing systems, and heat-actuated fan controls.

(3) Cleanout openings shall be provided every 20 feet (6.10 meters) and at changes in direction in the horizontal exhaust duct systems serving these hoods. Horizontal runs of ducts serving range hoods shall be kept to a minimum.

8.2.2.4 Fuel-fired equipment rooms. Rooms with fuel-fired equipment shall be provided with sufficient outdoor air to maintain equipment combustion rates and to limit workstation temperatures.

8.2.3 Thermal Insulation and Acoustical Provisions
See Section 1.6-2.2.1.

8.2.4 HVAC Air Distribution
8.2.4.1 Return air systems. For patient care areas, return air shall be via ducted systems.

8.2.4.2 HVAC ductwork

(1) General

(a) Air-handling duct systems shall be designed with accessibility for duct cleaning and shall meet the requirements of NFPA 90A.

(b) When smoke partitions are required, heating, ventilation, and air conditioning zones shall be coordinated with compartmentation insofar as practical to minimize need to penetrate fire and smoke partitions.

*(2) Duct humidifiers

(a) If duct humidifiers are located upstream of the final filters, they shall be at least 15 feet (4.57 meters) upstream of the final filters.

(b) Ductwork with duct-mounted humidifiers shall have a means of water removal.

(c) An adjustable high-limit humidistat shall be located downstream of the humidifier to reduce the potential for condensation inside the duct.

(d) All duct takeoffs shall be sufficiently downstream of the humidifier to ensure complete moisture absorption. Steam humidifiers shall be used.

(e) Reservoir-type water spray or evaporative pan humidifiers shall not be used.

(3) Fire and smoke dampers

(a) Fire and smoke dampers shall be constructed, located, and installed in accordance with the requirements of NFPA 101, 90A, and the specific damper's listing requirements.

(b) Fans, dampers, and detectors shall be interconnected so that damper activation will not damage ducts.

(c) Maintenance access shall be provided at all dampers.

(d) All damper locations shall be shown on design drawings.

(e) Dampers shall be activated by fire or smoke sensors, not by fan cutoff alone. Installation of switching systems for restarting fans shall be permitted for fire department use in venting smoke after a fire has been controlled. However, provisions should be made to avoid possible damage to the system due to closed dampers.

(4) Construction requirements. Ducts that penetrate construction intended for x-ray or other ray protection shall not impair the effectiveness of the protection.

8.2.4.3 Exhaust systems

(1) To enhance the efficiency of recovery devices required for energy conservation, combined exhaust systems shall be permitted.

(2) Local exhaust systems shall be used wherever possible in place of dilution ventilation to reduce exposure to hazardous gases, vapors, fumes, or mists.

(3) Fans serving exhaust systems shall be located at the discharge end and shall be readily serviceable.

8.2.4.4 Air outlets and inlets

(1) Fresh air intakes

(a) Fresh air intakes shall be located at least 25 feet (7.62 meters) from exhaust outlets of ventilating systems, combustion vents (including those serving rooftop air-handling equipment), medical-surgical vacuum systems, plumbing vents, or areas that may collect vehicular exhaust or other noxious fumes. (Prevailing winds and/or proximity to other structures may require greater clearances.)

(b) Plumbing vents that terminate at a level above the top of the air intake may be located as close as 10 feet (3.05 meters).

(c) The bottom of outdoor air intakes serving central systems shall be as high as practical, but at least 6 feet (1.83 meters) above ground level, or, if installed above the roof, 3 feet (91.44 centimeters) above roof level.

(2) Relief air. Relief air is exempt from the 25-foot separation requirement. Relief air is defined as air that otherwise could be returned (recirculated) to an air handling unit from the occupied space, but is being discharged to the outdoors to maintain building pressure, such as during outside air economizer operation.

(3) Exhaust outlets from areas that may be contaminated shall be above roof level, arranged to minimize recirculation of exhaust air into the building, and directed away from personnel service areas.

(4) Gravity exhaust. Where conditions permit, gravity exhaust shall be permitted for nonpatient areas such as boiler rooms, central storage, etc.

8.2.5 HVAC Filters
8.2.5.1 Filter efficiencies

(1) All central ventilation or air conditioning systems shall be equipped with filters with efficiencies equal to, or greater than, those specified in Table 2.1-3.

(2) Noncentral air-handling systems shall be equipped with permanent (cleanable) or replaceable filters with a minimum efficiency of MERV 3 (68 percent weight arrestance).

(3) Filter efficiencies, tested in accordance with ASHRAE 52.1, shall be average.

8.2.5.2 Filter frames. Filter frames shall be durable and proportioned to provide an airtight fit with the enclosing ductwork. All joints between filter segments and enclosing ductwork shall have gaskets or seals to provide a positive seal against air leakage.

8.2.5.3 Filter housing blank-off panels. Filter housing blank-off panels shall be permanently attached to the frame, constructed of rigid materials, and have sealing surfaces equal to or greater than the filter media installed in the filter frame.

8.2.5.4 Filter manometers. A manometer shall be installed across each filter bed having a required efficiency of 75 percent or more. Provisions shall be made to allow access for field testing.

8.2.6 Steam and Hot Water Systems
Boilers shall have the capacity, based upon the net ratings published by the Hydronics Institute or another acceptable national standard, to supply the normal heating, hot water, and steam requirements of all systems and equipment.

8.3 Electrical Systems

8.3.1 General
8.3.1.1 Applicable standards

(1) All electrical material and equipment, including conductors, controls, and signaling devices, shall be installed in compliance with applicable sections of NFPA 70 and NFPA 99.

(2) All electrical material and equipment shall be listed as complying with available standards of listing agencies or other similar established standards where such standards are required.

8.3.1.2 Testing and documentation. The electrical installations, including alarm, nurse call, staff emergency signed system, and communication systems, shall be tested to demonstrate that equipment installation and operation is appropriate and functional. A written record of performance tests on special electrical systems and equipment shall show compliance with applicable codes and standards.

8.3.2 Electrical Distribution and Transmission
8.3.2.1 Switchboards

(1) Location

  (a) Main switchboards shall be located in an area separate from plumbing and mechanical equipment and shall be accessible to authorized persons only.

  (b) Switchboards shall be convenient for use, readily accessible for maintenance, and away from traffic lanes.

  (c) Switchboards shall be located in dry, ventilated spaces free of corrosive or explosive fumes, gases, or any flammable material.

(2) Overload protective devices. These shall operate properly in ambient room temperatures.

8.3.2.2 Panelboards

(1) Panelboards serving normal lighting and appliance circuits shall be located on the same floor as the circuits they serve.

(2) Panelboards serving critical branch emergency circuits shall be located on each floor that has major users.

(3) Location of panelboards serving life safety emergency circuits on the floors above and/or below the loads to be served shall be permitted.

8.3.2.3 Ground-fault circuit interrupters

(1) Ground-fault circuit interrupters (GFCIs) shall comply with NFPA 70.

(2) When ground-fault circuit interrupters are used in critical areas, provisions shall be made to ensure

that other essential equipment is not affected by activation of one interrupter.

8.3.3 Power-Generating and -Storing Equipment
8.3.3.1 Emergency Electrical Service

(1) As a minimum, psychiatric hospitals or sections thereof shall have emergency electrical systems as required in NFPA 99, NFPA 101, and NFPA 110.

(2) Where the psychiatric facility is a distinct part of an acute care hospital, it may use the emergency generator system for required emergency lighting and power if such sharing does not reduce hospital services. Life support systems and their respective areas shall be subject to applicable standards of Section 2.1-10.3.

(3) An emergency electrical source shall provide lighting and/or power during an interruption of the normal electrical supply.

8.3.4 Lighting
8.3.4.1 General

(1) Lighting shall be engineered to the specific application.

(2) Recommended lighting levels for health care facilities developed by the Illuminating Engineering Society of North America (IES) shall be considered. Refer to the IES publication RP-29, *Lighting for Hospitals and Health Care Facilities.*

(3) Consideration shall be given to the special needs of the elderly. Excessive contrast in lighting levels that makes effective sight adaptation difficult shall be minimized. Refer to IES publication RP-28, *Lighting and the Visual Environment for Senior Living.*

8.3.4.2 Light fixtures. Light fixtures shall be secured or of sufficient height to prevent patient access.

8.3.4.3 Lighting for specific locations in the psychiatric hospital

(1) Patient rooms. Patient rooms shall have general lighting and night lighting. At least one nightlight fixture in each patient room shall be controlled at the room entrance.

(2) Nursing unit corridors. Corridors in nursing units shall have general illumination with provisions for reducing light levels at night.

(3) Exterior lighting. Approaches to buildings and parking lots and all occupied spaces shall have lighting fixtures that can be illuminated as necessary.

8.3.5 Electrical Equipment
8.3.5.1 General electrical equipment. Special design considerations for injury and suicide prevention shall be given to the electrical equipment in the psychiatric hospital, including light fixtures, electrical outlets, electrical appliances, nurse call systems and staff emergency assistance systems.

8.3.5.2 Special electrical equipment. Special equipment is identified in the sections on nursing units, support areas, rehabilitation therapy, laboratory, pharmacy, and imaging, if applicable. These sections shall be consulted to ensure compatibility between programmatically defined equipment needs and appropriate power and other electrical connection needs.

8.3.6 Receptacles (Convenience Outlets)
8.3.6.1 Receptacles in corridors

(1) Duplex-grounded receptacles for general use shall be installed approximately 50 feet (15.24 meters) apart in all corridors and within 25 feet (7.62 meters) of corridor ends.

(2) These outlets shall be tamper-resistant or equipped with ground-fault circuit interrupters (GFCIs).

8.3.6.2 Receptacles in patient rooms. Each patient room shall have duplex-grounded receptacles.

(1) Electrical receptacles in patient rooms shall be tamper-resistant or equipped with ground-fault circuit interrupters (GFCIs).

(2) There shall be one at each side of the head of each bed and one on every other wall.

(3) Receptacles may be omitted from exterior walls

where construction or room configuration makes installation impractical.

8.3.6.3. Emergency system receptacles. Electrical receptacle cover plates or electrical receptacles supplied from the emergency system shall be distinctively colored or marked for identification. If color is used for identification purposes, the same color shall be used throughout the facility.

8.3.7 Call Systems

*8.3.7.1 General. Use of alternate technologies for emergency or nurse call systems shall be permitted.

(1) Staff response call systems shall be low voltage, current limited.

(2) Control to limit unauthorized use shall be permitted.

8.3.7.2 Nursing unit. A nurse call system is not required in psychiatric nursing units, but if it is included the following shall apply:

(1) Provisions shall be made for easy removal or covering of call buttons.

(2) All hardware shall have tamper-resistant fasteners.

(3) Signal location

    (a) Calls shall activate a visible signal in the corridor at the patient's door and at an annunciator panel at the nurse station or other appropriate location.

    (b) In multi-corridor nursing units, additional visible signals shall be installed at corridor intersections.

8.3.7.3 Emergency call system

(1) If provided, the staff emergency call shall be designed so that a signal activated by staff at a

patient's calling station will initiate a visible and audible signal distinct from the regular nurse call system.

(2) The signal shall activate an annunciator panel at the nurse station or other appropriate location, a distinct visible signal in the corridor at the door to the room from which the signal was initiated, and at other areas defined by the functional program.

8.4 Telecommunications and Information Systems

8.4.1 Locations for terminating telecommunications and information system devices shall be provided.

8.4.2 An area shall be provided for central equipment locations. Special air conditioning and voltage regulation shall be provided when recommended by the manufacturer.

8.4.3 Data processing and/or automated laboratory or diagnostic equipment, if provided, may require safeguards from power line disturbances.

8.5 Electronic Safety and Security

8.5.1 Electronic Surveillance Systems

8.5.1.1 Electronic surveillance systems are not required in psychiatric nursing units, but if provided for the safety of the residents, any devices in resident areas shall be mounted in a tamper-resistant enclosure that is unobtrusive.

8.5.1.2 Electronic surveillance system monitoring devices shall be located so they are not readily observable by the general public or other patients.

8.5.1.3 If installed, electronic surveillance systems shall be supplied with power from the emergency electrical system in the event of a disruption of normal electrical power.

8.5.2 Fire Detection and Suppression System

8.5.2.1 Fire alarm and detection systems shall be provided in compliance with NFPA 101 and NFPA 72.

8.2.5.2 Fire extinguisher cabinets and fire alarm pull stations shall be located in staff areas or otherwise secured in patient-accessible locations.

APPENDIX

A8.3.7.1 If radio frequency systems are used, consideration should be given to electromagnetic compatibility between internal and external sources.

2.4 Rehabilitation Facilities

Appendix material, which appears in shaded boxes at the bottom of the page, is advisory only.

1. General Considerations

Rehabilitation facilities may be organized under hospitals (organized departments of rehabilitation), outpatient clinics, rehabilitation centers, and other facilities designed to serve either single- or multiple-disability categories, including but not limited to cerebrovascular, head trauma, spinal cord injury, amputees, complicated fractures, arthritis, neurological degeneration, genetic, and cardiac.

In general, rehabilitation facilities will have larger space requirements than general hospitals, have longer lengths of stay, and have environments that are less institutional and more residential.

2 Nursing Locations

2.1 Nursing Unit
Where inpatients are a part of the facility, each nursing unit shall provide the following:

2.1.1 Patient Rooms
Each patient room shall meet the following standards:

2.1.1.1 Capacity

(1) Maximum room occupancy shall be four patients.

(2) Larger units shall be permitted if justified by the functional program.

(3) At least two single-bed rooms with private toilet rooms shall be provided for each nursing unit.

2.1.1.2 Space requirements

(1) Area. Minimum room areas exclusive of toilet rooms, closets, lockers, wardrobes, alcoves, or vestibules shall be 140 square feet (13.01 square meters) in single-bed rooms and 125 square feet (11.61 square meters) per bed in multiple-bed rooms.

(2) Clearances. In multiple-bed rooms, a clearance of 3 feet 8 inches (1.12 meters) shall be maintained at the foot of each bed to permit the passage of equipment and beds.

2.1.1.3 Window(s). Each patient sleeping room shall have a window in accordance with Section 2.4-7.2.2.5.

2.1.1.4 Patient privacy. Visual privacy shall be provided for each patient in multiple-bed rooms.

2.1.1.5 Hand-washing station (s). Hand-washing stations shall be provided in each patient room.

2.1.1.6 Toilet room

(1) Each patient shall have access to a toilet room without having to enter the general corridor area.

(2) One toilet room shall serve no more than four beds and no more than two patient rooms.

(3) The toilet room shall contain a water closet and a hand-washing station. Omission of the hand-washing station shall be permitted where the toilet room serves single-bed and two-bed rooms if each such patient room contains a hand-washing station.

(4) Each toilet room shall be of sufficient size to ensure that wheelchair users will have access.

2.1.1.7 Patient storage locations

(1) Each patient shall have a wardrobe, closet, or locker with minimum clear dimensions of 1 foot 10 inches (55.88 centimeters) by 1 foot 8 inches (50.80 centimeters).

(2) An adjustable clothes rod and adjustable shelf shall be provided.

2.1.1.8 Nurse call system. A nurse call system shall be provided.

2.1.2 Examination/Treatment Room

2.1.2.1 General

(1) Omission of this room shall be permitted if all patient rooms are single-bed rooms.

(2) The examination room in the evaluation unit shall be permitted to serve this purpose if it is conveniently located.

2.1.2.2 Space requirements

(1) This room shall have a minimum floor area of 120 square feet (11.15 square meters), excluding space for vestibules, toilet, closets, and work counters (whether fixed or movable).

(2) The minimum room dimension shall be 10 feet (3.05 meters).

2.1.2.3 Facility requirements. The room shall contain a work counter; hand-washing station; storage facilities; and a desk, counter, or shelf space for writing.

2.1.3 Support Areas for the Nursing Unit

2.1.3.1 General

(1) Location

   (a) The support areas noted in this section (2.4-2.1.3) shall be provided in or readily available to each nursing unit.

   (b) Although identifiable spaces are required for each indicated function, consideration shall be given to alternative designs that accommodate some functions without designating specific areas or rooms.

   (c) Each support area may be arranged and located to serve more than one nursing unit, but at least one such support area shall be provided on each nursing floor.

(2) Size. The size and disposition of each support area shall meet the needs of the functional program.

2.1.3.2 Administrative center or nurse station

2.1.3.3 Charting facilities for nurses and doctors

2.1.3.4 Nurse office

2.1.3.5 Hand-washing stations

(1) Hand-washing stations shall be located near the nurse station and the drug distribution station.

(2) One hand-washing station shall be permitted to serve both areas.

2.1.3.6 Medication station. Provisions shall be made for convenient and prompt 24-hour distribution of medicine to patients. Distribution may be from a medicine preparation room, self-contained medicine dispensing unit, or by another approved system.

(1) A medicine preparation room

   (a) If used, this room shall be under the visual control of the nursing staff.

   (b) If used, this room shall contain a work counter, refrigerator, and locked storage for biologicals and drugs.

(2) A self-contained medicine dispensing unit. Location of such a unit shall be permitted at a nurse station, in the clean workroom, or in an alcove or other space under direct control of nursing or pharmacy staff.

2.1.3.7 Nourishment area. The nourishment station shall be accessible to patients and shall contain the following:

(1) Equipment for serving nourishment between scheduled meals

(2) Refrigerator

(3) Storage cabinets

(4) A hand-washing station

2.1.3.8 Ice machine. Ice maker-dispenser units shall be provided for patient service and treatment.

2.1.3.9 Clean workroom or clean holding room

2.1.3.10 Soiled workroom or soiled holding room

2.1.3.11 Equipment and supply storage

(1) Clean linen storage

   (a) A separate closet or an area within the clean workroom shall be provided for this purpose.

   (b) If a closed-cart system is used, storage in an alcove shall be permitted.

(2) Equipment storage room. A storage room shall be provided for equipment such as IV stands, inhalators, air mattresses, and walkers.

(3) Storage space for stretchers and wheelchairs. Parking for stretchers and wheelchairs shall be located out of the path of normal traffic.

(4) Storage for administrative supplies

2.1.4 Support Areas for Staff
2.1.4.1 Lounge and toilet room(s)

2.1.4.2 Staff storage facilities. Individual closets or compartments for safekeeping of the personal effects of nursing personnel shall be located convenient to the duty station or in a central location.

2.1.5 Support Areas for Patients
2.1.5.1 Patient toilet facilities

(1) A toilet room that does not require travel through the general corridor shall be accessible to each central bathing area.

(2) Doors to toilet rooms shall have a minimum width of 2 feet 10 inches (86.36 centimeters) to admit a wheelchair. The doors shall permit access from the outside in case of an emergency.

(3) A hand-washing station shall be provided for each water closet in each multi-fixture toilet room.

2.1.5.2 Patient bathing facilities

(1) Bathtubs or showers shall be provided at a ratio of one bathing facility for each eight beds not

otherwise served by bathing facilities within patient rooms.

(2) Each tub or shower shall be in an individual room or privacy enclosure that provides space for the private use of bathing fixtures, for drying and dressing, and for a wheelchair and an assistant.

(3) Showers in central bathing facilities shall be at least 4 feet (1.22 meters) square, curb-free, and designed for use by a wheelchair patients.

2.2 Special Patient Care Areas

2.2.1 Airborne Infection Isolation Rooms
2.2.1.1 Number. The need for and number of required airborne infection isolation rooms in the rehabilitation facility shall be determined by an infection control risk assessment.

2.2.1.2 Location. They may be located within individual nursing units and used for normal acute care when not required for isolation cases, or they may be grouped as a separate isolation unit.

2.2.1.3 Facility requirements. Where required, the airborne infection isolation room(s) shall comply with the general requirements of Section 2.1-3.2.2.

3 Patient Living Areas

3.1 Dining, Recreation, and Day Spaces
The following standards shall be met for patient dining, recreation, and day spaces (areas may be in separate or adjoining spaces):

3.1.1 Space Requirements
3.1.1.1 Inpatient spaces. A total of 55 square feet (5.11 square meters) per bed shall be provided.

3.1.1.2 Outpatient services. If dining is part of the day care program, a total of 55 square feet (5.11 square meters) per person shall be provided. If dining is not part of the program, at least 35 square feet (3.25 square meters) per person shall be provided for recreation and day spaces.

3.1.2 Hand-Washing Station

A hand-washing station shall be provided in each dining room.

3.1.3 Equipment and Supply Storage

Storage spaces shall be provided for recreational equipment and supplies.

3.2 Activity Areas

3.2.1 Activities for Daily Living Unit

A unit shall be provided for teaching daily living activities.

3.2.1.1 Facility requirements. The unit shall include the following:

(1) A bedroom

(2) A bath. The bathroom shall be in addition to other toilet and bathing requirements.

(3) A kitchen

(4) Space for training stairs

3.2.1.2 Equipment. Equipment shall be functional. The facilities shall be similar to those in a residential environment so patients can learn to use those at home.

3.3 Personal Services (Barber/Beauty) Areas

A separate room with appropriate fixtures and utilities shall be provided for patient grooming. The activities for daily living unit may serve this purpose.

4 Diagnostic and Treatment Locations

Functional units and support areas shall include the following:

4.1 Medical Evaluation Unit

Each rehabilitation facility shall contain a medical evaluation unit.

4.1.1 Examination Room(s)

4.1.1.1 Space requirements. Examination rooms shall have a minimum floor area of 140 square feet (13.01 square meters), excluding such spaces as the vestibule, toilet, closet, and work counter (whether fixed or movable). The minimum room dimension shall be 10 feet (3.05 meters).

4.1.1.2 Facility requirements. The room shall contain a hand-washing station; a work counter; storage facilities; and a desk, counter, or shelf space for writing.

4.1.2 Evaluation Room(s)

Where the facility is small and workload light, evaluation shall be permitted in examination room(s).

4.1.2.1 Layout. Evaluation rooms shall be arranged to permit appropriate evaluation of patient needs and progress and to determine specific programs of rehabilitation.

4.1.2.2 Facility requirements. Rooms shall include a desk and work area for the evaluators; writing and work space for patients; and storage for supplies.

4.1.3 Support Areas for the Medical Evaluation Unit

4.1.3.1 Office(s). These shall be provided for personnel.

4.2 Other Required Units

In addition to the medical evaluation unit, each rehabilitation facility shall contain one or more of the following units:

4.2.1 Psychological Services Unit

Office(s) and work space shall be provided for testing, evaluation, and counseling.

4.2.2 Social Services Unit

Office space(s) shall be provided for private interviewing and counseling.

4.2.3 Vocational Services Unit

Office(s) and work space shall be provided for vocational training, counseling, and placement.

4.3 Optional Units

The following units, if required by the functional program, shall be provided as outlined in these sections. The sizes of the various units shall depend upon the requirements of the functional program.

4.3.1 Physical Therapy Unit

4.3.1.1 General

(1) The size of the unit shall depend upon the requirements of the functional program.

(2) The elements listed in this section (2.4-4.3.1) shall be provided. Shared use of the facilities in Sections 2.4-4.3.1.5 and 4.3.1.6 by occupational therapy patients and staff shall be permitted if the functional program reflects this sharing concept.

4.3.1.2 Treatment area(s)

(1) Privacy. For thermotherapy, diathermy, ultrasonics, hydrotherapy, etc., cubicle curtains shall be provided around each individual treatment area.

(2) Hand-washing station(s) shall also be provided. One hand-washing station may serve more than one cubicle.

(3) Facilities for collection of wet and soiled linen and other material shall be provided.

(4) As a minimum, one individual treatment area shall be enclosed within walls and have a door for access—minimum size 80 square feet (7.43 square meters). Curtained treatment areas shall have a minimum size of 70 square feet (6.51 square meters).

4.3.1.3 Exercise area. Space requirements shall be designed to permit access to all equipment and be sized to accommodate equipment for physical therapy.

4.3.1.4 Therapeutic pool. A therapeutic pool shall be provided if required by the functional program. The size of the pool shall depend upon the requirements of the functional program.

4.3.1.5 Support areas for the physical therapy unit

(1) Waiting space

(2) Office space

(3) Equipment and supply storage

   (a) Storage for clean linen, supplies, and equipment shall be provided.

   (b) Wheelchair and stretcher storage shall be provided.

4.3.1.6 Support areas for patients. Patients' dressing areas, showers, lockers, and toilet rooms shall be provided as required by the functional program.

4.3.2 Occupational Therapy Unit
4.3.2.1 General

(1) The size of the unit shall depend upon the requirements of the functional program.

(2) The elements listed in this section (2.4-4.3.2) shall be provided. (Facilities in Sections 2.4-4.3.2.3 and 4.3.2.4 may be planned and arranged for shared use by physical therapy patients and staff if the functional program reflects this sharing concept.)

4.3.2.2 Activity areas

4.3.2.3 Support areas for the occupational therapy unit

(1) Waiting space

(2) Office space

(3) Equipment and supply storage

4.3.2.4 Support areas for patients
Patients' dressing areas, showers, lockers, and toilet rooms shall be provided as required by the functional program.

4.3.3 Prosthetics and Orthotics Unit
4.3.3.1 General

(1) The size of the unit shall depend upon the requirements of the functional program.

(2) The following elements shall be provided:

4.3.3.2 Work space for technician(s)

4.3.3.3 Space for evaluation and fitting. This shall include provision for privacy.

4.3.3.4 Support areas for the prosthetics and orthotics unit. Space for equipment, supplies, and storage shall be provided.

4.3.4 Speech and Hearing Unit
4.3.4.1 General

(1) The size of the unit shall depend upon the requirements of the functional program.

(2) The unit shall include the following:

4.3.4.2 Space for evaluation and treatment

4.3.4.3 Support areas for the speech and hearing unit

(1) Office(s) for therapists

(2) Equipment and supply storage

4.3.5 Dental Unit
4.3.5.1 Operatory. This shall contain a hand-washing station.

4.3.5.2 Laboratory and film processing facilities

4.3.6 Imaging Suite
4.3.6.1 Size. The size of the unit shall depend upon the requirements of the functional program. The sizes of the various areas shall depend on the requirements of the service to be provided.

4.3.6.2 Facility requirements. This unit shall contain imaging room(s) as required by the functional program. (See Section 2.1-5.5 for special requirements.) Areas for the following services, if required, shall be provided as outlined in Section 2.1-5.5.5.

(1) Electromyography

(2) CAT scan

(3) MRI

(4) Nuclear medicine

(5) Radiography

4.3.7 Laboratory Facilities
4.3.7.1 General

(1) Location. Facilities shall be provided within the rehabilitation department or through contract arrangement with a nearby hospital or laboratory service for hematology, clinical chemistry, urinalysis, cytology, pathology, and bacteriology.

(2) Size. The size of the unit shall depend upon the requirements of the functional program.

4.3.7.2 Minimum services
If laboratory facilities are provided through contract, the following minimum laboratory services shall be provided in the rehabilitation facility:

(1) Laboratory work counter(s). These shall have a sink and gas and electric service.

(2) Hand-washing stations

(3) Specimen collection facilities

    (a) Urine collection rooms shall be equipped with a water closet and hand-washing station.

    (b) Blood collection facilities shall have space for a chair and work counter.

(4) Storage cabinet(s) or closet(s)

4.3.8 Home Health Service

5 Service Areas

The following service areas, if required by the functional program, shall be provided as outlined.

5.1 Pharmacy Unit

5.1.1 General
The size and type of services to be provided in the pharmacy will depend on the drug distribution system chosen and whether the facility proposes to provide, purchase, or share pharmacy services.

5.1.2 Facility Requirements
If a pharmacy is required by the functional program, provisions shall be made for the following functional areas:

5.1.2.1 A compounding area

5.1.2.2 A packaging area

5.1.2.3 A quality control area

5.1.2.4 A dispensing area. This shall have a hand-washing station.

5.1.2.5 A drug information area

5.1.2.6 Order review area. An editing or order review area shall be provided.

5.1.2.7 Support areas for the pharmacy

(1) Administrative areas

(2) Storage areas

5.2 Dietary Unit

*5.2.1 General
Construction, equipment, and installation of food service facilities shall meet the requirements of the functional program.

5.2.2 Facility Requirements
The following facilities shall be provided as required to implement the food service selected:

5.2.2.1 Control station. A control station for receiving food supplies shall be provided.

5.2.2.2 Hand-washing station(s). Hand-washing station(s) shall be located in the food preparation area.

5.2.2.3 Food preparation facilities

(1) Conventional food preparation systems require space and equipment for preparing, cooking, and baking.

(2) Convenience food service systems such as frozen prepared meals, bulk packaged entrees, individually packaged portions, and contractual commissary services require space and equipment for thawing, portioning, cooking, and/or baking.

5.2.2.4 Patient meal service facilities. Facilities shall be provided for tray assembly and distribution.

5.2.2.5 Ware-washing space

(1) This shall be located in a room or alcove separate from the food preparation and serving area.

(2) Commercial dish-washing equipment shall be provided.

(3) A hand-washing station shall be conveniently available.

(4) Space shall also be provided for receiving, scraping, sorting, and stacking soiled tableware and for transferring clean tableware to the using areas.

5.2.2.6 Pot-washing facilities

5.2.2.7 Self-dispensing ice-making facilities. These may be in an area or room separate from the food preparation area but shall be easily cleanable and convenient to dietary facilities.

5.2.3 Support Areas for the Dietary Unit
5.2.3.1 Office(s). Office(s) or desk spaces shall be provided for the dietitian(s) or the dietary service manager.

5.2.3.2 Equipment storage. Storage areas shall be provided for cans, carts, and mobile tray conveyors.

5.2.3.3 Housekeeping room

(1) This shall be located within the dietary department.

(2) This shall contain a floor receptor or service sink and storage space for housekeeping equipment and supplies.

5.2.3.4 Waste storage facilities. These shall be located in a separate room easily accessible to the outside for direct waste pickup or disposal.

5.2.4 Support Areas for Staff
5.2.4.1 Separate dining space for staff

APPENDIX

A5.2.1 Services may consist of an on-site conventional food preparation system, a convenience food service system, or an appropriate combination thereof. On-site facilities should be provided for emergency food preparation and refrigeration.

5.2.4.2 Toilets. Toilets shall be provided for dietary staff. Hand-washing stations shall be immediately available.

5.3 Sterilizing Facilities

Where required by the functional program, a system for sterilizing equipment and supplies shall be provided. Its size shall depend upon the requirements of the functional program.

5.4 Linen Services

5.4.1 On-Site Processing

If linen is to be processed on site, the following shall be provided:

5.4.1.1 Soiled linen holding room. A room shall be provided for soiled linen receiving, holding, and sorting. This shall have a hand-washing station and cart-washing facilities.

5.4.1.2 Clean linen storage. A clean linen storage, issuing, and holding room or area shall be provided.

5.4.1.3 Laundry processing room. This shall be provided with commercial equipment that can process seven days' laundry within a regularly scheduled work week.

5.4.1.4 Hand-washing station. A hand-washing station shall be provided.

5.4.1.5 Supply storage. Storage shall be provided for laundry supplies.

5.4.1.6 Housekeeping room. This shall contain a floor receptor or service sink and shall provide storage space for housekeeping equipment and supplies.

5.4.2 Off-Site Processing

If linen is processed off the rehabilitation facility site, the following shall be provided:

5.4.2.1 Soiled linen holding room

5.4.2.2 Clean linen storage. Clean linen receiving, holding, inspection, and storage room(s) shall be provided.

5.5 Materials Management

*5.5.1 Waste Management

5.5.1.1 Collection and storage. The functional program shall stipulate the categories and volumes of waste for disposal and the methods of handling and disposal of waste.

(1) Location

    (a) Waste collection and storage locations shall be determined by the facility as a component of the functional program.

APPENDIX

A5.5.1 The underlying framework of waste management comprises waste minimization and segregation. Facilities should seek both to minimize all components of each waste stream and to separate different components of the total waste stream. At a minimum, the functional program should include consideration of regular trash, medical/infectious waste, hazardous waste, and low-level radioactive waste.

The program should address the development of effective collection, transport, pest control, and storage systems; waste management and contingency planning; protecting the health and safety of workers; and proper siting of all on-site waste treatment technologies.

Optimizing waste management has programmatic and space impacts throughout the facility, at points where waste is generated, collected, and staged for disposal. For facilities or municipalities with recycling programs in place, particular consideration

should be given to sorting and staging areas. The following elements are examples that may be considered:

a. Building should include adequate space to accommodate bins/carts for appropriate waste segregation such as recyclables, infectious waste, sharps, etc. Corridors and materials handling systems should be designed to achieve an efficient movement of waste from points of generation to storage or treatment while minimizing the risk to personnel.

b. Dedicated storage and flow space and cleaning/sanitation facilities should facilitate reuse of items such as medical products, food service items, and the like to eliminate disposables and reduce waste.

c. Space should be included for autoclaves, shredders, and other technologies for processing medical waste prior to removals to landfill. Secure storage should be provided for staging fluorescent lamps for recycling.

(b) At docks or other waste removal areas, the functional program shall stipulate the location of compactors, balers, sharps, and recycling container staging.

(c) Red bag waste shall be staged in enclosed and secured areas. Biohazardous and environmentally hazardous materials, including mercury, nuclear reagent waste, and other regulated waste types, shall be segregated and secured.

(2) Space requirements. The functional program shall outline the space requirements, including centralized waste collection and storage spaces. Size of spaces shall be determined based upon volume of projected waste and length of anticipated storage.

5.5.1.2 Regulated waste storage spaces

(1) If provided, regulated medical waste or infectious waste storage spaces shall have a floor drain, cleanable floor and wall surfaces, lighting, and exhaust ventilation, and should be safe from weather, animals and unauthorized entry.

(2) Refrigeration requirements for such storage facilities shall comply with state and/or local regulations.

5.5.1.3 Refuse chutes. The design and construction of trash chutes shall comply with NFPA 82.

5.6 Environmental Services

5.6.1 Housekeeping Room(s)
In addition to the housekeeping rooms called for in certain departments, housekeeping rooms shall be provided throughout the facility as required to maintain a clean and sanitary environment. Each shall contain the following:

5.6.1.1 A floor receptor or service sink

5.6.1.2 Storage space for housekeeping supplies and equipment

5.7 Engineering Services and Maintenance

5.7.1 Equipment Rooms
Rooms for boilers, mechanical equipment, and electrical equipment shall be provided.

5.7.2 Storage Room(s)
Storage rooms for building maintenance supplies and yard equipment shall be provided.

6 Administrative and Public Areas

6.1 Public Areas

6.1.1 Entrance
A grade-level entrance, sheltered from the weather and able to accommodate wheelchairs, shall be provided.

6.1.2 Lobby
The lobby shall include the following:

6.1.2.1 A reception and information counter or desk

6.1.2.2 Waiting space(s)

6.1.2.3 Public toilet facilities

6.1.2.4 Public telephone(s)

6.1.2.5 Provision for drinking water

6.1.2.6 Wheelchair storage space(s)

6.1.2.7 Convenience store. An expanded gift shop with toiletries and other items available to patients during extended stays shall be provided according to the requirements of the functional program.

6.2 Administrative and Related Support Areas

6.2.1 Interview Space(s)
Space for private interviews relating to social service, credit, and admissions shall be provided.

6.2.2 General or Individual Office(s)
General or individual offices for business transactions, records, and administrative and professional staff shall be provided.

6.2.3 Multipurpose Room(s)
Multipurpose room(s) for conferences, meetings, health education, and library services shall be provided.

6.2.4 Patient Storage Locations

Rehab patients' length of stay is longer than that of typical acute care patients. Space for storage of patients' personal effects shall meet the needs of the functional program.

6.2.5 General Storage

Separate space shall be provided for office supplies, sterile supplies, pharmaceutical supplies, splints and other orthopedic supplies, and housekeeping supplies and equipment.

6.2.6 Employee Facilities

In addition to the employee facilities such as locker rooms, lounges, toilets, or showers called for in certain departments, a sufficient number of such facilities to accommodate the needs of all personnel and volunteers shall be provided.

7 Construction Standards

7.1 Design and Construction, Including Fire-Resistant Standards

7.1.1 Construction Requirements

7.1.1.1 General. Except as noted below, construction of freestanding outpatient rehabilitation facilities shall comply with the applicable requirements of NFPA 101, and the standards contained herein, and the requirements of authorities of having jurisdiction. Rehabilitation facilities that accommodate inpatients shall comply with the construction requirements for general hospitals in Section 2.1-8.1.

7.1.1.2 Fire prevention/protection measures

(1) Compartmentation, exits, automatic extinguishing systems, and other details relating to fire prevention and fire protection in inpatient rehabilitation facilities shall comply with requirements listed in NFPA 101.

(2) In freestanding outpatient rehabilitation facilities, details relating to exits and fire safety shall comply with the appropriate occupancy chapter of NFPA 101 and the requirements outlined herein.

7.1.1.2 Interior finishes. Interior finish materials for inpatient facilities shall comply with the flame-spread limitations and the smoke-production limitations in NFPA 101.

7.1.1.3 Insulation materials. Building insulation materials, unless sealed on all sides and edges, shall have a flame-spread rating of 25 or less and a smoke-developed rating of 150 or less when tested in accordance with NFPA 255.

7.1.2 Provisions for Disasters

For design and construction standards relating to hurricanes, tornadoes, and floods, see Section 2.1-8.1.3.

7.2 General Standards for Details and Finishes

7.2.1 General

Patients in a rehabilitation facility will be disabled to differing degrees. Therefore, high standards of safety for the occupants shall be provided to minimize accidents. All details and finishes for renovation projects as well as for new construction shall comply with the following requirements insofar as they affect patient services:

7.2.2 Details

7.2.2.1 Corridor width. Items such as provisions for drinking water, telephone booths, vending machines, and portable equipment shall not restrict corridor traffic or reduce the corridor width below the required minimum.

7.2.2.2 Ceiling height. The minimum ceiling height shall be 7 feet 10 inches (2.39 meters), with the following exceptions:

(1) Corridors, storage rooms, and toilet rooms. Ceilings in corridors, storage rooms, toilet rooms, and other minor rooms shall be not less than 7 feet 8 inches (2.34 meters).

(2) Rooms with ceiling-mounted equipment/light fixtures. Ceilings of radiographic and other rooms containing ceiling-mounted equipment, including those with ceiling-mounted surgical light fixtures, shall have sufficient height to accommodate the equipment and/or fixtures.

(3) Boiler rooms. Boiler rooms shall have a ceiling clearance not less than 2 feet 6 inches (76.20 centimeters) above the main boiler header and connecting piping.

(4) Clearances. Suspended tracks, rails, and pipes located in the path of normal traffic shall be not less than 6 feet 8 inches (2.03 meters) above the floor.

7.2.2.3 Doors

(1) Door type

   (a) Doors between corridors and rooms or those leading into spaces subject to occupancy, except elevator doors, shall be swing-type.

   (b) Openings to showers, baths, patient toilets, and other small, wet-type areas not subject to fire hazard are exempt from this requirement.

(2) Door width

   (a) Minimum width of all doors to rooms needing access for beds shall be 3 feet 8 inches (1.12 meters).

   (b) Doors to rooms requiring access for stretchers and doors to patient toilet rooms and other rooms needing access for wheelchairs shall have a minimum width of 2 feet 10 inches (86.36 centimeters).

   (c) Where the functional program states that the sleeping facility will be for residential use (and therefore not subject to in-bed patient transport), patient room doors that are 3 feet (91.44 centimeters) wide shall be permitted if approved by the local authority having jurisdiction.

(3) Door swing. Doors, except those to spaces such as small closets not subject to occupancy, shall not swing into corridors in a manner that obstructs traffic flow or reduces the required corridor width.

(4) Door hardware

   (a) Patient bathing/toilet facilities

   (i) Rooms that contain bathtubs, sitz baths, showers, and water closets subject to patient use shall be equipped with doors and hardware that will permit access from the outside in an emergency.

   (ii) When such rooms have only one opening or are small, the doors shall open outward or be otherwise designed to open without pressing against a patient who may have collapsed within the room.

7.2.2.4 Thresholds and expansion joint covers. These shall be flush with the floor surface to facilitate use of wheelchairs and carts in new facilities.

7.2.2.5 Windows

(1) Operable windows are not required in patient rooms.

(2) Windows shall be designed to prevent accidental falls when open or shall be provided with security screens where deemed necessary by the functional program.

7.2.2.6 Insect screens. Windows and outer doors that may be frequently left open shall be provided with insect screens.

7.2.2.7 Glazing materials

(1) Doors, sidelights, borrowed lights, and windows glazed to within 1 foot 6 inches (45.72 centimeters) of the floor shall be constructed of safety glass, wired glass, or plastic glazing material that resists breaking or creates no dangerous cutting edges when broken. Similar materials shall be used in wall openings of playrooms and exercise rooms.

(2) Safety glass or plastic glazing material shall be used for shower doors and bath enclosures.

7.2.2.8 Hand-washing stations. Location and arrangement of hand-washing stations shall permit proper use and operation and meet the following:

(1) Particular care shall be given to clearance required for blade-type operating handles.

(2) Lavatories intended for use by disabled patients shall be installed in accordance with Section 1.1-4, Design Standards for the Disabled.

(3) Mirrors. Mirrors shall be arranged for convenient use by wheelchair patients as well as by patients in a standing position.

(4) Provisions for hand drying shall be included at all hand-washing stations.

(5) Lavatories and hand-washing stations shall be securely anchored to withstand an applied vertical load of not less than 250 pounds (113.40 kilograms) on the front of the fixture.

7.2.2.9 Grab bars

(1) Grab bars shall be provided in all patient toilets, bathtubs, showers, and sitz baths with a wall clearance of 1-1/2 inches (3.81 centimeters) clearance to walls.

(3) Grab bars shall be sufficiently anchored to sustain a concentrated load of 250 pounds (113.40 kilograms).

(4) Ends of grab bars shall be constructed to prevent snagging the clothes of patients.

(5) Special consideration shall be given to shower curtain rods that may be momentarily used for support. Recessed soap dishes shall be provided in showers and bathrooms.

7.2.2.10 Handrails

(1) Handrails shall be provided on both sides of corridors used by patients.

(2) A clear distance of 1-1/2 inches (3.81 centimeters) shall be provided between the handrail and the wall, and the top of the rail shall be about 2 feet 8 inches (81.28 centimeters) above the floor, except for special care areas such as those serving children.

(3) Ends of handrails shall be constructed to prevent snagging the clothes of patients.

7.2.2.11 Radiation protection

(1) Radiation protection requirements of x-ray and gamma ray installations shall conform to state and local laws.

(2) Provisions shall be made for testing the completed installation before use. All defects shall be corrected before acceptance.

7.2.2.12 Noise control

(1) Recreation rooms, exercise rooms, and similar spaces where impact noises may be generated shall not be located directly over patient bed areas unless special provisions are made to minimize such noise.

(2) Noise reduction criteria shown in Table 2.1-1 shall apply to partition, floor, and ceiling construction in patient areas.

7.2.2.13 Temperature control. Rooms containing heat-producing equipment (such as boiler or heater rooms and laundries) shall be insulated and ventilated to prevent any floor surface above from exceeding a temperature 10°F (6°C) above the ambient room temperature.

7.2.3 Finishes

7.2.3.1 Noncombustible or flame-retardant materials. Cubicle curtains and draperies shall be noncombustible or rendered flame retardant and shall pass both the large- and small-scale tests in NFPA 701.

7.2.3.2 Floors

(1) Floor materials shall be readily cleanable and appropriately wear-resistant for the location.

   (a) In all areas frequently subject to wet cleaning methods, floor materials shall not be physically affected by germicidal and cleaning solutions.

   (b) Wall bases in kitchens, soiled workrooms, and other areas that are frequently subject to wet cleaning methods shall be monolithic and coved with the floor, tightly sealed within the wall, and constructed without voids that can harbor insects.

(2) Floor surfaces in patient areas shall be smooth and without irregular surfaces to prevent tripping by patients using orthotic devices.

(3) Floors subject to traffic while wet, such as shower and bath areas, kitchens, and similar work areas, shall have a nonslip surface.

(4) Food preparation areas

   (a) Floors in food preparation or assembly areas shall be water-resistant.

   (b) Joints in tile and similar material in such areas shall also be resistant to food acids.

   (c) Floor construction in dietary and food preparation areas shall be free from spaces that can harbor pests.

7.2.3.3 Walls

(1) Wall finishes. Wall finishes shall be washable and, in the proximity of plumbing fixtures, shall be smooth and moisture-resistant.

(2) Dietary and food preparation areas. Finish, trim, and wall construction in these areas shall be free from spaces that can harbor pests.

7.2.3.4 Ceilings

(1) Ceilings throughout shall be readily cleanable.

(2) All overhead piping and ductwork in the dietary and food preparation area shall be concealed behind a finished ceiling.

(3) Finished ceilings may be omitted in mechanical and equipment spaces, shops, general storage areas, and similar spaces, unless required for fire-resistive purposes.

(4) Acoustical ceilings shall be provided for corridors in patient areas, nurse stations, day rooms, recreational rooms, dining areas, and waiting areas.

7.2.3.5 Penetrations. Floors and wall areas penetrated by pipes, ducts, and conduits shall be tightly sealed to minimize entry of pests. Joints of structural elements shall be similarly sealed.

8 Special Systems

8.1 General

8.1.1 Testing
8.1.1.1 Testing. Prior to acceptance of the facility, all special systems shall be tested and operated to demonstrate to the owner or his designated representative that the installation and performance of these systems conform to design intent.

8.1.1.2 Test results. Test results shall be documented for maintenance files.

8.1.2 Documentation
8.1.2.1 Upon completion of the special systems equipment installation contract, the owner shall be furnished with a complete set of manufacturers' operating, maintenance, and preventive maintenance instructions; parts lists; and complete procurement information, including equipment numbers and descriptions.

8.1.2.2 Operating staff persons shall also be provided with instructions for proper operation of systems and equipment. Required information shall include all safety or code ratings as needed.

8.1.3 Insulation
Insulation shall be provided surrounding special system equipment to conserve energy, protect personnel, and reduce noise.

8.2 Elevators

8.2.1 General
All buildings with patient facilities (such as bedrooms, dining rooms, or recreation areas) or critical services (such as diagnostic or therapy) located on other than the main entrance floor shall have electric or hydraulic elevators.

8.2.2 Number
The number of elevators required shall be determined from a study of the facility plan and of the estimated vertical transportation requirements.

8.2.3 Dimensions

8.2.3.1 Hospital-type elevator cars shall have inside dimensions that accommodate a patient bed with attendants. Cars shall be at least 5 feet 8 inches (1.73 meters) wide by 9 feet (2.74 meters) deep.

8.2.3.2 Car doors shall have a clear opening of not less than 4 feet (1.22 meters) wide and 7 feet (2.13 meters) high.

8.2.3.3 In renovations, existing elevators that can accommodate patient beds used in the facility will not be required to be increased in size.

*8.2.4 Elevator Controls

Elevator call buttons and controls shall not be activated by heat or smoke. Light beams, if used for operating door reopening devices without touch, shall be used in combination with door-edge safety devices and shall be interconnected with a system of smoke detectors.

8.2.5 Installation and Testing

8.2.5.1 Standards. Installation and testing of elevators shall comply with ANSI/ASME A17.1 for new construction and ANSI/ASME A17.3 for existing facilities. (See ASCE 7 for seismic design and control systems requirements for elevators.)

8.2.5.2 Testing. Field inspections and tests shall be made and the owner shall be furnished with written certification stating that the installation meets the requirements set forth in this section as well as all applicable safety regulations and codes.

8.3 Waste Processing

8.3.1 Waste Treatment and Disposal Technologies

Space and facilities shall be provided for disposal of waste.

***8.3.1.1** Incineration. On-site hospital incinerators shall comply with federal, state, and local regulatory and environmental requirements. The design and construction of incinerators shall comply with NFPA 82.

8.3.1.2 Other technologies. Types of non-incineration waste treatment technology(ies) shall be determined by the facility in conjunction with environmental, economic, and regulatory considerations. The functional program shall describe waste treatment technology components.

(1) Location

(a) Safe transfer routes, distances from waste sources, temporary storage requirements, and space requirements for treatment equipment shall be considered in determining the location for a non-incineration technology.

(b) The location of the technology shall not cause traffic problems as waste is brought in and out.

(c) Odor, noise, and the visual impact of medical waste operations on patients, visitors, public access and security shall be considered.

APPENDIX

A8.2.4 This is so the light control feature will be overridden or disengaged should it encounter smoke at any landing.

A8.3.1.1 The EPA has identified medical waste incineration as a significant contributor to air pollution worldwide. Health care facilities should seek to minimize incineration of medical waste, consistent with local and state regulations and public health goals.

When incinerators are used, consideration should be given to the recovery of waste heat from on-site incinerators used to dispose of large amounts of waste materials. Incinerators should be designed in a manner fully consistent with protection of public and environmental health, both on-site and off-site, and in compliance with

federal, state, and local statutes and regulations. Toward this end, permit applications for incinerators and modifications thereof should be supported by Environmental Assessments and/or Environmental Impact Statements (EISs) and/or Health Risk Assessments (HRAs) as may be required by regulatory agencies. Except as noted below, such assessments should utilize standard U.S. EPA methods, specifically those set forth in U.S. EPA guidelines, and should be fully consistent with U.S. EPA guidelines for health risk assessment. Under some circumstances, however, regulatory agencies having jurisdiction over a particular project may require use of alternative methods.

(2) Space requirements. Space needed for such technologies shall be determined by the equipment requirements, including associated area for opening waste entry doors, access to control panels, space for hydraulic lifts, conveyors, and operational clearances. Mobile or portable units, trailer-mounted units, underground installations, or all-weather enclosed shelters at an outdoor site may also be used, subject to local regulatory approvals.

(3) Ventilation. Exhaust vents, if any, from the treatment technology shall be located a minimum of 25 feet (7.62 meters) from inlets to HVAC systems. If the technology involves heat dissipation, sufficient cooling and ventilation shall be provided.

9 Building Systems

9.1 Plumbing

9.1.1 General
Unless otherwise specified herein, all plumbing systems shall be designed and installed in accordance with the International Plumbing Code.

9.1.2 Plumbing and Other Piping Systems
9.1.2.1 General piping and valves

(1) All piping, except control-line tubing, shall be identified.

(2) All valves shall be tagged, and a valve schedule shall be provided to the facility owner for permanent record and reference.

(3) No plumbing lines shall be exposed overhead or on walls where possible accumulation of dust or soil may create a cleaning problem or where leaks would create a potential for food contamination.

9.1.2.2 Hemodialysis/hemoperfusion piping. Where the functional program includes hemodialysis, continuously circulated filtered cold water shall be provided. Piping shall be in accordance with ANSI/AAMI RD62, *Water Treatment Equipment for Hemodialysis Applications.*

9.1.2.3 Potable water supply systems. The following standards shall apply to potable water supply systems:

(1) Capacity. Systems shall be designed to supply water at sufficient pressure to operate all fixtures and equipment during maximum demand. Supply capacity for hot- and cold-water piping shall be determined on the basis of fixture units, using recognized engineering standards. When the ratio of plumbing fixtures to occupants is proportionally more than required by the building occupancy and is in excess of 1,000 plumbing fixture units, a diversity factor is permitted.

(2) Valves. Each water service main, branch main, riser, and branch to a group of fixtures shall have valves.

   (a) Stop valves shall be provided for each fixture.

   (b) Appropriate panels for access shall be provided at all valves where required.

(3) Backflow prevention

   (a) Systems shall be protected against cross-connection in accordance with American Water Works Association (AWWA) Recommended Practice for Backflow Prevention and Cross-Connection Control.

   (b) Vacuum breakers or backflow prevention devices shall be installed on hose bibs and supply nozzles used for connection of hoses or tubing in housekeeping sinks, bedpan-flushing attachments, etc.

(4) Bedpan-flushing devices. Bedpan-flushing devices (may be cold water) shall be provided in each inpatient toilet room.

(5) Potable water storage. Potable water storage vessels (hot and cold) not intended for constant use shall not be installed.

9.1.2.4 Hot water systems. See Section 1.6-2.1.2.1.

9.1.2.5 Drainage systems. The following standards shall apply to drainage systems:

(1) Piping

    (a) Drain lines from sinks used for acid waste disposal shall be made of acid-resistant material.

    (b) Drain lines serving some types of automatic blood-cell counters shall be of carefully selected material that will eliminate potential for undesirable chemical reactions (and/or explosions) between sodium azide wastes and copper, lead, brass, solder, etc.

    (c) Insofar as possible, drainage piping shall not be installed within the ceiling or exposed in operating rooms, food preparation centers, food serving facilities, food storage areas, central services, electronic data processing areas, electric closets, and other sensitive areas. Where exposed overhead drain piping in these areas is unavoidable, special provisions shall be made to protect the space below from leakage, condensation, or dust particles.

(2) Floor drains

    (a) Floor drains shall not be installed in operating rooms.

    (b) If a floor drain is installed in cystoscopy, it shall contain a nonsplash, horizontal-flow flushing bowl beneath the drain plate.

    (c) Dietary area floor drains and/or floor sinks

        (i) Type. These shall be of a type that can be easily cleaned by removing the cover. Removable stainless steel mesh shall be provided in addition to grilled drain covers to prevent entry of large particles of waste that might cause stoppages.

        (ii) Location. Floor drains or floor sinks shall be provided at all "wet" equipment (as ice machines) and as required for wet cleaning of floors. Location of floor drains and floor sinks shall be coordinated to avoid conditions where locations of equipment make removal of covers for cleaning difficult.

(3) Autopsy table drain systems. Drain systems for autopsy tables shall be designed to positively avoid splatter or overflow onto floors or back siphonage and for easy cleaning and trap flushing.

(4) Sewers. Building sewers shall discharge into community sewerage. Where such a system is not available, the facility shall treat its sewage in accordance with local and state regulations.

(5) Grease traps. Kitchen grease traps shall be located and arranged to permit easy access without the need to enter food preparation or storage areas. Grease traps shall be of capacity required and shall be accessible from outside the building without need to interrupt any services.

(6) Plaster traps. Where plaster traps are used, provisions shall be made for appropriate access and cleaning.

9.1.2.6 Condensate drains. See Section 1.6-2.1.2.2.

9.1.3 Plumbing Fixtures
In addition to the requirements of Section 1.6-2.1.3, the following standards shall apply to plumbing fixtures in a rehabilitation hospital:

9.1.3.1 Clinical sinks

(1) Handles on clinical sinks shall be at least 6 inches (15.24 centimeters) long.

(2) Clinical sinks shall have an integral trap wherein the upper portion of the water trap provides a visible seal.

9.1.3.2 Scrub sinks. Freestanding scrub sinks and hand-washing stations used for scrubbing in procedure rooms shall be trimmed with foot, knee, or ultrasonic controls; single lever wrist blades are not permitted.

9.1.4 Medical Gas and Vacuum Systems
9.1.4.1 Medical gas and air systems. The installation, testing, and certification of nonflammable medical gas and air systems shall comply with the requirements of NFPA 99. (See Table 2.1-5 for rooms requiring station outlets.)

9.1.4.2 Clinical vacuum systems. Clinical vacuum system installations shall be in accordance with NFPA 99. (See Table 2.1-5 for rooms requiring station outlets.)

9.2 Heating, Ventilating, and Air-Conditioning (HVAC) Systems

9.2.1 General

9.2.1.1 Mechanical system design

(1) Efficiency. The mechanical system shall be designed for overall efficiency and life-cycle costing. Details for cost-effective implementation of design features are interrelated and too numerous (as well as too basic) to list individually.

    (a) Recognized engineering procedures shall be followed for the most economical and effective results. A well-designed system can generally achieve energy efficiency at minimal additional cost and simultaneously provide improved patient comfort.

    (b) Different geographic areas may have climatic and use conditions that favor one system over another in terms of overall cost and efficiency.

    (c) In no case shall patient care or safety be sacrificed for conservation.

    (d) Insofar as practical, the facility shall include provisions for recovery of waste cooling and heating energy (ventilation, exhaust, water and steam discharge, cooling towers, incinerators, etc.).

    *(e) Use of recognized energy-saving mechanisms such as variable air volume (VAV) systems, load shedding, programmed controls for unoccupied periods (nights and weekends, etc.), and use of natural ventilation shall be considered, site and climatic conditions permitting

    (f) Facility design considerations. These shall include site, building mass, orientation, configuration, fenestration, and other features relative to passive and active energy systems

(2) Air-handling systems

    *(a) These shall be designed with an economizer cycle where appropriate to use outside air. (Use of mechanically circulated outside air does not reduce need for filtration.)

    (b) VAV systems. The energy-saving potential of variable air volume systems is recognized, and the standards in this document are intended to maximize appropriate use of such systems. Any system used for occupied areas shall include provisions to avoid air stagnation in interior spaces where thermostat demands are met by temperatures of surrounding areas.

    (c) Noncentral air-handling systems (i.e., individual room units that are used for heating and cooling purposes) (fan-coil units, heat pump units, etc.). These units may be used as recirculating units only. All outdoor air requirements shall be met by a separate central air-handling system with proper filtration, as noted in Table 2.1-3.

(3) Vibration isolators. Mechanical equipment, ductwork, and piping shall be mounted on vibration isolators as required to prevent unacceptable structure-borne vibration.

(4) System valves. Supply and return mains and risers for cooling, heating, and steam systems shall be equipped with valves to isolate the various sections of each system. Each piece of equipment shall have valves at the supply and return ends.

(5) Renovation. If system modifications affect greater than 10 percent of the system capacity, designers

---

APPENDIX

A9.2.1.1 (1)(e) Systems with excessive installation and/or maintenance costs that negate long-range energy savings should be avoided.

A9.2.1.1 (2)(a) It may be practical in many areas to reduce or shut down mechanical ventilation under appropriate climatic and patient care conditions and to use open windows for ventilation.

shall utilize pre-renovation water/air flow rate measurements to verify that sufficient capacity is available and that renovations have not adversely affected flow rates in non-renovated areas.

9.2.1.2 Ventilation and space conditioning requirements. All rooms and areas in the facility used for patient care shall have provisions for ventilation.

(1) Ventilation rates. The ventilation systems shall be designed and balanced, as a minimum, according to the requirements shown in Table 2.1-2 and the applicable notes. The ventilation rates shown in Table 2.1-2 do not preclude the use of higher, more appropriate rates.

(2) Air change rates. Air supply and exhaust in rooms for which no minimum total air change rate is noted may vary down to zero in response to room load. For rooms listed in Table 2.1-2, where VAV systems are used, minimum total air change shall be within limits noted.

(3) Temperature and humidity levels. Space temperature and relative humidity shall be as indicated in Table 2.1-2.

(4) Air movement direction. To maintain asepsis control, airflow supply and exhaust shall generally be controlled to ensure movement of air from "clean" to "less clean" areas, especially in critical areas.

(5) Although natural ventilation for nonsensitive areas and patient rooms (via operable windows) shall be permitted, mechanical ventilation shall be considered for all rooms and areas in the facility.

9.2.1.3 Testing and documentation

(1) Upon completion of the equipment installation contract, the owner shall be furnished with a complete set of manufacturers' operating, maintenance, and preventive maintenance instructions, parts lists, and complete procurement information, including equipment numbers and descriptions. Required information shall include energy ratings as needed for future conservation calculations.

(2) Operating staff persons shall also be provided with written instructions for proper operation of systems and equipment.

9.2.2 Requirements for Specific Locations

9.2.2.1 Cough-inducing procedure rooms. Rooms used for sputum induction, aerosolized pentamidine treatments, or other cough-inducing procedures shall meet the requirements of Table 2.1-2 for airborne infection isolation rooms. If booths are used, refer to Section 2.1-5.8.1.

9.2.2.2 ETO sterilizer space. The ventilation system for the space that houses ethylene oxide (ETO) sterilizers shall be designed as follows:

(1) A dedicated exhaust system (one not connected to a return air or other exhaust system) shall be provided. Refer to 29 CFR Part 1910.1047.

(2) All source areas shall be exhausted, including the sterilizer equipment room, service/aeration areas, over the sterilizer door, and the aerator.

   (a) If the ETO cylinders are not located in a well-ventilated, unoccupied equipment space, an exhaust hood shall be provided over the cylinders.

   (b) The relief valve shall be terminated in a well-ventilated, unoccupied equipment space, or outside the building.

   (c) If the floor drain which the sterilizer(s) discharges to is not located in a well-ventilated, unoccupied equipment space, an exhaust drain cap shall be provided (coordinate with local codes).

(3) General airflow shall be away from the sterilizer operator(s).

(4) A dedicated exhaust duct system for ETO shall be provided. The exhaust outlet to the outside shall be at least 25 feet (7.62 meters) away from any air intake.

(5) An audible and visual alarm shall activate in the sterilizer work area, and in a 24-hour staffed

location, upon loss of airflow in the exhaust system.

9.2.2.3 Food preparation centers

(1) Exhaust hoods handling grease-laden vapors in food preparation centers shall comply with NFPA 96.

(2) All hoods over cooking ranges shall be equipped with grease filters, fire-extinguishing systems, and heat-actuated fan controls.

(3) Cleanout openings shall be provided every 20 feet (6.10 meters) and at changes in direction in the horizontal exhaust duct systems serving these hoods. Horizontal runs of ducts serving range hoods shall be kept to a minimum.

9.2.2.4 Fuel-fired equipment rooms. Rooms with fuel-fired equipment shall be provided with sufficient outdoor air to maintain equipment combustion rates and to limit work station temperatures.

9.2.3 Thermal Insulation and Acoustical Provisions
See Section 1.6-2.2.1.

9.2.4 HVAC Air Distribution

9.2.4.1 Return air systems. For patient care areas, all return ventilation shall be via ducted systems.

9.2.4.2 HVAC ductwork. See Section 1.6-2.2.2.1.

9.2.4.3 Exhaust systems

(1) General

(a) To enhance the efficiency of recovery devices required for energy conservation, combined exhaust systems shall be permitted.

(b) Local exhaust systems shall be used whenever possible in place of dilution ventilation to reduce exposure to hazardous gases, vapors, fumes, or mists.

(c) Fans serving exhaust systems shall be located at the discharge end and shall be readily serviceable.

9.2.4.4 Air outlets and inlets

(1) Fresh air intakes

(a) Fresh air intakes shall be located at least 25 feet (7.62 meters) from exhaust outlets of ventilating systems, combustion vents (including those serving rooftop air handling equipment), medical-surgical vacuum systems, plumbing vents, or areas that may collect vehicular exhaust or other noxious fumes. (Prevailing winds and/or proximity to other structures may require greater clearances.)

(b) Plumbing vents that terminate at a level above the top of the air intake may be located as close as 10 feet (3.05 meters).

(c) The bottom of outdoor air intakes serving central systems shall be as high as practical, but at least 6 feet (1.83 meters) above ground level, or, if installed above the roof, 3 feet (91.44 centimeters) above roof level.

(2) Relief air. Relief air is exempt from the 25-foot (7.62-meter) separation requirement. Relief air is defined as air that otherwise could be returned (recirculated) to an air handling unit from the occupied space, but is being discharged to the outdoors to maintain building pressure, such as during outside air economizer operation.

(3) Gravity exhaust. Where conditions permit, gravity exhaust shall be permitted for nonpatient areas such as boiler rooms, central storage, etc.

9.2.4.5 Ventilation hoods

(1) Exhaust hoods and safety cabinets

(a) Hoods and safety cabinets may be used for normal exhaust of a space providing minimum air change rates are maintained.

(b) If air change standards in Table 2.1-2 do not provide sufficient air for proper operation of exhaust hoods and safety cabinets (when in use), makeup air (filtered and preheated) shall be provided around these units to maintain the required airflow direction and exhaust velocity. Use of makeup air will avoid dependence upon infiltration from outdoors and/or from contaminated areas.

(c) Makeup systems for hoods shall be arranged to minimize "short circuiting" of air and to avoid reduction in air velocity at the point of contaminant capture.

(2) Laboratory fume hoods. Laboratory fume hoods shall meet the following general standards:

(a) General standards

(i) An average face velocity of at least 75 feet per minute (0.38 meters per second)

(ii) Connection to an exhaust system to the outside that is separate from the building exhaust system

(iii) Location of an exhaust fan at the discharge end of the system

(iv) Inclusion of an exhaust duct system of noncombustible corrosion-resistant material as needed to meet the planned usage of the hood

(b) Special standards for use with strong oxidants

(i) Fume hoods and their associated equipment in the air stream intended for use with perchloric acid and other strong oxidants shall be constructed of stainless steel or other material consistent with special exposures.

(ii) These hoods and equipment shall be provided with a water wash and drain system to permit periodic flushing of duct and hood.

(iii) Electrical equipment intended for installation within such ducts shall be designed and constructed to resist pene-

tration by water. Lubricants and seals shall not contain organic materials.

(iv) When perchloric acid or other strong oxidants are only transferred from one container to another, standard laboratory fume hoods and the associated equipment may be used in lieu of stainless steel construction.

(c) Special standards for use with infectious or radioactive materials. In new construction and major renovation work, each hood used to process infectious or radioactive materials shall meet the following requirements:

(i) A minimum face velocity of 90 to 110 feet per minute (0.45 to 0.56 meter per second) with suitable pressure-independent air modulating devices and alarms to alert staff of fan shutdown or loss of airflow.

(ii) Filters with a 99.97 percent efficiency (based on the DOP test method) in the exhaust stream, and shall be designed and equipped to permit the safe removal, disposal, and replacement of contaminated filters. Filters shall be as close to the hood as practical to minimize duct contamination.

(iii) For fume hoods intended for use with radioactive isotopes, construction of stainless steel or other material suitable for the particular exposure. These hoods shall comply with NFPA 801, Facilities for Handling Radioactive Materials. **Note:** Radioactive isotopes used for injections, etc., without probability of airborne particulates or gases may be processed in a clean-workbench-type hood where acceptable to the Nuclear Regulatory Commission.

9.2.5 HVAC Filters
9.2.5.1 Filter efficiencies

(1) All central ventilation or air conditioning systems shall be equipped with filters with efficiencies equal to, or greater than, those specified in Table 2.1-3.

(2) Noncentral air-handling systems shall be equipped with permanent (cleanable) or replaceable filters with a minimum efficiency of MERV 3 (68 percent weight arrestance).

(3) Filter efficiencies, tested in accordance with ASHRAE 52.1, shall be average.

9.2.5.2 Filter bed location. Where two filter beds are required, filter bed no. 1 shall be located upstream of the air conditioning equipment and filter bed no. 2 shall be downstream of any fan or blowers.

9.2.5.3 Filter frames. Filter frames shall be durable and proportioned to provide an airtight fit with the enclosing ductwork. All joints between filter segments and enclosing ductwork shall have gaskets or seals to provide a positive seal against air leakage.

9.2.5.4 Filter housing blank-off panels. Filter housing blank-off panels shall be permanently attached to the frame, constructed of rigid materials, and have sealing surfaces equal to or greater than the filter media installed in the filter frame.

9.2.5.5 Filter manometers. A manometer shall be installed across each filter bed having a required efficiency of 75 percent or more, including hoods requiring HEPA filters. Provisions shall be made to allow access for field testing.

9.2.6 Steam and Hot Water Systems
9.2.6.1 Boilers

(1) Capacity. Boilers shall have the capacity, based upon the net ratings published by the Hydronics Institute or another acceptable national standard, to supply the normal heating, hot water, and steam requirements of all systems and equipment. Their number and arrangement shall accommodate facility needs despite the breakdown or routine maintenance of any one boiler. The capacity of the remaining boiler(s) (reserve capacity) shall be sufficient to provide hot water service for clinical, dietary, and patient use; steam for sterilization and dietary purposes; and space heating for operating, recovery, and general patient rooms.

(2) Space heating requirements. Reserve capacity for facility space heating is not required in geographic areas where a design dry-bulb temperature of 25°F (-4°C) or more represents not less than 99 percent of the total hours in any one heating month as noted in the *ASHRAE Handbook—Fundamentals* under the "Table for Climatic Conditions for the United States."

9.2.6.2 Boiler accessories. These, including feed pumps, heat-circulating pumps, condensate return pumps, fuel oil pumps, and waste heat boilers, shall be connected and installed to provide both normal and standby service.

9.3 Electrical Systems

9.3.1 General
9.3.1.1 Applicable standards

(1) All electrical material and equipment, including conductors, controls, and signaling devices, shall be installed in compliance with applicable sections of NFPA 70 and NFPA 99.

(2) All electrical material and equipment shall be listed as complying with available standards of listing agencies or other similar established standards where such standards are required.

9.3.1.2 Testing and documentation. The electrical installations, including alarm, nurse call, and communication systems, shall be tested to demonstrate that equipment installation and operation is appropriate and functional. A written record of performance tests on special electrical systems and equipment shall show compliance with applicable codes and standards.

9.3.2 Electrical Distribution and Transmission
9.3.2.1 Switchboards

(1) Location

   (a) Main switchboards shall be located in an area separate from plumbing and mechanical equipment and shall be accessible to authorized persons only.

   (b) Switchboards shall be convenient for use, readily accessible for maintenance, away from traffic lanes

(c) Switchboards shall be located in dry, ventilated spaces free of corrosive or explosive fumes, gases, or any flammable material.

(2) Overload protective devices shall operate properly in ambient room temperatures.

9.3.2.2 Panelboards

(1) Panelboards serving normal lighting and appliance circuits shall be located on the same floor as the circuits they serve.

(2) Panelboards serving critical branch emergency circuits shall be located on each floor that has major users.

(3) Panelboards serving life safety emergency circuits may also serve floors above and/or below.

9.3.2.3 Ground-fault circuit interrupters

(1) Ground-fault circuit interrupters (GFCIs) shall comply with NFPA 70.

(2) Where GFCIs are used in critical areas, provisions shall be made to ensure that other essential equipment is not affected by activation of one interrupter.

9.3.3 Power Generating and Storing Equipment
9.3.3.1 Emergency electrical service

(1) As a minimum, nursing units or sections thereof shall have emergency electrical systems as required in NFPA 99, NFPA 101, and NFPA 110.

(2) Where the nursing unit is a distinct part of an acute-care hospital, it may use the emergency generator system for required emergency lighting and power, if such sharing does not reduce hospital services.

  (a) Such a shared system shall be designed with the capacity to meet the needs of both the hospital and the rehabilitation facilities.

  (b) Life support systems and their respective areas shall be subject to applicable standards of Section 2.1-10.

(3) An emergency electrical source shall provide lighting and/or power during an interruption of the normal electric supply.

9.3.4 Lighting
9.3.4.1 General. Lighting shall be engineered to the specific application. See Section 1.6-2.3.1.1.

9.3.4.2 Lighting for specific locations in the rehabilitation hospital

(1) Patient rooms. Patient rooms shall have general lighting and night lighting.

  (a) Reading light controls shall be accessible to the patient(s) without the patient having to get out of bed.

  (b) Incandescent and halogen light sources that produce heat shall be avoided to prevent burns to the patient and/or bed linen.

  (c) Unless specifically designed to protect the space below, the light source shall be covered by a diffuser or lens.

(2) Nursing unit corridors. Nursing unit corridors shall have general illumination with provisions for reducing light levels at night.

9.3.5 Receptacles
9.3.5.1 Corridors. Duplex-grounded receptacles for general use shall be installed approximately 50 feet (15.24 meters) apart in all corridors and within 25 feet (7.62 meters) of corridor ends.

9.3.5.2 Patient room. Each patient room shall have duplex-grounded receptacles.

(1) There shall be one at each side of the head of each bed and one on every other wall.

(2) Receptacles may be omitted from exterior walls where construction or room configuration makes installation impractical.

9.3.5.3 Emergency system receptacles. Electrical receptacle cover plates or electrical receptacles supplied from the emergency system shall be distinctively colored or marked for identification. If color is used for identification purposes, the same color shall be used throughout the facility.

9.3.6 Equipment

9.3.6.1 Data processing and/or automated laboratory or diagnostic equipment, if provided, may require safeguards from power line disturbances.

9.3.6.2 X-ray equipment. Fixed and mobile x-ray equipment installations shall conform to articles 517 and 660 of NFPA 70.

9.3.6.3 Special electrical equipment. Special equipment is identified in the sections in this chapter on nursing units, support areas, physical therapy, occupational therapy, and imaging, if applicable. These sections shall be consulted to ensure compatibility between programmatically defined equipment needs and appropriate power and other electrical connection needs.

9.3.7 Call Systems

9.3.7.1 General. Alternate technologies shall be permitted for emergency or nurse call systems. If radio frequency systems are utilized, consideration shall be given to electromagnetic compatibility between internal and external sources.

(1) A nurse call system shall be provided.

(2) Each bed shall be provided with a call device. Two call devices serving adjacent beds may be served by one call station.

(3) Calls shall activate a visible signal in the corridor at the patient's door or other appropriate location. In multicorridor nursing units, additional visible signals shall be installed at corridor intersections.

9.3.7.2 Emergency call system

(1) The emergency call shall be designed so that a signal activated at a patient's call station will initiate a visible and audible signal distinct from the regular nurse call system that can be turned off only at the patient call station.

(2) The signal shall activate an annunciator panel at the nurse station or other appropriate location, a visible signal in the corridor at the patient's door, and at other areas defined by the functional program.

(3) A nurse emergency call shall be provided at each inpatient toilet, bath, sitz bath, and shower room. This emergency call shall be accessible to a collapsed patient lying on the floor. Inclusion of a pull cord will satisfy this standard.

9.4 Telecommunications and Information Systems

9.4.1 Locations for terminating telecommunications and information system devices shall be provided.

9.4.2 An area shall be provided for central equipment locations. Special air conditioning and voltage regulation shall be provided when recommended by the manufacturer.

9.5 Fire Alarm and Detection Systems

Fire alarm and detection systems shall be provided in compliance with NFPA 72 and NFPA 101.

3

Ambulatory Care Facilities

3.1 Outpatient Facilities

Appendix material, which appears in shaded boxes at the bottom of the page, is advisory only.

1 General Considerations

1.1 Applicability

1.1.1 This part of the Guidelines applies to the outpatient unit in a hospital, a freestanding facility, or an outpatient facility in a multiple-use building containing an ambulatory health care facility as defined in the NFPA 101 Life Safety Code occupancy chapters.

*1.1.2 The general standards set forth in Sections 1 through 5 of this chapter (General Considerations, Diagnostic and Treatment Locations, Service Areas, Administrative and Public Areas, and Construction Standards) shall apply to each of the facility types below. Additions and/or modifications shall be made as described in this chapter and in the chapters for the specific facility types. Consideration shall be given to the special needs of anticipated patient groups/demographics as determined by the functional program.

- Primary Care Outpatient Centers (Chapter 3.2)
- Small Primary (Neighborhood) Outpatient Facilities (Chapter 3.3)
- Freestanding Outpatient Diagnostic and Treatment Facilities (Chapter 3.4)
- Freestanding Urgent Care Facilities (Chapter 3.5)
- Freestanding Birthing Centers (Chapter 3.6)
- Ambulatory Surgical Facilities (Chapter 3.7)
- Gastrointestinal Endoscopy Facilities (Chapter 3.9)
- Renal Dialysis (Acute and Chronic) Centers (Chapter 3.10)
- Psychiatric Outpatient Centers (Chapter 3.11)

1.1.3 Specialty facilities not identified above may have needs that are not addressed in this chapter. Development of such specialty facilities shall rely on a detailed and specific functional program to establish physical environment requirements beyond the general requirements identified in this chapter.

1.2 Outpatient Facility Classification

1.2.1 The outpatient facilities described in this part of

the Guidelines are used primarily by patients capable of traveling into, around, and out of the facility unassisted. This group includes the disabled confined to wheelchairs. Occasional facility use by stretcher patients shall not be used as a basis for more restrictive institutional occupancy classifications.

1.2.2 Where patients are rendered incapable of self-preservation due to the care process, facilities shall comply with the Ambulatory Health Care Occupancies section of NFPA 101 in addition to details herein. The Business Occupancy section of NFPA 101 applies to other types of outpatient facilities. Outpatient units that are part of another facility may be subject to the additional requirements of the other occupancy.

1.2.3 References are made to Chapter 2.1, General Hospitals, for certain service spaces. Those references are intended only for the specific areas indicated.

1.3 Functional Program
Each project sponsor shall provide a functional program for the facility. (See Section 1.2-2.)

1.4 Environment of Care

1.4.1 Patient Privacy
Each facility design shall ensure appropriate levels of patient acoustical and visual privacy and dignity throughout the care process, consistent with needs established in the functional program. See Sections 1.1-6 and 1.2-2.1.2.5 (4).

1.5 Shared/Purchased Services
When services are shared or purchased, modification or elimination of space and equipment to avoid unnecessary duplication shall be permitted.

APPENDIX

A1.1.2 The applicability of Sections 3.1-6 (Special Systems) and 3.1-7 (Building Systems) generally are specified in these sections and/or in the text of the individual facility type chapters.

1.6 Facility Access

1.6.1 Where the outpatient occupancy is part of another facility, separation and access shall be maintained as described in NFPA 101.

1.6.2 Building entrances used to reach the outpatient services shall be at grade level, clearly marked, and located so patients need not go through other activity areas. (Lobbies of multi-occupancy buildings may be shared.)

1.6.3 Design shall preclude unrelated traffic within the unit.

1.7 Site

*1.7.1 Location

1.7.2 Parking
1.7.2.1 In the absence of a formal parking study, parking for outpatient facilities shall be provided at the rate noted for each type of unit.

1.7.2.2 On-street parking, if available and acceptable to local authorities having jurisdiction, may satisfy part of this requirement unless described otherwise.

1.7.2.3 If the facility is located in a densely populated area where a large percentage of patients arrive as pedestrians, or if adequate public parking is available nearby, or if the facility is conveniently accessible via public transportation, adjustments to this standard may be made with approval of the appropriate authorities.

2 Diagnostic and Treatment Locations

Clinical and support areas shall be provided to support the functional program. The following spaces are common to most outpatient facilities:

| APPENDIX |

A1.7.1 Community outpatient units should ideally be conveniently accessible to patients via available public transportation.

A2.1.1 Door swings should be oriented to provide patient privacy.

A2.1.2 Door swings should be oriented to provide patient privacy.

A2.1.3 Door swings should be oriented to provide patient privacy.

2.1 Examination and Treatment Rooms

*2.1.1 General Purpose Examination Room(s)
2.1.1.1 Space requirements
(1) Area. Rooms for medical, obstetrical, and similar examinations, if provided, shall have a minimum floor area of 80 net square feet (7.43 square meters) excluding vestibules, toilets, closets, and fixed casework.

(2) Clearances. Room arrangement shall permit a minimum clearance of 2 feet 8 inches (81.28 centimeters) at each side and at the foot of the examination table.

2.1.1.2 Hand-washing station. A hand-washing station shall be provided.

2.1.1.3 Documentation space. A counter or shelf space for writing shall be provided.

*2.1.2 Special Purpose Examination Rooms
2.1.2.1 Space requirements

(1) Area. Rooms for special clinics such as eye, ear, nose, and throat examinations, if provided, shall have a minimum floor area of 80 net square feet (7.43 square meters). This square footage shall exclude vestibules, toilets, closets, and fixed casework.

(2) Clearances. Room arrangement shall permit a minimum clearance of 2 feet 8 inches (81.28 centimeters) at each side and at the foot of the examination table, bed, or chair.

2.1.2.2 Hand-washing station. A hand-washing station shall be provided.

2.1.2.3 Documentation space. A counter or shelf space for writing shall be provided.

*2.1.3 Treatment Room(s)
2.1.3.1 Space requirements

(1) Area. Rooms for minor surgical and cast procedures, if provided, shall have a minimum floor area of 120 square feet (11.15 square meters). This square footage shall exclude vestibule, toilet,

closets, and fixed casework. The minimum room dimension shall be 10 feet (3.05 meters).

(2) Clearance. Room arrangement shall permit a minimum clearance of 3 feet (91.44 centimeters) at each side and at the foot of the bed.

2.1.3.2 Hand-washing station. A hand-washing station shall be provided.

2.1.3.3 Documentation space. A counter or shelf for writing shall be provided.

2.1.4 Observation Room(s)
*2.1.4.1 Location. The room shall be convenient to a nurse or control station.

2.1.4.2 Space requirements. If provided, observation rooms for the isolation of suspect or disturbed patients shall have a minimum floor area of 80 square feet (7.43 square meters). This square footage shall exclude vestibule, toilet, closets, and fixed casework.

2.1.5 Airborne Infection Isolation Rooms
2.1.5.1 Applicability. In facilities with a functional program that includes treatment of patients with known infectious disease, the need for and number of such rooms shall be determined by an infection control risk assessment (ICRA).

2.1.5.2 Standards. Where airborne infection isolation room(s) are required, they shall comply with the general requirements of Section 2.1-3.2.2, except that a shower or tub shall not be required.

2.1.6 Protective Environment Rooms
2.1.6.1 Applicability. The need for and number of required protective environment rooms shall be determined by an infection control risk assessment.

2.1.6.2 Standards. When required, the protective environment room(s) shall comply with the general requirements of Section 2.1-3.2.3, except that a toilet, bathtub, or shower shall not be required.

2.1.7 Support Areas for Examination and Treatment Rooms
2.1.7.1 Nurse station(s). A work counter, communication system, space for supplies, and provisions for charting shall be provided.

2.1.7.2 Drug distribution station. This may be a part of the nurses station and shall include a work counter, sink, refrigerator, and locked storage for biologicals and drugs.

2.1.7.3 Sterilizing facilities. A system for sterilizing equipment and supplies shall be provided. Sterilizing procedures may be done on- or off-site, or disposables may be used to satisfy functional needs.

2.1.7.4 Clean storage. A separate room or closet for storing clean and sterile supplies shall be provided. This storage shall be in addition to that of cabinets and shelves.

2.1.7.5 Soiled holding. Provisions shall be made for separate collection, storage, and disposal of soiled materials.

2.1.7.6 Wheelchair storage space. Such storage shall be out of the direct line of traffic.

2.1.8 Support Areas for Patients
2.1.8.1 Toilet(s) for patient use. These shall be provided separate from public use toilet(s) and located to permit access from patient care areas without passing through publicly accessible areas.

*2.2 Imaging Facilities
Basic diagnostic procedures (these may be part of the outpatient service, off-site, shared, by contract, or by referral) shall be provided and shall include the following:

APPENDIX

A2.1.4.1 This is to permit close observation of patients. An examination room may be modified to accommodate this function. A toilet room with lavatory should be immediately accessible.

A2.2 Imaging Facilities
a. Access. Stretchers should have ready access to and from other areas of the facility. The emergency, surgery, cystoscopy, and outpatient clinics should be accessible to the imaging suite.

b. Layout. Particular attention should be paid to the management of outpatients for preparation, holding, and observation.

c. Location. Imaging should be located with consideration of ceiling height requirements, proximity to electrical services, and future expansion considerations.

2.2.1 Access

2.2.2 Radiographic Room(s)
See Section 2.1-5.5 for special requirements.

2.2.3 Support Areas for Imaging Facilities
2.2.3.1 Viewing and administrative areas(s)

2.2.3.2 Film and media processing facilities. These shall be provided as indicated in the functional program and as technology requires.

2.2.3.3 Storage facilities for exposed film. These shall be provided as indicated in the functional program and as technology requires.

2.2.4 Support Areas for Patients
2.2.4.1 Dressing rooms or booths. These shall be provided as required by the functional program, with convenient toilet access.

2.2.4.2 Toilet rooms. Toilet rooms with hand-washing stations shall be accessible to procedure room(s) if procedures provided may result in the need for immediate access to patient toilet facilities.

2.3 Laboratory
Facilities shall be provided within the outpatient department, or through an effective contract arrangement with a nearby hospital or laboratory service, for hematology, clinical chemistry, urinalysis, cytology, pathology, and bacteriology. If these services are provided on contract, the following laboratory facilities shall also be provided in (or be immediately accessible to) the outpatient facility:

2.3.1 Laboratory Work Counter(s)
These shall have sink, vacuum, gas, and electric services.

2.3.2 Hand-washing Station(s)
Hand-washing stations or counter sink(s) equipped for hand washing shall be provided.

2.3.3 Support Areas for the Laboratory
2.3.3.1 Storage cabinet(s) or closet(s)

2.3.3.2 Specimen collection facilities

(1) These shall have a water closet and lavatory.

(2) Blood collection facilities shall have seating space, a work counter, and hand-washing station.

3 Service Areas

3.1 Environmental Services

3.1.1 Housekeeping Room(s)
3.1.1.1 Number. At least one housekeeping room per floor shall be provided.

3.1.1.2 Facility requirements. Each housekeeping room shall contain a service sink and storage for housekeeping supplies and equipment.

3.2 Engineering Services and Maintenance
The following shall be provided (sharing of these with other services shall be permitted provided capacity is appropriate for overall use):

3.2.1 Equipment Rooms
Equipment room(s) for boilers, mechanical equipment, and electrical equipment shall be provided.

3.2.2 Equipment and Supply Storage
Storage room(s) for supplies and equipment shall be provided.

3.3 Materials Management

3.3.1 Waste Management
For information on treatment or disposal of waste, see Section 3.1-6.3.

3.3.1.1 Collection and storage

(1) Space and facilities shall be provided for the sanitary storage of waste in accordance with the functional program.

(2) These facilities shall use techniques acceptable to the appropriate health and environmental authorities.

3.3.1.2 Trash chutes. The design and construction of trash chutes shall comply with NFPA 82.

4 Administrative and Public Areas

4.1 Public Areas
The following shall be provided:

4.1.1 Entrance
This shall be located at grade level and be able to accommodate wheelchairs.

4.1.2 Reception. A reception and information counter or desk shall be provided.

*4.1.3 Waiting Space(s)

4.1.4 Public Toilets
Toilet(s) for public use shall be conveniently accessible from the waiting area without passing through patient care or staff work areas or suites.

4.1.5 Public Telephones
Conveniently accessible public telephone(s) shall be provided.

4.1.6 Provisions for Drinking Water
Conveniently accessible provisions for drinking water shall be provided.

4.1.7 Wheelchair Storage
Conveniently accessible wheelchair storage shall be provided.

*4.2 Administrative Areas

4.2.1 Interview Space(s)
Space(s) shall be provided for private interviews related to social service, credit, etc.

4.2.2 General or Individual Office(s)
Space providing adequate work area for business transactions, records storage, and administrative and professional staffs shall be provided.

4.2.3 Medical Records
Provisions shall be made for securing medical records.

4.2.4 Equipment and Supply Storage
General storage facilities for supplies and equipment shall be provided as identified in the functional program.

4.2.5 Support Areas for Staff
Special storage for staff personal effects with locking drawers or cabinets (may be individual desks or cabinets) shall be provided. Such storage shall be convenient to individual workstations and shall be staff controlled.

5 Construction Standards

5.1 Design and Construction, including Fire-Resistant Standards

5.1.1 Building Codes
5.1.1.1 Construction and structural elements of free-standing outpatient facilities shall comply with recognized building code requirements for offices (business occupancies) and the standards contained herein.

5.1.1.2 Outpatient facilities that are an integral part of a hospital or that share common areas and functions with a hospital shall comply with the construction standards for general hospitals. See applicable sections of Chapter 2.1.

5.1.2 Provision for Disasters
5.1.2.1 Earthquakes. Seismic force resistance of new construction for outpatient facilities shall comply with Section 1.1-5 and shall be given an importance factor of one. Where the outpatient facility is part of an existing building, that facility shall comply with applicable local codes.

5.1.2.2 Other natural disasters. Special design provisions shall be made for buildings in regions that have sustained loss of life or damage to buildings from hurricanes, tornadoes, floods, or other natural disasters.

APPENDIX

A4.1.3 Consideration should be given to special needs of specific patient groups in a shared/general waiting area, such as separation of adolescent and geriatric patients.

A4.2 Multipurpose room(s) should be provided for private interviews, conferences, meetings, and health education purposes. Where health education is accommodated, the room(s) should be equipped for audiovisual aids.

5.2 General Standards for Details and Finishes

5.2.1 Details
Details shall comply with the following standards:

5.2.1.1 Corridor width

(1) Minimum public corridor width shall be 5 feet (1.52 meters). Staff-only corridors shall be permitted to be 3 feet 8 inches (1.12 meters) wide.

(2) Items such as provisions for drinking water, telephone booths, vending machines, etc., shall not restrict corridor traffic or reduce the corridor width below the required minimum.

(3) Out-of-traffic storage space for portable equipment shall be provided.

5.2.1.2 Ceiling height. The minimum ceiling height shall be 7 feet 10 inches (2.39 meters), with the following exceptions:

(1) Corridors, storage rooms, toilet rooms, etc. Ceiling height in corridors, storage rooms, toilet rooms, and other minor rooms shall not be less than 7 feet 8 inches (2.34 meters).

(2) Rooms with ceiling-mounted equipment/light fixtures. Radiographic and other rooms containing ceiling-mounted equipment shall have ceilings of sufficient height to accommodate the equipment and/or fixtures.

(3) Boiler rooms. Boiler rooms shall have ceiling clearances not less than 2 feet 6 inches (76.20 centimeters) above the main boiler header and connecting piping.

(4) Clearances. Tracks, rails, and pipes suspended along the path of normal traffic shall be not less than 6 feet 8 inches (2.03 meters) above the floor.

5.2.1.3 Exits

(1) Each building shall have at least two exits that are remote from each other.

(2) Other details relating to exits and fire safety shall comply with NFPA 101 and the standards outlined herein.

5.2.1.4 Door width

(1) The minimum nominal door width for patient use shall be 3 feet (0.91 meter).

(2) If the outpatient facility serves hospital inpatients, the minimum nominal width of doors to rooms used by hospital inpatients transported in beds shall be 3 feet 8 inches (1.12 meters).

5.2.1.5 Glazing materials

(1) Doors, sidelights, borrowed lights, and windows glazed to within 18 inches (45.72 centimeters) of the floor shall be constructed of safety glass, wired glass, or plastic glazing material that resists breakage and creates no dangerous cutting edges when broken.

(2) Similar materials shall be used in wall openings of playrooms and exercise rooms unless otherwise required for fire safety.

(3) Glazing materials used for shower doors and bath enclosures shall be safety glass or plastic.

5.2.1.6 Hand-washing stations

(1) Hand-washing stations shall be located and arranged to permit proper use and operation.

(2) Particular care shall be taken to provide the required clearance for operation of blade-type handles.

(3) Provisions for hand drying shall be included at all hand-washing stations except scrub sinks.

5.2.1.7 Thresholds and joints. Threshold and expansion joint covers shall be flush with the floor surface to facilitate use of wheelchairs and carts.

5.2.1.8 Radiation protection. Radiation protection for x-ray and gamma ray installations shall comply with Section 2.1-5.5.

5.2.1.9 Protection from heat-producing equipment. Rooms containing heat-producing equipment (such as boiler or heater rooms) shall be insulated and ventilated to prevent occupied adjacent floor or wall surfaces from exceeding a temperature 10°F above the ambient room temperature.

5.2.2 Finishes

Finishes shall comply with the following standards:

5.2.2.1 Fire-retardant materials

(1) Cubicle curtains and draperies shall be noncombustible or flame-retardant and shall pass both the large- and small-scale tests required by NFPA 701.

(2) The flame-spread and smoke-developed ratings of finishes shall comply with Section 2.1-8.1. Where possible, the use of materials known to produce large amounts of noxious gases shall be avoided.

5.2.2.2 Floors

(1) Floor materials shall be readily cleanable and appropriately wear-resistant.

(2) In all areas subject to wet cleaning, floor materials shall not be physically affected by liquid germicidal and cleaning solutions.

(3) Floors subject to traffic while wet, including showers and bath areas, shall have a nonslip surface.

(4) Wall bases in areas frequently subject to wet cleaning shall be monolithic and coved with the floor, tightly sealed to the wall, and constructed without voids.

5.2.2.3 Walls. Wall finishes shall be washable and, in the proximity of plumbing fixtures, shall be smooth and moisture resistant.

5.2.2.4 Penetrations. Floor and wall areas penetrated by pipes, ducts, and conduits shall be tightly sealed to minimize entry of rodents and insects. Joints of structural elements shall be similarly sealed.

6 Special Systems

6.1 General

6.1.1 Applicability

As required by the functional program, special systems shall be installed in accordance with the following standards:

6.1.2 Testing

6.1.2.1 Prior to acceptance of the facility, all special systems shall be tested and operated to demonstrate to the owner or its designated representative that the installation and performance of these systems conform to design intent.

6.1.2.2 Test results. Test results shall be documented for maintenance files.

6.1.3 Documentation

6.1.3.1 Upon completion of the special systems equipment installation contract, the owner shall be furnished with a complete set of manufacturers' operating, maintenance, and preventive maintenance instructions, a parts lists, and complete procurement information, including equipment numbers and descriptions.

6.1.3.2 Operating staff persons shall also be provided with instructions for proper operation of systems and equipment. Required information shall include all safety or code ratings as needed.

6.1.4 Insulation

Insulation shall be provided surrounding special system equipment to conserve energy, protect personnel, and reduce noise.

6.2 Elevators

6.2.1 Dimensions

Cars shall have a minimum inside floor dimension of not less than 5 feet (1.52 meters).

6.2.2 Leveling Device

Elevators shall be equipped with a two-way automatic level-maintaining device with an accuracy of ±1/2 inch (±12.7 millimeters).

6.2.3 Elevator Controls

6.2.3.1 Elevator call buttons and controls shall not be activated by heat or smoke. Light beams, if used for operating door reopening devices without touch, shall be used in combination with door-edge safety devices and shall be interconnected with a system of smoke detectors. This is so the light control feature will be overridden or disengaged should it encounter smoke at any landing.

6.2.3.2 Elevator controls, alarm buttons, and telephones shall be accessible to wheelchair occupants and usable by the blind.

6.2.4 Installation and Testing

6.2.4.1 Standards. Installation and testing of elevators shall comply with ANSI/ASME A17.1 for new construction and ANSI/ASME A17.3 for existing facilities. (See ASCE/SEI 7 for seismic design and control system requirements for elevators.)

6.2.4.2 Documentation. Field inspections and tests shall be made and the owner shall be furnished with written certification stating that the installation meets the requirements set forth in this section as well as all applicable safety regulations and codes.

6.3 Waste Processing

Space and facilities shall be provided for the treatment or disposal of waste.

Note: For information on collection and storage of waste, see Section 3.1-3.3.1, Waste Management.

6.3.1 General

6.3.1.1 The functional program shall stipulate the categories and volumes of waste for disposal and shall stipulate the methods of disposal for each.

6.3.1.2 These facilities shall use techniques acceptable to the appropriate health and environmental authorities.

6.3.2 Medical Waste Disposal
6.3.2.1 General

APPENDIX

A6.3.2.4 When incinerators are used, consideration should be given to the recovery of waste heat from on-site incinerators used to dispose of large amounts of waste materials.

---

(1) Medical waste shall be disposed of by incineration or other approved technologies. Two or more institutions shall be permitted to share incinerators or other major disposal equipment.

(2) Use of incinerators or other major disposal equipment to dispose of other medical waste shall be permitted where local regulations permit.

6.3.2.2 Space requirements

(1) Incinerators with capacities of 50 pounds per hour or more shall be in a separate room or outdoors; those with lesser capacities shall be permitted to be in a separate area within the facility boiler room.

(2) Rooms and areas containing incinerators shall have adequate space and facilities for charging and cleaning incinerators, as well as necessary clearances for work and maintenance.

(3) Provisions shall be made for operation, temporary storage, and disposal of materials so that odors and fumes do not drift back into occupied areas.

(4) Existing approved incinerator installations that are not in separate rooms or outdoors may remain unchanged provided they meet the above criteria.

6.3.2.3 Equipment

(1) Incinerators or other major disposal equipment shall be designed for the actual quantity and type of waste to be destroyed.

(2) Equipment shall meet all applicable regulations.

(3) The design and construction of incinerators, if used, shall comply with NFPA 82 and conform to the standards prescribed by area air pollution regulations.

Note: For information about refuse chutes, see Section 3.1-3.3.1.2.

*6.3.2.4** Recovery of waste heat

*6.3.2.5 Environmental/health risk assessments

6.3.3 Nuclear Waste Disposal
See Code of Federal Regulations, title X, parts 20 and 35, concerning the handling and disposal of nuclear materials in health care facilities.

7 Building Systems

7.1 Plumbing

7.1.1 General
7.1.1.1 Applicability. These requirements do not apply to small primary (neighborhood) outpatient facilities or outpatient facilities that do not perform invasive applications or procedures. See Section 3.3-6.1 for requirements for small primary (neighborhood) outpatient facilities.

7.1.1.2 Standards. Unless otherwise specified herein, all plumbing systems shall be designed and installed in accordance with the International Plumbing Code.

7.1.2 Plumbing and Other Piping Systems
7.1.2.1 General piping and valves

(1) All piping, except control-line tubing, shall be identified.

(2) All valves shall be tagged, and a valve schedule shall be provided to the facility owner for permanent record and reference.

(3) No plumbing piping shall be exposed overhead or exposed on walls where possible accumulation of dust or soil may create a cleaning problem or where leaks would create a potential for food contamination.

7.1.2.2 Hemodialysis piping

(1) Where the functional program includes hemodialysis, continuously circulated filtered cold water shall be provided. Piping shall be in accordance with AAMI RD62.

(2) In new construction and renovation where hemodialysis or hemoperfusion are routinely performed, a separate water supply and drainage facility that does not interfere with hand-washing shall be provided.

7.1.2.3 Potable water supply systems. The following standards shall apply to potable water supply systems:

(1) Capacity. Systems shall be designed to supply water at sufficient pressure to operate all fixtures and equipment during maximum demand. Supply capacity for hot- and cold-water piping shall be determined on the basis of fixture units, using recognized engineering standards. Where the ratio of plumbing fixtures to occupants is proportionally more than required by the building occupancy and is in excess of 1,000 plumbing fixture units, a diversity factor is permitted.

(2) Valves. Each water service main, branch main, riser, and branch to a group of fixtures shall have valves.

    (a) Stop valves shall be provided for each fixture.

    (b) Appropriate panels for access shall be provided at all valves where required.

(3) Backflow prevention

    (a) Systems shall be protected against cross-connection in accordance with American Water Works Association (AWWA) *Recommended Practice for Backflow Prevention and Cross-connection Control.*

> **APPENDIX**
>
> **A6.3.2.5** Incinerators should be designed in a manner fully consistent with protection of public and environmental health, both on-site and off-site, and in compliance with federal, state, and local statutes and regulations. Toward this end, permit applications for incinerators and modifications thereof should be supported by environmental assessments and/or environmental impact statements (EISs) and/or health risk assessments (HRAs) as required by regulatory agencies. Except as noted below, such assessments should utilize standard U.S. EPA methods, specifically those set forth in U.S. EPA guidelines, and should be fully consistent with U.S. EPA guidelines for health risk assessment. Under some circumstances, however, regulatory agencies having jurisdiction over a particular project may require use of alternative methods.

(b) Vacuum breakers or backflow prevention devices shall be installed on hose bibs and supply nozzles used for connection of hoses or tubing in laboratories, housekeeping sinks, etc.

(4) Potable water storage vessels (hot and cold) not intended for constant use shall not be installed.

(5) Emergency eyewash and showers shall comply with ANSI Z358.1.

7.1.2.4 Hot water systems. See Section 1.6-2.2.1.

7.1.2.5 Drainage systems. The following standards shall apply to drainage systems:

(1) Piping

(a) Drain lines from sinks used for acid waste disposal shall be made of acid-resistant material.

(b) Drain lines serving some types of automatic blood-cell counters shall be of carefully selected material that will eliminate the potential for undesirable chemical reactions (and/or explosions) between sodium azide wastes and copper, lead, brass, solder, etc.

(c) Insofar as possible, drainage piping shall not be installed within the ceiling or exposed in operating and delivery rooms, nurseries, food preparation centers, food-serving facilities, food storage areas, central services, electronic data processing areas, electric closets, and other sensitive areas.

APPENDIX

A7.1.2.5 (2)(b) Floor drains in cystoscopy operating rooms have been shown to disseminate a heavily contaminated spray during flushing. Unless flushed regularly with large amounts of fluid, the trap tends to dry out and permit passage of gases, vapors, odors, insects, and vermin directly into the operating room. For new construction, if the users insist on a floor drain, the drain plate should be located away from the operative site and should be over a frequently flushed nonsplash, horizontal-flow type of bowl, preferably with a closed system of drainage. Alternative methods include (1) an aspirator/trap installed in a wall connected to the collecting trough of the operating table by a closed, disposable tube system or (2) a closed system using portable collecting vessels. (See NFPA 99.)

Where exposed overhead drain piping in these areas is unavoidable, special provisions shall be made to protect the space below from leakage, condensation, or dust particles.

(2) Floor drains

(a) Floor drains shall not be installed in operating and delivery rooms.

*(b) If a floor drain is installed in cystoscopy, it shall contain a nonsplash, horizontal-flow flushing bowl beneath the drain plate.

(c) Dietary area floor drains and/or floor sinks

(i) Type. These shall be of a type that can be easily cleaned by removing the cover. Removable stainless steel mesh shall be provided in addition to grilled drain covers to prevent entry of large particles of waste that might cause stoppages.

(ii) Location. Floor drains or floor sinks shall be provided at all "wet" equipment (as ice machines) and as required for wet cleaning of floors. Location of floor drains and floor sinks shall be coordinated to avoid conditions where locations of equipment make removal of covers for cleaning difficult.

(3) Sewers. Building sewers shall discharge into community sewerage. Where such a system is not available, the facility shall treat its sewage in accordance with local and state regulations.

(4) Kitchen grease traps

(a) Grease traps shall be of capacity required.

(b) These shall be located and arranged to permit easy access without the need to enter food preparation or storage areas.

(c) These shall be accessible from outside the building without need to interrupt any services.

(5) Plaster traps. Where plaster traps are used, provisions shall be made for appropriate access and cleaning.

7.1.2.6 Condensate drains. See Section 1.6-2.1.2.2.

7.1.3 Plumbing Fixtures

In addition to the requirements of Section 1.6-2.1.3, the following standards shall apply to plumbing fixtures in outpatient facilities:

7.1.3.1 Clinical sinks

(1) Handles on clinical sinks shall be at least 6 inches (15.24 centimeters) long.

(2) Clinical sinks shall have an integral trap wherein the upper portion of the water trap provides a visible seal.

7.1.3.2 Scrub sinks. Freestanding scrub sinks and lavatories used for scrubbing in procedure rooms shall be trimmed with foot, knee, or ultrasonic controls; single-lever wrist blades shall not be permitted.

7.1.4 Medical Gas and Vacuum Systems

7.1.4.1 Medical gas systems. If piped medical gas is used, the installation, testing, and certification of nonflammable medical gas and air systems shall comply with the requirements of NFPA 99. Station outlets shall be provided consistent with need established by the functional program. (See also Table 3.1-2.)

7.1.4.2 Vacuum systems. Central vacuum systems. Where the functional program requires, central clinical vacuum system installations shall be in accordance with NFPA 99.

7.2 Heating, Ventilating, and Air-Conditioning (HVAC) Systems

7.2.1 Applicability

These requirements do not apply to small primary (neighborhood) outpatient facilities or outpatient facilities that do not perform invasive applications or procedures. See Section 3.3-6.2 for requirements for small primary (neighborhood) outpatient facilities.

7.2.2 General

*7.2.2.1 Mechanical system design

(1) Efficiency. The mechanical system shall be designed for overall efficiency and life-cycle costing. Details for cost-effective implementation of design features are interrelated and too numerous (as well as too basic) to list individually.

(a) Recognized engineering procedures shall be followed for the most economical and effective results. A well-designed system can generally achieve energy efficiency at minimal additional cost and simultaneously provide improved patient comfort.

(b) Different geographic areas may have climatic and use conditions that favor one system over another in terms of overall cost and efficiency.

(c) In no case shall patient care or safety be sacrificed for conservation.

(d) Facility design features such as site, building mass, orientation, configuration, fenestration, and other features relative to passive and active energy systems shall be considered.

(e) Use of recognized energy-saving mechanisms such as variable-air-volume (VAV) systems, load shedding, programmed controls for unoccupied periods (nights and weekends, etc.), and use of natural ventilation shall be considered, site and climatic conditions permitting.

APPENDIX

A7.2.2.1 Mechanical system design

a. Remodeling and work in existing facilities may present special problems. As practicality and funding permit, existing insulation, weather stripping, etc., should be brought up to standard for maximum economy and efficiency. Consideration should be given to additional work that may be needed to achieve this.

b. Insofar as practical, the facility should include provisions for recovery of waste cooling and heating energy (ventilation, exhaust, water and steam discharge, cooling towers, incinerators, etc.).

c. Systems with excessive installation and/or maintenance costs that negate long-range savings should be avoided.

d. Use of mechanically circulated outside air does not reduce the need for filtration.

(2) Air-handling systems

   *(a) Air-handling systems shall be designed with an economizer cycle where appropriate to use outside air.

   (b) VAV systems. The energy-saving potential of VAV systems is recognized, and the standards herein are intended to maximize appropriate use of such systems. Any system used for occupied areas shall include provisions to avoid air stagnation in interior spaces where thermostat demands are met by temperatures of surrounding areas.

   (c) Non-central air-handling systems (i.e., individual room units used for heating and cooling purposes, such as fan-coil units, heat pump units, etc.) shall meet the following requirements: These units may be used as recirculating units only. All outdoor air requirements shall be met by a separate central air handling system with the proper filtration, as noted in Table 3.1-1.

(3) Vibration isolators. Mechanical equipment, ductwork, and piping shall be mounted on vibration isolators as required to prevent unacceptable structure-borne vibration.

(4) System valves. Supply and return mains and risers for cooling, heating, and steam systems shall be equipped with valves to isolate the various sections of each system. Each piece of equipment shall have valves at the supply and return ends.

7.2.2.2 Ventilation and space conditioning requirements. All rooms and areas used for patient care shall have provisions for ventilation.

(1) Ventilation rates. The ventilation rates shown in Table 2.1-2 shall be used only as minimum standards; they do not preclude the use of higher, more appropriate rates.

APPENDIX

A7.2.2.1 (2)(a) It may be practical in many areas to reduce or shut down mechanical ventilation during appropriate climatic and patient care conditions and to use open windows for ventilation.

---

(2) Air change rates. Air supply and exhaust in rooms for which no minimum total air change rate is noted may vary down to zero in response to room load. For rooms listed in Table 2.1-2 , where VAV systems are used, minimum total air change shall be within limits noted.

(3) Temperature and humidity. Space temperature and relative humidity shall be as indicated in Table 2.1-2 .

(4) Air movement direction. To maintain asepsis control, airflow supply and exhaust shall be controlled to ensure general movement of air from "clean" to "less clean" areas, especially in critical areas. The ventilation systems shall be designed and balanced according to the requirements in Table 2.1-2 and in the applicable notes.

(5) Natural ventilation. Although natural window ventilation for nonsensitive and patient areas shall be permitted, mechanical ventilation shall be provided for all rooms and areas in the facility.

(6) Renovation. For renovation projects, prior to the start of construction and preferably during design, airflow and static pressure measurements shall be taken at the connection points of new ductwork to existing systems. This information shall be used by the designer to determine if existing systems have sufficient capacity for intended new purposes, and so any required modifications to the existing system can be included in the design documentation.

7.2.2.3 Testing and documentation

(1) Upon completion of the equipment installation contract, the owner shall be furnished with a complete set of manufacturers' operating, maintenance, and preventive maintenance instructions, parts lists, and complete procurement information, including equipment numbers and descriptions. Required information shall include energy ratings as needed for future conservation calculations.

(2) Operating staff persons shall also be provided with written instructions for the proper operation of systems and equipment.

7.2.3 Ventilation Requirements for Specific Locations
*7.2.3.1 Operating rooms

(1) Air supply

    (a) In new construction and major renovation work, air supply for operating rooms shall be from non-aspirating ceiling diffusers with a face velocity in the range of 25 to 35 fpm (0.13 to 0.18 m/s), located at the ceiling above the center of the work area. Return air shall be near the floor level, at a minimum. Return air shall be permitted high on the walls, in addition to the low returns.

    (b) Each operating and delivery room shall have at least two return-air inlets located as far from each other as practical.

    (c) Turbulence and other factors of air movement shall be considered to minimize the fall of particulates onto sterile surfaces.

(2) Temperature. Temperature shall be individually controlled for each operating room.

(3) Ventilation rates

    (a) Operating room ventilation systems shall operate at all times, except during maintenance and conditions requiring shutdown by the building's fire alarm system.

    (b) During unoccupied hours, operating room air change rates may be reduced, provided that the positive room pressure is maintained as required in Table 2.1-2.

7.2.3.2 Cough-inducing procedure rooms. Rooms used for sputum induction, aerosolized pentamidine treatments, or other cough-inducing procedures shall meet the requirements of Table 2.1-2 for airborne infection isolation rooms. If booths are used, refer to Section 2.1-5.8.1.

7.2.3.3 Anesthesia storage rooms. The ventilation system for anesthesia storage rooms shall conform to the requirements of NFPA 99, including the gravity option. Mechanically operated air systems are optional in this room.

7.2.3.4 ETO sterilizer space. The ventilation system for the space that houses ethylene oxide (ETO) sterilizers shall be designed as follows:

(1) A dedicated (not connected to a return air or other exhaust system) exhaust system shall be provided. Refer to 29 CFR Part 1910.1047.

(2) All source areas shall be exhausted, including the sterilizer equipment room, service/aeration areas, and the space above the sterilizer door, as well as the aerator.

APPENDIX

A7.2.3.1 Ventilation for operating rooms

a. The operating and delivery room ventilation systems should operate at all times to maintain the air movement relationship to adjacent areas. The cleanliness of the spaces is compromised when the ventilation system is shut down. For example, airflow from a less clean space such as the corridor can occur, and standing water can accumulate in the ventilation system (near humidifiers or cooling coils).

b. The recommended air change rate in an operating room is 20 to 25 air changes per hour (ACH) for ceiling heights between 9 feet (2.74 meters) and 12 feet (3.66 meters). The system should provide a single directional flow regime, with both high and low exhaust locations. A face velocity of around 25 to 35 fpm (0.13 to 0.18 m/s) is sufficient from the non-aspirating diffuser array provided that the array size itself is set correctly. The non-aspirating diffuser array size should be set so that it covers at least the area footprint of the table plus a reasonable margin around it. In the cited study, this margin is 21 inches (0.53 meter) on the short side and 12 inches (0.3 meter) on the long side. If additional diffusers are required, they may be located outside this central diffuser array. Up to 30% of the central diffuser array may be allocated to non-diffuser items (medical gas columns, lights, etc.).

The recommended ventilation rates in the previous paragraph were derived from studies conducted by the National Institutes of Health titled "Comparison of Operating Room Ventilation Systems in the Protection of the Surgical Site" (Memarzadeh 2002) and "Effect of Operation Room Geometry and Ventilation System Parameter Variations on the Protection of the Surgical Site" (Memarzadeh 2004).

(a) If the ETO cylinders are not located in a well-ventilated, unoccupied equipment space, an exhaust hood shall be provided over the cylinders.

(b) The relief valve shall be terminated in a well-ventilated, unoccupied equipment space or outside the building.

(c) If the floor drain to which the sterilizer(s) discharges is not located in a well-ventilated, unoccupied equipment space, an exhaust drain cap shall be provided (coordinate with local codes).

(3) General airflow shall be away from the sterilizer operator(s).

(4) A dedicated exhaust duct system for ETO shall be provided. The exhaust outlet to the outside shall be at least 25 feet (7.62 meters) away from any air intake.

(5) An audible and visual alarm shall activate in the sterilizer work area, and in a 24-hour staffed location, upon loss of airflow in the exhaust system.

7.2.3.5 Food preparation centers. Exhaust hoods handling grease-laden vapors in food preparation centers shall meet the following requirements:

(1) Hoods shall comply with NFPA 96.

(2) All hoods over cooking ranges shall be equipped with grease filters, fire extinguishing systems, and heat-actuated fan controls.

(3) Cleanout openings shall be provided every 20 feet (6.10 meters) and at changes in direction in the horizontal exhaust duct systems serving these hoods. Each horizontal duct run shall have at least one cleanout opening. Horizontal runs of ducts serving range hoods shall be kept to a minimum.

APPENDIX

A7.2.5.3 (2) See Industrial Ventilation: A Manual of Recommended Practice, published by the American Conference of Governmental Industrial Hygienists (www.acgih.org), for additional information.

7.2.3.6 Fuel-fired equipment rooms. Rooms with fuel-fired equipment shall be provided with sufficient outdoor air to maintain equipment combustion rates and to limit workstation temperatures.

7.2.4 Thermal Insulation and Acoustical Provisions
See Section 1.6-2.2.1.

7.2.5 HVAC Air Distribution
7.2.5.1 Return air systems. All return air ventilation systems in patient care areas of outpatient surgery facilities shall be ducted.

7.2.5.2 HVAC ductwork. See Section 1.6-2.2.2.1.

7.2.5.3 Exhaust systems

(1) General

(a) To enhance the efficiency of recovery devices, required for energy conservation, combined exhaust systems shall be permitted.

(b) Local exhaust systems shall be used whenever possible in place of dilution ventilation to reduce exposure to hazardous gases, vapors, fumes, or mists.

(c) Fans serving exhaust systems shall be located at the discharge end and shall be readily serviceable.

(d) Airborne infection isolation rooms shall not be served by exhaust systems incorporating a heat wheel.

*(2) Anesthesia scavenging system. Each space routinely used for administering inhalation anesthesia and inhalation analgesia shall be served by a scavenging system to vent waste gases.

(a) If a vacuum system is used, the gas-collecting system shall be arranged so that it does not disturb patients' respiratory systems.

(b) Gases from the scavenging system shall be exhausted directly to the outside. The anesthesia evacuation system may be combined with the room exhaust system, provided that the part used for anesthesia gas scavenging exhausts directly to the outside and is not part of the recirculation system.

(c) Where anesthesia scavenging systems are required, air supply shall be at or near the ceiling. Return or exhaust air inlets shall be near the floor level.

(d) Scavenging systems are not required for areas where gases are used only occasionally, such as the emergency department, offices for routine dental work, etc.

7.2.5.4 Air outlets and inlets

(1) Fresh air intakes

(a) Fresh air intakes shall be located at least 25 feet (7.62 meters) from exhaust outlets of ventilating systems, combustion equipment stacks, medical-surgical vacuum systems, plumbing vents, or areas that may collect vehicular exhaust or other noxious fumes. (Prevailing winds and/or proximity to other structures may require greater clearances.)

(b) The requirement for a 25-foot (7.62-meter) separation also pertains to the distance between the intake and the exhaust and/or gas vent off packaged rooftop units.

(c) Plumbing and vacuum vents that terminate at a level above the top of the air intake may be located as close as 10 feet (3.05 meters).

(d) The bottom of outdoor air intakes serving central systems shall be as high as practical, but at least 6 feet (1.83 meters) above ground level or, if installed above the roof, 3 feet (0.91 meter) above roof level.

(2) Exhaust outlets. Exhaust outlets from areas that may be contaminated shall be above roof level, arranged to minimize recirculation of exhaust air into the building and directed away from personnel service areas.

(3) Gravity exhaust. Where conditions permit, gravity exhaust may be used for nonpatient areas such as boiler rooms, central storage, etc.

(4) Construction requirements. The bottom of air distribution devices (supply/return/exhaust) shall be at least 3 inches (7.62 centimeters) above the floor.

7.2.5.5 Ventilation hoods

(1) Exhaust hoods and safety cabinets

(a) Hoods and safety cabinets are permitted to be used for normal exhaust of a space provided minimum air change rates are maintained.

(b) If air change standards in Table 2.1-2 do not provide sufficient air for proper operation of exhaust hoods and safety cabinets (when in use), makeup air (filtered and preheated) shall be provided around these units to maintain the required airflow direction and exhaust velocity. Use of makeup air will avoid dependence upon infiltration from outdoor and/or from contaminated areas.

(c) Makeup systems for hoods shall be arranged to minimize "short circuiting" of air and to avoid reduction in air velocity at the point of contaminant capture.

(2) Laboratory fume hoods. Laboratory fume hoods shall meet the following general standards:

(a) General standards

(i) Average face velocity of 75 feet per minute (0.45 to 0.56 meters per second).

(ii) Connection to an exhaust system to the outside that is separate from the building exhaust system

(iii) Location of an exhaust fan at the discharge end of the system

(iv) Inclusion of an exhaust duct system of noncombustible corrosion-resistant material as needed to meet the planned usage of the hood.

(b) Special standards for use with strong oxidants

    (i) Fume hoods, and their associated equipment in the air stream intended for use with perchloric acid and other strong oxidants, shall be constructed of stainless steel or other material consistent with special exposures.

    (ii) These hoods and equipment shall be provided with a water wash and drain system to permit periodic flushing of duct and hood.

    (iii) Electrical equipment intended for installation within such ducts shall be designed and constructed to resist penetration by water. Lubricants and seals shall not contain organic materials.

    (iv) When perchloric acid or other strong oxidants are only transferred from one container to another, standard laboratory fume hoods and the associated equipment may be used in lieu of stainless steel construction.

(c) Special standards for use with infectious or radioactive materials. In new construction and major renovation work, each hood used to process infectious or radioactive materials shall meet the following requirements:

    (i) Each hood shall have a minimum face velocity of 90 to 110 feet per minute (0.45 to 0.56 meters per second) with suitable pressure-independent air-modulating devices and alarms to alert staff of fan shutdown or loss of airflow.

    (ii) Each hood shall have filters with a 99.97 percent efficiency (based on the DOP test method) in the exhaust stream, and be designed and equipped to permit the safe removal, disposal, and replacement of contaminated filters. Filters shall be as close to the hood as practical to minimize duct contamination.

    (iii) Fume hoods intended for use with radioactive isotopes shall be constructed of stainless steel or other material suitable for the particular exposure and shall comply with NFPA 801, *Facilities for Handling Radioactive Materials*. **Note:** Radioactive isotopes used for injections, etc., without probability of airborne particulates or gases may be processed in a clean-work-bench-type hood where acceptable to the Nuclear Regulatory Commission.

7.2.6 HVAC Filters
7.2.6.1 Filter efficiencies

(1) All central ventilation or air conditioning systems shall be equipped with filters with efficiencies equal to, or greater than, those specified in Table 3.1-1.

(2) Non-central air handling systems shall be equipped with permanent (cleanable) or replaceable filters with a minimum efficiency of MERV 3 (68 percent weight arrestance).

(3) Filter efficiencies, tested in accordance with ASHRAE 52.1, shall be average.

7.2.6.2 Filter bed location. Where two filter beds are required, filter bed no. 1 shall be located upstream of the air conditioning equipment and filter bed no. 2 shall be downstream of any fan or blowers.

7.2.6.3 Filter frames. Filter frames shall be durable and proportioned to provide an airtight fit with the enclosing ductwork. All joints between filter segments and enclosing ductwork shall have gaskets or seals to provide a positive seal against air leakage.

7.2.6.4 Filter manometers. A manometer shall be installed across each filter bed having a required efficiency of 75 percent or more, including hoods requiring HEPA filters. Provisions shall be made to allow access for field testing.

7.2.7 Steam and Hot Water Systems
See Section 1.6-2.2.3.

7.3 Electrical Systems

7.3.1 General
7.3.1.1 Applicable standards

(1) All electrical material and equipment, including conductors, controls, and signaling devices, shall be installed in compliance with applicable sections of NFPA 70 and NFPA 99.

(2) All electrical material and equipment shall be listed as complying with available standards of listing agencies or other similar established standards where such standards are required.

7.3.1.2 Testing and documentation. Electrical installations, including alarm and communication systems, shall be tested to demonstrate that equipment installation and operation is appropriate and functional. A written record of performance tests on special electrical systems and equipment shall show compliance with applicable codes and standards.

7.3.1.3 Power disturbance safeguards. Data processing and/or automated laboratory or diagnostic equipment, if provided, may require safeguards from power line disturbances.

7.3.2 Electrical Distribution and Transmission
7.3.2.1 Switchboards

(1) Location

   (a) Main switchboards shall be located in an area separate from plumbing and mechanical equipment and shall be accessible to authorized persons only.

   (b) Switchboards shall be convenient for use and readily accessible for maintenance but away from traffic lanes.

   (c) Switchboards shall be located in dry, ventilated spaces free of corrosive or explosive fumes or gases or any flammable material.

(2) Overload protective devices. These shall operate properly in ambient room temperatures.

7.3.2.2 Panelboards

(1) Panelboards serving normal lighting and appliance circuits shall be located on the same floor as the circuits they serve.

(2) Panelboards serving critical branch emergency circuits shall be located on each floor that has major users.

(3) Panelboards serving life safety emergency circuits may also serve floors above and/or below.

7.3.2.3 Ground-fault circuit interrupters

7.3.3 Power Generating and Storing Equipment
7.3.3.1 Emergency electrical service. Emergency lighting and power shall be provided for in accordance with NFPA 99, NFPA 101, and NFPA 110.

7.3.4 Lighting
7.3.4.1 General. See Section 1.6-2.3.1.1.

7.3.4.2 Lighting for specific locations in the outpatient facility

(1) Exam/treatment/trauma rooms. A portable or fixed examination light shall be provided for examination, treatment, and trauma rooms.

(2) Operating and delivery rooms. Operating and delivery rooms shall have general lighting in addition to special lighting units provided at surgical and obstetrical tables. General lighting and special lighting shall be on separate circuits.

7.3.4.3 Emergency lighting. See Section 1.6-2.3.1.2.

7.3.5 Receptacles (Convenience Outlets)
7.3.5.1 Duplex grounded-type receptacles (convenience outlets) shall be installed in all areas in sufficient quantities for tasks to be performed as needed.

7.3.5.2 Each examination and worktable shall have access to a minimum of two duplex receptacles.

7.3.6 Equipment

7.3.6.1 X-ray equipment. Fixed and mobile x-ray equipment installations shall conform to articles 517 and 660 of NFPA 70.

7.3.6.2 Inhalation anesthetizing locations. At inhalation anesthetizing locations, all electrical equipment and devices, receptacles, and wiring shall comply with applicable sections of NFPA 99 and NFPA 70.

7.3.6.3 Special electrical equipment. Special equipment is identified in the subsections of Section 2, Diagnostic and Treatment Locations, of this chapter. These sections shall be consulted to ensure compatibility between programmatically defined equipment needs and appropriate power and other electrical connection needs.

7.4 Telecommunications and Information Systems

7.4.1 Locations for terminating telecommunications and information system devices shall be provided.

7.4.2 A space shall be provided for central equipment locations. Special air conditioning and voltage regulation shall be provided when recommended by the manufacturer.

7.5 Fire Alarm System

Any fire alarm system shall be as required by NFPA 101 and installed per NFPA 72.

Table 3.1-1

Filter Efficiencies for Central Ventilation and Air Conditioning Systems in Outpatient Facilities

Area designation	No. filter beds	Filter bed no. 1 (MERV, %)	Filter bed no. 2[1] (MERV, %)
All areas for patient care, treatment, and/or diagnosis, and those areas providing direct service or clean supplies such as sterile and clean processing, etc.	2	8 (30%)	14 (90%)
Laboratories	1	13 (80%)	—
Administrative, bulk storage, soiled holding areas, food preparation areas, and laundries	1	8 (30%)	—

[1]These requirements do not apply to small primary (neighborhood) outpatient facilities or outpatient facilities that do not perform invasive applications or procedures.

Notes
1. Additional roughing or prefilters should be considered to reduce maintenance required for main filters.
2. MERV = minimum efficiency reporting value. MERVs are based on ASHRAE 52.2.
3. The filtration efficiency ratings are based on average dust spot efficiency per ASHRAE 52.1.

Table 3.1-2

Station Outlets for Oxygen, Vacuum, and Medical Air in Outpatient Facilities

Section	Location	Oxygen	Vacuum	Medical Air
3.1-2.1.1/2.1.2	General/special purpose examination	0	0	—
3.1-2.1.3	Treatment	0	0	—
3.1-2.1.5	Isolation	0[1]	0[1]	—
3.6-2.1	Birthing room	2	2	—
3.7-2.2	Examination in outpatient surgical facility	0[1]	0[1]	—
	Ambulatory operating rooms			
3.7-2.3.1.1	Class A–minor surgical procedure room	1	1	—
3.7-2.3.1.2	Class B–intermediate surgical procedure room	2	2	—
3.7-2.3.1.3	Class C–major surgical procedure room	2	3	—
3.7-2.4.1	Post-anesthesia recovery	1	1	—
3.7-2.4.2	Phase II recovery	0[1]	0[1]	—
—	Cysto procedure	1	3	—
	Urgent Care			
	Procedure room	1	1	1
—	Cast room	0[1]	0[1]	—
—	Catheterization room	1	2	2
	Endoscopy			
3.9-2.3	Procedure room	1	3	—
3.9-2.3.2	Holding/prep/recovery area	0[1]	0[1]	—
3.9-3.2.2	Decontamination area	—	—	—

[1]Portable source shall be available for the space.

3.2 Primary Care Outpatient Centers

Appendix material, which appears in shaded boxes at the bottom of the page, is advisory only.

1 General Considerations

The primary care center provides comprehensive community outpatient medical services.

1.1 Applicability
All standards set forth in Sections 1 through 5 of Chapter 3.1 (General, Diagnostic and Treatment Locations, Service Areas, Administrative and Public Areas, and Construction Standards) shall apply to primary care outpatient centers, with additions and modifications described herein. (See Chapter 3.3 for small primary (neighborhood) outpatient facilities.)

1.2 Functional Program
The number and type of diagnostic, treatment, and administrative areas shall be sufficient to support the services and estimated patient load described in the functional program.

1.3 Site

1.3.1 Parking
Parking spaces for patients and family shall be provided at the rate of not less than two parking spaces for each examination and each treatment room. In addition, one space shall be provided for each of the maximum number of staff persons on duty at any one shift. Adjustments, as described in Section 3.1-1.7.2, shall be permitted where public parking, public transportation, etc., reduces the need for on-site parking.

2 Diagnostic and Treatment Locations

*2.1 Examination and Treatment Rooms

> **APPENDIX**
>
> **A2.1** Examination rooms and services as described in Section 3.1-2.1 may be provided. In addition, offices and/or practitioner consultation rooms may be combined with examination rooms.

2.2 Imaging Facilities
Provisions shall be made for x-ray procedures as described in Section 3.1-2.2 in the Outpatient Facilities chapter. Services may be shared or provided by contract off-site.

2.3 Laboratory Facilities
Provisions shall be made for laboratory procedures as described in Section 3.1-2.3 in the Outpatient Facilities chapter. Services may be shared or provided by contract off-site.

2.4 Specimen Storage
Each outpatient unit shall have appropriate facilities for storage and refrigeration of blood, urine, and other specimens.

3 Administrative and Public Areas

3.1 Public Areas
Public areas shall be situated for convenient access and designed to promote prompt accommodation of patient needs, with consideration for personal dignity.

3.1.1 Entrances
3.1.1.1 Entrances shall be well marked and at grade level.

3.1.1.2 Where entrance lobby and/or elevators are shared with other tenants, travel to the outpatient unit shall be direct and accessible to the disabled. Except for passage through common doors, lobbies, or elevator stations, patients shall not be required to go through other occupied areas or outpatient service areas.

3.1.1.3 Entrances shall be convenient to parking and accessible via public transportation.

3.1.2 Reception
3.1.2.1 Reception/information counter. A reception and information counter or desk shall be located to provide visual control of the entrance to the outpatient unit and shall be immediately apparent from that entrance.

3.1.2.2 Control counter. A control counter shall be provided with access to patient files and records for scheduling of services. This shall be permitted to be part of the reception, information, and waiting room control.

3.1.3 Waiting Area
3.1.3.1 The waiting area for patients and escorts shall be under staff control.

3.1.3.2 The seating area shall contain not fewer than two spaces for each examination and/or treatment room.

3.1.3.3 Where the outpatient unit has a formal pediatrics service, a separate, controlled area for pediatric patients shall be provided.

3.1.3.4 Wheelchairs shall be accommodated within the waiting area.

3.1.4 Provisions for Drinking Water
Drinking water shall be available for waiting patients. In shared facilities, provisions for drinking water may be outside the outpatient area if convenient for use.

3.2 Administrative Areas
Each primary care outpatient facility shall make provisions to support administrative activities, filing, and clerical work as appropriate. (See also Section 3.1-4.2.) Administrative areas provided shall include the following:

3.2.1 Office(s)
3.2.1.1 Office(s), separate and enclosed, with provisions for privacy shall be provided.

3.2.1.2 Clerical space or rooms for typing and clerical work shall be provided separate from public areas to ensure confidentiality.

3.2.3 Multipurpose Rooms
Multiuse rooms for conferences, meetings, and health education shall be provided. One room may be primarily for staff use but also available for public access as needed. In smaller facilities, the room may also serve for consultation and other purposes.

3.2.4 Medical Records
Filing cabinets and storage shall be provided for the safe and secure storage of patient records with provisions for ready retrieval.

3.2.5 Supply Storage
Office supply storage (closets or cabinets) shall be provided within or convenient to administrative areas.

3.2.6 Support Areas for Staff
A staff toilet and lounge in addition to and separate from public and patient facilities.

4 Building Systems

4.1 Plumbing
All standards set forth in Section 3.1-7.1 of the Outpatient Facilities shall be met.

4.2 Heating, Ventilating, and Air-Conditioning Systems
All standards set forth in Section 3.1-7.2 of the Outpatient Facilities chapter shall be met.

3.3 Small Primary (Neighborhood) Outpatient Facilities

1 General Considerations

Facilities covered under this section are often contained within existing commercial or residential buildings as "storefront" units, but they may also be small, free-standing new or converted structures. The size of these units limits occupancy, thereby minimizing hazards and allowing for less stringent standards. Needed community services can therefore be provided at an affordable cost.

1.1 Size
The term small structure shall be defined as space and equipment serving four or fewer workers at any one time.

1.2 Applicability
Meeting all provisions of Sections 2 through 5 (Diagnostic and Treatment Locations, Service Areas, Administrative and Public Areas, and Construction Standards) of Chapter 3.1 for general outpatient facilities is desirable, but limited size and resources may preclude satisfying any but the basic minimums described. This section does not apply to outpatient facilities that are within a hospital, nor is it intended for larger, more sophisticated units.

1.3 Site

1.3.1 Location
The small neighborhood center is expected to be especially responsive to communities with limited income. It is essential that it be located for maximum accessibility and convenience. In densely populated areas, many of the patients might walk to services. Where a substantial number of patients rely on public transportation, facility location shall permit convenient access requiring a minimum of transfers.

1.3.2 Parking
1.3.2.1 Not less than one convenient parking space shall be provided for each staff member on duty at any one time, and no fewer than four spaces shall be provided for patients.

1.3.2.2 Parking requirements may be satisfied by street parking or by a nearby public parking lot or garage.

1.3.2.3 Where the facility is within a shopping center or similar area, customer spaces may meet parking needs.

2 Diagnostic and Treatment Locations

2.1 Examination and Treatment Rooms

2.1.1 Number
At least one examination room shall be available for each provider who may be on duty at any one time.

2.1.2 Function
Rooms may serve both as examination and treatment spaces (see Section 3.1-2.1.1).

2.1.3 Support Areas for Examination and Treatment Rooms
2.1.3.1 Toilet rooms

(1) A toilet room containing a hand-washing station shall be accessible from all examination and treatment rooms.

(2) Where a facility contains no more than three examination and/or treatment rooms, the patient toilet shall be permitted to serve waiting areas.

2.1.3.2 Clean work area. A clean work area with a counter, hand-washing station, and storage for clean supplies shall be provided. This may be a separate room or an isolated area.

2.1.3.3 Soiled holding room. A soiled holding room shall be provided (see Section 3.1-2.1.7.5).

2.1.3.4 Equipment and supply storage

(1) Sterile equipment and supplies. Sterile equipment and supplies shall be provided to meet functional requirements. Sterile supplies may be prepackaged disposables or processed off-site.

(2) Biological and drug storage. Locked storage for biologicals and drugs shall be provided.

2.2 Diagnostic Facilities

2.2.1 General
2.2.1.1 Functional program. The functional program shall identify diagnostic services that will not be provided within the facility.

2.2.1.2 Standards. When these services are provided within the facility, spaces to accommodate them shall meet the standards of Section 3.1-2.

2.2.2 Laboratory
Laboratory services and/or facilities shall meet the following standards:

2.2.2.1 Specimen collection. Urine collection rooms shall be equipped with a water closet and hand-washing station. Use of the toilet room provided within the examination and treatment room for specimen collection shall be permitted.

2.2.2.2 Blood collection. Blood collection facilities shall have space for a chair and work counter.

2.2.2.3 Other laboratory services. Services shall be available within the facility or through a formal agreement or contract with a hospital or other laboratory for hematology, clinical chemistry, urinalysis, cytology, pathology, and bacteriology.

3 Administrative and Public Areas

3.1 Public Areas
Public areas shall include the following:

3.1.1 Reception
A reception and information center or desk shall be provided.

3.1.2 Waiting Area
This space shall include provisions for wheelchairs.

3.2 Administrative Areas

3.2.1 Office
An office area for business transactions, records, and other administrative functions, separate from public and patient areas, shall be provided.

3.2.2 Equipment and Supply Storage
General storage facilities for office supplies, equipment, sterile supplies, and pharmaceutical supplies shall be provided.

3.2.3 Staff Storage
Locked storage (cabinets or secure drawers) convenient to workstations shall be provided for staff valuables.

4 Construction Standards

Every building and every portion thereof shall be designed and constructed to sustain all dead and live loads in accordance with accepted engineering practices and standards. If existing buildings are converted for use, consideration shall be given to the structural requirements for concentrated floor loadings, including x-ray equipment, storage files, and similar heavy equipment that may be added.

5 Building Systems

The following shall apply for the small outpatient facility in lieu of Section 3.1-7.

5.1 Plumbing
Plumbing and other piping systems shall meet the following standards:

5.1.1 Systems shall comply with applicable codes, be free of leaks, and be designed to supply water at sufficient pressure to operate all fixtures and equipment during maximum demand.

5.1.2 Backflow preventers (vacuum breakers) shall be installed on all water supply outlets to which hoses or tubing can be attached.

5.1.3 Water temperature at lavatories shall not exceed 110°F (43°C).

5.1.4 All piping registering temperatures above 110°F (43°C) shall be covered with thermal insulation.

5.2 Heating, Ventilating, and Air-Conditioning Systems
These shall meet the following standards:

5.2.1 A minimum indoor winter-design-capacity temperature of 75°F (24°C) shall be set for all patient areas. Controls shall be provided for adjusting temperature as appropriate for patient activities and comfort.

5.2.2 All occupied areas shall be ventilated by natural or mechanical means.

5.2.3 Air-handling duct systems shall meet the requirements of NFPA 90A.

5.3 Electrical Systems

5.3.1 Testing
Prior to completion and acceptance of the facility, all electrical systems shall be tested and operated to demonstrate that installation and performance conform to applicable codes and functional needs.

5.3.2 Lighting
5.3.2.1 Lighting shall be provided in all facility spaces occupied by people, machinery, and/or equipment, and in outside entryways.

5.3.2.2 Automatic emergency lighting shall be provided in every facility that has a total floor area of more than 1,000 square feet (92.9 square meters) and in every facility requiring stairway exit.

5.3.2.3 An examination light shall be provided for each examination and treatment room.

5.3.3 Receptacles
Sufficient duplex grounded-type receptacles shall be available for necessary task performance. Each examination and work table area shall be served by at least one duplex receptacle.

5.3.4 X-Ray Equipment
X-ray equipment installations, when provided, shall conform to NFPA 70.

3.4 Freestanding Outpatient Diagnostic and Treatment Facilities

Appendix material, which appears in shaded boxes at the bottom of the page, is advisory only.

1 Applicability

*1.1 Facility Type
This section applies to the outpatient diagnostic and treatment facility that is separate from the acute care hospital. This facility is a new and emerging form of outpatient center that is capable of accommodating a wide array of outpatient diagnostic services and minimally invasive procedures.

1.2 Standards
The general standards for outpatient facilities set forth in Sections 1 through 5 of Chapter 3.1 (General Considerations, Diagnostic and Treatment Locations, Service Areas, Administrative and Public Areas, and Construction Standards) shall be met for the freestanding outpatient diagnostic and treatment facility, with two modifications:

1.2.1 For those facilities performing diagnostic imaging and minimally invasive interventional procedures, all provisions of Sections 2.1-5.4 and 5.5 shall also apply, except that adjacencies to emergency, surgery, cystoscopy, and outpatient clinics are not required.

1.2.2 For those facilities performing nuclear medicine procedures, all provisions of Section 2.1-5.6 shall also apply, except that support services such as radiology, pathology, emergency department, and outpatient clinics are not required.

APPENDIX

A1.1 The range of services provided in these facilities is very dynamic and growing, including diagnostic cardiac catheterization, general radiography, fluoroscopy, mammography, CT scanning, magnetic resonance imaging (MRI), ultrasound, radiation therapy, and IV therapies. Facilities may specialize in only one of these areas or may provide a mix of services.

3.5 Freestanding Urgent Care Facilities

1 General Considerations

1.1 Applicability
This section applies to facilities that provide urgent care to the public but are not part of licensed hospitals, are not freestanding emergency services, or do not provide care on a 24-hour-per-day, seven-day-per-week basis.

1.2 Site

1.2.1 Signage
1.2.1.1 The facility shall post signs that clearly indicate the type and level of care offered and the hours of operation (if not 24 hours per day, seven days per week).

1.2.1.2 The facility shall post directional signs and information showing the nearest emergency department that is part of a licensed hospital.

1.2.2 Parking
1.2.2.1 Not less than one parking space shall be provided for each staff member on duty at any one time, and no fewer than two spaces shall be provided for each examination and each treatment room.

1.2.2.2 Additional spaces shall be provided for emergency vehicles.

1.2.2.3 Street, public, and shared lot spaces, if included as part of this standard, shall be exclusively for the use of the urgent care facility.

1.2.2.4 All required parking spaces shall be convenient to the urgent care entrance.

2 Diagnostic and Treatment Locations

2.1 Examination and Treatment Rooms
In addition to the requirements of Section 3.1-2.1, the following shall be provided:

2.1.1 Examination Rooms
2.1.1.1 Number. At least two examination rooms shall be provided.

2.1.1.2 Space requirements

(1) Area. The examination rooms shall have a clear floor area of 120 square feet (11.15 square meters) excluding vestibule, toilet, closet, and fixed casework (treatment room may also be utilized for examination).

(2) Clearances. Room arrangement shall permit a minimum clearance of 3 feet 6 inches (1.07 meters) at each side, head, and foot of the bed.

2.1.2 Procedure Room
At least one procedure room with the following characteristics shall be provided.

2.1.2.1 Capacity. Setup of the room to accommodate more than one patient shall be permitted.

(1) Utilities and services shall be provided for each patient.

(2) Provisions shall be included for patient privacy.

2.1.2.2 Space requirements

(1) Where a procedure room is set up for multi-patient use, each patient area shall have a minimum clear area of 250 net square feet (23.23 square meters) excluding vestibule, toilet, closet, and fixed casework.

(2) Room arrangement shall permit a minimum clearance of 3 feet 6 inches (1.07 meters) at each side, head, and foot of the bed.

2.1.2.3 Scrub stations. Hands-free scrub stations shall be located at each procedure room.

2.1.3 Observation Facilities
Facilities shall be provided for holding urgent care patients until they can be discharged or transferred to an appropriate hospital.

2.1.3.1 Number. Use of one or more examination/ treatment rooms for this purpose shall be permitted.

2.1.3.2 Facility requirements. Size, type, and equipment shall be as required for anticipated patient load and lengths of stay.

2.1.3.3 Functional requirements. Each observation bed shall permit the following:

(1) Direct visual observation of each patient from the nurse station, except where examination/treatment rooms are used for patient holding. View from the duty station may be limited to the door.

(2) Patient privacy

(3) Access to patient toilets

(4) Secure storage of patients' valuables and clothing

(5) Dispensing of medication

(6) Bedpan storage and cleaning

(7) Nourishment area (see Section 2.1-2.3.5). Meal provisions shall be made for patients held for more than four hours.

2.2 Imaging Facilities

2.2.1 Standards
Standards stipulated in Section 3.1-2.2 shall be met during all hours of operation.

2.2.2 Facility Requirements
Radiographic equipment shall be adequate for any part of the body including, but not limited to, fractures.

2.2.3 Support Areas for Patients
Separate dressing rooms are not required for unit(s) used only for emergency procedures.

2.3 Laboratory

2.3.1 Standards
See Section 3.1-2.3 for applicable standards.

2.3.2 Facility Requirements
In addition, immediate access to blood for transfusions and provisions for cross-match capabilities shall be provided.

2.4 Support Areas for Diagnostic and Treatment Locations

2.4.1 A Nurse Control and Workstation
2.4.1.1 This shall accommodate charting, files, and staff consultation activities.

2.4.1.2 It shall be located to permit visual control of clinical area and its access.

2.4.1.3 Communication links with the examination/treatment area, procedure room, reception control, laboratory, radiology, and on-call staff shall be provided.

2.4.2 Poison Control Center
A poison control center with immediately accessible antidotes and a file of common poisons shall be provided.

2.4.2.1 Communication links with regional and/or national poison centers and regional EMS centers shall be provided.

2.4.2.2 This service may be part of the nurse control and workstation.

2.4.3 Equipment Storage
2.4.3.1 Location for CPR emergency cart. A CPR emergency cart shall be provided. It shall be located away from public circulation areas but immediately accessible to all areas, including entrance and receiving areas.

2.4.3.2 Wheelchair and stretcher storage. In addition to wheelchair storage, a holding area shall be provided for stretchers within the clinical area, away from traffic and under staff control.

2.5 Support Areas for Staff
Facilities for on-call medical staff shall be provided.

3 Administrative and Public Areas

Administrative and public areas shall conform to the standards in Section 3.1-4, with the following additions.

3.1 Public Areas

3.1.1 Entrances

3.1.1.1 Entrances shall be well marked, illuminated, and covered to permit protected transfer of patients from ambulance and/or automobile.

3.1.1.2 The urgent care entrance shall have vision panels to minimize conflict between incoming and outgoing traffic and to allow for observation of the unloading area from the control station.

3.1.1.3 Accessibility

(1) Convenient access to wheelchairs and stretchers shall be provided at the urgent care entrance.

(2) If a platform is provided for ambulance use, a ramp for wheelchairs and stretchers shall be provided in addition to steps.

3.1.2 Lobby and Waiting Areas
These shall satisfy the following requirements:

3.1.2.1 Reception
Reception and information functions may be combined or separate. These areas shall meet the following requirements:

(1) These areas shall provide direct visual control of the urgent care entrance and access to the treatment area and the lobby. Urgent care entrance control functions shall include observation of arriving vehicles.

(2) Control stations normally include a triage function and shall be in direct communication with medical staff.

(3) A public toilet with hand-washing stations shall be provided.

(4) A convenient telephone shall be provided.

3.1.2.2 Waiting area(s)

(1) Urgent care waiting area

  (a) This shall include provisions for wheelchairs.

  (b) This shall be separate from the area provided for scheduled outpatient service.

(2) Diagnostic imaging waiting area. If the urgent care facility ICRA determines that the diagnostic imaging waiting area requires special consideration to reduce the risk of airborne infection transmission, public waiting areas shall be designed, ventilated, and maintained with available technologies such as enhanced general ventilation and air disinfection techniques similar to inpatient requirements for airborne infection isolation rooms. See the CDC "Guidelines for Preventing the Transmission of Mycobacterium tuberculosis in Health Care Settings" (full reference at 1.1-7.5.1).

3.1.3 Interview Facilities
Initial interviews may be conducted at the triage reception/control area.

3.1.3.1 Facilities for conducting interviews on means of reimbursement, social services, and personal data shall include provisions for acoustical privacy.

3.1.3.2 These facilities shall be permitted to be separate from the reception area but must be convenient to the urgent care service waiting area.

3.2 Administrative Areas

3.2.1 Offices
For standards concerning general and individual offices, see Section 3.1-4.2.2.

3.2.2 Multipurpose Rooms
Multipurpose room(s) shall be provided for staff conferences. This room may also serve for consultation.

3.2.3 Storage
For standards concerning general storage, see Section 3.1-4.2.4.

3.2.4 Support Areas for Staff

For standards concerning special storage for staff, see Section 3.1-4.2.5.

4 Construction Standards

4.1 General Standards for Details and Finishes

4.1.1 Doors to Patient Care Rooms

4.1.1.1 Door(s) to urgent care patient care rooms serving stretcher-borne patients shall not be less than 4 feet (1.22 meters) wide.

4.1.1.2 All other doors to patient service areas shall be not less than 3 feet (91.44 centimeters) wide.

5 Building Systems

5.1 Plumbing

See Section 3.1-7.1 for applicable plumbing standards.

5.2 Heating, Ventilating and Air-Conditioning Systems

See Section 3.1-7.2 for applicable mechanical standards.

5.3 Electrical Systems

See Section 3.1-7.3 for applicable electrical standards.

3.6 Freestanding Birthing Centers

The freestanding birthing center is "any health facility, place, or institution that is not a hospital and where births are planned to occur away from the mother's usual place of residence" (American Public Health Association, 1982).

*1 General Considerations

1.1 Applicability
All standards set forth in Sections 1 through 5 of Chapter 3.1 (General Considerations, Diagnostic and Treatment Locations, Service Areas, Administrative and Public Areas, and Construction Standards) shall be met for new construction of birthing centers, with modifications described in this chapter.

1.2 Site

1.2.1 Parking
Parking spaces for clients and families shall be provided at a rate of no fewer than two for each birth room. In addition, one space shall be provided for each of the maximum number of staff persons on duty at any given time. Adjustments, as described in Section 3.1-1.7.2, shall be permitted where public parking, public transportation, etc., reduce the need for on-site parking.

2 Clinical Facilities

The following elements shall be provided for clinical services as needed to satisfy the functional program:

2.1 Birthing Rooms

2.1.1 Number
A minimum of two birthing rooms shall be provided.

2.1.2 Layout
The plan for each birthing room shall be such that it will permit unimpeded emergency transfer by stretcher.

2.1.3 Space Requirements
Birthing rooms shall be adequate in size to accommodate one patient, her family, and attending staff.

2.1.3.1 Area and dimensions

(1) New construction. A minimum clear floor area of 160 square feet (48.76 square meters) shall be provided with a minimum dimension of 11 feet (3.35 meters), excluding vestibule, toilet, closet, and fixed casework.

(2) Renovation. A minimum floor area of 120 square feet (11.15 square meters), excluding vestibule, toilet, and closets, with a minimum dimension of 10 feet (3.05 meters) shall be provided.

2.1.3.2 Clearances. Room arrangement shall permit a minimum clearance of 3 feet (91.44 centimeters) at each side, head, and foot of the bed.

2.1.4 Oxygen, Vacuum, and Medical Air
Birthing rooms shall have available oxygen, vacuum, and medical air per Table 2.1-5, LDRP rooms.

2.1.5 Communication
Each birthing room shall be equipped with a system for communicating to other parts of the center and to an outside telephone line.

2.1.6 Equipment and Supply Storage
2.1.6.1 Each birthing room shall have storage space sufficient to accommodate belongings of occupants, bedding, equipment, and supplies needed for a family-centered childbirth.

2.1.6.2 An area for equipment and supplies for routine and remedial newborn care, separate from the equipment supplies for maternal care, shall be provided in each birthing room.

2.1.6.3 Medicine, syringes, specimen containers, and instrument packs shall be contained in storage areas not accessible to children.

2.2 Support Areas for Birthing Rooms

2.2.1 Scrub Areas
Hand-washing stations with hands-free faucets shall be conveniently accessible to the birthing rooms.

2.2.2 Clean Storage
A separate area for storing clean and sterile supplies shall be provided.

2.2.3 Soiled Holding
2.2.3.1 Provisions shall be made for separate collection, storage, and disposal of soiled materials.

2.2.3.2 Fluid waste may be disposed of in the toilet adjacent to the birth room.

2.2.4 Equipment and Supply Storage
2.2.4.1 Storage for drugs and biologicals. An area for locked storage of drugs and refrigeration of biologicals (separate from the nourishment area refrigerator) shall be provided.

2.2.4.2 Emergency equipment. An area for maternal and newborn emergency equipment and supplies (carts or trays) shall be designated out of the direct line of traffic and conveniently accessible to the birthing rooms.

2.3 Support Areas for Staff
A secure storage space for personal effects, toilet, shower, change, and lounge area sufficient to accommodate staff needs shall be provided.

2.4 Support Areas for Patients
Toilet, hand-washing station, and bath/shower facilities with appropriately placed grab bars shall be adjacent to each birthing room. Bath/shower facilities shall not be shared by more than two birthing rooms.

3 Service Areas

3.1 Sterilizing Facilities
Sterile supplies may be prepackaged disposables or processed off-site. If instruments and supplies are sterilized on-site, an area for accommodation of sterilizing equipment appropriate to the volume of the birth center shall be provided.

3.2 Laundry Facilities
Laundry may be done on- or off-site.

3.2.1 Soiled Holding Area
Soiled laundry shall be held in the soiled holding area until deposited in the washer.

3.2.2 Laundry Equipment
If laundry is done on-site, an area for laundry equipment with counter and storage space shelving shall be provided. Depending on the size and occupancy of the center, use of ordinary household laundry equipment shall be permitted.

4 Administrative and Public Areas

4.1 Public Areas
These shall include the areas listed in this section.

4.1.1 General
4.1.1.1 Provisions for the disabled. See Section 1.1-4.

4.1.1.2 Childproof electrical outlets. These shall be used in public areas of the freestanding birthing center.

4.1.2 Entrance
4.1.2.1 The entrance to the birthing center shall be at ground level, well marked and illuminated.

4.1.2.2 Provisions shall be made for emergency vehicle access.

4.1.3 Reception
A reception area with facility to accommodate outdoor wear shall be provided.

4.1.4 Family Room
A family room with a designated play area for children shall be provided.

4.1.5 Toilet and Hand-Washing Stations
Convenient access to toilet and hand-washing stations shall be provided.

4.1.6 Nourishment Area
A nourishment area shall be provided where families can store and serve light refreshment of their dietary and cultural preferences. The area shall include a sink

and counter space, range, oven or microwave, refrigerator, cooking utensils, disposable tableware or dishwasher, storage space, and seating area.

4.1.7 Telephone
Convenient access to telephone service shall be provided.

4.1.8 Provisions for Drinking Water
Convenient access to provisions for drinking water shall be provided.

4.2 Administrative Areas

4.2.1 Records
Space for performing administrative functions, charting, and secure record storage shall be provided.

3.7 Outpatient Surgical Facilities

Appendix material, which appears in shaded boxes at the bottom of the page, is advisory only.

1 General Considerations

*1.1 Applicability
The general standards set forth in Sections 1 through 5 of Chapter 3.1 (General Considerations, Diagnostic and Treatment Locations, Service Areas, Administrative and Public Areas, and Construction Standards) shall apply to outpatient surgical facilities, with additions and modifications described herein.

1.2 Functional Program

*1.2.1 Facility Requirements
Outpatient surgery is performed without anticipation of overnight patient care. The functional program shall describe in detail staffing, patient types, hours of operation, function and space relationships, transfer provisions, and availability of off-site services.

1.2.2 Size
The extent (number and types) of the diagnostic, clinical, and administrative facilities to be provided will be determined by the services contemplated and the estimated patient load as described in the functional program. Provisions shall be made for medical and nursing assessment, nursing care, preoperative testing, and physical examination for outpatient surgeries.

1.3 Environment of Care

1.3.1 Patient Privacy
Visual and acoustical privacy shall be provided by design and include the registration, preparation, examination, treatment, and recovery areas. See Section 1.1-6.

1.4 Shared Services
If the outpatient surgical facility is part of an acute care hospital or other medical facility, services may be shared to minimize duplication as appropriate.

1.4.1 Where outpatient surgical services are provided within the same area or suite as inpatient surgery, additional space shall be provided as needed.

1.4.2 If inpatient and outpatient procedures are performed in the same room(s), the functional program shall describe in detail scheduling and techniques used to separate inpatients and outpatients.

1.5 Facility Access and Layout

1.5.1 Facility Access
The outpatient surgical facility shall be designed to facilitate movement of patients and personnel into, through, and out of defined areas within the surgical suite. Signs shall be provided at all entrances to restricted areas and shall clearly indicate the surgical attire required.

*1.5.2 Layout
The outpatient surgical facility shall be divided into three designated areas—unrestricted, semi-restricted, and restricted—that are defined by the physical activities performed in each area.

APPENDIX

A1.1 Outpatient "surgical" facilities include centers that perform both invasive and noninvasive procedures. The distinction between centers is better defined by the type of anesthesia used during the procedures.

A1.2.1 Even though most outpatient procedures do not require an overnight stay, some require extended patient observation for up to "23 hours and 59 minutes" of care.

a. This extended care possibility should be addressed in a recovery care center that provides facilities for adequate sleeping, bathroom, and nutrition services for the patient.

b. Recovery care centers should have adequate waiting areas for family, including children and adolescents, and privacy (noise barriers and sight barriers) for meetings between physicians and other professionals with family. The areas should be large enough for translators or have available translation equipment.

c. A key element to housing patients is the communication system and the ability to obtain additional assistance as necessary.

1.6 Site

1.6.1 Parking

Four spaces shall be provided for each room routinely used for surgical procedures plus one space for each staff member. Additional parking spaces convenient to the entrance for pickup of patients after recovery shall be provided.

*2 Diagnostic and Treatment Locations

2.1 Diagnostic Facilities

Facilities for diagnostic services shall be provided on or off-site for pre-admission tests as required by the functional program.

2.2 Examination Room(s)

If patients will be admitted without recent and thorough examination, at least one room, ensuring both visual and acoustical privacy, shall be provided for examination and testing of patients prior to surgery. This may be an examination room or treatment room as described in Sections 3.1-2.1.1 and 3.1-2.1.3.

2.3 Operating Rooms (Ambulatory)

Note: When invasive procedures need to be performed on persons who are known or suspected of having airborne infectious disease, these procedures are ideally performed in a room meeting airborne infection isolation ventilation requirements or in a space using local exhaust ventilation. If the procedure must be performed in the operating suite, follow recommendations outlined in the CDC "Guidelines for Environmental Infection Control" or the CDC "Guidelines for Preventing the Transmission of Mycobacterium tuberculosis in Health Care Facilities."

*2.3.1 Size and Location

The size and location of the operating rooms shall depend on the level of care and equipment specified in the functional program. Operating rooms shall be as defined by the American College of Surgeons.

2.3.1.1 Class A operating rooms (minor surgical procedure rooms)

(1) Area and dimensions. These operating rooms shall have a minimum floor area of 150 square

---

A1.5.2 Outpatient Surgical Facility Layout

a. The unrestricted area includes a central control point established to monitor the entrance of patients, personnel, and materials into the restricted areas. Street clothes are permitted in this area, and traffic is not limited.

b. The semi-restricted area includes the peripheral support areas of the surgical suite and has storage areas for clean and sterile supplies, work areas for storage and processing of instruments, and corridors leading to the restricted areas of the surgical suite. Traffic in this area is limited to authorized personnel and patients. Personnel are required to wear surgical attire and cover all head and facial hair.

c. The restricted area includes operating and procedure rooms, the clean core, and scrub sink areas. Surgical attire and hair coverings are required. Masks are required where open sterile supplies or scrubbed persons may be located.

A2 Provisions should be made to separate pediatric from adult patients. Separate areas should include pre- and postoperative care areas and should allow for parental presence.

A2.3.1 American College of Surgeons Surgical Facility Classes

a. Class A–Provides for minor surgical procedures performed under topical and local infiltration blocks with or without oral or intramuscular preoperative sedation. Excluded are spinal, epidural axillary, stellate ganglion blocks, regional blocks (such as interscalene), supraclavicular, infraclavicular, and intravenous regional anesthesia. These methods are appropriate for Class B and C facilities.

b. Class B–Provides for minor or major surgical procedures performed in conjunction with oral, parenteral, or intravenous sedation or under analgesic or dissociative drugs.

c. Class C–Provides for major surgical procedures that require general or regional block anesthesia and support of vital bodily functions.

Note: Those facilities meeting the guidelines for Class B procedures automatically qualify for Class A procedures, and those facilities meeting the guidelines for Class C automatically qualify for Classes A and B.

feet (45.72 square meters) with a minimum clear dimension of 12 feet (3.65 meters). This square footage and minimum dimensions shall exclude vestibule and fixed casework.

(2) Clearances. There shall be a minimum clear distance of 3 feet 6 inches (1.07 meters) at each side, the head, and the foot of the operating table.

(3) Location. These minor surgical procedure rooms may be located within the restricted corridors of the surgical suite or in an unrestricted corridor adjacent to the surgical suite.

2.3.1.2 Class B operating rooms (intermediate surgical procedure rooms)

(1) Area and dimensions. These operating rooms shall have a minimum floor area of 250 square feet (23.23 square meters) with a minimum clear dimension of 15 feet (4.57 meters). This square footage and minimum dimension shall exclude vestibule and fixed casework.

(2) Clearances. Room arrangement shall permit a minimum clearance of 3 feet 6 inches (1.07 meters) at each side, the head, and the foot of the operating table.

(3) Location. These intermediate surgical procedure rooms shall be located within the restricted corridors of the surgical suite.

2.3.1.3 Class C operating rooms (major surgical procedure rooms)

(1) Area and dimensions. These operating rooms shall have a minimum clear area of 400 square feet (37.16 square meters) and a minimum dimension of 18 feet (5.49 meters). This square footage and minimum dimension shall exclude vestibule and fixed casework.

(2) Clearances. Room arrangement shall permit a minimum clearance of 4 feet (1.22 meters) at each side, the head, and the foot of the operating table.

(3) Location. These major surgical procedure rooms shall be located within the restricted corridors of the surgical suite.

2.3.2 Emergency Communication System

All operating rooms shall be equipped with an emergency communication system connected with the control station.

*2.3.3 Image Viewer

There shall be at least one medical image viewer in each room.

2.3.4 Mechanical System and Medical Gas Requirements

See Tables 2.1-2 and 3.1-2 for mechanical system and medical gas requirements.

2.4 Recovery Areas

2.4.1 Post-Anesthesia Recovery Room(s)

Room(s) for post-anesthesia recovery in outpatient surgical facilities shall be provided in accordance with the functional program.

2.4.1.1 General

(1) The recovery area shall be accessible directly from the semi-restricted area.

(2) A nurse utility/control station shall be provided with visualization of patients in acute recovery positions.

(3) Clearances noted around gurneys are between the normal use position of the gurney and any adjacent fixed surface, or between adjacent gurneys.

(4) If pediatric surgery is part of the program, separation from the adult section and space for parents shall be provided. Sound attenuation of the area and the ability to view the patient from the nursing station shall be considered.

2.4.1.2 Minimum requirements. The minimum requirements for post-anesthesia recovery position(s) are as follows:

> **APPENDIX**
>
> **A2.3.3** For surgeries dependent upon medical imaging, such as many orthopedic procedures, medical image viewers should be provided in each operating room.

*(1) Number. A minimum of one recovery station per operating room shall be provided.

(2) Area and clearances. Each post-anesthetic care unit (PACU) shall provide a minimum clear floor area of 80 square feet (7.43 square meters) for each patient station with a space for additional equipment described in the functional program and for clearance of at least 5 feet (1.52 meters) between patient stretchers and 4 feet (1.22 meters) between patient stretchers and adjacent walls (at the stretcher's sides and foot).

(3) Patient privacy. Provisions for patient privacy such as cubicle curtains shall be made.

(4) Hand-washing stations. Hand-washing stations with hands-free or wrist blade-operable controls shall be available, with at least one station for every four stretchers or portion thereof, and uniformly distributed to provide equal access from each patient position.

2.4.1.3 Support areas for post-anesthesia recovery rooms

(1) Facility requirements. The recovery areas shall include provisions for staff hand-washing station, medication preparation and dispensing, supply storage, soiled linen and waste holding, and charting and dictation.

(2) Equipment storage. The recovery areas shall include dedicated space as needed to keep equipment (warming cabinet, ice machine, crash cart, etc.) out of required circulation clearances.

2.4.2 Phase II recovery
2.4.2.1 General

(1) A Phase II or stepdown recovery room shall be provided.

APPENDIX

2.4.1.2 (1) In the absence of a functional program, recovery positions should be considered at a ratio of one per Class A operating room, two per Class B operating room, and three per Class C operating room. Up to half the total recovery positions may be provided in the Phase II recovery area.

(2) In Phase II or stepdown units, a nurse utility/control station with visualization of patients is not required.

2.4.2.2 Space requirements. The design shall provide a minimum of 50 square feet (4.65 square meters) for each patient in a lounge chair with space for additional equipment described in the functional program and for clearance of 4 feet (1.22 meters) between the sides of the lounge chairs and the foot of the lounge chairs.

2.4.2.3 Patient privacy. Provisions for patient privacy such as cubicle curtains shall be made.

2.4.2.4 Facility requirements. The step-down room shall contain hand-washing station(s), storage space for supplies and equipment, clinical work space, space for family members, and nourishment facilities.

2.4.2.5 Patient toilet room. A patient toilet room shall be provided in the Phase II recovery area for the exclusive use of patients. In facilities with two or fewer operating rooms and an outpatient surgery change area adjacent to the recovery area, the toilet required by Section 3.7-2.6.11 shall be permitted to meet this requirement.

2.5 Support Areas for Surgical Service Areas
The following shall be provided in surgical service areas:

2.5.1 Control Station
A control station shall be located to permit visual surveillance of all traffic entering the restricted corridor (access to operating rooms and other ancillary clean/sterile areas).

2.5.2 Scrub Facilities

(1) Station(s) shall be provided near the entrance to each operating room and may service two operating rooms if needed.

(2) Scrub facilities shall be arranged to minimize splatter on nearby personnel or supply carts.

2.5.3 Drug Distribution Station
A drug distribution station shall be provided.

(1) Provisions shall be made for storage and preparation of medications administered to patients.

(2) A refrigerator for pharmaceuticals and double-locked storage for controlled substances shall be provided.

(3) Convenient access to hand-washing stations shall be provided.

2.5.4 Soiled Workroom

A soiled workroom shall be provided. This may be the same workroom described in Section 3.7-3.1.2.1.

(1) The soiled workroom shall contain a clinical sink or equivalent flushing-type fixture, a work counter, a hand-washing station, and waste receptacle(s).

(2) The soiled workroom shall be located within the semi-restricted area.

2.5.5 Sterilizing Facilities

Space shall be provided for a high-speed sterilizer or other sterilizing equipment for immediate or emergency use, as called for in the functional program.

(1) This space shall be located in the restricted area.

(2) The space shall include a separate area for cleaning and decontamination of instruments prior to sterilization.

2.5.6 Fluid Waste Disposal Facilities

(1) These shall be convenient to the general operating rooms and post-anesthesia recovery positions.

(2) A clinical sink or equivalent equipment in a soiled workroom shall meet this requirement in the operating room area, and a toilet equipped with bedpan-cleaning device or a separate clinical sink shall meet the requirement in the recovery area.

2.5.7 Equipment and Supply Storage

2.5.7.1 Anesthesia equipment and supply storage. Provisions shall be provided for cleaning, testing, and storing anesthesia equipment and supplies, as defined by the functional program. This space shall be located within the semi-restricted area.

2.5.7.2 Medical gas storage. Provisions shall be made for the medical gas(es) used in the facility. Adequate space for supply and storage, including space for reserve cylinders, shall be provided.

2.5.7.3 General equipment and supply storage. Equipment storage room(s) shall be provided for equipment and supplies used in the surgical suite.

(1) Area. The combined area of equipment and supply storage room(s) shall have a minimum floor area of 50 square feet (15.24 square meters) for each operating room(s) up to two and an additional 25 square feet (7.62 square meters) per additional operating room.

(2) Location. Equipment storage room(s) shall be located within the semi-restricted area.

2.5.7.4 A stretcher storage area. A stretcher storage area shall be convenient for use and out of the direct line of traffic.

2.5.7.5 Wheelchair storage. Space shall be provided for temporary storage of wheelchairs.

2.5.7.6 Emergency equipment/supply storage. Provisions shall be made for convenient access to and use of emergency resuscitation equipment and supplies (crash cart(s) and/or anesthesia carts) at both the surgical and recovery areas.

2.5.8 Housekeeping Room

A housekeeping room containing a floor receptor or service sink and storage space for housekeeping supplies and equipment shall be provided exclusively for the surgical suite.

2.6 Support Areas for Surgical Staff

2.6.1 Staff Lounge and Toilet Facilities

These shall be provided in facilities having three or more operating rooms. The toilet room shall be near the recovery area.

2.6.2 Staff Clothing Change Area(s)

Appropriate change area(s) shall be provided for male and female staff working within the surgical suite (unisex changing room shall be permitted).

(1) The area(s) shall contain lockers, toilet(s), hand-washing station(s), and space for donning scrub attire.

(2) These area(s) shall be arranged to encourage a one-way traffic pattern so that personnel entering from outside the surgical suite can change and move directly into the surgical suite.

2.6.3 Staff Shower

At least one staff shower shall be provided that is conveniently accessible to the surgical suite and recovery areas.

2.7 Support Areas for Patients

2.7.1 Outpatient Surgery Change Area(s)

A separate area shall be provided for outpatients to change from street clothing into hospital gowns and to prepare for surgery.

2.7.1.1 This area shall include lockers, toilet(s), clothing change or gowning area(s), and space for administering medications.

2.7.1.2 Provisions shall be made for securing patients' personal effects.

3 Service Areas

3.1 Sterilizing Facilities

A system for sterilizing equipment and supplies shall be provided.

3.1.1 General

3.1.1.1 When sterilization is provided off site, a room for the adequate handling (receiving and distribution) and on-site storage of sterile supplies shall be provided that conforms to Section 3.7-3.1.2.3.

APPENDIX

A3.1.2.2 This room is exclusively for the inspection, assembly, and packaging of medical/surgical supplies and equipment for sterilization. The area should contain worktables or counters and storage facilities for backup supplies and instrumentation. An area for a drying cabinet or equipment may be required. The area should be spacious enough to hold sterilizer carts, if used, for loading or prepared supplies for sterilization.

3.1.1.2 Provisions shall be made for sanitizing clean and soiled carts and/or vehicles consistent with the needs of the particular transportation system.

3.1.2 On-Site Facilities

If on-site processing facilities are provided, they shall include the following:

3.1.2.1 Soiled workroom. This room (or soiled holding room that is part of a system for the collection and disposal of soiled material) is for the exclusive use of the surgical suite.

(1) The soiled workroom shall be located in the semi-restricted area.

(2) The soiled workroom shall contain a flushing-rim clinical sink or equivalent flushing-rim fixture, a hand-washing station, a work counter, and space for waste receptacles and soiled linen receptacles. Rooms used only for temporary holding of soiled material may omit the flushing-rim clinical sink and work counters. However, if the flushing-rim clinical sink is omitted, other provisions for disposal of liquid waste shall be provided.

(3) The room shall not have direct connection with operating rooms. Soiled and clean workrooms or holding rooms shall be separated. A self closing door or pass-through opening for decontaminated instruments is permitted between soiled and clean workrooms.

*3.1.2.2 Clean assembly/workroom. This room shall contain sterilization equipment.

(1) This room shall contain a hand-washing station, workspace, and equipment for terminal sterilizing of medical and surgical equipment and supplies.

(2) Clean and soiled work areas shall be physically separated.

(3) Access to this room shall be restricted.

(4) The clean assembly room shall have adequate space for the designated number of work areas as defined in the functional program, as well as space for storage of clean supplies, sterilizer carriages (if used), and instrumentation.

3.1.2.3 Storage for clean/sterile supplies

(1) Storage for packs, etc., shall include provisions for ventilation, humidity, and temperature control.

(2) The clean and sterile supply room shall have a minimum floor area of 100 square feet (30.48 square meters) or 50 square feet (15.24 square meters) per operating room, whichever is greater.

4 Administrative and Public Areas

The following shall be provided:

4.1 Public Areas

*4.1.1 Entrance
A covered entrance shall be provided for pickup of patients after surgery.

4.2 Administrative Areas

4.2.1 Interview Space
Interview space(s) for private interviews relating to admission shall be provided. This may be the same room required under Section 3.7-4.2.4.

4.2.2 Offices
General and individual office(s) for business transactions, records, and administrative and professional staff shall be provided.

4.2.2.1 These shall be separate from public and patient areas with provisions for confidentiality of records.

4.2.2.2 Enclosed office spaces shall be provided in accordance with the functional program.

4.2.3 Medical Records
A medical records area where medical documents can be secured shall be provided.

4.2.4 Multipurpose or Consultation Room(s)

4.2.5 General Storage
General administrative storage facilities shall be provided.

4.2.6 Support Areas for Staff
Special storage, including locking drawers and/or cabinets, for the personal effects of administrative staff.

5 Construction Standards

5.1 Design and Construction, including Fire-Resistant Standards

5.1.1 The outpatient surgical facility, whether freestanding or adjacent to a separate occupancy, shall comply with the New Ambulatory Health Care Occupancies section of NFPA 101 and with the standards herein.

5.1.2 Separation for hazardous areas and smoke separation shall conform to NFPA 101.

5.1.3 Flammable anesthetics shall not be used in outpatient surgical facilities.

5.2 General Standards for Details and Finishes
In addition to the standards in Section 3.1-5.2, the guidelines in this section shall be met.

5.2.1 Details
Details shall conform to the following guidelines:

5.2.1.1 Corridor width

(1) Minimum public corridor width shall be 5 feet (1.52 meters), except that corridors in the operating room section, where patients are transported on stretchers or beds, shall be 8 feet (2.44 meters) wide.

(2) Passages and corridors used exclusively for staff access shall be a minimum of 3 feet 8 inches (1.12 meters) in clear width.

APPENDIX

A4.1.1 Such roof overhang or canopy should extend as far as practicable to the face of the driveway or curb of the passenger access door of the transport vehicle. Vehicles in the loading area should not block or restrict movement of other vehicles in the drive or parking areas immediately adjacent to the facility.

5.2.1.2 Exits. The outpatient surgical facility shall have not fewer than two exits to the exterior. Exits shall conform to NFPA 101.

5.2.1.3 Door width

(1) Doors serving occupiable spaces shall have a minimum nominal width of 3 feet (91.44 centimeters).

(2) Doors requiring gurney/stretcher access shall have a nominal width of 3 feet 8 inches (1.12 meters).

5.2.1.4 Toilet rooms. Toilet rooms for patient use in surgery and recovery areas shall comply with the following:

(1) These toilet rooms shall be equipped with doors and hardware that permit access from the outside in emergencies.

(2) When such rooms have only one opening or are small, the doors shall open outward or be otherwise designed to open without pressing against a patient who may have collapsed within the room.

5.2.2 Finishes

Finishes shall conform to the following guidelines:

5.2.2.1 General. Finishes shall comply with NFPA 101.

5.2.2.2 Ceilings. Ceiling finishes shall be appropriate for the areas in which they are located and shall be as follows:

(1) Semi-restricted areas

   (a) Ceiling finishes in semi-restricted areas such as clean corridors, central sterile supply spaces, specialized radiographic rooms, and Class A operating rooms shall be smooth, scrubbable, nonabsorptive, nonperforated, capable of withstanding cleaning with chemicals, and without crevices that can harbor mold and bacteria growth.

   (b) If a lay-in ceiling is used, it shall be gasketed or clipped down to prevent the passage of particles from the cavity above the ceiling plane into the semi-restricted environment.

   (c) Perforated, tegular, serrated, or highly textured tiles shall not be used.

(2) Restricted areas. Ceilings in restricted areas such as operating rooms shall be monolithic, scrubbable, and capable of withstanding chemicals. Cracks or perforations in these ceilings are not allowed.

(3) Mechanical and electrical rooms. Suspended ceilings may be omitted in mechanical and electrical rooms/spaces unless required for fire safety purposes.

5.2.2.3 Floors. Floor finishes shall be appropriate for the areas in which they are located and shall be as follows:

(1) Floor finishes shall be cleanable.

(2) Floor finishes in areas such as clean corridors, central sterile supply spaces, specialized radiographic rooms, and Class A operating rooms shall be washable, smooth, and able to withstand chemical cleaning.

(3) Floor finishes in areas such as operating rooms, delivery rooms, and trauma rooms shall be scrubbable, able to withstand chemical cleaning, and monolithic, with an integral base.

(4) All floor surfaces in clinical areas shall be constructed of materials that allow the easy movement of all required wheeled equipment.

5.2.2.4 Walls. Wall finishes shall be appropriate for the areas in which they are located and shall be as follows:

(1) Wall finishes shall be cleanable.

(2) Wall finishes in areas such as clean corridors, central sterile supply spaces, specialized radiographic rooms, and minor surgical procedure rooms shall be washable, smooth, and able to withstand chemical cleaning.

(3) Wall finishes in areas such as operating rooms, delivery rooms, and trauma rooms shall be scrubbable, able to withstand chemical cleaning, and monolithic. See also Section 3.8-4.1.2.2.

6 Building Systems

6.1 Plumbing

See Section 3.1-7.1.

6.1.1 Medical Gas Systems

Flammable anesthetics shall not be used in outpatient surgical facilities.

6.2 Heating, Ventilating, and Air-Conditioning Systems

6.2.1 General

Heating, ventilating, and air-conditioning (HVAC) systems shall be as described for similar areas in Section 3.1-7.2 and Table 2.1-2, with the following exceptions:

6.2.1.1 The recovery lounge need not be considered a sensitive area.

6.2.1.2 Outpatient operating rooms shall be permitted to meet the standards for emergency trauma rooms.

6.2.2 Filters

See Table 3.1-1 for filter efficiency standards.

6.3 Electrical Systems

See Section 3.1-7.3.

6.4 Electronic Safety and Security

6.4.1 Fire Alarm System

A manually operated, electrically supervised fire alarm system shall be installed in each facility as described in NFPA 101.

3.8 Office Surgical Facilities

An office surgical facility is an outpatient facility that has within it physician office(s) and space(s) for the performance of invasive procedures.

1 General Considerations

1.1 Applicability
Facilities that may have more than three patients rendered incapable of self-preservation without assistance from others shall meet requirements of Chapter 3.7.

1.2 Size
The number and type of diagnostic, clinical, and administrative facilities to be provided shall be determined by the services contemplated and the estimated patient load as described in the functional program.

2 Diagnostic and Treatment Locations

2.1 Operating Rooms
Operating rooms shall meet requirements as decribed in Section 3.7-2.3.

2.2 Recovery Areas

2.2.1 Location
Post-operative recovery shall be be conducted in the operating room or in a specifically designated space. An operating room shall be used by no more than one post-operative patient at a time.

2.2.2 Facility Requirements
If the recovery area is located in a specifically designated space, the following requirements shall be met:

2.2.2.1 The recovery station shall be located in direct view of a nurse station.

2.2.2.2 Cubicle curtains or other provisions for privacy during post-operative care shall be provided.

2.3 Support Areas for Operating Rooms
The following shall be immediately accessible to the operating room(s):

2.3.1 Scrub Facilities
2.3.1.1 Hands-free scrub station(s) shall be provided outside of but near the entrance to each operating room.

2.3.1.2 One scrub station shall be permitted to service two operating rooms if needed.

2.3.1.3 Scrub station(s) shall be arranged to minimize incidental splatter on nearby personnel or supply carts.

2.3.1.4 The scrub station shall be permitted to meet the hand-washing station requirements of immediately adjacent area(s).

2.3.2 Drug Distribution Station
Provisions shall be made for storage and preparation of medications administered to patients.

2.3.2.1 A refrigerator for pharmaceuticals and double-locked storage for controlled substances shall be provided.

2.3.2.2 Convenient access to hand-washing stations shall be provided.

2.3.3 Clean Storage
A clean storage area, including space for preparing instruments and supplies for surgery, shall be provided.

2.3.4 Soiled Storage/Workroom
A soiled handling/storage area, including provision for disposal of fluid waste, shall be provided.

2.3.5 Equipment and Supply Storage
2.3.5.1 Medical gas supply

2.3.5.2 Crash cart. Space for crash cart, including outlets for battery charging, shall be provided.

2.4 Support Areas for Staff

A staff clothing change area shall be provided.

3 Service Areas

3.1 Sterilizing Facilities

A system for sterilizing equipment and supplies shall be provided.

3.1.1 General

3.1.1.1 When sterilization is provided off site, adequate handling (receiving and distribution) and on-site storage of sterile supplies must be accommodated and shall meet the minimum requirements for on-site facilities.

3.1.1.2 Provisions shall be made for the cleaning and sanitizing of clean and soiled carts and vehicles transporting supplies.

3.1.2 On-Site Facilities

If on-site processing facilities are provided, they shall include the following:

3.1.2.1 Soiled workroom

(1) This room shall be physically separated from all other areas of the facility.

(2) Workspace shall be provided to handle the cleaning and the gross cleaning, debridement, and disinfection of all medical/surgical instruments and equipment. The soiled workroom shall contain work surfaces(s), sink(s), and washer/sterilizer decontaminators, flush-type devices(s), or other decontamination equipment as appropriate to the functional program.

3.1.2.2 Clean/assembly workroom

(1) This workroom shall have a hand-washing station.

(2) This room shall contain appropriate and sufficient work space and equipment for terminal sterilizing of medical and surgical equipment and supplies.

(3) Clean and soiled work areas shall be physically separated.

(4) The clean assembly room shall have adequate space for the designated number of work areas as defined in the functional program.

3.1.2.3 Storage for clean/sterile supplies

(1) Storage for packs, etc., shall include provisions for ventilation, humidity, and temperature control.

(2) A system for sterilizing equipment and supplies shall be provided. When sterilization is provided off site, adequate handling and on-site storage of sterile supplies shall be provided.

(3) Provision shall be made for cleaning and sanitizing of carts and vehicles used for transporting supplies.

3.1.2.4 Soiled holding area

(1) Space shall be provided for handling and storage of soiled materials and equipment separate from areas designated for storage of clean and sterile materials and equipment.

(2) Appropriate receptacles for biohazardous waste shall be provided, and these shall be placed in the designated soiled holding area.

4 Construction Standards

4.1 General Standards for Details and Finishes

4.1.1 Details

4.1.1.1 Corridor width

(1) Items such as provisions for drinking water, telephone booths, vending machines, etc., shall not restrict corridor traffic or reduce the corridor width below the required minimum.

(2) Out-of-traffic storage space for portable equipment shall be provided to maintain required egress and/or functional corridor width.

4.1.1.2 Door width

(1) The minimum nominal door width for patient use shall be 3 feet (0.91 meter) except that doors

requiring gurney/stretcher access (as defined by the functional program) shall have a nominal width of 44 inches (1.11 meters).

(2) Toilet room doors for patient use shall open outward or be equipped with hardware that permits access from the outside in emergencies.

4.1.2 Finishes
4.1.2.1 Ceilings

(1) Ceiling finishes in general areas are optional and may be omitted in mechanical and electrical rooms/spaces unless required for fire-resistive purposes.

(2) Ceiling finishes in operating rooms shall conform with Section 3.7-5.2.2.2.

4.1.2.2 Walls. Wall finishes in operating room(s) shall be scrubbable, able to withstand harsh chemical cleaning, and monolithic.

4.1.2.3 Floors. Wall bases in operating rooms and areas frequently subjected to wet cleaning shall be monolithic and coved directly up from the floor, tightly sealed to the wall, and constructed without voids. Seam welds in sheet flooring shall utilize manufacturer's weld product recommendations. Vinyl composition tile (VCT) or similar products shall not be permitted in these areas.

4.1.2.4 Penetrations. Floor and wall areas penetrated by pipes, ducts, and conduits shall be tightly sealed to minimize entry of rodents and insects.

3.9 Gastrointestinal Endoscopy Facilities

Appendix material, which appears in shaded boxes at the bottom of the page, is advisory only.

1 General Considerations

1.1 Applicability
All standards set forth in Section 3.1-7 shall be met for new construction of endoscopy suites, with modifications described in this chapter.

1.2 Functional Program

1.2.1 Facility Requirements
Endoscopy is performed without anticipation of overnight patient care. The functional program shall describe in detail staffing, patient types, hours of operation, function and space relationships, transfer provisions, and availability of off-site services.

1.2.2 Size
The extent (number and types) of the diagnostic, clinical, and administrative facilities to be provided shall be determined by the services contemplated and the estimated patient load as described in the functional program. Provisions shall be made for patient examination, interview, preparation, testing, and obtaining vital signs of patients for endoscopic procedures.

*1.3 Environment of Care

1.4 Shared Services
If the endoscopy suite is part of an acute care hospital or other medical facility, services may be shared to minimize duplication as appropriate.

1.4.1 Where endoscopy services are provided within the same area or suite as surgical services, additional space shall be provided as needed.

1.4.2 If inpatient and outpatient procedures are performed in the same room(s), the functional program shall describe in detail scheduling and techniques used to separate inpatients and outpatients.

1.5 Facility Layout and Circulation

1.5.1 Layout
The endoscopy suite may be divided into three major functional areas: the procedure room(s), instrument processing room(s), and patient holding/preparation and recovery room or area.

1.5.2 Circulation and Restricted Access
The endoscopy suite shall be designed to facilitate movement of patients and personnel into, through, and out of defined areas within the procedure suite. Signs shall be provided at all entrances to restricted areas and shall clearly indicate the proper attire required.

1.6 Site

1.6.1 Parking
Four spaces shall be provided for each room routinely used for endoscopy procedures plus one space for each staff member. Additional parking spaces shall be provided convenient to the entrance for pickup of patients after recovery.

2 Diagnostic and Treatment Locations

2.1 Diagnostic Facilities
Facilities for diagnostic services shall be provided on- or off-site for pre-admission tests as required by the functional program.

2.2 Examination Room(s)
If patients will be admitted without recent and thorough examination, at least one room shall be provided for examination and testing of patients prior to their procedures, ensuring both visual and acoustical privacy. This may be an examination room or treatment room as described in Sections 3.1-2.1.1 and 3.1-2.1.3.

> **APPENDIX**
>
> **A1.3** Visual and acoustical privacy should be provided by design and include the registration, preparation, examination, treatment, and recovery areas.

2.3 Procedure Suite

Note: When procedures are to be performed on persons who are known to have or suspected of having airborne infectious diseases, these procedures shall be performed only in a room meeting airborne infection isolation ventilation requirements or in a space using local exhaust ventilation. See also the CDC "Guidelines for Preventing the Transmission of Mycobacterium tuberculosis in Health-Care Facilities."

2.3.1 Procedure Room(s)
2.3.1.1 Space requirements

(1) Area. Each procedure room shall have a minimum clear floor area of 200 square feet (15 square meters), excluding vestibule, toilet, closet, fixed cabinets, and built-in shelves.

(2) Clearances. Room arrangement shall permit a minimum clearance of 3 feet, 6 inches (1.07 meters) at each side, head, and foot of the stretcher/table.

2.3.1.2 Privacy. Procedure rooms shall be designed for visual and acoustical privacy for the patient.

2.3.1.3 Medical gases. Station outlets for oxygen and vacuum (suction) shall be available in the procedure room. See Table 3.1-2.

2.3.1.4 Hand-washing station. A separate dedicated hand-washing station with hands-free controls shall be available in the suite.

2.3.1.5 Patient toilet room. Direct access may be provided to a patient toilet room. (See also Section 3.9-2.3.3.3.)

2.3.1.6 Communication system. A system for emergency communication shall be provided.

2.3.1.7 Floors. Floor covering in the procedure suite shall be monolithic and joint free.

2.3.2 Patient Holding/Prep/Recovery Area
2.3.2.1 General

(1) This area shall meet the size requirements of a stepdown recovery area, Section 3.7-2.4.2.1.

(2) The following shall be provided in this area:

2.3.2.2 Patient positions

(1) Area and dimensions. A minimum clear floor area of 80 square feet (7.43 square meters) shall be provided for each patient station with a space for additional equipment described in the functional program and for clearance of at least 5 feet (1.52 meters) between patient stretchers and 4 feet (1.22 meters) between patient stretchers and adjacent walls (at the stretcher's sides and foot).

(2) Patient privacy. Provisions for patient privacy such as cubicle curtains shall be provided.

(3) Medical gases. Oxygen and suction per Table 3.1-2 shall be provided for each patient cubicle.

2.3.3 Support Areas for the Procedure Suite
2.3.3.1 Nurse station. Nurse control and charting area that provides view of patient positions shall be provided.

2.3.3.2 Medication station. Provisions shall be made for storage and preparation of medications administered to patients.

(1) A refrigerator for pharmaceuticals and double-locked storage for controlled substances shall be provided.

(2) Convenient access to hand-washing stations shall be provided.

2.3.3.3 Toilet facilities. These shall be permitted to be accessible from patient holding or directly from procedure room(s) or both.

2.3.3.4 Clean utility space. A clean utility room or area shall be provided.

2.3.3.5 Equipment storage. The following shall be provided:

(1) Stretcher storage area(s). Such areas shall be convenient for use and out of the direct line of traffic.

(2) Wheelchair storage. Space for temporary storage of wheelchairs shall be provided.

2.3.3.6 Housekeeping closet. A janitor/housekeeping closet shall be provided.

2.4 Support Areas for Staff

2.4.1 Staff Clothing Change Areas
Appropriate change areas shall be provided for staff working within the procedure suite. These shall include the following:

2.4.1.1 Hand-washing stations

2.4.1.2 Toilets

2.4.1.3 Lockers and space for changing clothes

2.4.1.4 Staff shower. At least one shower shall be conveniently accessible to the procedure suite and patient holding/prep/recovery areas.

2.4.2 Lounge and Toilet Facilities
These shall be provided in facilities having three or more procedure rooms.

2.5 Support Areas for Patients

2.5.1 Patient Change Areas
A separate area shall be provided for patients to change from street clothing into hospital gowns and to prepare for procedures.

2.5.1.1 This area shall include lockers, toilet(s), clothing change or gowning area(s), and space for administering medications.

2.5.1.2 Provisions shall be made for securing patients' personal effects.

3 Service Areas

3.1 Clean Storage and Soiled Holding Areas

3.1.1 General
3.1.1.1 Adequate space shall be provided for the storage and holding of clean and soiled materials.

3.1.1.2 Such areas shall be separated from unrelated activities and controlled to prohibit public contact.

3.1.2 Clean/Sterile Supplies
Storage for packs, etc., shall include provisions for ventilation, humidity, and temperature control.

3.1.3 Soiled Holding/Workroom
3.1.3.1 This room shall be physically separated from all other areas of the department.

3.1.3.2 The soiled workroom shall contain work surface(s), sink(s), flush-type device(s), and holding areas for trash, linen, and other contaminated waste.

3.2 Instrument Processing Room(s)

3.2.1 Processing Rooms
Dedicated processing room(s) for cleaning and decontaminating instruments shall be provided.

3.2.1.1 Number. Processing room(s) shall be permitted to serve multiple procedure rooms.

3.2.1.2 Size. The size of the processing room(s) shall be dictated by the amount of equipment to be processed.

3.2.1.3 Layout. The cleaning area shall allow for flow of instruments from the contaminated area to the clean assembly area and then to storage. A physical barrier shall be provided to prevent droplet contamination on the clean side. Clean equipment rooms, including storage, should protect the clean equipment from contamination.

3.2.2 Decontamination Area
The decontamination area shall be equipped with the following:

*__3.2.2.1__ Utility sink(s). Sink(s) shall be provided as appropriate to the method of decontamination used.

3.2.2.2 Hand-washing station. One freestanding hand-washing station shall be provided.

3.2.2.3 Work counter space(s).

APPENDIX

A3.2.2.1 This may require soaking sink(s), rinse sink(s), automated cleaning device(s), or a combination.

3.2.2.4 Equipment accommodations. Space and utility connections for automatic endoscope reprocessor, sonic cleaner, and sterilizers (where required by the functional program).

3.2.2.5 Ventilation system. See Table 2.1-2.

3.2.2.6 Medical gases. Provision for vacuum and/or compressed air, as appropriate to cleaning methods used.

3.2.2.7 Floors. Floor covering, monolithic and joint free with 6-inch (15.24-centimeter) integral cove base.

3.3 Equipment and Supply Storage

3.3.1 Equipment and Supplies for Endoscopy Procedures
Storage room(s) for equipment and supplies used in the procedure suite shall be provided.

3.3.2 Anesthesia Equipment and Supply Storage
Provisions shall be made for cleaning, testing, and storing anesthesia equipment and supplies.

3.3.3 Medical Gas Storage
Provisions shall be made for the medical gas(es) used in the facility. Adequate space for supply and storage, including space for reserve cylinders, shall be provided.

3.3.4 Resuscitation Equipment and Supply Storage
Provisions for convenient access to and use of emergency resuscitation equipment and supplies (crash cart(s) and/or anesthesia carts) shall be provided at both procedure and recovery areas.

3.4 Fluid Waste Disposal Facilities
Fluid waste disposal facilities shall be provided.

3.4.1 Location
These shall be convenient to the procedure rooms and recovery positions.

3.4.1.1 In the procedure area, a clinical sink or equivalent equipment in a soiled workroom shall meet this requirement.

3.4.1.2 In the recovery area, a toilet equipped with bedpan-cleaning device or a separate clinical sink shall meet this requirement.

3.5 Housekeeping Room
Space containing a floor receptor or service sink and storage space for housekeeping supplies and equipment shall be provided.

4 Administrative and Public Areas

4.1 Public Areas

4.1.1 Entrance
A covered entrance for pickup of patients after procedure shall be provided.

4.1.1.1 A roof overhang or canopy shall extend, at a minimum, to the face of the driveway or curb of the passenger access door of the transport vehicle.

4.1.1.2 Vehicles in the loading area shall not block or restrict movement of other vehicles in the drive or parking areas immediately adjacent to the facility.

4.2 Administrative Areas

4.2.1 Interview Space
Space(s) for private interviews relating to admission shall be provided. This may be the same room required under Section 3.9-4.2.4 (Multipurpose Rooms).

4.2.2 Offices
General and individual office(s) shall be provided for business transactions, records, and administrative and professional staff.

4.2.2.1 Provisions for confidentiality of records shall be made.

4.2.2.2 Enclosed office spaces shall be provided, consistent with need identified in the functional program.

4.2.3 Medical Records Area
A medical records area where medical documents can be secured shall be provided.

4.2.4 Multipurpose Rooms
Multipurpose or consultation room(s) shall be provided.

4.2.5 General Storage
General storage facilities shall be provided.

5 Construction Standards

5.1 Design and Construction, including Fire-Resistant Standards

5.1.1 The separate endoscopy facility or section shall comply with the "New Ambulatory Health Care Occupancies" section of NFPA 101 and requirements described herein.

5.1.2 Flammable anesthetics shall not be used in outpatient endoscopy facilities.

5.2 General Standards for Details and Finishes

All details and finishes shall meet the standards in Section 3.1-5.2 except as modified below.

5.2.1 Details

5.2.1.1 Corridor width

(1) Minimum public corridor width shall be 5 feet (1.52 meters), except that corridors where patients are transported on stretchers or beds shall be 8 feet (2.44 meters) wide.

(2) Passages and corridors used exclusively for staff access may be 3 feet 8 inches (1.12 meters) in clear width.

5.2.1.2 Doors

(1) Door width

   (a) Doors serving occupiable spaces shall have a minimum nominal width of 3 feet (91.44 centimeters).

   (b) Doors requiring gurney/stretcher access shall have a nominal width of 3 feet 8 inches (1.12 meters).

(2) Toilet room doors

   (a) Toilet rooms in procedure and recovery areas for patient use shall be equipped with doors and hardware that permit access from the outside in emergencies.

   (b) When such rooms have only one opening or are small, the doors shall open outward or be otherwise designed to open without pressing against a patient who may have collapsed within the room.

5.2.2 Finishes

5.2.2.1 Floors. Floor finishes shall be appropriate for the areas in which they are located and shall be as follows:

(1) Floor finishes shall be cleanable.

(2) Floor finishes in areas such as clean corridors and patient care areas shall be washable, smooth, and capable of withstanding chemical cleaning.

(3) Floor finishes in areas such as procedure rooms and the decontamination room shall be scrubbable, capable of withstanding chemical cleaning, and monolithic with an integral base.

5.2.2.2 Walls. Wall finishes shall be appropriate for the areas in which they are located and shall be as follows:

(1) Wall finishes shall be cleanable.

(2) Wall finishes in areas such as clean corridors, central sterile supply spaces, specialized radiographic rooms, and endoscopic procedure rooms shall be washable, smooth, and capable of withstanding chemical cleaning.

(3) Wall finishes in areas such as procedure rooms shall be scrubbable, capable of withstanding chemical cleaning, and monolithic.

5.2.2.3 Ceilings. Ceiling finishes shall be appropriate for the areas in which they are located and shall be as follows:

(1) Ceiling finishes in general areas are optional and may be omitted in mechanical and electrical rooms/spaces unless required for fire-resistive purposes.

(2) Ceiling finishes in procedure rooms, the decontamination room, and other semirestricted areas shall be capable of withstanding cleaning with chemicals and without crevices that can harbor

mold and bacteria growth. If a lay-in ceiling is provided, it shall be gasketed or clipped down to prevent the passage of particles from the cavity above the ceiling plane into the semirestricted environment. Perforated, tegular, serrated, cut, or highly textured tiles shall not be used.

6 Building Systems

6.1 Plumbing
See Section 3.1-7.1.

6.2 Heating, Ventilating, and Air-Conditioning Systems
Heating, ventilation, and air conditioning shall be as described for similar areas in Section 3.1-7.2 and Table 2.1-2, except that the recovery lounge need not be considered a sensitive area.

6.3 Electrical Systems
See Section 3.1-7.3.

6.4 Electronic Safety and Security

6.4.1 Fire Alarm System
A manually operated, electrically supervised fire alarm system shall be installed in each facility as described in NFPA 101.

3.10 Renal Dialysis (Acute and Chronic) Centers

Appendix material, which appears in shaded boxes at the bottom of the page, is advisory only.

1 General

1.1 Functional Program

1.1.1 Number of Stations
The number of dialysis stations shall be based upon the functional program and may include several work shifts per day.

1.1.2 Facility Size
Space and equipment shall be provided as necessary to accommodate the functional program, which may include outpatient dialysis, home treatment support, and dialyzer reuse services.

1.2 Site
The location shall offer convenient access for outpatients. Accessibility to the renal dialysis center from parking and public transportation shall be a consideration.

2 Diagnostic and Treatment Areas

2.1 Examination Room
An examination room with hand-washing stations and writing surface shall be provided with at least 100 square feet (9.29 square meters).

2.2 Treatment Area(s)

2.2.1 Layout
2.2.1.1 The treatment area shall be permitted to be an open area and shall be separate from administrative and waiting areas.

2.2.1.2 The open treatment area shall be designed to provide privacy for each patient.

2.2.2 Space Requirements
2.2.2.1 Individual patient treatment areas shall contain at least 80 square feet (7.44 square meters).

2.2.2.2 There shall be at least a 4-foot (1.22-meter) space between beds and/or lounge chairs.

2.2.3 Nurse Station(s)
Nurse station(s) shall be located within the dialysis treatment area and designed to provide visual observation of all patient stations.

2.2.4 Hand-Washing Stations
2.2.4.1 These shall be convenient to the nurse station and patient treatment areas.

2.2.4.2 There shall be at least one hand-washing station serving no more than four patient stations. These shall be uniformly distributed to provide equal access from each patient station.

2.3 Special Treatment Area(s)

2.3.1 Airborne Infection Isolation Room(s)
2.3.1.1 The number of and need for required airborne infection isolation rooms shall be determined by an ICRA.

2.3.1.2 Where required, the airborne infection isolation room(s) shall comply with the requirements of Section 2.1-3.2.2.

2.3.2 Bloodborne Infection Isolation Room(s)
Facilities that dialyze patients with known bloodborne pathogens shall have at least one separate room to use for those patients.

2.3.3 Home Training Room
If home training is provided at the center, the following requirements shall be met:

2.3.3.1 A private treatment area of at least 120 square feet (11.15 square meters) shall be provided for patients who are being trained to use dialysis equipment at home.

2.3.3.2 This room shall contain counter, hand-washing stations, and a separate drain for fluid disposal.

2.4 Support Areas for the Renal Dialysis Treatment Center

2.4.1 Medication Station
If required by the functional program, there shall be a medication dispensing station for the dialysis center.

2.4.1.1 A work counter and hand-washing stations shall be included in this area.

2.4.1.2 Provisions shall be made for the controlled storage, preparation, distribution, and refrigeration of medications.

2.4.2 Nourishment Station
If a nourishment station for the dialysis service is provided, it shall contain a sink, a work counter, a refrigerator, storage cabinets, and equipment for serving nourishment as required.

2.4.3 Clean Workroom or Clean Supply Room
A clean workroom and/or clean supply room shall be provided. Such rooms shall be separated from the soiled workroom and have no direct connection to it.

2.4.3.1 Clean workroom. If the room is used for preparing patient care items, it shall contain a work counter, a hand-washing station, and storage facilities for clean and sterile supplies.

2.4.3.2 Clean supply room. If the room is used only for storage and holding as part of a system for distribution of clean and sterile materials, the work counter and hand-washing station may be omitted.

2.4.4 Soiled Workroom
A soiled workroom shall be provided. It shall contain a flushing-rim sink, hand-washing station, work counter, storage cabinets, waste receptacles, and a soiled linen receptacle.

2.4.5 Housekeeping Room
A housekeeping closet shall be provided. The closet shall contain a floor receptor or service sink and storage space for housekeeping supplies and equipment.

2.5 Support Areas for Staff
Appropriate area(s) shall be available for staff clothing change and lounge functions. Clothing change area(s) shall contain lockers, shower, toilet, and hand-washing stations.

2.6 Support Areas for Patients

2.6.1 Patient Toilet
A patient toilet with hand-washing station shall be provided. It shall be equipped with an emergency call station.

2.6.2 Patient Storage Space
Storage for patients' belongings shall be provided.

3 Service Areas

3.1 Reprocessing Room
If dialyzers are reused, a reprocessing room shall be provided and sized to perform the functions required.

3.1.1 Layout
The room shall include one-way flow of materials from soiled to clean.

3.1.2 Facility Requirements
The room shall have provisions for refrigeration for temporary storage of dialyzers, decontamination/cleaning areas, sinks, processors, computer processors and label printers, a packaging area, and dialyzer storage cabinets.

3.1.3 Ventilation Requirements
Engineering controls shall be required to provide negative pressure relative to adjoining spaces and 100 percent exhaust to outside.

3.2 Equipment and Supply Storage

3.2.1 Locations
3.2.1.1 Supply areas or supply carts shall be provided.

3.2.1.2 Storage space out of the direct line of traffic shall be available for wheelchairs and stretchers, if stretchers are provided.

3.2.2 Clean Linen Storage
If blankets or other linen is used, a clean linen storage area shall be provided.

3.2.2.1 Location of the clean linen storage area within the clean workroom, a separate closet, or an approved distribution system shall be permitted.

3.2.2.2 If a closed cart system is used, storage in an alcove shall be permitted. It must be out of the path of normal traffic and under staff control.

3.2.3 Dialysis Solutions Preparation Room
Each facility using a central batch delivery system shall provide, either on the premises or through written arrangements, individual delivery systems for the treatment of any patient requiring special dialysis solutions. The mixing area shall include a sink, storage space, and holding tanks.

3.3 Equipment Repair Room
If required by the functional program, an equipment repair and breakdown room shall be equipped with a hand-washing station, deep service sink, work counter, and storage cabinet.

4 Administrative and Public Areas

4.1 Public Areas
A waiting room, toilet room with hand-washing stations, provisions for drinking water, public telephone, and seating accommodations for waiting periods shall be available or accessible to the dialysis center.

4.2 Administrative Areas
Office and clinical work space shall be available for administrative services.

5 Building Systems

5.1 Plumbing

*5.1.1 Piping
All dialysis system piping shall be readily accessible for inspection and maintenance. Design consideration shall be given to the disposal of liquid waste from the dialyzing process to prevent odor and backflow.

5.1.2 Plumbing
In new construction and renovation where hemodialysis or hemoperfusion are routinely performed, hand-washing stations shall have a separate water supply and drainage facility that does not interfere with hemodialysis piping. See Section 3.1-7.1.2.2 (2).

5.1.3 Water Treatment Equipment Room
The water treatment equipment shall be located in an enclosed room.

5.2 Heating, Ventilating and Air-Conditioning Systems

5.2.1 Reprocessing Room Ventilation Requirements
Engineering controls shall be required to provide negative pressure relative to adjoining spaces and 100 percent exhaust to outside.

APPENDIX

A5.1.1 All installed reverse osmosis water and dialysis solution piping should be accessible.

3.11 Psychiatric Outpatient Centers

Appendix material, which appears in shaded boxes at the bottom of the page, is advisory only.

The psychiatric outpatient center provides community outpatient psychiatric services.

1 General Considerations

1.1 Applicability
All standards set forth in Sections 1 through 5 of Chapter 3.1 (General Considerations, Diagnostic and Treatment Locations, Service Areas, Administrative and Public Areas, and Construction Standards) shall be met for psychiatric outpatient centers with the additions and modifications described herein. In no way are these standards to be interpreted to inhibit placing small neighborhood psychiatric outpatient centers (i.e., units with four or fewer employees) into existing commercial and residential facilities.

1.2 Functional Program
The number and type of diagnostic, clinical, and administrative areas shall be sufficient to support the services and estimated patient load described in the functional program.

1.3 Site

1.3.1 Parking
Parking spaces for patients and family shall be provided to meet the functional program.

2 Diagnostic and Treatment Areas

Facilities shall be provided only for those services specified in the functional program. Facilities provided shall meet the requirements of the specific diagnostic and clinical services as well as the standards set forth in Sections 3.1-7.1 and 3.1-7.2. Following are areas that shall be strongly considered for inclusion in any psychiatric outpatient center:

2.1 Consultation Room(s)

2.2 Group Rooms

2.2.1 Small Group Room(s)

2.2.2 Large Group Room(s)
These may also be used for activities.

2.3 Observation Room(s)
See Section 3.1-2.1.4.

2.4 Support Areas for the Psychiatric Outpatient Center

2.4.1 Nurse Station(s)
See Section 3.1-2.1.7.1.

2.4.2 Drug Distribution Station
See Section 3.1-2.1.7.2.

2.4.3 Multipurpose Rooms
Multiuse room(s) shall be provided for conferences, meetings, and health education.

2.4.3.1 One room may be primarily for staff use but also available for public access as needed.

2.4.3.2 If the program so indicates, these functions may take place in group room(s).

2.4.4 Nourishment Area(s)
Location of kitchenette(s) by the large group room(s) shall be permitted.

2.4.5 Clean Storage
See Section 3.1-2.1.7.4.

2.4.6 Soiled Holding
See Section 3.1-2.1.7.5.

2.4.7 Storage Areas
Wheelchair storage space shall be provided. See Section 3.1-2.1.7.6.

2.5 Support Areas for Staff

2.5.1 Staff Toilet and Lounge
2.5.1.1 Staff toilet and lounge shall be provided in addition to and separate from public and patient facilities.

*2.5.1.2 Centralized staff facilities are not required in small centers..

3 Administrative and Public Areas

3.1 Public Areas

3.1.1 Layout
Public areas shall be situated for convenient access and designed to promote prompt accommodation of patient needs, with consideration for personal dignity.

3.1.2 Entrances
3.1.2.1 Entrances shall be well marked, at grade level, and secured at least at the psychiatric outpatient unit.

3.1.2.2 Where entrance lobby and/or elevators are shared with other tenants, travel to the psychiatric outpatient unit shall be direct and accessible to the disabled. Except for passage through common doors, lobbies, or elevator stations, patients shall not be required to go through other occupied areas or outpatient service areas.

3.1.2.3 Entrance shall be convenient to parking and available via public transportation.

3.1.3 Reception
3.1.3.1 A reception and information counter or desk shall be located to provide visual control of the entrance to the psychiatric outpatient unit and shall be immediately apparent from that entrance.

3.1.3.2 A control counter shall have access to patient files and records for scheduling of services; this shall be permitted to be part of the reception, information, and waiting room control.

3.1.4 Waiting Area
3.1.4.1 The waiting area for patients and escorts shall be under staff control.

3.1.4.2 The seating shall contain no fewer than two spaces for each consultation room and no fewer than 1.5 spaces for the combined projected capacity at one time of the group rooms.

3.1.4.3 Where the psychiatric outpatient unit has a formal pediatrics service, a separate, controlled area for pediatric patients shall be provided.

3.1.4.4 The waiting area shall accommodate wheelchairs.

3.1.5 Public Toilet
Toilet(s) for public use shall be immediately accessible to the waiting area. In smaller units, the toilet may be unisex.

3.1.6 Drinking Water
Provisons for drinking water shall be available for waiting patients. In shared facilities, provisions for drinking water may be outside the outpatient area if convenient for use.

3.2 Administrative Areas
Each psychiatric outpatient center shall make provisions to support administrative activities, filing, and clerical work as appropriate. (See also Section 3.1-4.2.) Administrative areas shall include the following:

3.2.1 Interview Spaces
Space(s) for private interviews related to social service, credit, and so on shall be provided. Interviews may take place in an office or consultation room if the program so indicates.

3.2.2 Office Space
3.2.2.1 Office(s), separate and enclosed, with provisions for privacy, shall be provided.

3.2.2.2 Clerical space or rooms for typing and clerical work shall be separated from public areas to ensure confidentiality.

3.2.3 Patient Records
Records room(s) shall be provided with filing and storage for the safe and secure storage of patient records with provisions for ready retrieval.

> **APPENDIX**
>
> **A2.5.1.2** In small centers, staff may utilize shared toilet facilities.

3.2.4 Office Supply Storage

Office supply storage (closets or cabinets) shall be provided within or convenient to administrative services.

4 Construction Standards

4.1 Applicable Standards

The standards set forth in Section 3.1-5.2 shall be met with the additions and modifications described herein:

4.2 Security

4.2.1 The level of patient safety and security shall be set by the owner in the functional program.

4.2.2 Observation of all public areas, including corridors, shall be possible.

4.2.2.1 This can be accomplished by electronic surveillance if it is not obtrusive.

4.2.2.2 Niches and hidden areas in corridors shall be prohibited.

4.3 Details

4.3.1 Tamper Resistance and Suicide Prevention

4.3.1.1 If the functional program determines suicide or staff safety risks are present, ceilings, walls, floors, windows, etc., shall be tamper-resistant in patient treatment areas. In addition, any rods, doors, grab bars, handrails, etc., shall be constructed so they do not allow attempts at suicide and cannot be used as weapons.

4.3.1.2 Cubicle curtains and draperies shall not be used where a risk assessment in the functional program clearly identifies them as a potential risk.

3.12 Mobile, Transportable, and Relocatable Units

Appendix material, which appears in shaded boxes at the bottom of the page, is advisory only.

1 General Considerations

1.1 Applicability

1.1.1 Unit Types
This section applies to mobile, transportable, and relocatable structures, as defined below. The size of these units limits occupancy, thereby minimizing hazards and allowing for less stringent standards. Needed community services can therefore be provided at an affordable cost.

1.1.1.1 Mobile unit. A mobile unit is any pre-manufactured structure, trailer, or self-propelled unit equipped with a chassis on wheels and intended to provide shared medical services to the community on a temporary basis.

(1) These units are typically no larger than 8 feet wide by 48 feet long (2.44 meters by 14.63 meters).

(2) Some units are equipped with expanding walls.

(3) Typically these units are designed to be moved on a daily basis.

1.1.1.2 Transportable unit. A transportable unit is any pre-manufactured structure or trailer equipped with a chassis on wheels that is intended to provide shared medical services to the community on an extended temporary basis.

(1) The units are typically no larger than 12 feet wide by 60 feet long (3.66 meters by 18.29 meters).

(2) The units are designed to be moved periodically, depending on need.

1.1.1.3 Relocatable unit. A relocatable unit is any structure not on wheels that is built to be relocated at any time and to provide medical services. These structures vary in size.

*1.1.2 Standards

1.1.2.1 Meeting all provisions of Sections 2 through 5 of Chapter 3.1 (Diagnostic and Treatment Locations, Service Areas, Administrative and Public Areas, and Construction Standards) for general outpatient facilities is desirable, but limited size and resources may preclude satisfying any but the basic minimums described.

1.1.2.2 The classifications of these facilities shall be Business Occupancy as listed in the building codes and NFPA 101, Life Safety Code.

1.1.3 Maximum Size
These facilities shall be defined as space and equipment for services provided by four or fewer workers at any one time.

1.2 Site

1.2.1 Location
1.2.1.1 Access for the unit to arrive shall be taken into consideration for site planning. Turning radius of the vehicles, slopes of the approach (6 percent maximum), and existing conditions shall be addressed.

1.2.1.2 Consideration shall be given to location of the unit so that diesel exhaust of the tractor and/or unit generator is kept away from the fresh air intake of the facility.

1.2.2 Facility Access
Each site shall provide access to the unit for wheelchair/stretcher patients.

1.2.3 Environmental Standards
All mobile, transportable, and relocatable units shall be sited in full compliance with such federal, state, and

local environmental laws and regulations as may apply; for example, those listed in Section 1.3-4.

*1.2.4 Utility Requirements
1.2.4.1 Sites shall be provided with properly sized power, including emergency power, water, waste, telephone, and fire alarm connections, as required by local and state building codes.

1.2.4.2 Adequate protection shall be provided for utility hook-ups, cables, and wires by concealing them in conduits, burying them underground, or installing them overhead.

1.2.5 Foundation
*1.2.5.1 Sites shall have level concrete pads or piers and be designed for the structural loads of the facility. Construction of pads shall meet local, state, and seismic codes.

1.2.5.2 Each facility shall provide a means of preventing unit movement, either by blocking the wheels or by providing pad anchors.

1.2.6 Parking and Drop-off Zones
Sites shall provide hazard-free drop-off zones and adequate parking for patients. (See also 3.12-3.1.1.)

1.2.7 MRI Unit Site Considerations
1.2.7.1 Gauss fields of various strengths generated by magnetic resonance imaging (MRI) units shall be considered; both for the environmental effects on (interference with) the integrity of the scan, and for the potentially adverse effects of the field on adjacent electrical and/or magnetic devices and materials. Radio frequency interference shall be considered when planning a site.

1.2.7.2 Sites utilizing MRI systems shall consider providing adequate access for cryogen-servicing of the magnet. Cryogen dewars are of substantial weight and size.

APPENDIX

A1.2.4 It is recommended that each site requiring water and waste services to the unit provide a means of freeze protection in geographic areas where freezing temperatures occur.

A1.2.5.1 Concrete-filled steel pipe bollards are recommended for protection of the facility and the unit.

---

2 Diagnostic and Treatment Locations

2.1 Mobile Units

2.1.1 Hand-Washing Stations
2.1.1.1 Noninvasive procedure locations. Mobile units where noninvasive procedures are performed shall be provided with hand-washing stations unless each site can provide hand-washing stations within 25 feet (7.47 meters) of the unit.

2.1.1.2 Invasive procedure locations. When invasive procedures are performed in a mobile unit, all units shall be provided with hand-washing stations.

2.2 Transportable Units
Transportable units shall be provided with hand-washing stations.

2.3 Relocatable Units

2.3.1 Seismic and Structural Requirements
2.3.1.1 Seismic force resistance for relocatable units shall comply with Section 1.1-5 and shall be given an importance factor of one when applied to the seismic design formulas.

2.3.1.2 These units shall meet the structural requirements of local and state building codes.

2.3.2 Hand-Washing Stations
Relocatable units shall be provided with hand-washing stations.

2.4 Support Areas for Mobile, Transportable, and Relocatable Facilities

2.4.1 Cryogenic Equipment and Supply Storage
Storage for dewars, which are of substantial weight and size, shall be included in space planning.

3 Administrative and Public Areas

3.1 Public Areas

*3.1.1 Entrance
Patient protection from the elements during transport to and from the mobile unit shall be provided.

3.1.1.1 Use of means other than covered walkways shall be permitted to protect patients from the elements.

3.1.1.2 Snow shall be kept clear of pathways to and from the mobile unit. Effective means of abating ice shall be used when conditions exist.

3.1.2 Public Waiting Area

The facility shall provide waiting space for patient privacy as close to the unit docking area as possible.

3.1.3 Toilets

The facility shall provide patient/staff toilets as close to the unit docking area as possible.

4 Construction Standards

4.1 Design and Construction Standards

4.1.1 Applicable Codes

Existing facilities shall comply with applicable requirements of the Existing Business Occupancies chapter of NFPA 101, Life Safety Code. Where patients incapable of self-preservation are receiving inhalation anesthesia, the Existing Ambulatory Health Care Occupancies chapter of NFPA 101 shall apply.

4.1.2 Radiation Protection

Radiation protection for x-ray and gamma ray installations shall be in accordance with NCRP reports 49 and 91 in addition to all applicable local and state requirements.

4.2 General Standards for Details and Finishes for Unit Construction

Requirements below apply to all units unless otherwise noted:

4.2.1 Details
4.2.1.1 Doors

(1) Horizontal sliding doors and power-operated doors shall comply with NFPA 101.

(2) Units shall be permitted a single means of egress as permitted by NFPA 101.

(3) All glazing in doors shall be safety or wire glass.

4.2.1.2 Stairs

(1) Stairs for mobile and transportable units shall be in accordance with Table 3.12-1.

(2) There shall be no variation exceeding 3/16 inch (4.76 millimeters) in depth of adjacent treads or in the height of adjacent risers, and the tolerance between the largest and smallest tread shall not exceed 3/8 inch (9.52 millimeters) in any flight.

Exception: Where the bottom riser adjoins a public way, walk, or driveway having an established grade and serving as a landing, a variation in height of not more than 3 inches (7.62 centimeters) in every 3 feet (91.44 centimeters) and fraction of thereafter is permitted. Adjustable legs at the bottom of the stair assembly shall be permitted to allow for grade differences.

(3) Stairs and landings for relocatable units shall comply with NFPA 101.

(4) Handrails shall be provided on at least one side.

(5) Handrails shall be installed and constructed in accordance with NFPA 101, with the following exception: Provided the distance from grade to unit floor height is not greater than 4 feet 5 inches (1.35 meters), one intermediate handrail with a clear distance between rails of 19 inches (48.26 centimeters) maximum shall be permitted. (This exception is not applicable to existing units having a floor height of 5 feet 3 inches, or 1.60 meters, maximum.)

4.2.2 Finishes
4.2.2.1 Interior finish materials

(1) Interior finish materials shall be class A as defined in NFPA 101.

APPENDIX

A3.1.1 It is recommended that each site provide a covered walkway or enclosure to ensure patient safety from the outside elements. Protecting the patient from dust and wind also needs to be considered.

(2) Textile materials having a napped, tufted, looped, woven, nonwoven, or similar surface shall be permitted on walls and ceilings provided such materials have a class A rating and rooms or areas are protected by automatic extinguishment or sprinkler system.

(3) Fire-retardant coatings shall be permitted in accordance with NFPA 101.

(4) Curtains and draperies shall be noncombustible or flame retardant and shall pass both the large- and small-scale tests required by NFPA 101.

5 Building Systems

5.1 Plumbing

5.1.1 Plumbing and Other Piping Systems
Plumbing and other piping systems shall be installed in accordance with applicable model plumbing codes, unless specified herein.

5.1.1.1 Plumbing vents

(1) Mobile units. Venting through the roof shall not be required for mobile units requiring sinks. Waste lines shall be permitted to be vented through the sidewalls or other acceptable locations.

(2) Transportable and relocatable units. These shall be vented through the roof per model plumbing codes.

5.1.1.2 Water supply connection. Backflow prevention shall be installed at the point of water connection on the unit.

5.1.1.3 Waste connection. All waste lines shall be designed and constructed to discharge into the facility sanitary sewage system.

5.1.2 Medical Gas and Vaccuum Systems
Medical gases and suction systems, if installed, shall be in accordance with NFPA 99.

5.2 Heating, Ventilating, and Air-Conditioning Systems

5.2.1 Standards
5.2.1.1 Air-conditioning, heating, ventilating, duct-work, and related equipment shall be installed in accordance with NFPA 90B, Standard for the Installation of Warm Air Heating and Air Conditioning Systems.

5.2.1.2 All other requirements for heating and ventilation systems shall comply with Section 3.1-7.2.

5.3 Electrical Systems

5.3.1 General
5.3.1.1 Applicable standards

(1) All electrical material and equipment, including conductors, controls, and signaling devices, shall be installed in compliance with applicable sections of NFPA 70 and NFPA 99.

(2) All electrical material and equipment shall be listed as complying with available standards of listing agencies or other similar established standards where such standards are required.

5.3.1.2 Testing and documentation. The electrical installations, including alarm, nurse call, and communication systems, shall be tested to demonstrate that equipment installation and operation is appropriate and functional. A written record of performance tests on special electrical systems and equipment shall show compliance with applicable codes and standards.

*5.3.1.3** Power disturbance safeguards

5.3.2 Electrical Distribution and Transmission
5.3.2.1 Switchboards

(1) Location

(a) Main switchboards shall be located in an area separate from plumbing and mechanical equipment and shall be accessible to authorized persons only.

(b) Switchboards shall be convenient for use and readily accessible for maintenance but away from traffic lanes.

(c) Switchboards shall be located in dry, ventilated spaces free of corrosive or explosive fumes, gases, or any flammable material.

(2) Overload protective devices. These shall operate properly in ambient room temperatures.

5.3.2.2 Panelboards
Panelboards serving normal lighting and appliance circuits shall be located on the same level as the circuits they serve.

5.3.3 Power Generating and Storing Equipment
5.3.3.1 Emergency electrical service. Emergency lighting and power shall be provided for in accordance with NFPA 99, NFPA 101, and NFPA 110.

5.3.4 Lighting
5.3.4.1 General

(1) Lighting shall be engineered to the specific application.

(2) Recommended lighting levels for health care facilities developed by the Illuminating Engineering Society of North America (IES) shall be considered. Refer to IES publication RP-29, *Lighting for Hospitals and Health Care Facilities.*

(3) Consideration shall be given to the special needs of the elderly. Excessive contrast in lighting levels that makes effective sight adaptation difficult shall be minimized. Refer to IES publication, RP-28, *Lighting and the Visual Environment for Senior Living.*

(4) Approaches to buildings and parking lots and all occupied spaces shall have lighting fixtures that can be illuminated as necessary.

5.3.4.2 Lighting for examination, treatment and trauma rooms. A portable or fixed examination light

shall be provided for examination, treatment, and trauma rooms.

5.3.5 Receptacles (Convenience Outlets)
5.3.5.1 Duplex grounded-type receptacles (convenience outlets) shall be installed in all areas in sufficient quantities for tasks to be performed as needed.

5.3.5.2 Each examination and work table shall have access to a minimum of two duplex receptacles.

5.3.6 Equipment
5.3.6.1 X-ray equipment. Fixed and mobile x-ray equipment installations shall conform to articles 517 and 660 of NFPA 70.

5.3.6.2 Inhalation anesthetizing locations. At inhalation anesthetizing locations, all electrical equipment and devices, receptacles, and wiring shall comply with applicable sections of NFPA 99 and NFPA 70.

5.4 Telecommunications and Information Systems

5.4.1 Locations for terminating telecommunications and information system devices shall be located on the unit that the devices serve and shall be accessible to authorized personnel only.

5.4.2 Special air conditioning and voltage regulation shall be provided when recommended by the manufacturer.

5.5 Electronic Safety and Security

5.5.1 Fire Alarm System
5.5.1.1 The fire alarm system shall be as described in NFPA 101 and, where applicable, NFPA 72.

5.5.1.2 Fire protection equipment

(1) Manual fire extinguishers shall be provided in accordance with NFPA 101.

(2) Fire detection, alarm, and communications capabilities shall be installed and connected to facility central alarm system on all new units in accordance with NFPA 101.

Table 3.12-1
Stair Requirements for Mobile and Transportable Units

	New Units	Existing Units
Minimum width clear of all obstructions, except projections not exceeding 3 1/2 inches (8.89 centimeters) at or below handrail height on each side	2 feet 10 inches (86.36 centimeters)	2 feet 3 inches (68.58 centimeters)
Minimum headroom	6 feet 8 inches (2.03 meters)	6 feet 8 inches (2.03 meters)
Maximum height of risers	9 inches (22.86 centimeters)	9 inches (22.86 centimeters)
Minimum height of risers	4 inches (10.16 centimeters)	4 inches (10.16 centimeters)
Minimum tread depth	9 inches (22.86 centimeters)	7 inches (17.78 centimeters)
Doors opening immediately onto stairs without a landing	No	Yes

4

Other Health Care Facilities

4.1 Nursing Facilities

Appendix material, which appears in shaded boxes at the bottom of the page, is advisory only.

1 General Considerations

*1.1 Applicability
This chapter covers the continuum of nursing services listed below, which may be provided within freestanding facilities or as distinct parts of a general hospital or other health care facility.

1.1.1 Continuum of Nursing Services
The continuum of nursing services and facilities may be distinguished by the levels of care, staff support areas, and service areas provided and classified as:

1.1.1.1. Nursing and skilled nursing facilities

1.1.1.2. Special care facilities. These include the following:

(1) Subacute care facilities (Section 4.1-3.1)

(2) Alzheimer's and other dementia units (Section 4.1-3.2)

1.1.2 Minimum Standards for New Facilities
The text of this chapter represents minimum requirements for new construction and shall not be applied to existing facilities unless major construction renovations (see Section 1.1-3) are undertaken.

1.2 Auxiliary Services
When the nursing facility is part of, or contractually linked with, another facility, services such as dietary, storage, pharmacy, linen, and laundry may be shared insofar as practical. In some cases, all ancillary service requirements will be met by the principal facility and the only modifications necessary will be within the nursing facility. In other cases, programmatic concerns and requirements may dictate separate service areas.

1.3 Environment of Care

1.3.1 Flexibility
Nursing facilities shall be designed to provide flexibility in order to meet the changing physical, medical, and psychological needs of their residents.

1.3.2 Supportive Environment
The facility design shall produce a supportive environment to enhance and extend quality of life for residents and facilitate wayfinding while promoting privacy, dignity, and self-determination.

1.3.2.1 The architectural design—through the organization of functional space, the specification of ergonomically appropriate and arranged furniture and equipment, and the selection of details and finishes— shall eliminate as many barriers as possible to effective access and use by residents of all space, services, equipment, and utilities appropriate for daily living.

1.3.2.2 Design shall maximize opportunities for ambulation and self-care, socialization, and independence and minimize the negative aspects of an institutional environment.

*1.3.3 Long-Term Care Space Needs
While there are similarities in the spatial arrangement of hospitals and nursing facilities, the service requirements of long-term care residents require additional special design considerations.

1.4 Functional Program
The sponsor for each project shall provide a functional program for the facility (see Section 1.2-2).

1.5 Shared Services
Each nursing facility shall, as a minimum, contain the elements described within the applicable paragraphs

---

APPENDIX

A1.1 Specific requirements for each of the special care facility types are addressed in the paragraphs noted. For basic requirements, see chapters 1.1 through 1.6. For requirements regarding swing beds, see Section 2.1-1.2.2. Related sections include the following: Chapter 4.2 for hospice care; Chapter 4.3 for assisted living; and Chapter 4.4 for adult day health care.

A1.3.3. When a section of an acute care facility is converted for use as a nursing facility, it may be necessary to reduce the number of beds to provide space for long-term care services.

of this section. However, when a project calls for sharing or purchasing services, appropriate modifications or deletions in space and parking requirements shall be permitted.

1.6 Site

1.6.1 Location
See Sections 1.3-2 and 1.3-4 for requirements regarding location and environmental pollution control.

1.6.2 Roads
Roads shall be provided within the property for access to the main entrance and service areas. Fire department access shall be provided in accordance with local requirements. The property or campus shall be marked to identify emergency services or departments.

1.6.3 Parking
In the absence of local requirements, each nursing facility shall have parking space to satisfy the needs of residents, employees, staff, and visitors. The facility shall provide a minimum of one space for every four beds.

1.7 Renovation
See Section 1.1-3.

1.8 Provisions for Disasters
See Section 1.1-5.

1.9 Codes and Standards
See Section 1.1-7.

1.10 Equipment
See Chapter 1.4.

1.11 Planning, Design, and Construction
See Chapter 1.5.

1.12 Record Drawings and Manuals
See Section 1.5-5.

2 Resident Units

Resident units are groups of resident rooms, staff support areas, service areas, and resident support areas whose size and configuration are based upon organizational patterns of staffing, functional operations, and communications as provided in the functional program for the facility.

2.1 General

2.1.1 Applicability
Each resident unit in a nursing or skilled nursing facility shall comply with the following.

2.1.2 Resident Unit Size
In the absence of local requirements, consideration shall be given to restricting the size of the resident unit to 60 beds or a maximum travel distance from the staff station to a resident room door of 150 feet (45.72 meters).

*2.1.3 Layout
2.1.3.1 Arranging groups of resident rooms adjacent to decentralized service areas, optional satellite staff work areas, and optional decentralized resident support areas is acceptable.

2.1.3.2 In new construction, resident units shall be arranged to avoid unrelated travel through resident units.

2.2 Typical Resident Rooms
Each resident room shall meet the following requirements:

*2.2.1 Capacity
2.2.1.1 In new construction and renovations, maximum room occupancy shall be two residents.

2.2.1.2 Where renovation work is undertaken and the present capacity is more than two residents, maximum room capacity shall be no more than the present capacity with a maximum of four residents.

*2.2.2 Space Requirements
2.2.2.1 Area and dimensions

(1) Room area and dimensions shall be determined by analyzing the needs of the resident(s) to move about the room in a wheelchair, gain access to at least one side of the bed, turn and wheel around the bed, gain access to a window and to the resident's toilet room, wardrobe locker, or closet and to the resident's possessions or equipment, including chair, dresser, and nightstand.

(2) Room size and configuration shall permit resident(s) options for bed location(s) and make provision for visual privacy.

2.2.2.2 Clearances

(1) In multiple-bed rooms, clearance shall allow for the movement of beds and equipment without disturbing residents.

APPENDIX

A2.1.3 Clusters and Staffing Considerations

a. Clustering refers to several concepts wherein the design of traditional nursing home floor plans (straight halls, double- or single-loaded corridors) is reorganized to provide benefits to both residents and to the effectiveness with which people care for them. Clustering is done to achieve better image, faster service, shorter walking/wheeling distances, and more subtle handling of linen. It can also afford more localized social areas and optional decentralized staff work areas.

b. A functioning cluster as described here is more than an architectural form where rooms are grouped around social areas without reference to caregiving. In a functioning cluster, the following will be accomplished:

–Utility placement is better distributed for morning care: Clean and soiled linen rooms are located closer to the resident rooms, minimizing staff steps and maximizing the appearance of corridors (carts are not scattered through halls).

–Unit scale and appearance reinforces smaller groups of rooms seen as being grouped or related: Clusters should offer identifiable social groups for both staff and older people, thereby reducing the sense of largeness often associated with centralized facilities.

–Geographically effective staffing: The staffing pattern and design reinforce each other so that nursing assistants can offer primary nursing care and relate to a given set of rooms. Their room assignments are grouped together and generally do not require unequal travel distances to basic utilities. Staff "buddying" is possible. Buddying involves sharing responsibilities such as lifting a non-weight-bearing person or covering for someone while the buddy provides off-unit transport or is on a break.

–Staffing that works as well at night as during the day: An effective cluster design incorporates multiple staffing ratios. A unit might have 42 beds, but with clustering, could staff effectively in various ratios of licensed nurses to nurses assistants: 1:7 days (six clusters); 1:14 or 1:21 nights (three or two neighborhoods).

c. Clustering can also have some other benefits:

–Cluster design can provide more efficient "gross/net area" when a variety of single and/or double rooms are "nested."

–Cluster design can be useful when a project is to have a high proportion of private occupancy rooms, because it reduces distances to staff work areas or nursing stations.

–Clusters provide a method of distributing nursing staff through a building, nearer to bedrooms at night, so they can be responsive to vocal calls for assistance and toileting. (Central placement of staff requires greater skill in using traditional call systems than many residents possess.)

–Cluster units of a given size may "stack" or be placed over each other, but might have different staffing for varying care levels.

–If digital call systems are used (such as those allowing reprogramming of what room reports to which zone or nursing assistant's work area), then one unit might easily be changed over time, such as when client needs justify higher ratios of nursing assistants to older people. For example, a 48-bed unit might start at 1:8 staffing but also respond to 1:6 staffing needs. In some units, staffing might also be slightly uneven, such as where 60-bed units are comprised of clusters of 1:7 and 1:8 during days.

d. Architectural form and clustering: Clusters involve architectural form and may have an impact on overall building shape.

–The longer length of stay of nursing home residents compared with hospital clients is one factor that makes clustering rooms in more residential groups particularly appropriate. However, the visual advantages of units without long corridors has also attracted hospital planners. In both facility types, architectural clustering may help both staff and residents socially identify a space or sub-unit within a larger unit.

–Though architectural clustering may involve grouping rooms, this should not result in windowless social areas, or the incorporation of all social options in a windowless social area directly outside of the bedroom doorways.

A2.2.1 Changes to the maximum number of residents per room may be made upon a determination by the authority having jurisdiction that such an alternate room configuration provides a preferable environment for residents with unusual care requirements. Single resident rooms with an individual toilet room are encouraged. In two-bed rooms, consideration should be given to creating room configurations that maximize individual resident privacy, access to windows, room controls, and equivalent space.

A2.2.2 For purposes of planning minimum clearances around beds, unless specified otherwise by the functional program, the rectangular dimensions of the bed are width: 3 feet 4 inches (1.01 meters) and length: 8 feet (2.44 meters).

(2) Clear access to one side of the bed shall be provided along 75 percent of its length.

(3) Mechanical and fixed equipment shall not obstruct access to any required element.

(4) These guidelines shall allow arrangement of furniture that may reduce these access provisions, without impairing access provisions for other occupants.

2.2.3 Layout
Beds shall be no more than two deep from windows in new construction and three deep from windows in renovated construction.

2.2.4 Window(s)
Each room shall have a window that meets the requirements of Section 4.1-8.2.2.4.

APPENDIX

A2.2.7.2 A mirror for resident use shall be provided in the toilet room.

A2.2.7.4 While ADAAG, UFAS, and ANSI accessibility standards were all developed with the intention of providing greater access for individuals with disabilities, their standards are based upon assumed stature and strength, whereby dimensional and grab bar requirements are intended to facilitate wheelchair-to-toilet transfers by individuals with sufficient upper body strength and mobility to effect such a transfer. The typical nursing home resident is unlikely to have such capabilities, thus requiring the assistance of one or more staff. Insufficient clearance at the side of the toilet can restrict staff mobility and access, and can result in injury. There are ongoing efforts aimed at educating regulators and advisory panels to the difficulties caused by inappropriate standards required within environments serving frail and geriatric populations.

Alternative grab bar configurations should address the following scenarios:

a. When a resident is capable of independent transfer facilitated by the grab bar and side-wall location required by accessibility standards, a removable/temporary wall structure and grab bar can be installed alongside the toilet.

b. When a resident requires partial assistance in transfer, fold-down grab bars on one or both sides of the toilet would facilitate such transfers.

2.2.5 Resident Privacy
Visual privacy shall be provided for each resident in multiple-bed rooms. Design for privacy shall not restrict resident access to the toilet, room entrance, window, or other shared common areas in the resident room.

2.2.6 Hand-Washing Station
A hand-washing station shall be provided in each resident room. Omission of this station shall be permitted in a single-bed or two-bed room when a hand-washing station is located in an adjoining toilet room that serves that room only.

2.2.7 Toilet Room
Each resident shall have access to a toilet room without the need to enter the corridor area.

2.2.7.1 One toilet room shall serve no more than two residents in new construction and no more than four beds or two resident rooms in renovation projects.

*2.2.7.2 The toilet room shall contain a water closet and hand-washing station and (where permitted) a horizontal surface for the personal effects of each resident.

2.2.7.3 Doors to toilet rooms may be hinged or, where local requirements permit, sliding or folding doors may be used, provided adequate provisions are made for acoustic privacy and resident safety.

*2.2.7.4 Toilets used by residents shall be provided sufficient clearance on both sides of the water closet to enable physical access and maneuvering by staff, who may have to assist the resident in wheelchair-to-water closet transfers and returns. Where independent transfers are feasible, alternative grab bar configurations shall be permitted.

2.2.8 Resident Storage Locations
Each resident shall be provided a separate wardrobe, locker, or closet.

2.2.8.1 This storage shall have minimum clear dimensions of 1 foot 10 inch (55.88 centimeters) depth by 1 foot 8 inch (50.80 centimeters) width.

2.2.8.2 A clothes rod and shelf shall be provided at heights accessible to the resident. Accommodations shall be made for storage of full-length garments. The shelf may be omitted if the unit provides at least two drawers.

*2.2.9 Medical Gases
Resident rooms designated for ventilator dependency shall have provisions for the administration of oxygen and suction.

2.3 Support Areas—General

2.3.1 Size and Features
The size and features of each staff support area shall depend upon the number and types of residents served.

2.3.2 Space Requirements
Identifiable spaces are required for each indicated function, but consideration shall be given to multiple-use design solutions that provide equivalent, though unspecified, areas. Except where the word room or office is used, support functions may be accommodated in a multipurpose area.

2.3.3 Location
Staff support areas may be arranged and located to serve more than one resident unit, but at least one such support area shall be located on each resident floor unless noted otherwise. The following staff support areas shall be located in or readily accessible to each resident unit.

2.4 Support Areas for Resident Units

*2.4.1 Staff Work Area(s)
Resident units shall have staff work areas in central or decentralized direct care locations.

2.4.1.1 Central staffing. Where caregiving is organized on a central staffing model, such work areas shall provide for charting or transmitting charted data and any storage or administrative activities.

*2.4.1.2 Decentralized staffing. Where caregiving is decentralized, supervisory work areas need not accommodate charting activities nor have direct visualization of resident rooms. Rather, such functions shall be accomplished at decentralized direct care staff work areas, which shall provide for charting or transmitting charted data and any storage or administrative activities required by the functional program.

2.4.2 Medication Station
Provision shall be made for 24-hour distribution of medications. A medicine preparation room, a self-contained medicine-dispensing unit, or other system shall be used for this purpose.

2.4.2.1 Medicine preparation room

(1) The medicine preparation room, if used, shall be visually controlled from the staff work area.

(2) It shall contain a work counter, sink, refrigerator, and locked storage for controlled drugs.

(3) It shall have a minimum area of 50 square feet (4.65 square meters).

2.4.2.2 Self-contained medicine dispensing unit

(1) Location of a self-contained medicine-dispensing unit, if used, shall be permitted at the staff work area, in the clean workroom, in an alcove, or in other space convenient for staff control.

(2) Convenient access to hand-washing stations shall be provided. (Standard cup-sinks provided in many self-contained units are not adequate for hand-washing.)

2.4.3 Nourishment Area

2.4.3.1 The nourishment area shall contain a work counter, refrigerator, storage cabinets, and a sink for serving nourishment between meals.

2.4.3.2 The nourishment station shall include space for trays and dishes used for nonscheduled meal service and may also be used as a pantry for food service adjacent to a resident's dining room or area.

2.4.3.3 Ice machine. Ice for residents' consumption shall be provided by ice-maker units. Where accessible to residents and the public, ice-maker units shall be self-dispensing. Ice makers shall be located, designed, and installed to minimize noise (and may serve more than one nourishment station).

2.4.3.4 Hand-washing stations. Hand-washing stations shall be in or immediately accessible from the nourishment station.

2.4.4 Clean Workroom or Clean Supply Room

2.4.4.1 Clean workroom. If the room is used for preparing resident care items, it shall contain a work counter, a hand-washing station, and storage facilities for clean and sterile supplies.

2.4.4.2 Clean supply room. If the room is used only for storage and holding as part of a system for distribution of clean and sterile materials, the work counter and hand-washing station may be omitted.

2.4.5 Soiled Utility or Soiled Holding Room(s)

It shall contain a clinical sink or equivalent flushing-rim fixture with a rinsing hose or a bedpan sanitizer, hand-washing station, soiled linen receptacles, and waste receptacles in number and type as required by the functional program.

2.4.6 Equipment and Supply Storage

2.4.6.1 Clean linen storage. A separate closet or designated area shall be provided. If a closed-cart system is used, storage may be in an alcove where staff control can be exercised.

2.4.6.2 Supply storage. Storage space(s) for supplies and recreation shall be provided near their points of use, as required by the functional program.

2.4.6.3 Wheelchair and other equipment storage. Space for wheelchairs and other equipment shall be provided away from normal traffic.

2.5 Support Areas for Staff

2.5.1 Staff Lounge Area(s)

These areas may be shared by more than one resident unit or service.

2.5.2 Staff Storage

Lockable closets, drawers, or compartments shall be provided for safekeeping of staff personal effects such as handbags.

2.5.3 Toilet Room(s)

These shall contain water closets with hand-washing stations for staff and may be unisex.

2.6 Support Areas for Residents

*2.6.1 Resident Bathing Facilities

2.6.1.1 A minimum of one bathtub or shower shall be provided for every 20 residents (or major fraction thereof) not otherwise served by bathing facilities in resident rooms.

2.6.1.2 Residents shall have access to at least one bathing unit (room) per floor or unit, sized to permit assisted bathing in a tub or shower.

(1) The bathtub in this room shall be accessible to residents in wheelchairs.

(2) The shower shall accommodate a shower gurney with fittings for a resident in a recumbent position.

2.6.1.3 Other showers or tubs shall be in an individual room(s) or enclosure(s) with space for private use of the bathing fixture and, for drying and dressing, and for access to a grooming location containing a hand-washing station, mirror, and counter or shelf.

*2.6.1.4 A separate toilet shall be provided within or directly accessible to each resident's bathing facility without requiring entry into the general corridor.

2.6.2 Storage for Resident Needs

Storage space(s) for resident needs shall be provided near their points of use, as required by the functional program.

2.6.3 Resident Telephone

Provisions shall be made convenient to each nursing unit to allow residents to make and receive telephone calls in private, unless otherwise indicated by the functional program.

3 Special Care Facilities

*3.1 Subacute Care Facilities

3.2 Alzheimer's and Other Dementia Units

*3.2.1 Safety

Safety concerns must be emphasized because of poor judgment inherent in those with dementia:

3.2.1.1 Hazard avoidance. Areas or pieces of furniture that could be hazardous to these residents shall be eliminated or designed to minimize possible accidents.

3.2.1.2 Doors. Resident security shall be addressed through systems that secure the unit and comply with life safety codes. Should the functional program (see Section 1.2-2) justify limiting the movements of any resident(s) for their safety, any door locking arrangements shall be in full compliance with applicable requirements of NFPA 101. A secure unit shall contain appropriate activity area(s), dining, bathing, soiled linen/utility, and staff work area.

3.2.2 Windows

Operable windows shall be permitted and shall comply with Section 4.1-8.2.2.4.

*3.2.3 Outdoor Spaces

Secure outdoor gardens and lounge areas shall be available for residents of the Alzheimer's/dementia resident unit.

APPENDIX

A2.6.1.4 This toilet may also serve as the toilet-training facility.

A3.1 Since subacute care comprises programs in various settings, the design of such units/facilities should focus on two major components:

a. The unit/facility should comply with all applicable nursing home requirements contained in this chapter to the extent these do not conflict with the clinical program.

b. The facility/unit should comply with the requirements dictated by the functional program required by Section 1.2-2.

A3.2.1 The latest edition of the Life Safety Code recognizes the need to lock doors in Alzheimer's units. Consideration should be given to making locks on wardrobes, closets, or cupboards inconspicuous.

A3.2.3 Outdoor spaces may include gardens on grade or on roof decks, or solaria, porches, balconies, etc. Lounge space may be a winterized sun room, a designated lounge space separate from the dining room, or a day room, where other residents may be sitting. Secure, accessible outdoor space can provide a calming change in environment and also a convenient place for agitated residents to walk.

A3.2.4 Major characteristics of persons with Alzheimer's and other dementias are lack of attention span and an inability to orient themselves within space. The environment should provide attention-grabbing landmarks and wayfinding cues and information to aid in navigation from point to point. Sensory cuing that is used in other long-term care resident areas should be incorporated for persons with dementia. Dementia program activities may include memory stimulation, music therapy, art therapy, horticultural therapy, etc. Space for dining and activities in dedicated dementia units may be provided within the unit or in a location directly accessible to the residents of the unit per the minimum standards described elsewhere in Chapter 4.1. Consideration should be given to:

a. Landmarks. Design elements that provide clear reference points in the environment (e.g., a room, a large three-dimensional object, large picture, or other wall-mounted artifact).

b. Signs. When appropriate, large characters and redundant word/picture combinations should be used on signs.

c. Environmental design challenge. Residents with mental impairment often find it difficult to sit for long periods of time or to sit at all without becoming restless. Although it is not a universal trait, it is so common and requires so much staff time that environmental solutions should be explored in all areas to give cognitively impaired people interesting places and things on which to focus their attention.

*3.2.4 Activity Space
Activity space for resident use in dementia programs shall be provided.

4 Resident Living Areas

*4.1 Resident Dining and Recreation Areas

4.1.1 Space Requirements
4.1.1.1 The space needed for dining and recreation shall be determined by considering the following:

(1) The needs of residents to use adaptive equipment and mobility aids and receive assistance from support and service staff

(2) The extent to which support programs shall be centralized or decentralized

(3) The number of residents to be seated for dining at one time, as required by the functional program

Note: Nothing in these Guidelines is intended to restrict a facility from providing additional square footage per resident beyond what is required herein for dining rooms, activity areas, and similar spaces.

*4.1.1.2 In new construction, the total area set aside for dining, resident lounges, and recreation shall be at least 35 square feet (3.25 square meters) per bed with a minimum total area of at least 225 square feet (20.90 square meters). At least 20 square feet (1.86 square meters) per bed shall be available for dining.

*4.1.1.3 For renovations, at least 14 square feet (1.30 square meters) per bed shall be available for dining.

*4.2 Activity Areas

4.2.1 Space Requirements
If required by the functional program, the minimum requirements for new construction shall include the following. However, nothing in these Guidelines is intended to restrict a facility from providing additional square footage per resident beyond what is required herein for activities.

4.2.2 Activity Spaces
Space and equipment shall be provided for carrying out each of the activities defined in the functional program.

4.2.3 Small Group Activity Space
A space for small group and "one-on-one" activities shall be readily accessible to the residents.

A4.1 It is important to provide outdoor views from dining, recreation, and living spaces.

A4.1.1.2 While the guidelines provide a minimum requirement of 20 square feet (1.85 square meters) per bed for dining space, it is likely that facilities designed to this standard will be required to serve the resident population in more than one shift. In practice, the dining room should be sized at a minimum of 28 net square feet (2.60 square meters) per resident seated at one time. Additional space may be required for outpatient day care programs.

A4.1.1.3 Additional space may be required for outpatient day care programs.

A4.2 Activity programs focus on the social, spiritual, and creative needs of residents and clients and provide quality, meaningful experiences for them. These programs may be facility-wide or for smaller groups.

If included in the functional program, the activity department is generally responsible for coordination of activities for large groups as well as small groups and personalized individual programs involving one resident and one therapist. These activities may be conducted in other portions of the building (e.g., dining rooms, recreation spaces, lounges, etc.), but dedicated spaces are preferred for efficient operation of quality programs. Large space requirements (e.g., libraries, chapels, auditoriums, and conference, classroom, and/or training spaces) depend upon the programming decisions of the sponsors as reflected in the functional program for the facility.

A4.2.4 If required by the functional program, include space for files, records, computers, and administrative activities; a storage space for supplies and equipment; and a quiet space for residents to maximize conversations. This quiet space may be incorporated within space for administrative activities.

Note: Hearing loss in the elderly is well documented. Quiet space is very important to enable conversation.

*4.2.4 Activity Storage
Storage for large items used for large group activities (e.g., recreation materials and exercise equipment; supplies for religious services) shall be placed near the location of the planned activity and at the point of first use.

4.2.5 Resident Toilet Room(s)
Toilet room(s) that are convenient to activity spaces shall be provided for residents.

*4.3 Personal Services (Barber/Beauty) Areas
Facilities and equipment for resident hair care and grooming shall be provided separate from the resident rooms.

4.3.1 These shall be permitted to be unisex and located adjacent to central resident activity areas, provided that location and scheduling preserve patient dignity.

4.3.2 Resident toilets shall be located convenient to the hair and grooming area(s).

5 Diagnostic and Treatment Locations

5.1 Rehabilitation Therapy
Each nursing facility that provides physical and/or occupational therapy services for rehabilitating long-term care residents shall have areas and equipment that conform to program intent. Where the nursing facility is part of a general hospital or other facility, services may be shared as appropriate.

5.1.1 Physical and Occupational Therapy Provisions for Residents
As a minimum, the following shall be located on-site, convenient for use:

5.1.1.1 Space and equipment for carrying out each type of therapy that may be prescribed

5.1.1.2 Hand-washing stations. These shall be within the therapy unit.

5.1.1.3 Provisions for resident privacy

5.1.1.4 Provisions for wheelchair residents

5.1.1.5 Support areas for rehabilitation therapy

(1) Space for files, records, and administrative activities

(2) Equipment and supply storage

(3) Housekeeping rooms, in or near unit

5.1.1.6 Support areas for residents

(1) Resident toilet room(s). These shall be usable by wheelchair occupants.

5.1.2 Physical and Occupational Therapy Provisions for Outpatients
If the program includes outpatient treatment, additional provisions shall include the following:

5.1.2.1 Convenient facility access usable by the disabled

5.1.2.2 Support areas for patients

(1) Waiting area for outpatients and public. This shall be in addition to and separate from required resident support and activity areas. Public toilets shall be provided convenient to these waiting areas.

(2) Facilities for dressing and lockers for storing patients' clothing and personal effects

(3) Toilet facilities dedicated for outpatient use

(4) Showers, if required by the functional program

6 Service Areas

6.1 Dietary Facilities
The following services shall be provided:

6.1.1 General
Food service facilities and equipment shall conform with these standards and other applicable food and sanitation codes and standards and shall provide food service for residents.

APPENDIX

A4.3 Consideration should be given to the special ventilation and exhaust requirements of these areas.

6.1.1.1 Food receiving, storage, and preparation areas shall facilitate quality control.

6.1.1.2 Provision shall be made for transport of hot and cold foods as required by the functional program.

6.1.1.3 Separate dining areas shall be provided for staff and for residents.

6.1.1.4 The design and location of dining facilities shall encourage resident use.

6.1.1.5 Facilities shall be furnished to provide nourishment and snacks between scheduled meal service.

6.1.1.6 The dietary facility shall be easy to clean and to maintain in a sanitary condition.

6.1.2 Functional Elements

If the dietary department is on-site, the following facilities, in the size and number appropriate for the type of food service selected, shall be provided:

6.1.2.1 Control station. A control station shall be provided for receiving and controlling food supplies.

6.1.2.2 Hand-washing station(s). Hand-washing station(s) shall be located in the food preparation area.

6.1.2.3 Food preparation facilities. These facilities shall be provided to accommodate the method of food preparation specified in the functional program.

(1) Conventional food preparation systems require space and equipment for preparing, cooking, and baking.

(2) Convenience food service systems using frozen prepared meals, bulk packaged entrees, individual packaged portions, or those using contractual commissary services require space and equipment for thawing, portioning, cooking, and baking.

6.1.2.4 Ice-making facilities. These may be located in the food preparation area or in a separate room. They

APPENDIX

A6.1.3.2 (1) Facilities in remote areas may require proportionally more food storage facilities.

shall be easily cleanable and convenient to the dietary function.

6.1.2.5 Assembly and distribution. Facilities for assembly and distribution of patient meals

6.1.2.6 Dining space. Separate dining spaces shall be provided for residents and staff.

6.1.2.7 Ware-washing space. Ware-washing space shall be provided in a room or an alcove separate from the food preparation and serving area.

(1) Commercial-type ware-washing equipment shall be provided.

(2) Space shall be provided for receiving, scraping, sorting, and stacking soiled tableware and for transferring clean tableware to the using areas.

(3) Convenient hand-washing stations shall be provided.

6.1.2.8 Pot-washing facilities

6.1.3 Support Areas for Dietary Facilities
6.1.3.1 Offices(s). Office(s) or desk spaces for dietitian(s) and/or a dietary service manager.

6.1.3.2 Storage

*(1) Food storage. Storage space, including cold storage, shall be provided for at least a four-day supply of food.

(2) Storage areas and sanitizing facilities for cans, carts, and mobile-tray conveyors.

(3) Waste, storage, and recycling facilities (per local requirements) located in a separate room easily accessible to the outside for direct pickup or disposal.

6.1.3.3 Housekeeping room. A housekeeping room shall be located within the dietary department. It shall include a floor receptor or service sink and storage space for housekeeping equipment and supplies.

6.1.4 Support Areas for Staff
6.1.4.1 Staff toilet. Toilet for dietary staff shall be provided convenient to the kitchen area.

6.2 Linen Services

6.2.1 General
Each facility shall have provisions for storing and processing clean and soiled/contaminated linen for resident care. Processing may be done within the facility, in a separate building on- or off-site, or in a commercial or shared laundry. At a minimum, the following elements shall be included:

6.2.2 Laundry Facility
6.2.2.1 General

(1) Layout. Equipment shall be arranged to permit an orderly work flow and minimize cross-traffic that might mix clean and soiled operations.

(2) If linen is processed in a laundry facility within the facility, the following shall be provided:

6.2.2.2 Receiving, holding, and sorting room. A receiving, holding, and sorting room shall be provided for control and distribution of soiled linen. Discharge from soiled linen chutes may be received within this room or in a separate room adjacent to it.

6.2.2.3 Washers/extractors. Washers/extractors shall be located between the soiled linen receiving and clean processing areas. Personal laundry, if decentralized, may be handled within one room or rooms, as long as separate, defined areas are provided for handling clean and soiled laundry.

6.2.2.4 Supply storage. Storage shall be provided for laundry supplies.

6.2.2.5 Inspection and mending area. An area shall be provided for linen inspection and mending.

6.2.3 Support Areas for Internal Processing
6.2.3.1 Soiled holding room(s). Separate central or decentralized room(s) shall be provided for receiving and holding soiled linen for pickup or processing.

(1) Such room(s) shall have proper ventilation and exhaust.

(2) Discharge from soiled linen chutes shall be received in a separate room.

6.2.3.2 Central clean linen storage. A central clean linen storage and issuing room(s) shall be provided in addition to the linen storage required at individual resident units.

6.2.3.3 Linen carts

(1) Storage. Provisions shall be made for parking of clean and soiled linen carts separately and out of traffic.

(2) Cleaning. Provisions shall be made for cleaning of linen carts on premises (or exchange of carts off premises).

6.2.3.4 Hand-washing stations. Hand-washing stations shall be provided in each area where unbagged, soiled linen is handled.

6.2.4 Support Areas for Off-Site Processing
If linen is processed off-site or in a separate building on-site, the following shall be provided:

6.2.4.1 Service entrance. A service entrance, protected from inclement weather, for loading and unloading of linen. This can be shared with other services and serve as the loading dock for the facility.

6.2.4.2 Control station. A control station for pickup and receiving shall be provided. This can be shared with other services and serve as the receiving and pickup point for the facility.

6.3 Materials Management

6.3.1 Waste Management
Facilities shall be provided for sanitary storage of waste and recyclables using techniques and capacities acceptable to the appropriate health and environmental authorities.

Note: For waste treatment and disposal requirements, see Section 4.1-9.3.

6.4 Environmental Services

6.4.1 Housekeeping Rooms
6.4.1.1 Location. Housekeeping rooms shall be provided throughout the facility as required to maintain a clean and sanitary environment.

6.4.1.2 Number. At least one housekeeping room shall be provided for each floor.

6.4.1.3 Facility requirements. Each housekeeping room shall contain a floor receptor or service sink and storage space for housekeeping equipment and supplies.

6.5 Engineering Services and Maintenance

The following shall be provided as necessary for effective service and maintenance functions:

6.5.1 Equipment Locations

Room(s) or separate building(s) shall be provided for boilers, mechanical, and electrical equipment.

6.5.2 General Maintenance Area

A general maintenance area shall be provided for repair and maintenance.

6.5.3 Receiving Areas

If required by the functional program, a loading dock and receiving and breakout area(s) shall be provided. These may be shared with other services.

6.5.4 Equipment, Supply, and Facility Records Storage

6.5.4.1 Provisions shall be made for protected storage of facility drawings, records, manuals, etc.

6.5.4.2 Storage room for building maintenance supplies. **Note:** Storage for solvents and flammable liquids shall comply with applicable NFPA codes.

6.5.4.3 General storage space(s) for furniture and equipment such as intravenous stands, inhalators, air mattresses, walkers, medical supplies, and housekeeping supplies and equipment.

6.5.4.4 Yard equipment and supply storage areas, located so that equipment may be moved directly to the exterior.

7 Administrative and Public Areas

The following shall be provided:

7.1 Public Areas

7.1.1 Vehicular Drop-Off and Pedestrian Entrance
This shall be at grade level, sheltered from inclement weather, and accessible to the disabled.

7.1.2 Administrative/Public Lobby Area
This shall include the following:

7.1.2.1 A counter or desk for reception and information

7.1.2.2 Public waiting area(s)

7.1.2.3 Public toilet facilities

7.1.2.4 Public telephone(s)

7.1.2.5 Provisions for drinking water

7.2 Administrative Areas

7.2.1 General or Individual Office(s)
7.2.1.1 These shall be provided for business transactions, admissions, social services, medical and financial records, and administrative and professional staff. Provisions for private interviews shall be included.

7.2.1.2 Space for clerical files and staff office space shall be provided as required by the functional program.

7.2.2 Multipurpose Room(s)
A multipurpose room for conferences, meetings, and health education purposes shall be provided as required by the functional program; it shall include provisions for the use of visual aids. One multipurpose room may be shared by several services.

7.2.3 Supply Room
Space for storage of office equipment and supplies shall be provided as required by the functional program.

8 Construction Standards

8.1 Applicable Codes

All parts of the nursing facility shall be designed and constructed to sustain dead and live loads in accordance with applicable building codes and accepted engineering practices and standards, including requirements for seismic forces and applicable sections of NFPA 101.

8.2 General Standards for Details and Finishes

8.2.1 General

8.2.1.1 Resident facilities require features that encourage ambulation of long-term residents.

8.2.1.2 Signage and other wayfinding features shall be provided to aid self-ambulating residents and avoid confusing or disorienting them.

*8.2.1.3 Potential hazards to residents, such as sharp corners, slippery floors, loose carpets, and hot surfaces shall be avoided.

8.2.1.4 Renovations shall not diminish the level of compliance with these standards below that which existed prior to the renovation. However, features in excess of those for new construction are not required to be maintained in the completed renovation.

8.2.2 Details
8.2.2.1 Corridors

(1) Width. The placement of drinking fountains, public telephones, and vending machines shall not restrict corridor traffic or reduce the corridor width below the minimum stipulated in NFPA 101.

*(2) Handrails. Where corridors are defined by walls, handrails shall be provided on both sides of all corridors normally used by residents.

    (a) A minimum clearance of 1-1/2 inches (3.81 centimeters) shall be provided between the handrail and the wall.

    (b) Rail ends shall be returned to the wall or floor.

8.2.2.2 Ceiling height. The minimum ceiling height shall be 7 feet 10 inches (2.39 meters), with the following exceptions:

(1) Corridors, storage rooms, toilet rooms. Ceilings in these spaces shall be at least 7 feet 8 inches (2.34 meters). Ceilings in normally unoccupied spaces may be reduced to 7 feet (2.13 meters).

(2) Rooms containing ceiling-mounted equipment. These shall have the ceiling height required to ensure proper functioning of the ceiling-mounted equipment.

(3) Boiler rooms. Boiler rooms shall have ceiling clearances of at least 2 feet 6 inches (76.2 centimeters) above the main boiler header and connecting pipe.

(4) Clearances. Building components and suspended tracks, rails, and pipes located along the path of normal traffic shall be not less than 7 feet (2.13 meters) above the floor.

(5) Renovation. In renovation projects, all new work shall comply, insofar as practical, with subparagraphs 8.2.2.2 (1) through (4) above. Where existing conditions make compliance impractical or impossible, exceptions shall be considered. However, in no case shall ceiling heights be reduced more than 4 inches (2.54 centimeters) below the minimum requirement for new construction.

(6) Doorways and other openings. Architecturally framed and trimmed openings in corridors and rooms shall be permitted, provided a minimum clear opening height of 7 feet (2.13 meters) is maintained.

8.2.2.3 Doors. Doors to all rooms containing bathtubs, sitz baths, showers, and toilets for resident use shall be hinged, sliding, or folding.

8.2.2.4 Windows. Resident rooms or suites in new construction shall have window(s).

(1) Operable windows or vents that open from the inside shall be restricted to inhibit possible resident escape or suicide.

APPENDIX

A8.2.1.3 Hot surfaces are intended to include those surfaces to which residents have normal access that exceed 110°F (43°C). This requirement does not extend to medical or therapeutic equipment.

A8.2.2.1 (2) Consideration should be given to increasing clearances for arthritic residents and for mounting handrails lower than required by ADA to enable frail residents to lean on the handrails for support when ambulating.

(2) Windows shall have sills located above grade, but no higher than 36 inches (91.44 centimeters) above the finished floor.

8.2.2.5 Screens. Windows and outer doors that may be left open shall have insect screens.

*8.2.2.6 Glazing materials

(1) Glazing in doors, sidelights, borrowed lights, and windows where glazing is less than 18 inches (45.72 centimeters) from the floor shall be constructed of safety glass, wire glass, tempered glass, or plastic glazing material that resists breaking and creates no dangerous cutting edges when broken.

(2) Similar materials shall be used in wall openings in activity areas (such as recreation rooms and exercise rooms) if permitted by local requirements.

(3) If doors are provided for shower and tub enclosures, glazing shall be safety glass or plastic.

8.2.2.7 Hand-washing stations

(1) Clearances. Hand-washing stations shall be constructed with sufficient clearance for blade-type operating handles.

(2) Mirror(s). Each resident hand-washing station shall have a mirror. Mirror placement shall allow for convenient use by both wheelchair occupants and ambulatory persons. Tops and bottoms may be at levels usable by individuals either sitting or standing, or additional mirrors may be provided for wheelchair occupants. One separate full-length mirror may serve for wheelchair occupants.

(3) Hand drying. Provisions for hand drying shall be included at all hand-washing stations. These shall be paper or cloth towels enclosed to protect against dust or soil and to ensure single-unit dispensing.

8.2.2.8 Grab bars

(1) Grab bars shall be installed in all resident toilets, showers, tubs, and sitz baths.

*(2) For wall-mounted grab bars, a minimum 1-1/2 inch (3.81 centimeters) clearance from walls shall be provided.

(3) Bars, including those which are part of fixtures such as soap dishes, shall have the strength to sustain a concentrated load of 250 pounds (113.4 kilograms).

*(4) Toilets used by residents shall be provided sufficient clearance on both sides of the water closet to enable physical access and maneuvering by staff, who may have to assist the resident in wheelchair-to-water-closet transfers and return.

APPENDIX

A8.2.2.6 Where local requirements permit, wire-free, fire-rated safety glazing should be used to enhance the home-like residential appearance preferred by residents and visitors.

A8.2.2.8 (2) Consideration should be given to increasing clearances for arthritic residents.

A8.2.2.8 (4). While ADAAG, UFAS, and ANSI accessibility standards were all developed with the intention of providing greater access for individuals with disabilities, their standards are based upon assumed stature and strength, whereby dimensional and grab bar requirements are intended to facilitate wheelchair-to-toilet transfers by individuals with sufficient upper body strength and mobility to effect such a transfer. The typical nursing home resident is unlikely to have such capabilities, thus requiring the assistance of one or more staff. Insufficient clearance at the side of the toilet can restrict staff mobility and access, and can result in injury. There are ongoing efforts aimed at educating regulators and advisory panels to the difficulties caused by inappropriate standards required within environments serving frail and geriatric populations.

Alternative grab bar configurations should address the following scenarios:

a. When a resident is capable of independent transfer facilitated by the grab bar and side-wall location required by accessibility standards, a removable/temporary wall structure and grab bar can be installed alongside the toilet.

b. When a resident requires partial assistance in transfer, fold-down grab bars on one or both sides of the toilet would facilitate such transfers.

When independent transfers are feasible, alternative grab bar configurations shall be permitted.

8.2.2.9 Thresholds and joints. Thresholds and expansion joint covers shall be designed to facilitate use of wheelchairs and carts and to prevent tripping.

8.2.2.10 Anchorage. Lavatories, hand-washing stations, and handrails that a resident could use for support shall be securely anchored.

8.2.2.11 Insulation and ventilation. Rooms containing heat-producing equipment (such as boiler rooms, heater rooms, and laundries) shall be insulated and ventilated to prevent the floors of occupied areas overhead and the adjacent walls from exceeding a temperature of $10°F$ ($6°C$) above the ambient room temperature of such occupied areas.

8.2.3 Materials and Finishes
8.2.3.1 Floors

(1) Floor materials shall be readily cleanable and appropriate for the location.

(2) Floors in areas used for food preparation and assembly shall be water-resistant. Floor surfaces, including tile joints, shall be resistant to food acids.

(3) In all areas subject to frequent wet-cleaning methods, floor materials shall not be physically affected by germicidal cleaning solutions. Floors subject to traffic while wet (such as shower and bath areas, kitchens, and similar work areas) shall have a slip-resistant surface.

8.2.3.2 Walls

(1) Wall finishes shall be washable and, if near plumbing fixtures, shall be smooth and moisture-resistant.

(2) Wall bases in areas subject to routine wet cleaning shall be coved and tightly sealed.

(3) Wall construction, finish, and trim, as well as floor construction, in dietary and food storage areas shall be free from rodent- and insect-harboring spaces.

8.2.3.3 Penetrations and joints. Floor and wall openings for pipes, ducts, and conduits shall be tightly sealed to resist fire and smoke and to minimize entry of pests. Joints of structural elements shall be similarly sealed.

8.2.3.4 Ceilings

(1) The finishes of all exposed ceilings and ceiling structures in resident rooms and staff work areas shall be readily cleanable with routine housekeeping equipment.

(2) Finished ceilings shall be provided in dietary and other areas where dust fallout might create a problem.

8.2.3.5 Signage. Directional and identification signage shall comply with Americans with Disabilities Act (ADA) guidelines.

8.2.3.6 Furnishings

(1) Applicable standard. Materials provided for finishes and furnishings, including mattresses and upholstery, shall comply with NFPA 101.

(2) Carpet. Carpet and padding in resident areas shall be glued down or stretched taut and free of loose edges or wrinkles that might create hazards or interfere with the operation of wheelchairs, walkers, wheeled carts, etc.

(3) Drapery. Cubicle curtains and draperies shall be noncombustible or flame-retardant as prescribed in both the large- and small-scale tests in NFPA 701.

9 Special Systems

9.1 General

9.1.1 Testing
9.1.1.1 Prior to acceptance of the facility, all special systems shall be tested and operated to demonstrate to the owner or designated representative that the installation and performance of these systems conform to design intent.

9.1.1.2 Test results shall be documented for maintenance files.

9.1.2 Documentation

9.1.2.1 Upon completion of the special systems equipment installation contract, the owner shall be furnished with a complete set of manufacturers' operating, maintenance, and preventive maintenance instructions, a parts list, and complete procurement information, including equipment numbers and descriptions.

9.1.2.2 Operating staff shall also be provided with instructions for proper operation of systems and equipment. Required information shall include all safety or code ratings as needed.

9.1.3 Insulation

Insulation shall be provided surrounding special system equipment to conserve energy, protect personnel, and reduce noise.

9.2 Elevators

9.2.1 General

All buildings having resident use areas on more than one floor shall have electric or hydraulic elevator(s).

*9.2.2 Number

Engineered traffic studies are recommended, but in their absence the following guidelines for minimum number of elevators shall apply:

9.2.2.1 At least one elevator sized to accommodate a bed, gurney, and/or medical carts and wheelchair users shall be installed where residents are housed on any floor other than the main entrance floor.

9.2.2.2 At least two elevators, one of which shall be of the hospital type, shall be installed where 60 to 200 residents are housed on floors other than the main entrance floor.

9.2.2.3 At least three elevators, one of which shall be of the hospital type, shall be installed where 201 to 350 residents are housed on floors other than main entrance floor.

9.2.2.4 For facilities with more than 350 residents housed above the main entrance floor, the number of elevators shall be determined from a study of the facility plan and from the estimated vertical transportation requirements.

9.2.2.5 When the nursing facility is part of a general hospital, elevators may be shared and the standards of Section 2.1-9.2 shall apply.

9.2.3 Dimensions and Clearances

*9.2.3.1 Hospital-type elevator cars shall have inside dimensions that accommodate a resident bed with attendants. The clear inside dimension of such cars shall be at least 5 feet 4 inches (1.62 meters) wide by 8 feet 5 inches (2.43 meters) deep.

9.2.3.2 Car doors shall have a clear opening of not less than 3 feet 8 inches (1.12 meters).

9.2.3.3 Other elevators required for passenger service shall be constructed to accommodate wheelchairs.

9.2.4 Leveling Device

Elevators shall be equipped with an automatic two-way leveling device with an accuracy of ±1/4 inch (7 millimeters).

9.2.5 Handrails

Elevators shall have handrails on all sides without entrance door(s).

9.2.6 Installation and Testing

Installation and testing of elevators shall comply with ANSI/ASME A17.1 (for new construction) or ANSI/ASME 17.3 (for existing buildings). (See ASCE/SEI 7 for seismic design and control system requirements for elevators.)

9.3 Waste Processing

Facilities shall be provided for treatment or disposal of waste and recyclables using techniques and capacities acceptable to the appropriate health and environmental authorities.

APPENDIX

A9.2.2 These standards may be inadequate for moving large numbers of people in a short time; adjustments should be made as appropriate.

A9.2.3.1 Handrail projections of up to 3.5 inches (8.89 centimeters) should not be construed as diminishing the clear inside dimensions.

Note: For waste collection and storage requirements, see Section 4.1-6.3.

10 Building Systems

10.1 Plumbing

10.1.1 General
Unless otherwise specified herein, all plumbing systems shall be designed and installed in accordance with the International Plumbing Code.

10.1.2 Plumbing and Other Piping Systems
10.1.2.1 General piping and valves

(1) All piping, except control-line tubing, shall be identified.

(2) All valves shall be tagged, and a valve schedule shall be provided to the facility owner for permanent record and reference.

10.1.2.2 Hot water systems. See Section 1.6-2.1.2.1 and Table 4.1-3.

10.1.2.3 Potable water supply systems

(1) Capacity. Systems shall be designed to supply water at sufficient pressure to operate all fixtures and equipment during maximum demand. Supply capacity for hot- and cold-water piping shall be determined on the basis of fixture units, using recognized engineering standards. When the ratio of plumbing fixtures to occupants is proportionally more than required by the building occupancy and is in excess of 1,000 plumbing fixture units, a diversity factor shall be permitted.

(2) Valves. Each water service main, branch main, riser, and branch to a group of fixtures shall have valves.

 (a) Stop valves shall be provided for each fixture.

 (b) Appropriate panels for access shall be provided at all valves where required.

(3) Backflow prevention

 (a) Systems shall be protected against cross-connection in accordance with American Water Works Association (AWWA) Recommended Practice for Backflow Prevention and Cross-connection Control.

 (b) Vacuum breakers or backflow prevention devices shall be installed on hose bibs and supply nozzles used for connection of hoses or tubing in housekeeping sinks, bedpan-flushing attachments, etc.

(4) Potable water storage. Potable water storage vessels (hot and cold) not intended for constant use shall not be installed.

10.1.2.4 Drainage systems

(1) Piping. Insofar as possible, drainage piping shall not be installed within the ceiling or exposed in food preparation centers, food serving facilities, food storage areas, central services, electronic data processing areas, electric closets, and other sensitive areas. Where exposed overhead drain piping in these areas is unavoidable, special provisions shall be made to protect the space below from leakage, condensation, or dust particles.

(2) Sewers. Building sewers shall discharge into community sewerage. Where such a system is not available, the facility shall treat its sewage in accordance with local and state regulations.

(3) Grease traps. Kitchen grease traps shall be located and arranged to permit easy access.

10.1.3 Plumbing Fixtures
In addition to the requirements of Section 1.6-2.1.3, the following standards shall apply:

10.1.3.1 Clinical sinks. Clinical sinks shall have an integral trap wherein the upper portion of the water trap provides a visible seal.

10.1.4 Medical Gas and Vacuum Systems
Any installation of nonflammable medical gas, air, or clinical vacuum systems shall comply with the requirements of NFPA 99. When any piping or supply of medical gases is installed, altered, or augmented, the

altered zone shall be tested and certified as required by NFPA 99.

10.2 Heating, Ventilating, and Air-Conditioning (HVAC) Systems

10.2.1 General
10.2.1.1 Mechanical system design

(1) Efficiency. The mechanical system shall be subject to general review for operational efficiency and appropriate life-cycle cost. Details for cost-effective implementation of design features are interrelated and too numerous (as well as too basic) to list individually.

    (a) Recognized engineering procedures shall be followed for the most economical and effective results. A well-designed system can generally achieve energy efficiency with minimal additional cost and simultaneously provide improved resident comfort.

    (b) In no case shall resident care or safety be sacrificed for conservation.

    (c) Facility design consideration shall include site, building mass, orientation, configuration, fenestration, and other features relative to passive and active energy systems.

(2) Air-handling systems

    (a) Where appropriate, controls for air-handling systems shall be designed with an economizer cycle that uses outside air to reduce heating and cooling system loads. Innovative design that provides for additional energy conservation while meeting the intent of these standards for acceptable resident care shall be considered. (Filtering will be necessary when outside air is used as part of the mechanical ventilation system.)

    *(b) Non-central air-handling systems (i.e., individual room units that are used for heating and cooling purposes, such as fan-coil units, heat pump units, etc.). These units may be used as recirculating units only. All outdoor air requirements shall be met by a separate central air-handling system with the proper filtration, as noted in Table 4.1-2.

(3) System valves. Supply and return mains and risers for cooling, heating, and steam systems shall be equipped with valves to isolate the various sections of each system. Each piece of equipment shall have valves at the supply and return ends.

(4) Renovation. If system modifications affect greater than 10 percent of the system capacity, designers shall utilize pre-renovation water/air flow rate

measurements to verify that sufficient capacity is available and that renovations have not adversely affected flow rates in non-renovation areas.

10.2.1.2 Ventilation and space conditioning requirements. All rooms and areas in the facility shall have provision for positive ventilation.

(1) Ventilation rates. The ventilation systems shall be designed and balanced, as a minimum, according to the requirements shown in Table 4.1-1. The ventilation rates shown in Table 4.1-1 do not preclude the use of higher rates as appropriate.

*(2) Temperature and humidity. Space temperature and relative humidity shall be as indicated in Table 4.1-1.

(3) Air movement direction. To maintain asepsis control, airflow supply and exhaust should generally be controlled to ensure movement of air from "clean" to "less clean" areas.

(4) Although use of natural window ventilation shall be permitted when weather and outside air quality permit, mechanical ventilation shall be provided for all rooms and areas in the facility.

10.2.2 Requirements for Specific Locations
10.2.2.1 Food preparation centers

(1) Exhaust hoods handling grease-laden vapors in food preparation centers shall comply with NFPA 96.

(2) All hoods over cooking ranges shall be equipped with grease filters, fire-extinguishing systems, and heat-actuated fan controls.

(3) Cleanout openings shall be provided every 20 feet (6.10 meters) and at changes in direction in the horizontal exhaust duct systems serving these hoods. Horizontal runs of ducts serving range hoods shall be kept to a minimum.

(4) Food preparation facilities shall have ventilation systems whose air supply mechanisms are interfaced appropriately with exhaust hood controls or relief vents so that exfiltration or infiltration to or from exit corridors does not compromise the exit

corridor restrictions of NFPA 90A, the pressure requirements of NFPA 96, or the maximum defined in Table 4.1-1.

10.2.2.2 Fuel-fired equipment rooms. Rooms with fuel-fired equipment shall be provided with sufficient outdoor air to maintain equipment combustion rates and to limit workstation temperatures.

10.2.3 Thermal and Acoustical Insulation
In addition to the requirements of Section 1.6-2.2.1, the following requirement shall apply:

10.2.3.1 In facilities undergoing major renovations, existing accessible insulation shall be inspected, repaired, and/or replaced as appropriate.

10.2.4 HVAC Air Distribution
10.2.4.1 HVAC ductwork. See Section 1.6-2.2.2.1.

10.2.4.2 Exhaust systems

(1) To enhance the efficiency of recovery devices required for energy conservation, combined exhaust systems shall be permitted.

(2) Fans serving exhaust systems shall be located at the discharge end and shall be readily serviceable.

10.2.4.3 Air outlets and inlets

(1) Fresh air intakes

(a) Fresh air intakes shall be located at least 25 feet (7.62 meters) from exhaust outlets of ventilating systems, combustion equipment stacks, medical vacuum systems, plumbing vents, or areas that may collect vehicular exhaust or other noxious fumes. (Prevailing winds and/or proximity to other structures may require greater clearances.)

(b) The bottom of outdoor air intakes serving central ventilating systems shall be as high as practical, but at least 6 feet (1.83 meters) above ground level or, if installed above the roof, 3 feet (91.44 centimeters) above roof level.

(2) Exhaust outlets. Exhaust outlets from areas that may be contaminated shall be above roof level, arranged to minimize recirculation of exhaust air into the building.

10.2.5 HVAC Filters
10.2.5.1 Filter efficiencies

(1) All central ventilation or air conditioning systems shall be equipped with filters with efficiencies equal to, or greater than, those specified in Table 4.1-2.

(2) Noncentral air-handling systems shall be equipped with permanent (cleanable) or replaceable filters rated at a minimum efficiency of MERV 3 (68 percent arrestance). These units may be used as recirculating units only.

(3) Filter efficiencies, tested in accordance with ASHRAE Standard 52.1, shall be average.

10.2.5.2 Filter frames

(1) Filter frames shall be durable and proportioned to provide an airtight fit with the enclosing ductwork. All joints between filter segments and the enclosing ductwork shall have gaskets or seals to provide a positive seal against air leakage.

(2) Provisions shall be made to allow access for field testing.

10.2.6 Steam and Hot Water Systems
10.2.6.1 Boilers. See Section 1.6-2.2.3.

10.3 Electrical Systems

10.3.1 General
10.3.1.1 Applicable standards

(1) All material and equipment, including conductors, controls, and signaling devices, shall be installed to provide a complete electrical system in accordance with NFPA 70 and NFPA 99.

(2) Electrical systems for nursing facilities shall comply with applicable sections of NFPA 70.

10.3.1.2 Testing and documentation. All electrical installations and systems shall be tested to verify that the equipment has been installed and that it operates as designed.

10.3.2 Electrical Requirements for Specific Nursing Facility Locations
10.3.2.1 Ventilator-dependent resident bedrooms

(1) Dedicated circuit(s). This paragraph shall apply to both new and existing facilities serving ventilator-dependent patients.

  (a) A minimum of one dedicated essential system circuit per bed for ventilator-dependent patients shall be provided in addition to the normal system receptacle at each bed location required by NFPA 70. This circuit shall be provided with a minimum of two duplex receptacles identified for emergency use.

  (b) Additional essential system circuits/receptacles shall be provided where the electrical life support needs of the patient exceed the minimum requirements stated in this paragraph.

(2) Essential electrical system connections

  (a) Heating equipment provided for ventilator-dependent patient bedrooms shall be connected to the essential electrical system. This paragraph shall apply to both new and existing facilities.

  (b) Task lighting connected to the essential electrical system shall be provided for each ventilator-dependent patient bedroom. This paragraph shall apply to both new and existing facilities.

10.3.3 Power-Generating and Storing Equipment
10.3.3.1 Emergency electrical service

(1) Applicable standards. At a minimum, nursing facilities or sections thereof shall have emergency electrical systems as required in NFPA 101 and Chapter 16, Nursing Home Requirements, of NFPA 99.

(2) Shared service. When the nursing facility is a distinct part of an acute care hospital, it may use the emergency generator system for required emergency

lighting and power if such sharing does not reduce hospital services. Life support systems and their respective areas shall be subject to applicable standards of Section 2.1-10.3.

(3) Lighting. An emergency electrical source shall provide lighting and/or power during an interruption of the normal electrical supply.

(4) Stored fuel

(a) Where stored fuel is required, storage capacity shall permit continuous operation for at least 24 hours.

(b) Fuel storage for electricity generation shall be separate from heating fuels.

(c) If the use of heating fuel for diesel engines is considered after the required 24-hour supply has been exhausted, positive valving and filtration shall be provided to avoid entry of water and/or contaminants.

10.3.3.2 Generators. Exhaust systems (including loca-

tions, mufflers, and vibration isolators) for internal combustion engines shall be designed and installed to minimize objectionable noise. Where a generator is routinely used to reduce peak loads, protection of patient areas from excessive noise may become a critical issue.

10.3.4 Lighting
10.3.4.1 General

(1) Lighting shall be engineered to the specific application. Unless alternative lighting levels are justified by the approved functional program, Table 4.1-4 shall be used as a guide to minimum required ambient and task lighting levels in all rooms, spaces, and exterior walkways.

(2) Recommended lighting design practices, including minimum lighting levels for nursing facilities and other senior living environments, developed by the Illuminating Engineering Society of North America (IESNA) shall be considered. Refer to ANSI/IESNA RP-28, Lighting and the Visual Environment for Senior Living.

*(3) Approaches to buildings and parking lots, and all

APPENDIX

A10.3.4.1 (3)

a. Excessive differences in lighting levels should be avoided in transition areas between parking lots, building entrances and lobbies or corridors, in transition zones between driveways and parking garages, etc. As the eye ages, pupils become smaller and less elastic, making visual adaptation to dark spaces slower. Upon entering a space with a considerably lower lighting level, elderly residents may need to stop or move to one side until their eyes adapt to excessive lighting changes. Elderly pedestrians may need several minutes to adjust to significant changes in brightness when entering a building from a sunlit walkway or terrace.

b. Consideration should be given to increasing both indoor and outdoor illumination levels in such transition spaces to avoid excessive differences between electric lighting levels and natural daytime and nighttime illumination levels. In addition, it is very helpful for pedestrians to have conveniently located places to wait, giving them time to adjust their eyes to different lighting environments. Seating areas off busy lobbies or corridors can minimize the potential for accidents by giving them the time they need.

c. Care should be taken to minimize extremes of brightness within spaces and in transitions between spaces. Excessive brightness contrast from windows or lighting systems can disorient residents.

d. Research has established that older adults sleep best in total darkness. Therefore, to minimize resident sleep disruption, night lights should (1) provide very low levels of illumination; (2) be located so as to minimize light scatter and reflections on room surfaces; and (3) be switched off when not needed. However, even when properly specified, located, and operated, night lights often disturb resident sleep. Therefore, many providers prefer to have staff wear portable light sources instead of using night lights that were installed primarily to satisfy a code requirement.

e. Lighting that creates glare and colors that do not differentiate between horizontal and vertical planes, or between objects and their backgrounds (such as handrails or light switches from walls, hardware from doors, faucets from sinks, or control knobs from appliances) should be avoided, unless therapeutic benefits can be demonstrated. (For example, it has been demonstrated that deliberately camouflaged door hardware may help control wandering and elopements by some cognitively impaired residents in Alzheimer's care facilities.)

occupied spaces within buildings, shall have fixtures for lighting. Consideration shall be given to both the quantity and quality of lighting, including the following:

(a) Even and consistent lighting levels

(b) Glare control

(c) Special lighting needs of the elderly

(d) Area-specific lighting solutions

(e) Use of daylighting in all resident rooms and resident use areas

(f) Life-cycle costs of lighting

(g) Other lighting design practices as defined and described in ANSI/IESNA RP-28

10.3.4.2 Lighting requirements for specific locations

*(1) Resident rooms. Resident rooms and toilet rooms shall have general lighting, task lighting, and night lighting.

A10.3.4.2 (1)

a. Care should be taken to avoid injury from lighting fixtures. Light sources that may burn residents or ignite bed linen by direct contact should be covered or protected.

b. Ambient light levels are determined on a horizontal plane above the floor. The use of this method in the types of areas described should result in values of average illuminance within 10 percent of the values that would be obtained by dividing the area into 2-foot (0.6-meter) squares, taking a reading in each square, and averaging.

c. The measuring instrument should be positioned so that when readings are taken, the surface of the light-sensitive cell is in a horizontal plane and 30 inches (760 millimeters) above the floor. This can be facilitated by means of a small portable stand of wood or other material that will support the cell at the correct height and in the proper plane. Daylight may be excluded during illuminance measurements. Readings can be taken at night or with shades, blinds, or other opaque covering on the fenestration.

(a) At least one task light shall be provided for each resident.

(b) Task light controls shall be readily accessible to residents.

(c) At least one low-level night light fixture in each room shall be located close to the floor and controlled at the room entrance. When the approved functional program stipulates staff shall use portable light sources, omission of night lights in resident rooms shall be permitted.

(d) All light controls in resident areas shall be quiet-operating.

(2) Resident unit corridors

(a) Resident unit corridors shall have general illumination with provisions for reducing light levels at night. Corridors and common areas used by residents shall have even light distribution to avoid glare, shadows, and scalloped lighting effects.

(b) Highly polished flooring or floors with glossy sheen shall not be used.

10.3.5 Receptacles
Receptacles (convenience outlets) shall be provided as follows:

10.3.5.1 Receptacles in resident rooms. Each resident room shall have duplex-grounded receptacles. There shall be one at each side of the head of each bed and one on every other wall. Receptacles may be omitted from exterior walls where construction makes installation impractical.

10.3.5.2 Receptacles in corridors. Duplex-grounded receptacles for general use shall be installed approximately 50 feet (15.24 meters) apart in all corridors and within 25 feet (7.62 meters) of corridor ends.

10.3.5.3 Emergency system receptacles. Electrical receptacle coverplates or electrical receptacles supplied from the emergency system shall be distinctively colored or marked for identification. If color is used for identification purposes, the same color shall be used throughout the facility.

10.3.5.4 Ground fault interrupters. Ground fault interrupters shall comply with NFPA 70.

10.3.6 Call System
A nurse/staff call system shall be provided.

10.3.6.1 General. Alternate technologies may be considered for emergency or nurse call systems. If radio frequency systems are used, consideration shall be given to electromagnetic compatibility between internal and external sources.

10.3.6.2 Patient room call station

(1) Each bed location and/or resident shall be provided with a call device. Two call devices serving adjacent beds or residents may be served by one calling station.

(2) Calls shall be initiated by a resident activating either a call device attached to a resident's call station or a portable device that sends a call signal to the call station and shall either:

    (a) Activate a visual signal in the corridor at the resident's door or other appropriate location. In multi-corridor or cluster resident units, additional visual signals shall be installed at corridor intersections; or

    (b) Activate a pager worn by a staff member, identifying the specific resident and/or room from which the call has been placed.

10.3.6.3 Emergency call system. An emergency call system shall be provided at each resident toilet, bath, sitz bath, and shower room.

(1) This system shall be accessible to a resident lying on the floor. Inclusion of a pull cord or portable radio frequency pushbutton will satisfy this standard.

(2) The emergency call system shall be designed so that a call activated by a resident will initiate a signal distinct from the regular staff call system and that can be turned off only at the resident's location.

(3) The signal shall activate an annunciator panel or screen at the staff work area or other appropriate location and at other areas defined by the functional program. In addition, the signal shall activate either a visual signal in the corridor at the resident's door or other appropriate location or a staff pager indicating the calling resident's name and/or room location.

10.4 Communications Systems

10.4.1 Telecommunication and Information Systems
10.4.1.1 Locations for terminating telecommunications and information system devices shall be provided.

10.4.1.2 A space shall be provided for central equipment locations. Special air conditioning and voltage regulation shall be provided when recommended by the manufacturer.

10.5 Electronic Safety and Security

10.5.1 Fire Alarm System
Fire alarm and detection systems shall be provided in compliance with NFPA 101 and NFPA 72.

Table 4.1-1
Ventilation Requirements for Areas Affecting Resident Care in Nursing Facilities[1]

Area designation	Air movement relationship to adjacent area[2]	Minimum air changes of outdoor air per hour[3]	Minimum total air changes per hour[4]	All air exhausted directly to outdoors[5]	Recirculated by means of room units[6]	Relative humidity[7] (%)	Design temperature[8] (degrees F/C)
RESIDENT UNITS							
Resident room	–	2	2	–	–	—[7]	70-75 (21–24)
Resident unit corridor	–	–	4	–	–	—[7]	—
Resident gathering areas	–	4	4	–	–	–	—
Toilet room	In	–	10	Yes	No	–	–
RESIDENT LIVING AREAS							
Dining rooms	–	2	4	–	–	–	75
Activity rooms, if provided	–	4	6	–	–	–	—
Personal services (barber/beauty)	In	2	20	Yes	No	—	—
DIAGNOSTIC AND TREATMENT LOCATIONS							
Physical therapy	In	2	6	–	–	–	75 (24)
Occupational therapy	In	2	6	–	–	–	75 (24)
SUPPORT AREAS							
Soiled workroom or soiled holding	In	2	10	Yes	No	—	—
Clean workroom or clean holding	Out	2	4	–	–	(Max) 70	75 (24)
Bathing rooms	In	–	10	Yes	No	—	75 (24)
SERVICE AREAS							
Sterilizer exhaust room	In	–	10	Yes	No	–	–
Linen and trash chute room, if provided	In	–	10	Yes	No	–	–
Laundry, general, if provided	–	2	10	Yes	No	–	–
Soiled linen sorting and storage	In	–	10	Yes	No	–	–
Clean linen storage	Out	–	2	Yes	No	–	–
Food preparation facilities[9]	–	2	10	Yes	Yes	–	–
Dietary warewashing	In	–	10	Yes	Yes	–	–
Dietary storage areas	–	–	2	Yes	No	–	–
Housekeeping rooms	In	–	10	Yes	No	–	–

[1] The ventilation rates in this table cover ventilation for comfort, as well as for asepsis and odor control in areas of nursing facilities that directly affect resident care and are determined based on nursing facilities being predominantly "no smoking" facilities. Where smoking may be allowed, ventilation rates will need adjustments. Areas where specific ventilation rates are not given in the table shall be ventilated in accordance with ASHRAE Standard 62, Ventilation for Acceptable Indoor Air Quality, and *ASHRAE Handbook—HVAC Applications.* Occupational Health and Safety Administration standards and/or National Institute for Occupational Safety and Health criteria require special ventilation requirements for employee health and safety within nursing facilities.

[2] Design of the ventilation system shall, insofar as possible, provide that air movement is from "clean to less clean" areas. However, continuous compliance may be impractical with full utilization of some forms of variable air volume and load-shedding systems that may be used for energy conservation. Areas that do require positive and continuous control are noted with "Out" or "In" to indicate the required direction of air movement in relation to the space named. Rate of air movement may, of course, be varied as needed within the limits required for positive control. Where indication of air movement direction is enclosed in parentheses, continuous directional control is required only when the specialized equipment or device is in use or where room use may otherwise compromise the intent of movement from clean to less clean. Air movement for rooms with dashes and nonpatient areas may vary as necessary to satisfy the requirements of those spaces. Additional adjustments may be needed when space is unused or unoccupied and air systems are de-energized or reduced.

[3] To satisfy exhaust needs, replacement air from outside is necessary. Table 4.1-1 does not attempt to describe specific amounts of outside air to be supplied to individual spaces except for certain areas such as those listed. Distribution of the outside air, added to the system to balance required exhaust, shall be as required by good engineering practice.

[4] Number of air changes may be reduced when the room is unoccupied if provisions are made to ensure that the number of air changes indicated is reestablished any time the space is being utilized. Adjustments shall include provisions so that the direction of air movement shall remain the same when the number of air changes is reduced. Areas not indicated as having continuous directional control may have ventilation systems shut down when space is unoccupied and ventilation is not otherwise needed.

[5] Air from areas with contamination and/or odor problems shall be exhausted to the outside and not recirculated to other areas. Note that individual circumstances may require special consideration for air exhaust to outside.

[6] Because of cleaning difficulty and potential for buildup of contamination, recirculating room units shall not be used in areas marked "No." Isolation rooms may be ventilated by reheat induction units in which only the primary air supplied from a central system passes through the reheat unit. Gravity-type heating or cooling units such as radiators or convectors shall not be used in special care areas.

[7] See 4.1-A10.2.1.2 (2) for additional information.

[8] Where temperature ranges are indicated, the systems shall be capable of maintaining the rooms at any point within the range. A single figure indicates a heating or cooling capacity of at least the indicated temperature. This is usually applicable where residents may be undressed and require a warmer environment. Nothing in these Guidelines shall be construed as precluding the use of temperatures lower than those noted when the residents' comfort and medical conditions make lower temperatures desirable. Unoccupied areas such as storage rooms shall have temperatures appropriate for the function intended.

Table 4.1-2

Filter Efficiencies for Central Ventilation and Air-Conditioning Systems in Nursing Facilities

Area designation	Minimum number of filter beds	Filter efficiencies in MERV (%)	
		Filter bed no. 1	Filter bed no. 2
All areas for resident care, treatment, and/or diagnosis, and those areas providing direct service or clean supplies	2	7 (30%)	13 (80%)
Administrative, bulk storage, soiled holding, laundries, food preparation areas	1	7 (30%)	

Notes

1. MERV = minimum efficiency reporting value. MERVs are based on ASHRAE 52.2.

2. The filtration efficiency ratings are based on average dust spot efficiency per ASHRAE 52.1.

Table 4.1-3

Hot Water Use—Nursing Facilities

	Resident care areas	Dietary	Laundry
Liters per hour per bed[1]	11.9	7.2	7.6
Gallons per hour per bed[1]	3	2	2
Temperature (°Centigrade)	35-43[2]	60[3]	60[4]
Temperature (°Fahrenheit)	95-110[2]	140 (min.)[3]	140 (min.)[4]

[1] Quantities indicated for design demand of hot water are for general reference minimums and shall not substitute for accepted engineering design procedures using actual number and types of fixtures to be installed. Design will also be affected by temperatures of cold water used for mixing, length of run and insulation relative to heat loss, etc. As an example, total quantity of hot water needed will be less when temperature available at the outlet is very nearly that of the source tank and the cold water used for tempering is relatively warm.

[2] The range represents the maximum and minimum allowable temperatures.

[3] Provisions shall be made to provide 180°F (82°C) rinse water at warewasher (may be by separate booster) unless a chemical rinse is provided.

[4] Provisions shall be made to provide 160°F (71°C) hot water at the laundry equipment when needed. (This may be by steam jet or separate booster heater.) However, it is emphasized that this does not imply that all water used would be at this temperature. Water temperatures required for acceptable laundry results will vary according to type of cycle, time of operation, and formula of soap and bleach as well as type and degree of soil. Lower temperatures may be adequate for most procedures in many facilities but higher temperatures should be available when needed for special conditions. Minimum laundry temperatures are for central laundries only.

Table 4.1-4
Minimum Maintained Average Illuminance

	Ambient Light in		Task Light in	
	Lux	Footcandles	Lux	Footcandles
Exterior entrance (night)	100	10		
Interior entry (day)[1]	1000	100		
Interior entry (night)	100	10		
Exit stairways and landings	300	30		
Elevator interiors	300	30		
Parking garage entrance	500	50		
Exterior walkways	50	5		
Administration (active hours)	300	30	500	50
Active areas (day only)	300	30	500	50
Visitor waiting (day)	300	30		
Visitor waiting (night)	100	10		
Resident room				
Entrance	300	30		
Living room	300	30	750	75
Bedroom	300	30	750	75
Wardrobe/closet	300	30		
Bathroom	300	30		
Makeup/shaving area	300	30	600	60
Shower/bathing rooms	300	30		
Kitchen area	300	30	500	50
Barber/beautician (day)	500	50		
Chapel or quiet area (active hours))	300	30		
Hallways (active hours)	300	30		
Hallways (sleeping hours)	100	10		
Dining (active hours)	500	50		
Medicine preparation	300	30	1000	100
Nurse station (day)	300	30	500	50
Nurse station (night)	100	10	500	50
Physical therapy area (active hours)	300	30	500	50
Occupational therapy (active hours)	300	30	500	50
Examination room (dedicated)	300	30	1000	100
Janitor's closet	300	30		
Laundry (active hours)	300	30	500	50
Clean/soiled utility	300	30		
Commercial kitchen	500	50	1000	100
Food storage (nonrefrigerated)	300	30		
Staff toilet area	200	20	600	60

[1] Use of daylight is encouraged in entryways to provide a transition between outside and inside illumination levels.

Notes
1. Ambient light levels are minimum averages measured at 76 cm (30 in.) above the floor in a horizontal plane. Task light levels are absolute minimums taken on the visual task. For makeup/shaving, the measurement is to be taken on the face in a vertical position.
2. It should be understood that the values listed are minimums. The optimum solution for task lighting is to give users control over the intensity and positioning of the light source to meet their individual needs.

Reproduced with permission from ANSI/IESNA RP-28-01, *Recommended Practice for Lighting and the Visual Environment for Senior Living*.

4.2 Hospice Facilities

Appendix material, which appears in shaded boxes at the bottom of the page, is advisory only.

Hospice care is a medically directed, interdisciplinary program of palliative care and services for terminally ill individuals and their family members or significant others.

Hospice care supports terminally ill persons through the dying process with a focus on maintaining dignity and quality of life while providing palliation or controlling unpleasant symptoms to the extent possible. Hospice care is provided by a team of professionals that may include nurses, social workers, certified nursing assistants, dietitians, therapists, volunteers, and clergy, as well as physicians who may visit on a scheduled basis or in response to a crisis. No curative interventions are used.

Inpatient hospices are part of a continuum of palliative care. They have been developed as new facilities and through renovation.

1 General Considerations

1.1 Applicability
This chapter shall apply to inpatient freestanding hospices. At the discretion of the authority having jurisdiction, the design concepts presented herein shall be permitted to be applied to a hospice located in other health care facilities.

1.2 Auxiliary Services
See Section 4.1-1.2.

1.3 Environment of Care
See Section 4.1-1.3.

1.4 Functional Program
See Section 4.1-1.4.

1.5 Shared Services
See Section 4.1-1.5.

1.6 Site

1.6.1 Location
See Section 4.1-1.6.1.

1.6.2 Roads
See Section 4.1-1.6.2.

1.6.3 Parking
See Section 4.1-1.6.3.

1.7 Renovation
See Section 1.1-3.

1.8 Provision for Disasters
See Section 1.1-5.

1.9 Codes and Standards
See Section 1.1-7.

1.10 Equipment
See Chapter 1.4.

1.11 Planning, Design, and Construction
See Chapter 1.5.

1.12 Record Drawings and Manuals
See Section 1.5-5.

2 Hospice Unit(s)

Each facility shall comply with the following:

*2.1 Unit Size
In the absence of local requirements, consideration shall be given to restricting the size of the care unit to 25 beds.

APPENDIX

A2.1 Overwhelming fatigue is the most predominant complaint of hospice residents. Use of assistive devices is often humiliating for residents. Arranging groups of resident rooms adjacent to decentralized service areas, optional satellite staff work areas, and optional decentralized resident support areas is desirable.

2.2 Resident Rooms
Each resident room shall meet the following requirements:

2.2.1 Capacity
Maximum room occupancy shall be one resident unless justified by the functional program and approved by the licensing authority. In no case shall bedrooms exceed two resident beds. See Section 4.1-2.2.

2.2.2 Space Requirements
Room size shall be based on the program of care, distinctive in-room furniture, and clothing storage requirements.

2.2.2.1 If consistent with the functional program, accommodation for dining shall be provided in the resident room.

2.2.2.2 Seating for visitors, with provision for at least one sleeping accommodation in resident rooms, shall be provided.

2.2.2.3 Access shall be provided to both sides of the resident bed.

*2.2.3 Windows
See Section 4.1-6.3.3.

2.2.4 Resident Privacy
See Section 4.1-2.2.5.

2.2.5 Hand-Washing Station
See Section 4.1-2.2.6.

2.2.6 Toilet Room
See Section 4.1-2.2.7.

2.2.7 Resident Storage
See Section 4.1-2.2.8.

2.2.8 Safety
See Section 4.1-3.2.1.

2.3 Airborne Infection Isolation Room(s)
The need for and number of required airborne infection isolation room(s) shall be determined by an infection control risk assessment. Where required, the airborne infection isolation room(s) shall comply with the general requirements of Section 2.1-3.2.2.

2.4 Support Areas for Hospice Units
Support areas shall be provided according to Sections 4.1-2.3 through 4.1-2.6 when required by the functional program.

3 Resident Living Areas

3.1 Resident Kitchen and Dining Areas
See Section 4.1-4.1. Where locally allowed, residential "homelike" kitchen and dining facilities shall be permitted to accommodate residents and their visitors.

3.2 Personal Services (Barber/Beauty) Areas
If these services are required by the functional program, see Section 4.1-4.3.

*3.3 Outdoor Spaces
Outdoor areas shall be available for residents.

4 Diagnostic and Treatment Locations

4.1 Therapy
If these services are required by the functional program to maximize current levels of function, see Section 4.1-5.1.

5 Service Areas

5.1 Dietary Facilities
The following facilities shall be provided:

APPENDIX

A2.2.3 Exterior windows should provide views to the natural environment and light when possible. Residents who are confined to their beds need a venue for visual stimulation. Plantings and other attempts to provide objects of visual interest should be made when exterior views of the natural environment are not possible due to existing building adjacencies.

A3.3 Due to the significant benefits of the natural environment, consideration should be given to providing access to the outdoors. Accessible outdoor space can provide a calming change in environment and also a convenient place for agitated or anxious patients to walk. Furthermore, gardens symbolize the full cycle of life and death and can be a source of serenity and spiritual calm.

5.1.1 Food Preparation Facilities

5.1.1.1 If food preparation is provided on site, the facility shall dedicate space and equipment for the preparation of meals.

5.1.1.2 The physical environment for food service and food service equipment shall comply with locally adopted food and sanitary regulations.

5.1.2 Ice-Making Facilities

These may be located in the food preparation area or in a separate room and shall be easily cleanable and convenient to the dietary function.

5.1.2.1 Ice-making facilities shall be self-dispensing if available for use by residents and/or visitors.

5.1.2.2 Ice-making facilities under the control of the dietary staff and not available for use by residents and/or visitors may be bin type or self-dispensing.

5.1.3 Distribution

Provision shall be made for transport of hot and cold foods, as required by the functional program.

5.1.4 Dining Areas

5.1.4.1 The design and location of dining facilities shall encourage resident use.

5.1.4.2 Separate dining areas shall be provided for staff and residents.

6 Construction Standards

6.1 General Standards for Details and Finishes

6.1.1 Doors
See Section 4.1-8.2.2.3.

6.1.2 Grab Bars
See Section 4.1-8.2.2.8.

7 Building Systems

7.1 Plumbing
See Section 4.1-10.1.

7.2 Heating, Ventilating, and Air-Conditioning (HVAC) Systems
See Section 4.1-10.2.

7.3 Electrical Systems
See Section 4.1-10.3.

7.4 Telecommunication and Information Systems
See Section 4.1-10.4.

7.5 Fire Alarm System
See Section 4.1-10.5.

4.3 Assisted Living

Appendix material, which appears in shaded boxes at the bottom of the page, is advisory only.

*1 General Considerations

1.1 Applicability

1.1.1 Continuum of Care
For the purposes of this chapter, assisted living facilities are a vital and growing component of the continuum of care, providing a supportive residential environment for consumer-directed services.

1.1.2 Minimum Standards for New Facilities
1.1.2.1 This chapter acknowledges that the many resident-driven variations of assisted living facilities that can be found represent the programmatic needs and preferences of the individuals who choose to live in them. Therefore, the requirements and recommendations contained herein are intended to represent base-level standards that will ensure the safety, accessibility, and residential aspects of all assisted living facilities.

1.1.2.2 This chapter identifies the minimum requirements for assisted living facilities and recognizes various configurations of assisted living facilities, which must comply with applicable state and local requirements. Acknowledging that occupancy and building construction requirements vary among jurisdictions,

it is the intent of this chapter to establish minimal standards for safety and accessibility for a residential care environment, regardless of facility scope and scale. The common goal of this chapter and individual local and state requirements is to facilitate accountability as well as protection of the consumer.

1.2 Functional Program
The sponsor of each project shall provide a functional program that defines the scope and scale of the facility, facilitates the application of licensure and occupancy approvals by authorities having jurisdiction, and addresses applicability provisions of this chapter. See Section 1.2-2 for additional information.

1.3 Environment of Care
See Chapter 1.2 for general requirements.

1.3.1 Supportive Environment
1.3.1.1 Assisted living facilities are unique in that services provided are in large part driven by the service needs and lifestyle preferences of the residents being served. The architectural environment shall support these services and levels of care provided within the facility.

1.3.1.2 Assisted living facilities shall be designed and constructed to provide a supportive residential environment that is conducive to day-to-day activities consistent with the cultural, emotional, and spiritual needs of the individuals who need assistance. This supportive environment shall promote independence, privacy, and dignity; balance autonomy with safety; and provide choice for all residents in a manner that encourages family and community involvement.

1.3.2 Barrier-Free Environment
The architectural environment shall eliminate as many barriers as possible to effective access and use of the space, services, equipment, and utilities appropriate for daily living.

1.4 Auxiliary Services
Services such as home health, hospice, dietary, storage,

APPENDIX

A1 Assisted living facilities can be very different from one state to another and within each state. In some states, the building itself is not licensed; rather, the entity that provides services is licensed. In addition, the design of assisted living facilities varies, taking into consideration cultural, geographic, socioeconomic, and ethnic differences.

Assisted living facilities provide care for individuals who may need or desire assistance with medications and activities of daily living (e.g., eating, bathing, dressing, toileting, and ambulating). Some facilities care only for people requiring minimal assistance, while others may offer more intensive services, including dementia-specific care. The design and construction of assisted living facilities, as much as possible, should reflect the needs and preferences of the individuals who reside in the facility.

---

pharmacy, linen, and laundry in accordance with the functional program may be contractually provided or shared insofar as practical with other licensed or unlicensed entities.

1.5 Shared Services
When a facility shares or purchases services, appropriate modifications or deletions in space and parking requirements shall be permitted.

APPENDIX

A1.9 Codes and Standards

a. Appropriate code. There has been a great deal of discussion about which building code or life safety code is appropriate for the design and construction of assisted living facilities. Facilities serving similar resident groups and providing similar services are considered residential occupancies in some jurisdictions and institutional occupancies in others.

The model codes do not adequately recognize the unique nature of assisted living as a distinct occupancy classification. Institutional codes place overly restrictive and costly requirements on facility construction. Residential codes, however, may not require adequate protection.

b. Residential construction type. To provide the flexibility needed to serve residents whose physical and mental capabilities may change over time, to eliminate the requirement for authorities having jurisdiction to continually monitor the evacuation capabilities of residents within assisted living facilities, and to provide additional protection for facilities occupied by physically and mentally frail occupants who may require physical assistance from others, use of a "Residential Plus" construction type is recommended for assisted living facilities with 24-hour staff. A "Residential Plus" occupancy allows use of residential construction, with the addition of several technological and institutional requirements. These additional requirements provide for prompt detection, notification, and suppression of fire within a facility and allow use of a "defend-in-place" approach that minimizes the need for evacuation of occupants.

c. Safety features. Assisted living facilities utilizing residential occupancy and construction types should be permitted with the addition of the following safety features:

Protection of the facilities throughout with a supervised automatic fire suppression system with quick-response sprinklers in smoke compartments containing sleeping rooms. Automatic fire suppression systems in facilities with more than 16 occupants should be installed in accordance with NFPA 13.

Smoke barriers subdividing every story into at least two smoke compartments. Such smoke compartments should be not more than 22,500 square feet (6,858 square meters), and the travel distance from any point in each smoke compartment to a smoke barrier door should not exceed 200 feet (61 meters).

d. Resident waiting areas. The therapeutic and programmatic benefits of providing waiting areas and similar spaces open to the corridor have long been recognized within long-term care facilities. Spaces open to the corridor significantly enhance resident mobility and accessibility to programs, encouraging resident participation.

Spaces open to corridors should be allowed within assisted living facilities utilizing residential occupancy and construction types where the following criteria are met:

The spaces are not used as sleeping rooms or hazardous or incidental use areas, and the space is arranged so access to required exits is not obstructed.

The corridors and areas open to corridors are equipped with quick response sprinklers and an automatic smoke detection system, which automatically notifies emergency forces.

e. Programmatic considerations may call for the control of egress from some facilities or portions of facilities. Where such egress control is desired, the following should be followed:

The means of egress should not be locked except when clinical reasons are well documented and when such egress control is not a substitute for appropriate staffing.

When the means of egress is locked, a keyed or electronically released locking device must automatically open upon activation of the fire alarm system or loss of power.

No device operation sign should be posted when 24-hour awake and trained staff supervises the locking device.

f. Accessibility. Assisted living facilities should consider residents with varying and possibly increasing levels of acuity. To maximize the potential for aging in place, particular attention should be paid to overall accessibility. Locations where individuals may not require physical assistance from others in emergency situations typically require compliance with standards for multifamily housing (a specific subset is now used as "safe harbor" for Fair Housing architectural requirements). In addition, the Uniform Federal Accessibility Guidelines shall apply for structures built with federal assistance. Locations where individuals require physical assistance from others in emergency situations may require compliance with the Americans with Disabilities Act Accessibility Guidelines (ADAAG).

1.6 Site

1.6.1 Location
Assisted living facilities shall obtain applicable land use approval from the relevant jurisdiction. See Chapter 1.3 for other general requirements.

1.6.2 Roads
Roads shall be provided within the property for access to the main entrance and service areas. Fire department and emergency vehicle access shall be provided in accordance with local requirements. See Chapter 1.3 for other general requirements.

1.6.3 Parking
Each assisted living facility shall have parking space to satisfy the needs of the residents, families, staff, and

APPENDIX

A2.1 Space Requirements
Assisted living has developed into a variety of models that are designed to meet differing social, economic, and therapeutic considerations. The many varieties of assisted living may generally be categorized into the following two types, although some facilities may combine elements from these approaches.

Apartment model. Apartment model facilities provide private resident units ranging in size from efficiency to two- or three-bedroom apartments. These apartments typically have cooking facilities (sometimes limited to a microwave) and are often indistinguishable from apartment units available to the general population. Common group activity areas that residents may utilize in addition to their private apartments are provided to promote the social and programmatic aspects of the facility.

Group living model. Group living model facilities provide smaller private spaces that are sometimes limited to a private or shared resident bedroom area. The focus of daily life is provided within shared activity spaces that are residential-scaled and organized similar to a typical house. These smaller-scale "homes" may be freestanding or grouped together in attached or detached configurations. At times, commons or community facilities are provided to allow residents to participate in activities outside of their "home."

Alternative models. Many alternative facility configurations have been created that incorporate aspects from each of these approaches. These guidelines are intended to allow and encourage the continued evolution of this facility type without locking into a particular program or model.

visitors. In the absence of local requirements or a formal parking study, a minimum of one space for every four resident units (or beds) shall be provided. See Chapter 1.3 for other general requirements.

1.7 Renovation
See Section 1.1-3.

1.8 Provisions for Disasters
See Section 1.1-5.

*1.9 Codes and Standards

1.9.1 General
A code-compliant, safe, and accessible environment shall be provided.

1.9.1.1 A facility that seeks accreditation, certification, licensure, or other credentials shall comply with applicable design and construction standards.

1.9.1.2 When institutional codes are required, the facility shall maintain the residential environment desired by residents.

1.9.2 Accessibility Codes
The facility shall comply with applicable federal, state, and local requirements (see Section 1.1-4).

1.10 Equipment
Assisted living facilities shall be equipped and furnished with facility and occupant items in accordance with the functional program. See Chapter 1.4 for other issues to consider.

1.11 Planning, Design, and Construction
See Chapter 1.5.

1.12 Record Drawings and Manuals
See Section 1.5-5.

2 Resident Living Environment

*2.1 General

2.1.1 Space Requirements
Facility spatial requirements shall be determined by the functional program.

2.1.2 Layout

Areas for the care and treatment of users not residing in the facility shall not interfere with or infringe upon the space of residents living in the facility.

2.2 Resident Rooms or Apartments

The facility shall provide adequately sized bedrooms or apartments (dwelling units) that allow for sleeping, afford privacy, provide access to furniture and belongings, and accommodate the care and treatment provided to the resident.

2.2.1 Capacity

Bedrooms shall be limited to single or double occupancy.

*2.2.2 Space Requirements

2.2.2.1 Resident room size (area and dimensions) shall permit resident(s) to move about the room with the assistance of a walker or wheelchair, allowing access to at least one side of a bed, window, closet or wardrobe, chair, dresser, and nightstand.

2.2.2.2 Room size and configuration shall permit resident(s) options for bed location(s) and shall comply with spatial requirements of the authority having jurisdiction.

2.2.2.3 Where cooking is permitted in resident rooms (apartments), additional floor area shall be provided for cooking and dining. The cooking area shall be equipped with a dedicated sink and cooking and refrigeration appliances.

2.2.3 Layout

Bedrooms shall not be used as passageways, corridors, or access to other bedrooms.

2.2.4 Windows

Resident bedrooms shall have a window that provides natural light with a maximum sill height of 3 feet (91.44 centimeters) above the finished floor.

*2.2.5 Toilet Room

Each resident shall have access to a toilet room.

2.2.5.1 A minimum of one toilet room shall be provided for every four residents not otherwise served by toilet rooms adjoining resident rooms.

2.2.5.2 The toilet room shall contain a water closet, lavatory, and a horizontal surface for the personal effects of each resident.

2.2.6 Resident Storage

Each resident shall be provided separate and adequate enclosed storage volume within the resident room.

2.3 Support Areas for Resident Rooms/Apartments

2.3.1 Staff Work Area(s)

These areas shall be provided in accordance with the functional program.

2.3.1.1 Lockable storage shall be provided for resident records.

2.3.1.2 Direct visualization of resident rooms or corridors from staff work areas is not required.

2.3.2 Medication Preparation

When required by the functional program, provision shall be made for 24-hour distribution of medications. A medicine preparation room, a self-contained medicine dispensing unit, or other system may be used for this purpose.

APPENDIX

A2.2.2 In cases where double-occupancy resident rooms are provided, configurations should be utilized that provide individual privacy and control of the environment. The design should not restrict access to shared, common elements within the room.

A2.2.2.3 Cooking equipment in resident rooms should be installed in a manner that allows it to be disabled by facility management as deemed necessary or appropriate.

A2.2.5 Toilet Room

a. Doors. Doors to toilet rooms may be hinged or, where local requirements permit, sliding, pocket, or folding doors may be used for toilet rooms in resident rooms, provided adequate provisions are made for acoustic and visual privacy and resident safety and usability.

b. Clearances. Toilets used by residents should have sufficient clearance on both sides of the water closet to enable physical access and maneuvering by staff, who may need to assist the resident in wheelchair-to-water closet transfers and returns.

c. Grab bars. Where independent transfers are feasible, alternative grab bar configurations should be permitted.

2.3.2.1 Medicine preparation room

(1) The medicine preparation room, if used, shall provide for security.

(2) It shall contain a work counter, sink, refrigerator, and locked storage for controlled drugs.

2.3.2.2 Medicine dispensing unit. A self-contained medicine dispensing unit, if used, may be located at the staff work area, in the clean workroom, in an alcove, or in other space convenient for staff control. (Standard "cup" sinks provided in many self-contained units are not adequate for hand-washing.)

2.4 Support Areas for Staff

2.4.1 Staff Lounge Area
When required by the functional program, a staff lounge area shall be provided.

2.4.2 Toilet Room(s)
Toilet room(s) for staff and public use shall be provided.

2.4.2.1 These shall contain water closets with a hand-washing station.

2.4.2.2 Toilet rooms may be unisex and shared by public and residents.

2.4.3 Staff Storage
Lockable closets, drawers, or compartments shall be provided for safekeeping of staff personal effects such as handbags.

APPENDIX

A3.1 Dementia Units
These are secure units specifically designed for individuals with dementia. However, in some assisted living facilities, a significant percentage of individuals with some level of dementia may not reside in a dementia unit. Thus, the entire assisted living facility should be designed to facilitate the highest level of functioning for all residents. The living environment should be equipped with special features such as personalized resident bedrooms, features that support resident orientation to their surroundings, secured storage, safe outside areas, and security considerations to support individuals with varying levels of cognitive impairment.

2.5 Support Areas for Residents

2.5.1 Bathing facilities
2.5.1.1 Location. Bathing facilities shall be provided on each floor where resident sleeping areas are located.

2.5.1.2 Number. One bathtub or shower shall be provided for every eight residents (or fraction thereof) not otherwise served by bathing facilities in resident rooms. A bathtub shall be provided for resident use when required by the functional program.

2.5.1.3 Space requirements. Bathing fixtures shall be located in individual rooms or enclosures with space for private use of the bathing fixture and for drying and dressing, as well as convenient access to a grooming location with a lavatory, mirror, and counter or shelf.

2.5.1.4 Toilet. A toilet shall be provided within or directly accessible to each resident bathing facility without requiring entry into the general corridor.

3 Special Care Facilities

*3.1 Alzheimer's and Other Dementia Units
A secure unit is a distinct living environment designed for the particular needs and behaviors of residents with dementia. Dementia units within assisted living facilities shall, in addition to the assisted living requirements, comply with the following:

3.1.1 Controlled Egress
Dementia units shall provide an appropriate controlled-egress system on all required exit doors and doors leading to other areas of the facility unless prior approval of an alternative method for prevention of resident elopement from the unit has been obtained from the authority having jurisdiction.

3.1.2 Windows
All operable windows shall be equipped with mechanisms to limit exterior window openings, to prevent elopement and accidental falls.

3.1.3 Leisure and Dining Space
A dementia unit operated as a portion of an assisted living facility must provide self-contained leisure and dining room space, unless it can be demonstrated to

the satisfaction of the authority having jurisdiction that use of shared common areas is appropriate to the needs of all residents.

3.1.4 Support Services and Areas
For operational efficiency, location of support services and areas within adjacent program areas shall be permitted.

3.1.5 Toilet and Bathing Fixtures
Alternative toilet and bathing fixture ratios (residents per fixture) shall be allowed in accordance with the functional program.

4 Resident Living Areas

4.1 Dining Areas

4.1.1 General
4.1.1.1 Space for dining, separate from social areas, shall be provided.

4.1.1.2 Dining areas shall be configured in accordance with the functional program.

4.1.1.3 Natural light shall be provided in resident dining areas.

4.1.2 Space Requirements
4.1.2.1 Dining areas shall provide 20 square feet (1.86 square meters) per occupant using the space at one time.

4.1.2.2 In a facility with more than 16 residents, dining and social areas shall not be confined to a single room.

4.1.3 Toilet Rooms
Toilet room(s) shall be provided convenient to dining and social areas.

4.2 Activity and Social Areas

4.2.1 Space Requirements
4.2.1.1 Activity areas shall accommodate both group and individual activities.

4.2.1.2 A minimum of 20 square feet (1.86 square meters) per facility resident shall be provided for activity areas for socialization, passive and active recreation, and social activities.

4.2.2 Outdoor Areas
Outdoor areas shall be provided for residents, visitors, and staff. Outdoor spaces may include solaria, porches, and balconies or gardens on grade or on roof decks.

4.2.3 Toilet Rooms
Toilet room(s) shall be provided convenient to activity areas.

4.3 Storage
The facility shall provide storage space for equipment and supplies required for the care of residents as required by the functional program.

5 Service Areas

5.1 Dietary Facilities
The food preparation and service area shall be provided with sufficient and suitable space and equipment to maintain efficient and sanitary operation of all required functions, in compliance with the applicable state and local sanitary codes.

5.2 Linen Services
Space shall be provided for laundry services, as defined by the functional program.

5.2.1 Contractual Linen Services
If contractual services are used, the facility shall provide the following:

5.2.1.1 An area for soiled linen awaiting pickup

5.2.1.2 A separate area for storage and distribution of clean linen

5.2.2 On-Site Linen Services
If on-site services are provided, the facility shall provide the following:

5.2.2.1 Areas dedicated to laundry that are separate from food preparation areas

5.2.2.2 A laundry area for facility-processed bulk laundry. This shall be divided into separate soiled (sort and washer area) and clean (drying, folding, and mending area) rooms.

5.2.2.3 Separate soaking and hand-washing sinks and housekeeping room located convenient to laundry areas

5.2.3 Personal Laundry Areas

If shared personal laundry areas are provided, these areas shall be equipped with a washer and dryer for use by residents and a conveniently located hand-washing station.

5.3 Materials Management

5.3.1 Waste Management

Accommodations shall be made for the collection and storage of waste produced within the facility. Space shall be provided for enclosed waste storage that is separate from food preparation, personal hygiene, and other clean functions. See Section 4.1-6.3.1.

5.4 Environmental Services

5.4.1 Housekeeping Rooms

5.4.1.1 Space shall be provided for storage of housekeeping supplies and equipment.

5.4.1.2 A designated service sink shall be provided.

5.5 Engineering Services and Maintenance

Assisted living facilities shall provide the area necessary to effectively house building systems and maintenance functions in accordance with the functional program. See Section 4.1-6.5.

6 Administrative and Public Areas

6.1 Public Notice Area

Areas shall be provided that are suitable for posting required notices, documents, and other written materials in public locations visible to and accessible to residents, staff, and visitors.

6.2 Private Meeting Space(s)

Private space shall be provided for residents to meet with others.

APPENDIX

A9.3 To promote individual autonomy and control, consideration should be given to providing individual temperature control for resident sleeping rooms.

---

7 Construction Standards

7.1 Applicable Codes
See Section 4.1-8.1.

7.2 General Standards for Details and Finishes

7.2.1 See Section 4.1-8.2.

7.2.2 Assisted living facilities shall incorporate features and finishes that optimize sensory function and facilitate mobility, including ambulation and self-propulsion, as well as features that optimize independent wayfinding.

7.2.3 Potential hazards to residents, including sharp corners, slippery floors, loose carpets, and exposed hot surfaces, shall be avoided.

8 Special Systems

8.1 Elevators
Multistory assisted living facilities shall be provided with independent access to all resident use floors.

8.2 Waste Processing
Accommodations shall be made for the disposal of waste produced within the facility. See Section 4.1-9.3.

9 Building Systems

9.1 General
Assisted living facilities shall have building systems that are designed and installed in such a manner as to provide for the safety, comfort, and well-being of the residents. See Section 4.1-10.

9.2 Plumbing
Plumbing and other piping systems shall comply with applicable codes and regulations. See Sections 1.6-2.1 and 4.1-10.1.

*9.3 Heating, Ventilating, and Air-Conditioning Systems
Assisted living facilities shall have an HVAC system(s) to prevent the concentrations of contaminants and temperatures that impair health or cause discomfort to residents and employees. Airflow shall move generally from clean to soiled locations. See Section 1.6-2.2.

9.3.1 Heating System

The facility shall have a permanently installed heating system capable of maintaining an interior temperature of 72° Fahrenheit (22° Celsius) under heating design temperatures.

9.3.2 Cooling System

The facility shall be configured and equipped with a cooling system capable of maintaining an interior temperature of 75° F (24° C) under cooling design temperatures.

9.4 Electrical Systems

9.4.1 Power-Generating Equipment

9.4.1.1 Emergency electrical service. If life support equipment is permitted by the functional program, emergency power shall be provided.

*9.4.2 Lighting

9.4.2.1 General

*(1) Lighting shall be engineered to the specific application. Unless alternative lighting levels are justified by the approved functional program, Table 4.1-4 shall be used as a guide to minimum required ambient and task lighting levels in all rooms, spaces, and exterior walkways.

(2) Approaches to buildings and parking lots and all occupied spaces within buildings shall have fixtures for lighting. Consideration shall be given to both the quantity and quality of lighting, including the following:

(a) Even and consistent lighting levels

APPENDIX

A9.4.2 Lighting

a. Excessive differences in lighting levels should be avoided in transition areas between parking lots, building entrances and lobbies, or corridors; in transition zones between driveways and parking garages, etc. As the eye ages, pupils become smaller and less elastic, making visual adaptation to dark spaces slower. Upon entering a space with a considerably lower lighting level, elderly residents may need to stop or move to one side until their eyes adapt to excessive lighting changes. Elderly pedestrians may need several minutes to adjust to significant changes in brightness when entering a building from a sunlit walkway or terrace.

b. Consideration should be given to increasing both indoor and outdoor illumination levels in such transition spaces to avoid excessive differences between electric lighting levels and natural daytime and nighttime illumination levels. In addition, it is very helpful for pedestrians to have conveniently located places to wait, giving them time to adjust their eyes to different lighting environments.

c. Care should be taken to minimize extremes of brightness within spaces and in transitions between spaces. Excessive brightness contrast from windows or lighting systems can disorient residents.

d. Lighting that creates glare and colors that do not differentiate between horizontal and vertical planes, or between objects and their backgrounds (such as handrails or light switches from walls, hardware from doors, faucets from sinks, bathroom fixtures from wall colors, or control knobs from appliances) should be avoided, unless therapeutic benefits can be demonstrated. (For example, it

has been demonstrated that deliberately camouflaged door hardware may help control wandering and elopements by some cognitively impaired residents in Alzheimer's care facilities.)

e. Care should be taken to avoid injury from lighting fixtures. Light sources that may burn residents or ignite bed linen by direct contact should be covered or protected.

f. Ambient light levels are determined on a horizontal plane above the floor. The use of this method in areas such as those listed in Table 4.1-4 should result in values of average illuminance within 10 percent of the values that would be obtained by dividing the area into 2-foot (0.6-meter) squares, taking a reading in each square, and averaging.

The measuring instrument should be positioned so that when readings are taken, the surface of the light-sensitive cell is in a horizontal plane and 30 inches (760 millimeters) above the floor. This can be facilitated by means of a small portable stand of wood or other material that will support the cell at the correct height and in the proper plane. Daylight may be excluded during illuminance measurements. Readings can be taken at night or with shades, blinds, or other opaque covering on the fenestration.

A9.4.2.1 (1) The Illuminating Engineering Society of North America (IESNA) has developed recommended lighting design practices, including minimum lighting levels for senior living environments. Refer to ANSI/IESNA RP-28, Lighting and the Visual Environment for Senior Living, for additional information.

(b) Glare control

(c) Special lighting needs of the elderly

(d) Area-specific lighting solutions

(e) Use of daylighting in all resident rooms and resident use areas

(f) Life-cycle costs of lighting

(g) Other lighting design practices as defined and described in ANSI/IESNA RP-28, Lighting and the Visual Environment for Senior Living

9.4.2.2 Lighting requirements for specific locations

*(1) Resident rooms and toilet rooms

(a) Resident rooms and toilet rooms shall have provisions for general lighting and task lighting.

(b) All light controls in resident areas shall be quiet-operating.

(2) Resident unit corridors

(a) Resident unit corridors shall have general illumination with provisions for reducing light levels at night.

(b) Corridors and common areas used by residents shall have even light distribution to avoid glare, shadows, and scalloped lighting effects.

(c) Highly polished flooring or floors with glossy sheen shall not be used.

*9.4.3 Call System

9.5 Telecommunication and Information Systems

Telecommunication and information systems shall be provided in accordance with the functional program. See Section 4.1-10.4.

9.6 Fire Alarm and Detection Systems

Fire alarm and detection systems shall be provided in accordance with applicable codes and regulations. See Section 4.1-10.5.

4.4 Adult Day Health Care Facilities

Appendix material, which appears in shaded boxes at the bottom of the page, is advisory only.

Adult day health care (ADHC) services are group programs designed to meet the needs of functionally and/or cognitively impaired adults. Adult day health care facilities provide a caring, non-institutional setting for individuals who, for their own safety and well-being, can no longer be left at home alone. Adult day health care facilities offer protected settings and include a mixture of health and support services. Many offer specialized services such as programs for individuals with Alzheimer's disease, developmental disabilities, traumatic brain injury, mental illness, HIV/AIDS, and vision and hearing impairments. Adult day health care facilities are an integral component of the continuum of care for the elderly and disabled.

1 General Considerations

1.1 ADHC Types

1.1.1 Multifunctional Facilities
A structured comprehensive, nonresidential program that provides for a variety of health, social, and support services in a protective setting. This type of facility is large enough to accommodate changing service needs.

1.1.2 Specialty Facilities
Structured comprehensive, nonresidential program that provides for a variety of health, social, and support services, as well as specialty services for a target population. These types of facilities have unique needs that affect usable activity space requirements.

1.2 Functional Program

1.2.1 Each adult day health care center, when it is located in a facility housing other services, shall have its own identifiable space. When permitted by the functional program, support spaces shall be permitted to be shared.

*1.2.2 The facility shall have sufficient space, furnishings, and equipment to accommodate the range of program activities and services for the number of participants as required by the functional program. This space shall include designated area(s) to be utilized when the privacy of the participants requires it.

1.2.3 Participants are defined as the number of people exclusive of staff occupying the space at the same time.

*1.3 Facility Access
When possible, the ADHC facility shall be located on the street level or shall be equipped with ramps or elevators to allow easy access for persons with disabilities.

2 Care Locations

2.1 Activity Space(s)

2.1.1 Space Requirements
2.1.1.1 Net usable space. Only spaces commonly used by participants are to be included as net usable activity space. Reception areas, storage areas, offices, restrooms, corridors, and service areas shall not be included. When a kitchen is used for activities other than meals, 50 percent of the floor area shall be counted as activity space.

2.1.1.2 Area. Minimum square footage requirements shall be based on the services offered by the adult day health care facility.

(1) Multifunctional ADHC facilities. At least 100 square feet (30.48 square meters) shall be provided for each of the first five participants and 60 square feet (18.28 square meters) of net usable program activity space for each participant thereafter.

(2) Specialty ADHC facilities. At least 30 square feet (9.14 square meters) shall be provided for each participant, but no facility shall have less than 300 square feet (91.44 square meters) of net usable activity space.

(3) Net usable area for additional functions

   (a) For social/recreational areas in an ADHC, an additional 20 square feet (6.09 square meters) shall be provided per participant to accommodate the programmed activities.

   (b) For mental health/Alzheimer's ADHCs, an additional 40 square feet (12.19 square meters) of space shall be provided per participant.

   (c) For physical rehabilitation therapy ADHCs, an additional 50 square feet (15.24 square meters) of space per participant shall be provided for activity space needed for equipment and treatment.

   (d) For developmental disability ADHCs, an additional 70 square feet (21.33 square meters) of space shall be provided per participant to ensure the therapeutic milieu is maintained.

2.1.2 Hand-Washing Station(s)
All communal activity areas shall have convenient access to a hand-washing station.

2.2 Rest or Private Area
There shall be a rest area and/or a designated area to permit privacy and to isolate participants who become ill or disruptive or who require rest.

APPENDIX

A2.4.1 If the facility capacity is 40 participants or greater, a separate staff lounge should be provided.

2.2.1 Location
2.2.1.1 This area shall be permitted to be part of the medical/health treatment room or nurse station.

2.2.1.2 This area shall be located in a place that can be clearly monitored and that is near a toilet room.

2.2.2 Area
This area shall be considered part of the usable activity space.

2.3 Support Areas for Care Locations

2.3.1 Meeting Room
A space shall be available for participants and family/caregivers to have private meetings with staff.

2.3.2 Equipment and Supply Storage
Storage space shall be available for program and operating supplies.

2.4 Support Areas for Staff

*2.4.1 Staff Lounge

2.4.2 Staff Toilet
At least one dedicated staff toilet shall be provided.

2.5 Support Areas for Participants

2.5.1 Participant Toilet Rooms
2.5.1.1 Number. The facility shall have at least one toilet and one lavatory for every ten participants.

2.5.1.2 Type. The facility shall provide a variety of toilet room types (e.g., independent, fully accessible, one-person assist, or two-person assist) as required by the functional program. All facilities shall include at least one toilet room that can accommodate a two-person assisted transfer between wheelchair and toilet.

2.5.1.3 Location. Participant toilet rooms shall be located no more than 40 feet (12.19 meters) away from the activity area.

2.5.1.4 Call system. Emergency call stations shall be provided in any toilet rooms used by participants.

*2.5.2 Bathing Facilities

2.5.2.1 A shower or bathtub area shall be provided in all adult day health care facilities. If the functional program indicates the need for bathing services, an assisted bathing facility shall be provided.

2.5.2.2 Call system. Emergency call stations shall be provided in bathing facilities used by participants.

3 Diagnostic and Treatment Locations

3.1 Treatment Room or Nurse Station
The ADHC shall have a medical/health treatment room or nurse station.

3.2 Support Areas for Diagnostic and Treatment Locations

3.2.1 Medication and Equipment Storage
3.2.1.1 This area shall be able to contain first aid materials and medical supplies and equipment.

3.2.1.2 This area shall provide for secure medication storage, including space that separates oral medications from topical agents, a refrigerator for medication storage, double-locking storage for narcotics, and adequate space to store medications brought in by participants. This storage can be a room, locked cabinetry, or a locked medication cart.

3.2.1.3 This area shall contain a hand-washing station.

4 Service Areas

*4.1 Dining Areas

4.2 Environmental Services

4.2.1 Housekeeping Room
A housekeeping closet shall be provided that will contain a service sink and provide for the locked safe storage of housekeeping items.

5 Administrative and Public Areas

5.1 Public Areas

5.1.1 Telephone(s)
A telephone(s) shall be available for participant(s) in an area that affords privacy during use.

5.1.2 Provisions for Drinking Water
Drinking water shall be easily accessible to the participants.

5.1.3 Outdoor Areas
Outdoor recreation and/or relaxation area for participants, if provided, shall be accessible to indoor areas. Outdoor areas shall have a fence or landscaping to create a boundary that prevents participant elopement.

6 Construction Standards

6.1 Details

6.1.1 Handrails
6.1.1.1 All stairways and ramps shall have handrails.

6.1.1.2 Hallways shall have handrails located on at least one side.

6.2 Finishes

6.2.1 Floors

APPENDIX

A2.5.2 Access to a washer and dryer is preferable when the participants have incontinence or physical limitations that predispose them to soiling with blood, body fluids, or food spills (e.g., swallowing or chewing problems, shakes or tremors).

A4.1 Dining should occur in a space that is visually and spatially distinct from the activity areas. No single dining setting should serve more than 16 participants to decrease the potential for unpredictable social and sensory stimulation. Dining tables should be reserved for meals and snacks and rarely, if ever, used for programmed activities.

Refer to K. Diaz Moore, "Design Guidelines for Adult Day Services" in *AIA 005: Report on University Research* for additional information and further detail on toilets, dining, and the zone of transition.

6.2.1.1 All stairways and ramps shall have nonslip surfaces.

6.2.1.2 Floor surfaces, including carpets, accessed by ADHC participants shall be slip-resistant. Highly polished flooring or floors with glossy sheen shall not be used. Area rugs shall not be used.

7 Building Systems

7.1 Plumbing

7.1.1 Hot Water
Hot water at shower, bathing, and hand-washing facilities shall not exceed 110° F (43° C).

7.2 Heating, Ventilating, and Air-Conditioning Systems

7.2.1 Ventilation
Ventilation by mechanical means shall be provided. Air conditioning and heating equipment shall be adequate and capable of maintaining the temperature in each room used by participants between 72° F (22° C) and 78° F (26° C).

7.3 Electrical Standards

*7.3.1 Lighting
Lighting shall be engineered to the specific application. Table 4.1-4 shall be used as a guide to minimum required ambient and task lighting levels in all rooms, spaces, and exterior walkways.

Glossary

Specific terms and definitions are provided below to facilitate consistency in the interpretation and application of the Guidelines.

Administrative areas: Designated spaces such as offices and meeting rooms that accommodate admission and discharge processes, medical records storage, medical and nursing administration, business management and financial services, human resources, purchasing, community services, education, and public relations.

Airborne infection isolation room: A single-occupancy room for patient care in which environmental factors are controlled to minimize transmission of infectious agents spread from person to person by droplet nuclei associated with coughing and inhalation. (Such rooms typically have specific requirements for controlled ventilation, air pressure, and air filtration.)

Ambulatory care: A defined health care encounter of less than 24 hours in duration that requires direct professional health care support within a specific facility.

Ambulatory surgical facility: Any surgical facility organized for the purpose of providing invasive surgical care to patients with the expectation that they will be recovered sufficiently to be discharged in less than 24 hours.

Bed size: Minimum rectangular dimensions for planning minimum clearances around beds—40 inches (101.6 centimeters) wide by 96 inches (2.43 meters) long.

Bioterrorism: The use, or threat of use, of biological agents to intimidate a political entity or population group.

Clear floor area: The built floor area available for functional use in a defined space. Such area shall not include other defined spaces (e.g., anterooms, vestibules, toilet rooms, closets, alcoves) or built-in equipment (e.g., lockers, wardrobes, fixed casework).

Cubicle: A patient location that is used for short-term patient-focused activities (e.g., observation or recovery) and can be delineated by ceiling-hung curtains or screens. Cubicles should be designed to accommodate patient privacy, mobility, flexible use, and ease of access.

Documentation area: A work area associated with or near a patient care area where information specific to patients is recorded, stored, and reviewed to facilitate ready access by authorized individuals.

Differential pressure: A measurable difference in air pressure that creates a directional airflow between adjacent spaces.

Emergency call system: Devices that are activated to indicate the need for staff assistance. Such devices produce an audible or visual indication (or both) or may be connected or transmit to an area alert monitor.

Environment of care: Those features in a built health care facility that are created, structured, and maintained to support and enhance quality health care.

Facility: A discrete physical entity composed of various functional units as described within these Guidelines.

Hand-washing station: An area that provides a sink with hot and cold water supply and a faucet that facilitates easy on/off/mixing capabilities. The station also provides cleansing agents and means for drying hands.

Hand sanitation station: A dispensing location for a waterless, antiseptic hand rub product that is applied to reduce the number of microorganisms present on the hands.

Health care facility: Any facility type listed in the table of contents of this book.

Housekeeping: Services anywhere within a health care facility that provide general cleaning and tidying and supply identified cleaning materials (e.g., soaps, towels). (While routine disinfection protocols can be included in such a definition, the definition is not intended to include complex, non-routine disinfection procedures nor the non-routine disposition of hazardous materials such as potentially toxic drugs or other chemicals and radioactive wastes.)

Infection control risk assessment: A multidisciplinary organizational process that focuses on reducing risk from infection throughout facility planning, design, and construction (including renovation) activities. The environment, infectious agents, and human factors and the impact of the proposed project are considered by a multidisciplinary team that includes, at minimum, those with expertise in infectious disease, infection control, patient care, epidemiology, facility design, engineering, construction, and safety, as circumstances dictate.

Invasive procedure: For the purposes of this document, any procedure that penetrates the protective surfaces of a patient's body (i.e., skin, mucous membrane, cornea) and that is performed within an aseptic field (procedural site). Not included in this category are placement of peripheral intravenous needles or catheters, dialysis, bronchoscopy, endoscopy (e.g., sigmoidoscopy), insertion of urethral catheters, and similar procedures.

Minimum clearance: The shortest unencumbered distance between the outermost dimensions of a specified object (often a patient bed) and specified, fixed reference points (e.g., walls, cabinets, sinks, and doors).

Monolithic ceiling: A ceiling constructed with a surface free of fissures, cracks, and crevices. Any penetrations such as lights, diffusers, and access panels shall be sealed or gasketed. ("Lay-in" ceilings are not considered "monolithic.")

Nursing locations: Departments, units, rooms, spaces, or areas in which patient observation, nursing care, and treatment services rendered involve direct contact between patients/residents and staff.

Observation unit: An area usually associated with an emergency department where one or more patients can be clinically monitored, assessed, and treated by staff for up to 24 hours.

Operating room: A room specifically designed for the performance of surgical procedures. (This includes most types of surgical procedures but especially those involving administration of anesthesia, multiple personnel, recovery room access, and a fully controlled environment.)

Patient care area: An area used primarily for the provision of clinical care to patients. Such care includes monitoring, evaluation, and treatment services.

Perioperative: Referring to patient care and other related support activities immediately before, during, or after an operative procedure.

Protective environment: A specialized patient care area that can safely accommodate highly immunosuppressed patients (patients with severe neutropenia, bone marrow transplant patients, or patients with childhood acute AML).

Provision of drinking water: Availability of readily accessible potable water for patient, staff, and visitor needs. This may be provided in a variety of ways, including fountains and bottled water.

Public areas: Designated spaces freely accessible to the public. These include parking areas, secured entrances and areas, entrance lobbies, reception and waiting areas, public toilets, snack bars, cafeterias, vending areas, gift shops and other retail locations, health education libraries and meeting rooms, chapels, and gardens.

Restricted area: A designated space with limited access eligibility. Such space has one or more of the following attributes: specific signage; physical barriers; security controls and protocols that delineate requirements for monitoring, maintenance, attire, and use. (The term is often applied to operating rooms and suites.)

Sealed (tight) room: A room that meets specific ventilation requirements and has minimum air leakage to achieve a particular designed air quality, airflow direction, and pressure differential.

Service areas: Designated spaces that house auxiliary functions that do not routinely involve contact with patients, residents, clients, or the public (e.g., supply, processing, storage, and maintenance services such as pharmacy, dietary, bulk sterile processing, laundry processing and storage, housekeeping, engineering operations, and waste storage/holding facilities).

Subacute care: A category of care requiring less intensity of care/resources than acute care. It falls within a continuum of care determined by patient acuity, clinical stability, and resource needs.

Support areas (nursing units, diagnostic and treatment areas, etc.): Designated spaces or areas in which staff members perform auxiliary functions that support the main purpose of the unit or other location.

Support areas (patient/resident and visitor): Designated spaces for the use of patients, residents, clients, registrants, or visitors (e.g., clothing change areas, dining rooms, toilet rooms, lounges) or families and visitors (e.g., waiting areas and lounges, children's play areas, toilet rooms).

Support areas (staff): Designated spaces for the personal use of staff personnel (e.g., clothing change areas, toilets, showers, lounges, dining areas).

Surgical suite: A space that includes an operating room(s) and support areas.

Swing bed: A patient bed that may be used for varying levels of clinical acuity. The built environment for such a bed must be consistent with the highest level of care acuity planned or provided.

Unit: An area or space usually dedicated to a single defined organizational function.

Index

nourishment areas in, 3.6–4.1.6

parking for, 3.6–1.2.1

patient support areas in, 3.6–2.4

staff support areas in, 3.6–2.3

sterilization facilities in, 3.6–3.1

Blood storage

in general hospitals, 2.1–5.11.2.4 (2)

in small hospitals, 2.2–3.5.1.2

Blueprints. *See* Drawings, architectural

Boilers

accessories for, 1.6–2.2.3.2

capacity of, 1.6–2.2.3.1 (1)

Bone marrow transplant units, 2.1–A3.2.3.6

Building service equipment, 1.4–2.1

Building systems, commonly required, 1.6–2. *See also*

Electrical systems, HVAC systems, Plumbing

Cable placement, in design considerations, 1.4–A1.3.1

Call systems. *See also* Emergency call system

in assisted living facilities, 4.3–9.4.3, 4.3–A9.4.3

in general hospitals, 2.1–10.3.8

for bone marrow transplant units,
2.1–A3.2.3.6 (i)

in critical care units, 2.1–3.4.2.1 (5)

in nursing facilities, 4.1–10.3.6

in psychiatric hospitals, 2.3–2.4.1.1, 2.3–8.3.7

in rehabilitation facilities, 2.4–9.3.7

Cardiac catheterization lab, 2.1–5.4.1, 2.1–5.5.7

Ceiling height

in general hospitals, 2.1–8.2.2.2

in nursing facilities, 4.1–8.2.2.2

in outpatient facilities, 3.1–5.2.1.2

in psychiatric seclusion rooms, 2.3–2.2.1.5 (4)

in rehabilitation facilities, 2.4–7.2.2.2

Ceilings

in gastrointestinal endoscopy facilities, 3.9–5.2.2.3

in general hospitals

in bone marrow transplant unit,
2.1-A3.2.3.6

in decontamination room,
2.1-A5.1.3.7 (5)d

in dietary areas, 2.1–8.2.3.4 (2)

in imaging suite, 2.1-5.5.1.4 (2)

finishes for, 2.1–8.2.3.4 (3)(a),
2.1-8.2.3.4 (4)

lay-in, 2.1–8.2.3.4 (3)(b)

in NICUs, 2.1-3.4.6.1 (7)(c)

in psychiatric patient areas, 2.1–8.2.3.6

in restricted areas, 2.1–8.2.3.4 (4)

in semirestricted areas, 2.1–8.2.3.4 (3)

in nursing facilities, 4.1–8.2.3.4

in office surgical facilities, 3.8-4.1.2.1

in outpatient surgical facilities, 3.7–5.2.2.2

in psychiatric hospitals, 2.3–6.2.3.1

in rehabilitation facilities, 2.4–7.2.3.4

Cesarean/delivery suites, 2.1–4.3

Change areas

in dialysis centers, 3.10-2.5

in gastrointestinal endoscopy facilities, 3.9–2.4.1,
3.9-2.5.1

in general hospitals

in cesarean/delivery suite, 2.1-4.3.7.2,
2.1-4.3.7.3

in surgical suite, 2.1-5.3.6.3, 2.1-5.3.7.1

in cardiac cath lab, 2.1-5.4.1.5 (1)

in dialysis unit, 2.1-5.9.5

in office surgery facilities, 3.8-2.4

in outpatient surgery facilities, 3.7-2.6.2, 3.7-2.7.1

Chemical safety provisions, for laboratory suites,
2.1–5.11.2.3 (1)

Clustering, in nursing facilities, 4.1–A2.1.3

Commissioning

areas included in, 1.5–A4.e

definition of, 1.5–4, 1.5–A4.c

of mechanical systems, 1.5–4.1

systems included in, 1.5–A4.d

of ventilation systems, 1.5–4.1.1, 1.5–4.1.2

Communications center, for emergency room, 2.1–5.1.3.5

Communication system, emergency, for hospitals, 2.1–8.1.3.2

Compressor room, for hyperbaric suites, 2.1–A5.10 (g)

Condensate drains, 1.6–2.1.2.2

Conservation

energy, 1.2–3.1.4, 1.2–3.1.4.1, 1.2–A3.1.4

water, 1.2–A3.1.3

Construction

infection control risk assessment and, 1.5–.2.2.2

ventilation of construction zone, 1.5–A3.2

Construction documents. *See* Drawings, architectural

Consultation rooms/areas, 1.2-A2.1.2.5 (4) . *See also*

Multipurpose rooms

in general hospitals

in hyperbaric suite, 2.1-A5.10

in imaging suite, 2.1-5.5.8.4

in nuclear medicine area, 2.1-5.6.4.5 (1),
2.1-5.6.5.5 (3)

in pediatric critical care unit,
2.1-3.4.5.2 (2)

in pharmacy, 2.1-6.1.5.6

in postpartum unit, 2.1-4.2.4.4

in psychiatric hospitals, 2.3–2.7.4.3

in psychiatric outpatient center, 3.11-2.1

in small hospitals, 2.2-3.6.3

Continuing care nursery, 2.1–3.6.7

Contrast media preparation areas, 2.1–5.5.8.9

Conversion, occupancy, 1.1–3.5

Copying machines, air quality and, 1.2–A3.1.5

Corridors

electrical receptacles in, 2.1–10.3.7.1

lighting in, 2.1–10.3.5.2 (2)

Corridor width

in general hospitals, 2.1–8.2.2.1

in outpatient facilities, 3.1–5.2.1.1

in endoscopy facilities, 5.9-3.2.1.1

in office surgical facilities, 3.8-4.1.1.1

in outpatient surgical facilities,
3.7–5.2.1.1

in rehabilitation facilities, 2.4–7.2.2.1

in small hospitals, 2.2–6.2

Coronary care units, 2.1–3.4.3

for toilet rooms, 2.1–2.2.1.3
types of, 2.1–8.2.2.3 (1)
in mobile units, 3.12–4.2.1
in outpatient surgical facilities, 3.7–5.2.1.3
in psychiatric hospitals, 2.3–6.2.2.1
for seclusion rooms, 2.3–2.2.1.5 (3)
in rehabilitation facilities, 2.4–7.2.2.3
in urgent care facilities, 3.5–4.1.1
Drainage systems
in general hospitals, 2.1–10.1.2.5
in nursing facilities, 4.1-10.1.2.4
in outpatient facilities, 3.1-7.1.2.5
in rehabilitation facilities, 2.4-9.1.2.5
Drains
autopsy table, 2.1–10.1.2.5 (3)
condensate, 1.6–2.1.2.2
in cystoscopy operating rooms, 2.1–10.1.2.5 (2)(b),
2.1–A10.1.2.5 (2)(b)
floor, 2.1–10.1.2.5 (2)
Drawings, architectural
equipment on, 1.4–1.3
life safety plan on, 1.5–5.1.2
recordkeeping of, 1.5–5.1
Dressing rooms. *See also* Change areas
for imaging suites, 2.1–5.5.10.3
for nuclear medicine suites, 2.1–5.6.4.7 (2)
Duct linings, 1.6–2.2.1.2
Ductwork. *See also* HVAC systems
humidifiers in, 1.6–2.2.2.1 (2), 1.6–A2.2.4.1 (2)
overview of, 1.6–2.2.2.1
Earthquakes, 1.1–5.1.3, 1.1–5.3.1
and mobile units, 3.12–2.3.1
Education therapy, in psychiatric hospitals, 2.3–3.4.6
Electrical systems, 1.6-2.3
in assisted living facilities, 4.3-9.4
in general hospitals, 2.1–10.3
emergency generators, 2.1–10.3.4.1
hand-washing stations dependent on,
2.1–10.3.6.3
in hospitals, 2.1–10.3
panelboards in, 2.1–10.3.3.2
receptacles, 2.1–10.3.7
standards for, 2.1–10.3.1.1
switchboards in, 2.1–10.3.3.1
testing of, 2.1–10.3.1.2
X-ray equipment and, 2.1–10.3.6.1
in hospice facilities, 4.2-7.3
in mobile units, 3.12–5.3
in nursing facilities, 4.1–10.3.2
in outpatient facilities, 3.1–7.3, 3.3-6.3
in gastrointestinal endoscopy facilities,
3.9-6.3
in outpatient surgical facilities, 3.7-6.3
in urgent care facilities, 3.5-5.3
in psychiatric hospitals, 2.3–8.3
in rehabilitation facilities, 2.4–9.3
in small hospitals, 2.2-8.3
testing and documentation of, 2.1-10.3.1.2,
2.3-8.3.1.2, 2.4-9.3.1.2, 3.1-7.3.1.2, 3.12-5.3.1.2,
4.1-10.3.1.2

Electrophysiology labs, 2.1–5.4.1.3
Elevators
in general hospitals
controls of, 2.1–9.2.5
critical care units and, 2.1–3.4.1.5,
2.1–A3.4.1.5
dimensions of, 2.1–9.2.3.
doors of, 2.1–9.2.3.2, 2.1–A9.2.3.2
installation of, 2.1–9.2.6
leveling device in, 2.1–9.2.4
number of, 2.1–9.2.2
as required, 2.1–9.2.1
in nursing facilities, 4.1–9.2
in outpatient facilities, 3.1–6.2
in psychiatric hospitals, 2.3–7.2, 2.3–A7.2.3.2
in rehabilitation facilities, 2.4–8.2
Emergency access, site selection and, 1.3–3.4
Emergency assistance system, 2.1–10.3.8.5
Emergency call system, 2.1–10.3.8.3. *See also* Call systems
Emergency exits, for hyperbaric facilities, 2.1–A5.10
Emergency generators, 2.1–10.3.4.1
Emergency lighting, 1.6–2.3.1.2
Emergency resuscitation alarm, 2.1–10.3.8.6
Emergency rooms
access to, 2.1–5.1.3.2
airborne infection control in, 2.1–5.1.2.6,
2.1–5.1.3.8
bereavement room in, 2.1–A5.1.3.11 (1)
classifications of, 2.1–A5.1.1.1
clean workrooms in, 2.1–5.1.3.9 (6)
communications center, 2.1–5.1.3.5
decontamination area for, 2.1–5.1.3.7 (5),
2.1–A5.1.3.7 (5)
definition of, 2.1–5.1.1.1
definitive emergency care, 2.1–5.1.3
diagnostic and treatment areas in, 2.1–5.1.3.7
entrance, 2.1–5.1.2.2, 2.1–5.1.3.3
equipment storage in, 2.1–5.1.3.9 (8)
fast-track area for, 2.1–A5.1.3
freestanding, 2.1–5.2
observation units in, 2.1–5.1.3.8 (2), 2.1–A5.1.3.8 (2)
pediatric treatment area in, 2.1–A5.1.3.7 (6)
reception area, 2.1–5.1.2.3, 2.1–5.1.3.4
security for, 2.1–5.1.3.9 (2), 2.1–A5.1.3.9 (2)
in small hospitals, 2.2–3.2
surge capacity for, 2.1–A5.1
trauma rooms in, 2.1–5.1.3.7 (2)
treatment room in, 2.1–5.1.2.5
triage area, 2.1–5.1.3.4 (2), 2.1–A5.1.3.4
ventilation requirements for, 2.1–2*t*
waiting area, 2.1–5.1.3.6
Endoscopy facilities, 3.9
Endourologic operating rooms, 2.1–5.3.2.4
Energy conservation, 1.2–3.1.4, 1.2–3.1.4.1, 1.2–A3.1.4
Engineering services
in hospitals, 2.1–6.7
in rehabilitation facilities, 2.4–5.7
in small hospitals, 2.2–4.3
Entrance
for general hospitals, 2.1–7.1.1

Hoods, ventilation, 2.1–10.2.4.5
Hospice facilities, 4.2
Hospitals, general
    administrative areas in, 2.1–7.2
    admissions area in, 2.1–7.2.1
    airborne infection isolation rooms in, 2.1–3.2.2, 2.1–3.3.3
    angiography facilities in, 2.1–5.5.2
    bone marrow transplant units in, 2.1–A3.2.3.6
    call systems in, 2.1–10.3.8
    catheterization lab, cardiac, 2.1–5.4.1, 2.1–5.5.7
    central services in, 2.1–6.3
    clean supply rooms in, 2.1–2.3.7
    clean workrooms in, 2.1–2.3.7
    construction standards for, 2.1–8
    coronary care units in, 2.1–3.4.3
    critical care units in, 2.1–3.4
    dialysis unit in, 2.1–5.9
    dietary facilities in, 2.1–6.2
    documentation areas in, 2.1–2.3.2
    doors in, 2.1–8.2.2.3
    drainage systems for, 2.1–10.1.2.5
    electrical systems in, 2.1–10.3
    elevators in, 2.1–9.2
    emergency communication system for, 2.1–8.1.3.2
    emergency rooms in, 2.1–5.1
    engineering services in, 2.1–6.7
    entrance to, 2.1–7.1.1
    environmental services in, 2.1–6.6
    equipment storage in, 2.1–2.3.9
    fire protection measures for, 2.1–8.1.2.2
    floors in, 2.1–8.3.2
    freestanding emergency service in, 2.1–5.2
    glazing materials in, 2.1–8.2.2.7
    hallway width in, 2.1–8.2.2.1
    hearing services departments in, 2.1–5.7.5
    housekeeping rooms in, 2.1–2.3.10
    HVAC systems in, 2.1–10.2
    hyperbaric suites in, 2.1–5.10, 2.1–A5.10
    imaging facilities in, 2.1–5.4, 2.1–5.5
    incinerators in, 2.1–9.3.1.1, 2.1–A9.3.1.1
    in-hospital skilled nursing units in, 2.1–3.9
    intermediate care units in, 2.1–3.3
    interview areas for, 2.1–7.2.2
    laboratory suites in, 2.1–5.11
    laundry facilities in, 2.1–6.4.4
    linen services in, 2.1–6.4
    linen storage in, 2.1–2.3.9.1
    lobby in, 2.1–7.1.2
    maintenance department in, 2.1–6.7
    materials management in, 2.1–6.5
    medical gas, 2.1–10.1.4.1
    medical/surgical nursing units in, 2.1–3.1
    medication stations in, 2.1–2.3.4
    morgue in, 2.1–5.12
    MRI suites in, 2.1–5.5.5
    newborn intensive care units in, 2.1–3.4.6
    noise controls in, 2.1–8.2.2.11
    nourishment areas in, 2.1–2.3.5
    nuclear medicine in, 2.1–5.6
    nurseries in, 2.1–3.6
    nurse stations in, 2.1–2.3.1
    obstetrical unit in, 2.1–4.1
    occupational therapy area in, 2.1–5.7.3
    operating rooms in, 2.1–5.3.2
    orthotics departments in, 2.1–5.7.4
    parking considerations, 2.1–1.3.1, 2.1–A1.3.1
    patient rooms in, 2.1–2.2, 2.1–3.1.1
    pharmacies in, 2.1–6.1
    plumbing in, 2.1–10.1
    prosthetics departments in, 2.1–5.7.4
    protective environment rooms in, 2.1–3.2.3
    psychiatric nursing units in, 2.1–3.8
    public areas in, 2.1–7.1
    radiopharmacies in, 2.1–5.6.2
    radiotherapy suites in, 2.1–5.6.5
    records area in, 2.1–7.2.5
    rehabilitation therapy departments in, 2.1–5.7
    respiratory therapy services in, 2.1–5.8
    service areas in, 2.1–6
    site selection, 2.1–1.3
    soiled workrooms in, 2.1–2.3.8
    sound transmission limitations in, 2.1–1t
    special patient care areas, 2.1–3.2
    speech services departments in, 2.1–5.7.5
    staff support areas in, 2.1–2.4, 2.1–3.1.4
    station outlets in, 2.1–5t
    sterilization rooms in, 2.1–6.3.1.2, 2.1–A6.3.1.2
    storage in, 2.1–6.5.2
    surgical suites in, 2.1–5.3.1
    telecommunications systems in, 2.1–10.4
    toilet rooms in, 2.1–2.2.1
    transfers to smaller hospitals, 2.2–1.3.1
    ultrasound suites in, 2.1–5.5.6
    vacuum systems in, 2.1–10.1.4.2
    vending machines in, 2.1–6.2.2.11
    ventilation in, 2.1–10.2.1.2
    waiting rooms in, 2.1–7.1.3
    waste management in, 2.1–6.5.3, 2.1–A6.5.3.1
    windows in, 2.1–8.2.2.5
    X-ray facilities in, 2.1–5.5.4
Hospitals, psychiatric. *See* Psychiatric hospitals
hospitals, small inpatient primary care, 2.2
    administrative areas in, 2.2–5.2
    building codes for, 2.2–6.1
    clean workrooms in, 2.2–2.5.8
    critical care in, 2.2–2.3.4
    emergency room in, 2.2–3.2
    engineering services in, 2.2–4.3
    entrance for, 2.2–5.1.1
    examination rooms in, 2.2–3.1
    helicopter pads at, 2.2–1.3.1.2
    housekeeping in, 2.2–2.5.11, 2.2–4.2.1
    HVAC systems in, 2.2–8.2
    ice machines in, 2.2–2.5.7
    imaging facilities in, 2.2–3.4, 2.2–A3.4.1
    laboratory facilities in, 2.2–3.5
    medication stations in, 2.2–2.5.5, 2.2–3.1.5.2

resident units in, 4.1–2
roads for, 4.1–1.6.2
toilet rooms in, 4.1–2.2.7
ventilation in, 4.1–1*t*
walls in, 4.1–8.2.3.2
waste management in, 4.1–6.3.1, 4.1–9.3
windows in, 4.1–8.2.2.4
Nursing homes. *See* Assisted living facilities; Nursing facilities; Rehabilitation facilities
Nursing units
    in general hospitals
        critical care, 2.1-3.4
        intermediate care, 2.1-3.3
        medical/surgical, 2.1–3.1
        ventilation requirements for, 2.1–2*t*
        pediatric and adolescent, 2.1-3.7
        postpartum, 2.1-4.2
        psychiatric, 2.1-3.8
        skilled nursing, *See* Nursing facilities
    in rehabilitation facilities, 2.4–2.1
    in small hospitals, 2.2–2
Observation areas
    in critical care units, 2.1–3.4.2.4 (1)(b), 2.1–A3.4.2.4 (1)
    in emergency room, 2.1–5.1.3.8 (2), 2.1–A5.1.3.8 (2)
    in outpatient facilities, 3.1–2.1.4
    in small hospitals, 2.2–3.1.4
    in urgent care facilities, 3.5–2.1.3
Obstetrical units, 2.1–4.1. *See also* Birthing Centers
    airborne infection isolation rooms in, 2.1–A4.2.2
    cesarean/delivery suite, 2.1–4.3
    delivery rooms in, 2.1–4.3.2
    infant resuscitation space in, 2.1–4.3.4
    medication stations in, 2.1–A4.2.4.5
    patient support areas in, 2.1–4.2.6
    postpartum unit, 2.1–4.2
    recovery rooms in, 2.1–4.3.5
    in small hospitals, 2.2–2.3.5
    types of, 2.1–A4.1
    ventilation requirements for, 2.1–2*t*
Occupational therapy areas
    in general hospitals, 2.1–5.7.3
    in nursing facilities, 4.1–5.1
    in psychiatric hospitals, 2.3–3.4.3
    in rehabilitation facilities, 2.4–4.3.2
Office surgical facilities, 3.8
Open-heart surgery, pump rooms for, 2.1–5.3.2.2 (2)
Operating rooms
    anesthesia workrooms for, 2.1–5.3.5.11
    class B, 3.7–2.3.1.2
    class C, 3.7–2.3.1.3
    electrical receptacles in, 2.1–10.3.7.2 (9)
    for endourologic procedures, 2.1–5.3.2.4
    HVAC considerations for, 2.1–10.2.2.4, 2.1–A10.2.2.4 (3)(a)
    lighting for, 2.1–10.3.5.2 (4)
    for orthopedic surgery, 2.1–5.3.2.2 (5)(a), 2.1–5.3.2.3
    for outpatient surgical facilities, 3.7–2.3

phase II recovery areas, 2.1–5.3.3.3
post-anesthetic care units for, 2.1–5.3.3.2
pre- and postoperative holding areas, 2.1–5.3.3
pump rooms for, 2.1–5.3.2.2 (2)
scrub facilities for, 2.1–5.3.5.4
space requirements for, 2.1–5.3.2.1 (1)(a)
for special procedures, 2.1–5.3.2.2
ventilation for, 3.1–A7.2.3.1
walls in, 2.1–8.2.3.3 (3)
X-ray viewers in, 2.1–5.3.2.1 (1)(c)
Orthopedic surgical rooms, 2.1–5.3.2.2 (5)(a), 2.1–5.3.2.3
Orthotics units
    in general hospitals, 2.1–5.7.4
    in rehabilitation facilities, 2.4–4.3.3
Outdoor areas
    in nursing facilities, 4.1–3.2.3, 4.1–A3.2.3
    in psychiatric hospitals, 2.3–2.1.3, 2.3–A2.1.3, 2.3–A2.3.3
Outlets (electrical)
    in critical care units, 2.1–10.3.7.2 (3)
    in dialysis units, 2.1–10.3.7.2 (10)
    in emergency room, 2.1–10.3.7.2 (7)
    in general hospitals, 2.1–10.3.7
    in mobile units, 3.12–5.3.5
    in nursing facilities, 4.1–10.3.5
    in patient rooms, 2.1–10.3.7.2 (1)
    in psychiatric hospitals, 2.3–8.3.6
    in rehabilitation facilities, 2.4–9.3.5
    in small primary care outpatient facilities, 3.3–5.3.3
Outpatient facilities
    accessibility of, 3.1–1.6
    administrative areas in, 3.1–4.2
    airborne infection isolation rooms in, 3.1–2.1.5
    air-handling systems in, 3.1–7.2.2.1 (2), 3.1–A7.2.2.1 (2)
    ceiling height in, 3.1–5.2.1.2
    classification of, 3.1–1.2
    diagnostic, freestanding, 3.4
    disaster provisions for, 3.1–5.1.2
    electrical systems in, 3.1–7.3
    elevators in, 3.1–6.2
    environmental services in, 3.1–3.1
    environment of care in, 3.1–1.4
    examination rooms in, 3.1–2.1
    filter efficiencies for, 3.1–1*t*
    finishes in, 3.1–5.2.2
    floors in, 3.1–5.2.2.2
    glazing in, 3.1–5.2.1.5
    hallways in, 3.1–5.2.1.1
    hand-washing stations in, 3.1–5.2.1.6
    housekeeping in, 3.1–3.1.1
    HVAC systems in, 3.1–7.2
    imaging facilities in, 3.1–2.2, 3.1–A2.2
    incinerators in, 3.1–A6.3.2.5
    lighting in, 3.1–7.3.4
    location of, 3.1–A1.7.1
    materials management in, 3.1–3.3
    observation rooms in, 3.1–2.1.4
    in outpatient facilities, 3.1–2.3

parking for, 3.1–1.7.2
patient support areas in, 3.1–2.2.4
plumbing in, 3.1–7.1
primary care
    entrances in, 3.2–3.1.1
    imaging facilities in, 3.2–2.2
    neighborhood, 3.3
    parking for, 3.2–1.3.1
    reception area in, 3.2–3.1.1.3
    waiting areas in, 3.2–3.1.3
protective environment rooms in, 3.1–2.1.6
psychiatric, 3.11
surgical, 2.1–5.3.1.3
    administrative areas ion, 3.7–4.2
    ceilings in, 3.7–5.2.2.2
    doors in, 3.7–5.2.1.3
    environment of care in, 3.7–1.3
    examination rooms in, 3.7–2.2
    finishes in, 3.7–5.2.2
    floors in, 3.7–5.2.2.3
    hallways in, 3.7–5.2.1.1
    HVAC systems in, 3.7–6.2
    layout of, 3.7–1.5.2, 3.7–A1.5.2
    operating rooms in, 3.7–2.3
    parking for, 3.7–1.6.1
    patient support areas for, 3.7–2.7
    privacy in, 3.7–1.3.1
    recovery areas in, 3.7–2.4
    scrub facilities for, 3.7–2.5.2
    soiled workrooms in, 3.7–2.5.4
    staff support areas in, 3.7–2.6
    sterilization rooms in, 3.7–3.1
    toilet rooms in, 3.7–5.2.1.4
    walls in, 3.7–5.2.2.4
toilets in, 3.1–2.1.8.1
treatment rooms in, 3.1–2.1.3
vacuum systems in, 3.1–7.1.4
ventilation in, 3.1–7.2.2.2
waiting areas in, 3.1–A4.1.3
waste management in, 3.1–6.3
water treatment in, 3.1–A7.1.2.4 (4)
Outpatient respiratory therapy areas, 2.1–5.8.2
Oxygen station outlets, 2.1–5t
Parking
    for assisted living facilities, 4.3–1.6.3
    for birthing centers, 3.6–1.2.1
    for gastrointestinal endoscopy facilities, 3.9–1.6.1
    for general hospitals, 2.1–1.3.1, 2.1–A1.3.1
    for nursing facilities, 4.1–1.6.2
    for outpatient care facilities, 3.1–1.7.2
    for outpatient surgical facilities, 3.7–1.6.1
    in primary care outpatient facilities, 3.2–1.3.1
    for psychiatric hospitals, 2.3–1.6.1
    site selection and, 1.3–3.3
    for small hospitals, 2.2–1.3.2
    for small primary care outpatient facilities, 3.3–1.3.2
    for urgent care facilities, freestanding, 3.5–1.2.2
Patient care areas, special, in general hospitals, 2.1–3.2
Patient rooms. *See* Rooms (patient/resident)

Pediatric critical care units, 2.1–3.4.5
Pediatric nursery, 2.1–3.6.8
Pediatric treatment rooms, in ER, 2.1–A5.1.3.7 (6)
Pediatric units, in psychiatric hospitals, 2.3–2.3
Permits, environmental pollution and, 1.3–4.1.3
PET scans, 2.1–A5.6.1.1, 2.1–A5.6.3
Pharmacies
    in general hospitals, 2.1–6.1
    in psychiatric hospitals, 2.3–4.1
    in rehabilitation facilities, 2.4–5.1
Phase II recovery areas, 2.1–5.3.3.3, 3.7–2.4.2
Phasing, renovation and, 1.5–3.1
Physical therapy
    in general hospitals, 2.1–3.9.3, 2.1–5.7.2
    in nursing facilities, 4.1–5.1
    in psychiatric hospitals, 2.3–3.4.2
    in rehabilitation facilities, 2.4–4.3.1
Piping
    dead-end, 1.6–2.1.2.1 (3)
    for dialysis, 2.1–10.1.2.2
    in dialysis centers, 3.10–5.1.1, 3.10–A5.1.1
    for drainage systems, 2.1–10.1.2.5 (1)
    identification of, 2.1–10.1.2.1 (1), 2.1–10.1.2.1 (2)
Plumbing
    in dialysis centers, 3.10–5.1, 3.10–A5.1.1
    in general hospitals
        code compliance, 1.6–2.1.1
        condensate drains, 1.6–2.1.2.2
        for dialysis unit, 2.1–5.9.8.1,
          2.1–10.1.2.2, 2.1–A5.9.8.1
        fixtures, 1.6–2.1.3
        hot water systems, 1.6–2.1.2.1
        infection control in, 1.6–A2.1.2.1 (4)
        for PET facilities, 2.1–A5.6.3
        piping in, 2.1–10.1.2.1
    in mobile units, 3.12–5.1
    in nursing facilities, 4.1–3t, 4.1–10.1
    in outpatient facilities, 3.1–7.1
    in psychiatric hospitals, 2.3–8.1.2
    in rehabilitation facilities, 2.4–9.1
    in small hospitals, 2.2–8.1
Pollution
    air quality and, 1.2–A3.1.5
    control, and site selection, 1.3–4
    mercury elimination, 1.3–4.2, 1.3–A4.2
    permit acquisition and, 1.3–4.1.3
Positron emission tomography (PET), 2.1–A5.6.1.1,
    2.1–A5.6.3
Post-anesthetic care units (PACUs), 2.1–5.3.3.2
Postoperative holding areas, 2.1–5.3.3
Power sources, constant, 1.4–3.2.2
Preoperative holding areas, 2.1–5.3.3
Prescriptive standards, 1.1–7.3.2
Primary care outpatient facilities
    entrances in, 3.2–3.1.1
    imaging facilities in, 3.2–2.2
    neighborhood, 3.3
    parking for, 3.2–1.3.1
    reception area in, 3.2–3.1.1.3

Relocation Matrix

Since the 2006 edition has been totally reorganized, the following matrix has been provided to help users of previous editions find information that has been moved to a different location.

2001 Edition	2006 Edition		4.2.A	1.4-2.1
1.1	1.1-1		4.2.B	1.4-2.2
1.1.A	1.1-1.3		4.2.C	1.4-2.3
1.1.B	1.1-1.1.2; 1.1-1.1.3		4.3	1.4-3.1
1.1.C	1.1-1.3.5		4.4	1.4-1.3.2.1
1.1.D	1.1-1.3.4.4		4.5	1.4-3.2
1.1.E	1.1-1.3.4.3		5.1	1.5-2
1.1.F	1.2-2		5.2	1.5-3
1.2	1.1-1.3.1.3 (2)		5.3	1.5-4
1.3.A	1.1-3.1		5.4	1.5-3.4
1.3.B	1.1-3.4		6.1	1.5-5.1
1.3.C	1.1-3.2		6.2	1.5-5.2
1.3.D	1.1-3.3		6.3	1.5-5.3
1.3.E	1.1-3.5.2		7.1	2.1-1
1.3.F	1.1-3.5		7.2	2.1-3
1.3.G	1.1-3.1.2		7.2.B2	2.1-2.3.2; 2.1-3.1.5.1
1.3.H	1.1-3.6		7.2.B14	2.1-2.3.10.1
1.3.I	1.1-3.7		7.2.B17	2.1-2.3.10.2
1.4	1.1-4		7.2.B18	2.1-2.3.10.3
1.5	1.1-5		7.2.B21	2.1-2.3.10.4
1.6.A	1.1-7.1		7.3	2.1-3.4
1.6.B	1.1-7.2		7.4	2.1-3.6
1.6.C	1.1-7.3		7.5	2.1-3.7
1.6.D	1.1-7.4		7.6	2.1-3.8
1.6.E	1.1-7.5		7.7	2.1-5.3.1
2.1	1.2-3.1.4		7.8	2.1-4.1
3.1	1.3-2		7.8.A2	2.1-4.2
3.2	1.3-3		7.8.A3	2.1-4.3
3.2.A	1.3-3.1		7.8.A4	2.1-4.4
3.2.B	1.3-3.3		7.9	2.1-5.1
3.3	1.3-4		7.10	2.1-5.4, 2.1-5.5
3.3.A	1.3-4.1		7.10.A	2.1-5.5.1
4.1	1.4-1		7.10.B	2.1-5.5.2
4.1.A	1.4-1.2		7.10.C	2.1-5.5.3
4.1.B	1.4-1.3.1.1; 1.4-1.3.3		7.10.D	2.1-5.5.4
4.1.C	1.4-3.1		7.10.E	2.1-5.5.5
4.1.D	1.4-1.3.2.2		7.10.F	2.1-5.5.6
4.2	1.4-2		7.10.G	2.1-5.5.8

7.10.G1	2.1-5.5.10.1	7.24	2.1-6.6.1
7.10.G4	2.1-5.5.10.2	7.25	2.1-7.3
7.10.G5	2.1-5.5.10.3	7.26	2.1-6.6.2
7.10.G6	2.1-5.5.9.1	7.27	2.1-6.7
7.10.H	2.1-5.4.1; 2.1-5.5.7	7.28	2.1-8.2
7.11	2.1-5.6	7.28.A1	2.1-8.1.2.2
7.12	2.1-5.11	7.28.A12	2.1-6.4.5, 2.1-6.5.3.2
7.13	2.1-5.7	7.28.B	2.1-8.2.3
7.14	2.1-5.9	7.29	2.1-8.1
7.15	2.1-5.8	7.30	2.1-9
7.16	2.1-5.12	7.30.C	2.1-6.5.3
7.17	2.1-6.1	7.30.C1	2.1-6.5.3.1
7.18	2.1-6.2	7.30.C2	2.1-9.3.1
7.18.B2	2.1-6.2.3.3 (1)	7.30.C3	2.1-9.3.2
7.18.B3	2.1-6.2.3.3 (3)	7.31	2.1-10
7.18.B4	2.1-6.2.3.3 (4)	7.31.A1	2.1-10.2.1
7.18.B18	2.1-6.2.3 (7)	7.31.B	1.6-2.2.1; 2.1-10.2.3
7.19	2.1-7	7.31.B1	1.6-2.2.1.1
7.20	2.1-7.2.5	7.31.B2	1.6-2.2.1.1 (1)
7.21	2.1-6.3	7.31.B3	1.6-2.2.1.1 (2)
7.21A	2.1-6.3.1	7.31.B4	1.6-2.2.1.2 (1), (2)
7.21.B	2.1-6.3.2	7.31.B5	1.6-2.2.1.2 (3)
7.21.B1	2.1-6.2.2.1	7.31.B6	1.6-2.2.1.1 (3)
7.21.B5	2.1-6.2.2.3	7.31.B7	1.6-2.2.1.2 (4)
7.21.B6	2.1-6.2.2.4	7.31.C	2.1-10.2.6
7.21.B7	2.1-6.2.2.5	7.31.C1	1.6-2.2.3.1
7.21.B8	2.1-6.2.2.6	7.31.C2	1.6-2.2.3.2
7.21.B9	2.1-6.2.2.11	7.31.D	1.6-2.2; 2.1-10.2
7.21.B10	2.1-6.2.2.7	7.31.D2	2.1-10.2.4.3 (1)
7.21.B11	2.1-6.2.2.8	7.31.D3	2.1-10.2.4.4 (1)
7.21.B12	2.1-6.2.2.9	7.31.D8	1.6-2.2.2.1 (2); 2.1-10.2.5
7.21.B14	2.1-6.2.2.2	7.31.D11	1.6-2.2.2.1 (4)
7.21.B15	2.1-6.2.3.1	7.31.E	1.6-2.1
7.21.B16	2.1-6.2.4.1	7.31.E1	1.6-2.1.3; 2.1-10.1.3
7.21.B19	2.1-6.2.2.10	7.31.E2	2.1-10.1.2.3
7.21.C	2.1-6.2.3.2	7.31.E3	1.6-2.1.2.1; 2.1-4
7.21.D	2.1-6.3.2.2	7.31.E4	2.1-10.1.2.5
7.22	2.1-6.5.2	7.31.E5	2.1-10.1.4.1
7.22.A	2.1-6.5.1.1	7.31.E6	2.1-10.1.4.2
7.22.B	2.1-6.5.1.2	7.31.E7	2.1-10.1.2.1
7.22.C	2.1-6.5.2.2	7.31.E8	2.1-10.1.2.2
7.22.D	2.1-6.5.2.3	7.31.E10	1.6-2.1.2.2; 2.1-10.1.2.6
7.23	2.1-6.4	7.32	1.6-2.3; 2.1-10.3

7.32.D1	1.6-2.3.1.1	9.2.I	3.1-5.1
7.32.D9	1.6-2.3.1.2; 1.6-2.3.1.3	9.2.J	3.1-5.1.2
7.32.I	2.1-10.5.2	9.3.A	3.2-1; 3.7-1.1
7.32.J	2.1-10.4	9.3.B	3.2-1.3.1
7.33	2.1-5.10	9.3.C	3.2-3.2
7.34.E	2.1-10.1	9.3.D	3.2-3.1
8.1	4.1-1	9.3.E	3.2-2.2
8.2	4.1-2	9.3.F	3.2-2.1
8.3.A	4.1-4.1	9.4.A	3.3-1
8.3.B	4.1-2.4.6.2; 4.1-2.6.2	9.4.B	3.3-1.3.1
8.4	4.1-4.2	9.4.C	3.3-1.3.2
8.5	4.1-5.1	9.4.D	3.3-4
8.6	4.1-4.3	9.4.E	3.3-2.1
8.7	4.1-3.1	9.4.F	3.3-2.2
8.8	4.1-3.2	9.4.I	3.3-6.2
8.9	4.1-6.1	9.4.I2	3.3-6.1
8.10	4.1-7	9.4.J	3.3-6.3
8.11	4.1-6.2	9.4.J4	3.3-6.3.4
8.12	4.1-6.4.1	9.5.A	3.7-1; 3.7-1.2.1; 3.7-1.3.1;
8.13	4.1-6.5		3.7-1.5.1; 3.7-1.5.2
8.14	4.1-8.2	9.5.B	3.7-1.2.2
8.15	4.1-8.2.3	9.5.C	3.7-1.6.1
8.30	4.1-9.1	9.5.D	3.7-4
8.30.B	4.1-9.2; 4.1-10.2.3	9.5.E	3.7-3.1
8.30.C	4.1-6.3.1	9.5.F	3.7-2
8.31	4.1-10.2	9.5.G	3.7-2.1
8.31.C	4.1-10.2.6	9.5.H1	3.7-5.2.1
8.31.E	4.1-10	9.5.H2	3.7-5.2.2
8.32	4.1-10.3	9.5.I	3.7-6.1
8.32.I	4.1-10.5	9.5.J	3.7-6.3
8.32.J	4.1-10.4	9.5.K	3.7-6.4.1
Table 8.2	Table 4.1-2	9.5.L	3.7-6.2
9.1	3.1-1	9.8.A	3.4-1.2
9.2	3.1-4	9.7.A	3.6-1.2.1
9.2.A	3.1-4	9.7.B	3.6-4.1
9.2.A9	3.1-7.1.2.2 (2)	9.7.B4	3.6-2.3
9.2.B	3.1-2	9.7.B5	3.6-4.2.1
9.2.C	3.1-2.2	9.7.B6	3.6-2.2.4.1
9.2.D	3.1-2.3	9.7.B7	3.6-2.2.2
9.2.E	3.1-3.1.1	9.7.B8	3.6-2.2.3
9.2.G	3.1-3.2	9.7.B9	3.6-3.1
9.2.G3	3.1-6.3	9.7.B10	3.6-3.2
9.2.H	3.1-5.2	9.7.C	3.6-2

9.30.A	3.1-6.1
9.30.B	3.1-6.2
9.30.C	3.1-3.3.1; 3.1-6.3
9.31.A–D	3.1-7.2
9.31.E	3.1-7.1
9.32A–H	3.1-7.3
9.32.I	3.1-7.6
9.32.J	3.1-7.5
11.1	2.3-1
11.1.A	2.3-1.1
11.1.B	2.3-1.2
11.1.C	2.3-1.6.1
11.1.D	2.3-1.4
11.1.E	2.3-3.1.3
11.1.F	2.3-1.5; 2.3-7.2; 2.3-7.2.3.1; 2.3-7.3.2; 2.3-9.2.5.2
11.2	2.3-2
11.2.A	2.3-2.1.1
11.2.B	2.3-2.7
11.2.B6	2.3-2.8.2
11.2.B7	2.3-2.8.1
11.2.B8	2.3-2.8.3
11.2.B9	2.3-2.7.9
11.2.B10	2.3-2.7.10
11.2.B11	2.3-2.7.6
11.2.B12	2.3-2.7.11.1
11.2.B13	2.3-2.7.7
11.2.B14	2.3-2.7.8
11.2.B15	2.3-2.9.2
11.2.B16	2.3-2.9.1
11.2.B17	2.3-2.7.4.5
11.2.B18	2.3-2.9.3
11.2.B19	2.3-2.9.4
11.2.B20	2.3-2.7.11.2
11.2.B22	2.3-2.7.11.3
11.2.B23	2.3-2.7.12
11.2.B24	2.3-2.7.4.1
11.2.B25	2.3-2.7.4.2
11.2.B26	2.3-2.7.4.3
11.2.B27	2.3-2.7.4.4
11.2.C	2.3-2.2.1
11.2.D	2.3-2.2.2
11.3	2.3-2.3
11.3.A	2.3-1
11.3.B	2.3-2.3.2
11.3.C	2.3-2.3.3
11.4	2.3-2.4
11.4.A	2.3-2.4.1
11.4.B	2.3-2.4.2
11.5	2.3-2.5
11.6	2.3-3.2
11.7	2.3-3.3
11.9	2.3-3.4
11.9.A	2.3-3.4.1
11.9.B	2.3-3.4.7
11.9.B1	2.3-3.4.7.4
11.9.B2	2.3-3.4.7.1
11.9.B3	2.3-3.4.7.2
11.9.B4	2.3-3.4.9
11.9.B5	2.3-3.4.7.5
11.9.B6	2.3-.4.8.2
11.9.B7	2.3-3.4.8.1
11.9.B8	2.3-3.4.7.4
11.9.C	2.3-3.4.2
11.9.D	2.3-3.4.3.
11.9.E	2.3-3.4.4
11.9.F	2.3-3.4.5
11.9.G	2.3-3.4.6
11.10	2.3-5.1
11.11	2.3-5.2
11.12	2.3-6
11.13	2.3-6.1
11.14	2.3-5.3
11.15	2.3-5.5.1
11.16	2.3-5.4
11.17	2.3-5.6.1
11.18	2.3-6.2
11.19	2.3-5.6.2
11.20	2.3-5.7
11.21	2.3-5.5.2
11.22	2.3-7.2
11.23	2.3-7.1
11.30	2.3-8
11.30.A	2.3-8.1
11.30.B	2.3-8.2
11.30.C	2.3-8.3

11.31.A	2.3-9.2.1
11.31.B	2.3-9.2.3
11.31.C	2.3-9.2.6
11.31.D1	2.3-9.2.1.2
11.31.D2	2.3-9.2.4.3
11.31.D3	2.3-9.2.4.4
11.31.D4	2.3-9.2.5
11.31.D5	2.3-9.2.1.4 (2)
11.31.D6	2.3-9.2.4.1
11.31.D8	2.3-9.2.4.1 (3)
11.31.D9	2.3-9.2.2.3
11.31.D10	2.3-9.2.2.4
11.31.D11	2.3-9.2.4.4 (4)
11.31.D12	2.3-9.2.1.1(2)(b)
11.31.D13	2.3-9.2.2.1
11.31.D14	2.3-9.2.2.2
11.31.D15	2.3-9.2.1.1 (2) (c)
11.31.E	2.3-9.1.2
11.31.E1	2.3-9.1.3
11.31.E2	2.3-9.1.2.2
11.31.E3	2.3-9.1.2.3
11.31.E4	2.3-9.1.2.4
11.31.E5	2.3-9.1.4.1
11.31.E6	2.3-9.1.4.2
11.31.E7	2.3-9.1.2.1
11.31.E8	2.3-9.1.2.5
11.31.E9	2.3-9.1.2.6
11.32	2.3-9.3
11.32.B	2.3-9.3.2.1
11.32.C	2.3-9.3.2.2
11.32.D	2.3-9.3.4
11.32.E	2.3-9.3.6
11.32.F	2.3-9.3.5
11.32G	2.3-9.3.7
11.32.H	2.3-9.3.3.1
11.32.I	2.3-9.5.2
11.32.J	2.3-9.4
11.32.K	2.3-9.5.1
12.1	3.12-1 through 3.12-4
12.31	3.12-5.1 through 3.12-5.2
12.32	3.12-5.3 through 3.12-5.5

Form for Requests for Formal Interpretations of the
Guidelines for Design and Construction of Health Care Facilities

Name _____

Company/organization _____

Address _____

City_____ State _____ Zip_____

Telephone _____ FAX _____ E-mail _____

Guidelines edition (year) _____ Chapter–section reference _____

Did this question arise from an actual field situation or ☐ Yes ☐ No
from discussion(s) with an authority having jurisdiction (AHJ)? ☐ Yes ☐ No
If yes, please provide the name, address, and telephone number of the AHJ:

_____

State the purpose of your request for formal interpretation:

_____

_____

_____

_____

Question:

_____

_____

_____

_____

Signature _____ Date _____

Visit www.fgi-guidelines.org or www.aia.org/aah for instructions on requesting an interpretation. Rules for requesting a formal interpretation are also posted on both Web sites.

Form for Proposals to Change the *Guidelines for Design and Construction of Health Care Facilities*, 2006 ed.

Name _____

Company/organization _____

Address _____

City_____ State _____ Zip_____

Telephone _____ FAX _____ E-mail _____

All proposals must refer to specific parts of the 2001 edition of the Guidelines. Each separate proposal requires a separate copy of this form. Only proposals that appear on this form (or in this format) can be considered.

1. Chapter–section reference: _____ Page no.: _____
2. Proposal recommends (check one):

    new text _____ revised text _____ deleted text _____

3. Proposals (Make a clear statement of what you want done in the document; be specific! Provide new or edited language that will accomplish your goal.):

4. Substantiation for proposal (State why you think your proposed addition, change, or deletion of text is necessary. Explain how your proposal solves the problem you identify.):

I agree to give FGI all and full rights—including rights of copyright—in this proposal, and I understand that I acquire no rights in any publication of the AIA in which this proposal in this manner or similar or analogous form is used.

Signature _____ Date _____

Visit the Facility Guidelines Institute Web site at www.fgi-guidelines.org. Instructions for making a proposal can be found on the site.

Facility Guidelines Institute (FGI)—the Author

The Facility Guidelines Institute, a not-for-profit, 501 (c)(3) corporation, was founded in 1998 by the executive committee of the Health Guidelines Revision Committee (HGRC) to provide leadership and continuity in the Guidelines revision process. FGI represents the authors of the Guidelines (the HGRC) as the legal author and holds the copyright for Guidelines 2006. (The multidisciplinary HGRC remains solely responsible for the content of the Guidelines for Design and Construction of Health Care Facilities.) FGI functions as a contractual, fundraising, and coordinating entity to develop and enhance the content and format of the Guidelines document and provides ancillary services that encourage and improve its application and use. FGI uses revenue derived from sales of the Guidelines to support the revision process and to fund research in support of evidence-based guidelines.

The American Institute of Architects (AIA)— the Publisher

For almost 150 years, members of the American Institute of Architects have worked with each other and their communities to create more valuable, healthy, secure, and sustainable buildings and cityscapes. The AIA Academy of Architecture for Health (AIA/AAH) strives to improve the quality of health care through design by developing, documenting, and disseminating knowledge on the practice of health care architecture; educating health care architects and related constituencies; improving the design of health care environments; affiliating and advocating with others with a shared vision; and promoting research. Members of the AIA/AAH participate in the Guidelines revision process, and the Academy cosponsors workshops on the Guidelines when a new edition is released. The AIA actively aids the work of the HGRC through staff and financial support, preparation and review of draft revisions to the document, and publication of the book.

KSI Architecture & Planning
310 1st Ave S #332 Seattle, WA 98104
206.624.5454